THE HOME COUNTIES

The Regions of Britain

THE
HOME
COUNTIES

MARCUS CROUCH

With photographs by the Author

Robert Hale & Company, Publishers
London

ISBN 0 7091 4869 0

Robert Hale & Company
63 Old Brompton Road
London SW7

PRINTED IN GREAT BRITAIN BY
EBENEZER BAYLIS AND SON LIMITED
THE TRINITY PRESS, WORCESTER, AND LONDON

Contents

Contents

Illustrations

7

FOR
DEAN HARRISON

I

Metropolitan England

THE conceit of the Londoner is different from that of other townsmen. The Mancunian will defend his city against all-comers, whatever he may call it in the privacy of his home, but he is on the defensive. Assurance sits, as Eliot might have said, uneasily on the Bradfordian. Immense local pride goes with the need to assert itself to the detriment of other places. Londoners never defend their city because it never occurs to them that it needs defence. The bland assumption that here is the centre of the real world has no parallel since the decline of Rome.

Hence the Home Counties. Other counties fall into informal groups: the North-east, the West Country and so on. Only around London do the counties turn on a single urban axis. These are the 'Home' counties; others are Away. It is not surprising that the Londoner should propagate this idea; it is astonishing that the rest of the country should have accepted it without protest.

The concept of the Home Counties seems to have been borrowed from the legal world. The Home Circuit has been, at least from the eighteenth century, the circuit of the counties around London. Which counties these are has varied from time to time, according to convenience and volume of business. The popular use of the term Home Counties has been similarly flexible. Originally the Home Counties

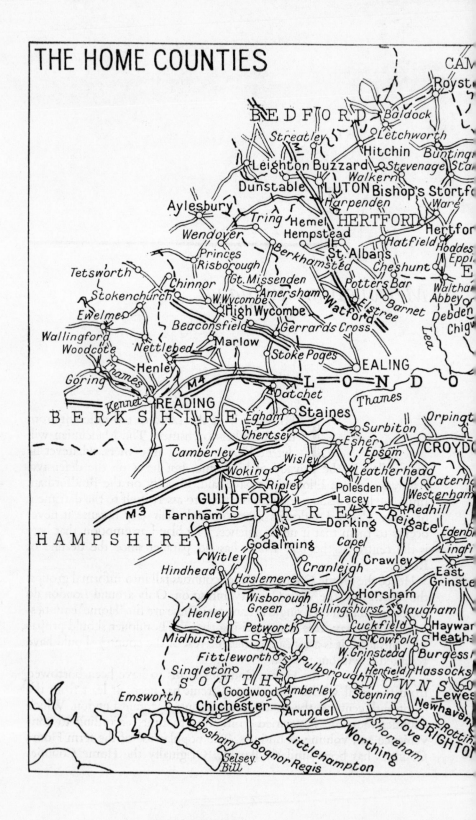

THE HOME COUNTIES

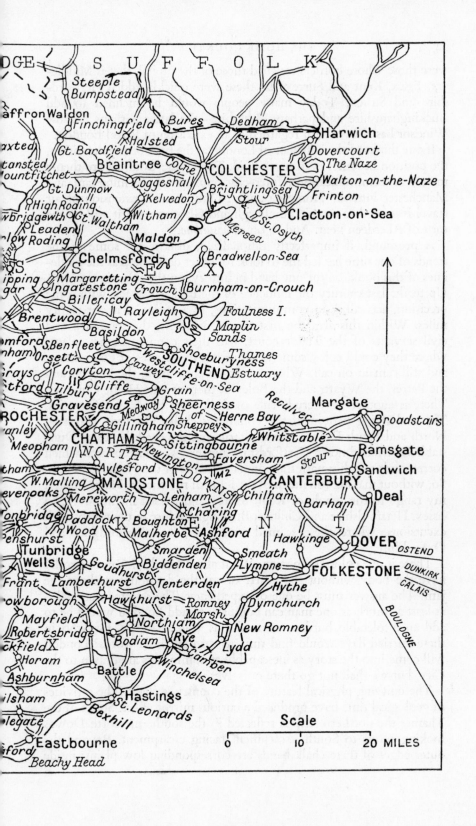

SUFFOLK

Steeple Bumpstead
affron Walden
Finchingfield
Bures
Dedham
Harwich
axted
Halsted
Stour
Dovercourt
stansted
Gt. Bardfield
Colne
The Naze
ountfitchet
Braintree
COLCHESTER
Walton-on-the-Naze
Gt. Dunmow
Coggeshall
Brightlingsea
Frinton
High Roding
Kelvedon
wbridgewth Gt. Waltham
Witham
St. Osyth
Clacton-on-Sea
Leaden
Maldon
Mersea I.
low Roding
S Chelmsford
Bradwell-on-Sea
ipping
S E X
gar Margaretting
Crouch
Burnham-on-Crouch
Ingatestone
Billericay
Rayleigh
Foulness I.
Brentwood
Maplin Sands
Basildon
omford S. Benfleet
Shoeburyness
Thames
ham Orsett
Westcliffe-on-Sea
Canvey
Estuary
rays
Coryton
SOUTHEND
tford
Cliffe
Grain
Tilbury
Gravesend
Sheerness
Reculver
Margate
ROCHESTER
Medway
I. of
Herne Bay
Broadstairs
anley
Gillingham
Sheppey
Whitstable
Ramsgate
Meopham
CHATHAM
Sittingbourne
Faversham
Sandwich
NORTH
Newington
Stour
tham
Aylesford
DOWNS
CANTERBURY
Deal
W. Malling
MAIDSTONE
M2
evenoaks
Mereworth
Lenham
Chilham
Barham
nbridge
Paddock
Boughton
Charing
Hawkinge
DOVER
Penshurst
Wood
Malherbe
Ashford
OSTEND
Tunbridge
Smarden
Smeath
FOLKESTONE
DUNKIRK
Wells
Goudhurst
Biddenden
Lympne
CALAIS
Frant
Lamberhurst
Tenterden
Hythe
owborough
Hawkhurst
Romney
Dymchurch
BOULOGNE
Mayfield
Northiam
Marsh
Robertsbridge
Bodiam
Rye
New Romney
ckfield
Camber
Lydd
Horam
Battle
Winchelsea
Ashburnham
ilsham
Hastings
legate
St. Leonards
Scale
Bexhill
Eastbourne
0   10   20 MILES
Beachy Head

were those whose borders touched those of the capital, that is Middlesex, Essex, Kent and Surrey. To these were quickly added Hertfordshire and Sussex. Today many people would be inclined to add Buckinghamshire and perhaps Berkshire—the latter perhaps because Windsor has always been regarded as an extension of Royal London.

If one thinks of the influence of London as the basis of any definition, the position becomes even more fluid. The Home Counties are then a matter of communications. Inter-city trains bring Birmingham and Manchester into the Home Counties. Only a small extension of air travel is needed to recruit Edinburgh and Glasgow, and it will be the turn of Aberdeen next. And so on *ad absurdum*.

A profound, if imperfectly rationalized, distaste for some of the trends of our time has led me to look for other definitions as the guidelines of this book, on the one hand in history, on the other in geology. Up to the last century the influence of the capital was felt with some precision, according to communications, in a radius of about eighty miles. Within this area the first true commuters, the statesmen and civil servants of the Tudor court, had their country homes, places where they could enjoy some respite from the stresses of government and still remain on call. Where one finds these men, the Smyths and the Petres, the Wyatts and the Boleyns, there are the Home Counties. There is another very crude rule of thumb for the Home Counties. The underlying pattern of this country is chalk. The twin waves of North and South Downs, the Chilterns and the chalk bands of Dunstable Down and north Hertfordshire and Essex enclose an area which corresponds roughly with the popular concept of the Home Counties. So, without making too much of the logic of my choice, I have limited my range to the whole of Kent, Surrey and Sussex in the south, to Essex, Hertfordshire and Chiltern Buckinghamshire in the north, with excursions, where these seemed irresistible, into Bedfordshire and Oxfordshire.

There is one colossal omission. What about London? Can one really have the body without the heart? or eat the doughnut without the jam? The answer must be one of expediency. The selected material is at least as much as one man can compass; to add London would be to add an intolerable burden, on reader as well as writer, for who in these hurried days would find time to read all those words? London will come into the story as inescapably as commuters are drawn to the City, but we shall not go there ourselves.

The unifying physical feature of the country is chalk. The activities of geological time have produced a curious mirror effect. South of the Thames the northern strip is reflected in the southern, North Downs looking across to South, escarpment facing escarpment. Beyond the outer edges of these chalk bands are corresponding low plains; inside them the facing slopes of the lower greensand hills, strongly defined to the north, faint on the south. In the middle rise the shrunken stumps of the wealden dome. The scenic features of this country lie in parallel strips running east and west, as if they were the fingers of a hand resting on the chalk hills of Hampshire.

North of the Thames the pattern is less conspicuous and symmetrical. The visible chalk forms an arc sweeping round the perimeter of an area from the Thames to Cambridgeshire, with outward-facing escarpment. The inward hills, rather like those of the North Downs, form a complex of mostly dry valleys, and the characteristic chalk undulations gradually fade into the mild plain of the Thames valley. Except for the chalk of its north-western corner, Essex stands outside the general pattern, with low gravel hills merging into the alluvial flat of an indented coast.

Apart from the Thames, which acts both as focus and divider of the region, the rivers of the Home Counties are conspicuous only in their estuaries. Historically and scenically, they are, however, of great importance, and they deserve a more detailed appreciation than they have usually received. The eastern rivers, which demonstrate most violently the contrast between insignificant upper waters and wide estuaries, all behave in an exemplary fashion, flowing from the low hills of their sources eastwards to find the North Sea. The southern rivers, on the other hand, take the most perverse courses. The Medway, for example, rising in the Forest Ridge of Sussex, flows south-east into the wealden plain, where it appears to have a clear course into the Channel; it then turns north, makes its way through the high greensand ridge and the higher North Downs to enter the Thames estuary. The others are only comparatively less eccentric. Wey, Mole, Darent and Stour all go north through the Downs; Arun, Adur, Ouse and Cuckmere all flow south through gaps in the South Downs. The East Sussex Rother, which alone seems to follow the normal behaviour of rivers in finding the easiest route to the sea, has a history of excessive waywardness which led to the ruin of several major ports. The Chilterns have largely been waterless in historic times; only the Wye and the Chess make any impression on the scene. As for Hertfordshire, the Lea gathers a few small tributaries on the way to the Thames, but its importance comes from the activities of the 'navvies'. Without the Lea and Stort Navigation, neither stream would be any more significant today than the Colne or the Ver.

This emphasizes the dominant fact of Home Counties scenery. This is, even more than most of England, man-made country. From the line of the coast to the shape of a field, these counties reflect the ruthless persistence of men in fighting and controlling the forces of nature. Romney Marsh and Welwyn Garden City have this in common, that both were made and not created. There can scarcely be surprise that not all achievements are of equal merit. When man sets out to embellish his environment he sometimes produces a Stourhead, sometimes an example of municipal 'carpet' gardening. There is as wide a range of quality in landscape design as in any other manifestation of art. Similarly when man uses land, to grow food or to steal its minerals, the results may be visually attractive and catastrophic.

Recent technological changes—I will not say advances—have accentuated these features of the landscape. The trend towards big farm units has resulted in the transformation of large areas of the country, substituting wide open fields for the neat patchwork of hedges, ditches and wayside trees which seems to have been the immemorial pattern of England—although it is at most barely three hundred years old. Sometimes, as in parts of North Essex and Thanet, the new scale suits the natural landscape; sometimes, as in the Weald, the big fields run counter to the lines of the land. Everywhere the change is having profound and long-term ecological effects which all of us, if we live at all, may live to regret.

The recent and growing interest in our industrial past may cloud our minds to the dangers implicit in many new developments. As we shall see elsewhere, the iron industry which turned the Weald temporarily into a Black Country contributed in the long term to the beauty of this loveliest of southern areas. This should not lead to complacency about the effects of modern industrial enterprises, compared with which wealden iron was a cottage industry. The destiny of the chalk country is tied up inevitably, and has been for more than two centuries, with the cement industry. The glistening cliffs which break the uniform green of the face of the North Downs are a legacy of this, and it seems to me that the scene would be poorer without them. In the absence of rigid controls a technically advanced cement industry would quickly swallow up the downs themselves. Whether this would be an appropriate price to pay for industrial progress is a question for everyone to ask, not just the 'authorities' in whose hands decisions rest. The downland rivers have laid down, over millennia, great beds of gravel, a raw material vital to twentieth-century economy. Gravel extraction is a hideous but comparatively brief operation. When the operators move on they leave behind a wide shallow lake through which the stream meanders unseen. Modern planning standards usually require a high degree of making-good, and the resulting landscape may not be unsightly. Indeed, sailing clubs will regard it as a positive improvement. Lovers of fine country, who perhaps outnumber the sailors, may not be of the same opinion. The enormous lakes of the Thames valley and the Buckinghamshire boundary with Middlesex have been a feature of the scene too long for us to recall what they replaced. But in the

South Downs

Marsh: Pevensey Level

Darent valley in Kent a comparison exists ready-made. The lower valley, towards Dartford and the Thames flats, is extensively occupied with flooded workings. Higher up, where the stream passes through the downs between Otford and Eynsford, the valley has mostly escaped exploitation. To many sound judges of landscape this is among the best of Kentish scenes, fertile and finely proportioned. The relationship between the stream, trees and hedges, meadows and fields, farm buildings and villages, and the steep shelves of the downs, is most delicately balanced, and the scale is easily distorted, as one can see at Eynsford. This valley lies under threat from the gravel extractors. If these fears are realized, the ultimate effect may not be totally deplorable, and the watersportsman, and perhaps the naturalist, will gain another playground; in the process a very characteristic and very beautiful aspect of rural life, which resists the pressures of an expanding metropolis just across the encircling hills, will have gone for ever.

The keynote of this region is change. The pursuit of this book has taken me back to a few places which I had not seen for forty years and more. Some of them corresponded with astonishing precision to my memories. Others were so totally different that I could find no familiar feature by which to measure my reaction. In other parts of the region I have witnessed changes, sometimes creeping, sometimes proceeding in a series of bursts, but in general moving at an accelerating rate. Not all change, it must be stated emphatically, is for the worse. Much of this country is in a more healthy state than it has ever been. Where farmers have looked beyond the immediate profit to the long-term welfare of the land, the soil has responded magnificently. Farm buildings are in fine repair—some of the new ones are admittedly hideous. Derelict buildings and dilapidated cottages are the rarest of sights. This latter is in itself an illustration of a south-eastern dilemma. The smallest country cottage, the most worm-eaten barn or oast, is valuable not because of the needs of the land but because of the hunger in every Londoner for a place in the country. Steadily year by year the number of residents who have no economic involvement in the land on which they sit grows, the number of those who work on that land decreases. One may regret these inescapable facts, while at the same time rejoicing that these one-time workaday buildings, lodges, turn-pike cottages, barns, kilns, which match their setting so exquisitely, have not been allowed to fall into ruin, or given place to 'residential developments', but have come into appreciative and loving hands. Anyone who studies the currently popular collections of Victorian and Edwardian topographical photographs and their earlier counterparts, the Georgian prints, will know that in the countryside picturesqueness was a mask of decay. The prettiest places were those with the thickest tangle of ivy, the most deeply eroded stone. Even if we find the

modern rural scene just a little too smugly perfect, it is difficult to
regret the passing of picturesque squalor.

The Home Counties are a battlefield of warring interests. Never in
the history of the world have more people been aware of the importance of a healthy environment; never have there been such appalling threats of pollution. Government departments, local authorities
and preservation societies are dedicated to the preservation of fine
buildings; fine buildings are destroyed daily in the name of development. Our precious heritage of rural rights of way has at last received
a definitive record by the will of Parliament, and officials have been
charged with their protection; hundreds of miles of paths disappear
for ever under the plough and the bulldozer. The catalogue of anomalies
might be extended indefinitely. The same is true to a degree of every
part of the country, but in the south-eastern corner every problem is
blown up to larger-than-life size.

Any examination of a region of Britain, however superficial, must
take account of the characteristics of the inhabitants. How does Home
Counties man compare with his counterpart in the North-east or in
Cumbria? The safest answer must be that there is no typical Home
Counties man. The process of intermingling which has contributed to
the destruction of regional characteristics in every part of the country
except perhaps North Wales and the Highlands has operated most
powerfully here. The South-east has been cosmopolitan for longer
than any other region. First the flow of invaders, hostile and pacific,
from the continent of Europe, then the counter-flow of Londoners into
the country, later still the steady migration from economically less
stable places to the promised land of the affluent south; all have helped
so to mix and muddle the blood of these counties that few can confidently claim to be men of Kent or Hertfordshire men except by virtue
of residence. There are some exceptions to this gross generalization.
In the Weald, and in the middle of eastern Essex, one has a better
chance than elsewhere to hear something like genuine dialect speech
and to encounter traditional ways of thought to match, and these
mostly among the very elderly. Local patriotism is seldom more than
skin-deep. Some may profess their pride in belonging to one of the
Home Counties, and many more will, without making a fuss about it,
have a very deep love of the unspectacular loveliness of their home
or adopted scene; but this is nothing to compare with the aggressive
and exclusive local pride of the Yorkshireman or his neighbour across
the Pennines. A stranger dropped without warning into a Rotary meeting or a Women's Institute would be hard put to it to guess whether he
was in Essex or Sussex; the matters under discussion would be common
to both and indeed to all the Home Counties.

One thing unites the native and immigrant—I use the word in a

non-racial sense because except in a few places like Slough and Gravesend these counties have not as yet acquired a race problem: an interest
and a pride in the past. All the Home Counties have been involved in
the formation of the nation and they retain not only memories but to a
surprising degree visible monuments of past history. The village which
possesses no local-history society is a poor and spiritless place, and there
are few such. If the present is too comfortable and profitable to be
colourful, here to hand is a world of action and passion. The Home
Counties, especially those with a sea-coast, were in the front line of
history from the beginnings of history—and beyond—until the last of
the flying bombs and rockets exploded in 1945. Waves of invaders
passed across the country in all the centuries of prehistory. The battles
of Roman, Saxon, Danish and Norman invasions were fought in those
fields and woods. The scars of later wars are still visible in the landscape.
So are the marks of more peaceable invaders, Flemings and Huguenots,
who brought their skills and their energies to stimulate new industries
in return for freedom from religious persecution. The violence of
change has as yet failed to destroy the pattern of the past which lies
just below the surface of the modern counties.

Legislative reformers are rarely equipped with a sense of history.
As I write, this country moves towards 1st April 1974 when a reorganized structure of local government comes officially into being. I
have no doubt at all that in time the new system will prove to be more
efficient and less humane than the old. The Local Government Act is
the greatest attempt for centuries to destroy the pattern of the past, and
with reorganization towns and cities which have been part of the web
of history will cease to have an administrative identity. The Cinque
Port of Hythe will be a part of District Number Nine, a district which
has somewhat affectedly and inaccurately revived the old lathe name of
Shepway. The Saxon port of Maldon, the Roman town of Colchester,
the Norman town of Bramber, all disappear from the administrative
map. But not from the hearts of those who live there. The idea that
citizens will change their loyalties by Act of Parliament is one which
could only occur to a bureaucrat. Of course Sandwich will remain
Sandwich, however meagrely the port may be represented on the new
District Council of Dover. No one resists change more than those who
live in the middle of it. No doubt many citizens in 1832 took pride in
the rottenness of their boroughs.

There are more fundamental enemies of local integrity than the
Local Government Act. The Home Counties face a crisis as great as
that posed by the invasions of Saxons and Vikings, and the enemies
this time are not to be vanquished by force of arms. The agricultural
face of the country is already changing on the instructions of the
European Community. Giant Continental lorries have made life in

main road villages almost intolerable. The Channel Tunnel and its approaches will destroy some of the finest landscape and natural habitat in the south country. Maplin will sterilize what is perhaps the most fertile soil in England, will destroy one of the most important centres of bird population in the world, and will turn the remote and lovely Roche peninsula into a jungle of brick and concrete. And are these changes even for the material benefit of the South-east? It is highly questionable.

In the face of all these profound changes, the writing of a book such as this is full of hazards. Between writing and publishing anything may happen. I have to the best of my ability described country which seems to me, at the time of writing, to possess commendable qualities of landscape and architecture. I cannot guarantee that by the time the words are printed the landscape will not be defiled or the buildings demolished. What started as a hymn of praise may end as a requiem.

What can be said is that in 1973, when I renewed my friendship with these counties, there was much lovely country still stubbornly resisting the pressures of urban and industrial civilization. Many towns and villages had kept their ancient centres inviolate, whatever horrors were perpetrated on the outskirts. Great and historic buildings defied the centuries and bore witness to the vision and the confident faith of our ancestors. Perhaps most notably, and most surprisingly, the minor buildings of the Home Counties—the small manor houses, the cottages, barns, oasts, dovecotes—displayed the resource, and the versatility, and the local individuality of their creators, in the charm and variety of their design and materials. So the true quality of Kent is to be found in Chilham and Lenham as much as in Canterbury and Knole, the quality of Essex in Great Bromley as well as Colchester, of Sussex in Shipley as well as Chichester.

Basic dilemmas face the writer about a region as large, populous and complex as the Home Counties. It is not so much a problem of selection, great as this is, but of approach. Two kinds of books might be written about the inner commuter belt. One would be sociological, exploring the conflicts generated by transplantation into new communities and the rootlessness of the great housing estates. The other, historical, would unravel the strands of the past which lie within the fabric of the present. For the former I lack the expertise, for the latter the patience. Then there might be a fascinating book about the supreme commuter towns like Brighton and St Albans and the changes which have taken place by virtue of their increasing involvement with London and their corresponding diminution of concern with their immediate environment.

Such valuable studies are not within my range. At best I am able to look selectively at the present in order to find in it evidence of the past.

I am acutely conscious that I lay excessive emphasis on the past, but here lie my own interests—and, I suspect, those of many readers. Much of the modern development of the Home Counties—I except the industrial buildings and such major engineering achievements as roads and bridges—is unlovely and, except as a phenomenon of the times, uninteresting to the general observer. What fascinates me is the persistence of the past, its patterns often clearly visible beneath later accretions. And in the Home Counties history has always been writ large. Local history in these parts is often also national history.

My original intention was to treat the subject in a conventionally topographical way, choosing a series of rural rides which would reveal the countryside and its buildings in their most attractive aspects. In the writing a slightly different pattern has emerged. Each part of the country seemed to have a specific as well as a general story to tell. Firm as was my intention to toe the topographical line, and, I fear, my publisher's intention that I should do so, I felt unable to ignore the vociferous demands of the country through which I travelled to look at it in this particular light. With each emerging theme an historical period became associated. So the exploration of western Surrey and West Sussex became identified with the navigations and the canal age. A journey through Sussex from west to east turned into a search for Saxon saints. The main A2 road from London to Canterbury inevitably invoked memories of the medieval pilgrims to Becket's shrine. North of the Thames two vertical strips of most delectable country produced evidence of the lost forest of Essex and the resourcefulness of Essex builders in brick, the one largely a story of Dark Age and medieval times, the other belonging mainly to Tudor, Stuart and Georgian England. In Hertfordshire I indulged an almost forgotten affection for Charles Lamb and for country which I, too, had walked in childhood. The Chiltern woodlands held memories of poets and politicians. Lastly, the lovely and undervalued northern and western fringe of the Home Counties was linked and demarcated by the ancient, and newly revived, trackway of the Icknield Way.

To give continuity to each chapter I have presented each in the form of a journey. With the exception of the little circuit of the wealden hop country, these journeys are not offered as serious practical suggestions. Only an exceptionally vigorous and insensitive motorist would 'do' the tour of stately homes and departed families in Chapter 6 in a single day. The journeys are practicable but most undesirable. Much better to take a few pages and use them as the starting point of independent explorations. One of the joys of the region is that the unexpected lies around every corner.

The obvious drawback to my plan is that so much must be left out. It is only too likely that the potential reader will find that his favourite

village, or more probably his favourite town—for I am not overfond
of towns—is missing. I am aware of painful deficiencies of this kind.
The most obvious omission is Brighton, a place which displays comprehensively the characteristics and the dilemmas of commuterdom.
Nowhere else could one find so completely the phenomenon of
Londoners recreating their metropolis beside the sea. And, setting aside
sociology, where else can one find a living museum of architecture
from the Regency to the present, illustrating each successive fashion in
its finest and its most mediocre achievements? These houses, elegant,
shoddy or deplorable, can be peopled with a colourful population of
wits, eccentrics and rogues, all delighting in the ministrations of
Doctor Brighton, all acknowledging their debt to Prinny himself who
first—as Rex Whistler recorded in his last and most devastating painting, now in the Royal Pavilion—awakened the Spirit of Brighton. But
Brighton calls not for a paragraph or a chapter but a book.

It is customary in books of this kind to conclude with the ack-
nowledgement of indebtedness to authorities and colleagues for help
and inspiration. Being of a solitary and independent nature I have
persistently, and doubtless to my loss, gone it alone. I am only too
conscious of the fact that my picture of the most populous corner of
England is almost without inhabitants—at least modern inhabitants; it
is full of ghosts. This is to offer no discourtesy to my wife who
patiently accompanied my journeys and endured, mostly without complaint, long days, irregular meals, and frequent, unpremeditated
decisions to explore one more narrow byroad, one more nettle-grown
track.

For those who wish to check their reactions to scenery and history
against those of earlier travellers I have added a very short selection
from the vast library of Home Counties literature.

And now the road lies open, the downs rise high and free, the barley
rustles in the breeze. Let us be out and away into this extraordinarily
persistent, enduring, infinitely fascinating country of Metropolitan
England.

2

Pilgrims' Road

ONLY the most dedicated, or masochistic, of drivers would travel by choice along the A2 today. Even the M2 offers greater scenic attractions in addition to a swifter passage. Yet the A2 can claim to be among the oldest, and potentially one of the most interesting, roads in England. Whether or not there was a trackway before the Romans—and there is an inevitability about the road which makes one believe that it has been here for ever—it was certainly the key to the maintenance of the Roman peace and, unlike many Roman roads, it was not abandoned with the decline of Rome. The road is bound up with the story of Kent and of England throughout the Middle Ages, and there was only a small and temporary reduction in use after the loss of English possessions in France. In the present century Watling Street lost a little in favour of the A20 through Maidstone and Folkestone, but with the construction of the M2 motorway, which solved the problem of the notorious bottleneck at Rochester Bridge, the balance has again been tilted towards the northern route.

The road which is now often enough choked with traffic has seen congestion in its own way as great in the past, even if the traffic was then a great deal slower and the obstructions created by human obtuseness and the failure to maintain the great legacy of the Romans. In no century could it have been totally deserted, and for much of the Middle

Ages it was frequented by men variously jolly, aggressive and devout: the Canterbury pilgrims.

For all the restlessness of modern times there is nothing in this country today comparable to the medieval pilgrim. For a near parallel one must go to the East where, but for differences of colour and creed, Chaucer's pilgrims still take the road—or the train or plane—in order to attain virtue by attendance at the holy places of Islam or of the Lord Buddha.

An astonishingly large part of the population of feudal England was always on the move. The peasant might be bound for life to the soil and the manor and his lord, but the rest of society was frequently on the road. Kings and prelates migrated from palace to palace, eating the country bare like locusts. The soldier traded his sword. Scholars sought out the rare manuscript and the inspired teacher. Others went on pilgrimage, in fulfilment of a personal vow or an imposed penance, out of pure devotion, or for the hell of it.

The holy places of Christendom based their attractiveness almost exclusively on the possession of relics. It was all very well for Jerusalem and Rome which were the hubs of the world. Lesser places were in competition and the competition was hot. Relics sometimes existed by the natural order of history. The great abbey of St Edmundsbury owned of right the bones of Edmund, king and martyr, who had ruled East Anglia. Holiness has a habit of snowballing; one saint attracts another, and so generations of Welsh saints took the road to Bardsey. Less fortunate places, having no saint readily to hand, buy a share in the business, and out of this comes the grotesquely macabre trade in relics which flourished in the early Middle Ages. (We shall meet a fantastic example of this later in Sussex.)

Canterbury had advantages over almost all her English rivals. It was not chance that the city became the springboard for the conversion of the southern English, because Augustine's mission came to the Kentish capital at the express wish of the Queen of Kent, herself a Christian. It was chance which confirmed Canterbury as the seat of the Primate of All England; Augustine intended to set up his chair in London, but the original plan did not work out. So Augustine saw his days out—and they were very few—in Kent, and he was buried in his own abbey of St Peter and St Paul in Canterbury. Around him, in due course, lay his lieutenants and the saints and archbishops and kings of Kent. The possessions of so many holy relics gave the abbey an advantage which no other abbot or prior in the country could regard as fair.

The monopoly of St Augustine's Abbey was not broken until the year 758, and then only by a subterfuge. Archbishop Cuthbert decided that it was time for archbishops to be buried in their own cathedral. On his deathbed he briefed the monks of Christ Church carefully, and they huddled his corpse away quickly and secretly. By the time the abbot of St Augustine's smelt a rat and came around to claim his dues it was too late. Cuthbert was safely buried, and St Augustine's had suffered a wound which, although only after many centuries, was to prove fatal.

If archbishops and saints make valuable attractions martyrs are precious beyond computation. Canterbury acquired its first great martyr with the death of Alphege in 1011. Alphege, a man of rich humanity and surpassing courage, was in Canterbury when the city fell by assault and treachery to the Danes. He was taken away to the Danish camp at Greenwich where, refusing to yield to threat and persuasion, he was literally boned to death. Followers smuggled his body away to London and he was buried in St Paul's. There he lay until Canute, looking for a way to help consolidate the kingdom which he had won by force, arranged for a ceremonial reburial in Canterbury. It was an occasion of the greatest splendour, and the seal was set on Canterbury's glory when the king gave his own crown to be set on the great rood in Christ Church nave.

Other saints followed: Anselm who lay, as of right, in his own cathedral. (Lanfranc too, a greater man but perhaps too efficient to qualify for canonization.) St Wilfrid, who belonged in history either to York or Ripon or Selsey, was presented to Canterbury by Archbishop Odo. As for poor St Blaise, he had no Kentish or even English affiliations but this did not save him from being bought in the European relic market and transferred to Canterbury.

All these were precious assets, but they were as nothing compared with St Thomas. Archbishop Thomas Becket had not been, in terms of solid benefits, a notable archbishop in Canterbury. By his death he changed the history of the city. There had been holy archbishops before, and troublesome archbishops, but not a saintly cantankerous archbishop who got himself murdered in his own cathedral. The event was supremely well stage-managed, and one cannot doubt that it was done quite deliberately by Thomas himself. The monks of Christ Church wisely put him in the safety of his grave without delay, and only just in time because the murderers' friends were round next morning to try to get possession of the body. Miracles followed quickly. When King Henry II did penance at the tomb and submitted to scourging by the monks, the fortune of Christ Church was made.

One should not yield to the temptation to jeer at the monks and the relic-mongers. Their object was not, at first anyway, economic. They were concerned with something more important than the gifts of pilgrims; they sought the power of prayer. Monks were committed to a life of work. Part of this was physical toil; the rest was *Opus Dei*, the work of God. Every day of every year, from dawn to dusk and again at midnight, prayers flew up to heaven from every monastery in Christendom. It was every monk's conviction that his prayer was vastly strengthened by the intercession of the saints, and how better to gain this than by possessing the saint's earthly relics?

So the prayers of Christ Church, powerful enough before 1170, were reinforced immeasurably when the holy blissful martyr was laid in the crypt of Canterbury Cathedral. As the offerings of pilgrims flowed in, it was perhaps inevitable that the keepers of the shrine should increasingly take pleasure in the wealth of their priory and pay less regard to the Work of God until, by the time Erasmus and his friend Colet made their pilgrimage in the early years of the sixteenth century, miracles and mysteries had given place to farce and sick comedy. But for three centuries Canterbury was the principal place of pilgrimage in England, outclassing Glastonbury and Walsingham, and Becket's crown attracted devotion only less than did the bones—spurious I fear—of St James the Apostle at Compostella.

The practices described by Erasmus were certainly due for reform. In their proceedings against Becket, however, the Commissioners of Henry VIII went beyond reform. They were concerned not merely to abolish superstition but to destroy the reputation of a cleric who had effectively opposed a king. Henry VIII, vigorously establishing his supremacy in the Church, was not willing to have past history quoted to his detriment. So the great shrine in the Chapel of the Holy Trinity in Christ Church was destroyed and its gold and jewels carted away by the wagon-load. Becket was posthumously tried for treason and con- victed, and his bones vanished, perhaps for ever. Images of the saint, who throughout the Middle Ages had been the most popular in England and greatly regarded abroad, were systematically destroyed. It was less easy to abolish his memory. For three centuries Thomas had been almost the most greatly favoured of English given names, and this tradition, even if its origin was largely forgotten, could not be obliterated. Among the foremost men in Henry's counsels were seven Thomases, and of all those who suffered because of the King's matri- monial adventures, the only man who succeeded in cuckolding him was a Thomas.

A topographical expedition in the train of the Canterbury pilgrims suffers a little as a result of the King's particular antipathy. Of the shrines which at one time must have lined the road almost literally nothing remains. A search for solid reminders of the Becket cult would take us far beyond the bounds of the region and would even then be largely unproductive. Indeed the modern pilgrim, although as ready as ever in the past to go to Canterbury, may well not feel attracted to this particular martyr. With twentieth-century hindsight one may feel that common sense and practical politics were on the King's side in the great debate, and that Becket, pursuing a course with the single-mindedness which marked every stage in his career, was trying to hold back the tide of history. By deliberately courting martyrdom he used a weapon which the King might well call unfair. The modern pilgrim goes to Canterbury in pursuit of great architecture; or the memory of other saints—Alphege, Anselm, William Temple—whose viewpoint, however remote in time, may be closer to his own; or in search of an idea. Few pilgrims are entirely dissatisfied with the experience.

For the start of this journey I would not go with Chaucer to South-wark in search of a vanished Tabard Inn, but begin a few miles along the road on one of the great historic sites of England, Blackheath. This was home ground for Chaucer who, in the years of his prosperity, had a house at Greenwich. Blackheath was notorious as a haunt of ruffians; Chaucer was beaten up and robbed in the neighbourhood in 1390. He was carrying government money at the time, and was lucky to have his story accepted by the authorities. He was still living in London when the Kentish contingent of peasant demonstrators assembled on the heath under Wat Tyler, but he moved into Kent soon afterwards and took a substantial part in county affairs. He became a justice of the peace in 1385 and was elected one of two Members of Parliament for Kent a year later.

It is reasonable to suppose that Chaucer's official duties as a civil servant, especially when he succeeded William of Wykeham as Clerk of the King's Works, took him through Kent, probably in the company of Henry Yevele who was engaged on the rebuilding of Canterbury nave during 1391. (One of Chaucer's duties was to pay Yevele for his work on Westminster Hall and other royal buildings.) One may indulge a fancy of these two men, each uniquely distinguished in his own field, riding together along Watling Street and observing, on Chaucer's part with a most keen and humorous eye, the motley traffic Canterbury-bound. Chaucer dropped enough casual hints into the linking passages of the *Canterbury Tales* to show his familiarity with the road. It is even possible that he made a formal pilgrimage himself on the death of his wife Philippa in 1387.

Chaucer's pilgrims took the ancient route across Blackheath and over Shooters Hill. Did they perhaps make a diversion towards the river to visit Lesnes Abbey? The modern pilgrim, unhappy among these miles of featureless brick, might well do so, for the remains, although barely above ground level, are of considerable interest and their setting is surprisingly pleasing.

The old pilgrims had always to look out for a place to hear Mass. At Crayford they could enter the very ancient parish church, dedicated to Augustine's colleague Paulinus who became the apostle to the Northumbrians. A little along the way was Dartford with church and priory. Beyond, and off the Roman road, was another church, of no special sanctity but one which the modern traveller will certainly go off his route to see. St Mary's Church at Stone stands incongruously in the midst of chalk pits used and disused. It has the oddest profile imaginable, with a rather ungracious tower and a chancel roof raised, unexpectedly and almost absurdly, high above the line of the nave. One almost turns away in despair; only the elegant doorway restrains. Inside it is quite another matter. Here is a building of a quality unmatched in Kent outside the cathedral. Stone Church was rebuilt in the reign of Henry III during the brief flowering of the Decorated phase of Gothic architecture. It has an exuberance which, because we turned so quickly to the more rigid conventions of Perpendicular, seems un-English. The nave piers soar and blossom into florid capitals. The windows have exquisite shafts, slim and gleaming. Most memorable of all, the walls of the choir break out into an elegant riot of blind arcading, deep sculpted with flowers and foliage among which strange creatures lurk. It is all wonderfully exhilarating, if not quite fitting for a church of so modest a scale. The similarity of much of the detail to that in Westminster Abbey, remodelled at just this time, can scarcely be coincidental. Did the Westminster masons have a trial run here, or did they toss off Stone as a splendid afterthought?

The church apart, nothing in Stone is likely to attract the modern traveller. Thameside Kent between Dartford and Gravesend is a strange and largely depressing area. The line of Watling Street passes to the south over the long slope of Telegraph Hill, now hugely changed by motorway-type improvements and with a quite lovely footbridge sweeping across it at the crown of the rise; the alternative road towards the river goes past waste ground, sad pubs, modern housing estates which seem to lack any convictions architectural or planning, and the weird moonscape of abandoned chalk-pits. In one of these, near Swanscombe, were discovered the fragmentary remains of a woman who can at present claim to be the earliest known inhabitant of this island. The reign of *homo sapiens* which she involuntarily inaugurated stumbles towards its whimpering close among the belching cement chimneys—visually magnificent but I should not care to live too near them—and the characterless streets. Even here the incongruity which makes of every journey through England a series of adventures produces a surprise. Where the houses of Swanscombe peter out on the edge of the chalk-belt, beside a block of very new council offices which are themselves a surprise, so pleasant is their design, is Swanscombe Church, a small building showing convincing evidence of pre-Conquest origins. The pilgrims must often have cut across the fields from the old road to hear Mass in a building old in their day. The pilgrims were too early to enjoy the present showpiece of Swanscombe Church. Here is the ornate tomb of Sir Antony Weldon, a kitchen knight of Elizabeth and James I. He lies on one elbow, his face lined with the cares of so many meals designed to satisfy the inner prince. Above are his arms and that symbol of a chivalry already long dead, his helmet.

The Weldons of Swanscombe came into the Kentish story more conspicuously in the following century when they took a leading part in Civil War and Commonwealth in the Parliamentary interest.

Watling Street, in its modernized form, acts as a largely successful *cordon sanitaire*. To the north is a strip of highly developed, largely undistinguished housing interspersed with gigantic holes in the ground. To the south the country is still surprisingly untouched by recent change. Orchard and arable turn the village of Southfleet into an island, and lanes wander south and east out of sight of the urban sprawl —except where an outlier of Northfleet erupts suddenly out of the fields at Istead Rise.

Here the modern traveller, if he is not desperate to get to a destination, has a choice. There is the fascination of Thameside and the traffic of London river, well seen from gardens on the waterfront of Gravesend. To this may be added a motley collection of memories, of poor Pocahontas, Indian princess who came to England, tasted the tawdry splendours of James I's court and liked them not, took ship for home and succumbed to the diseases of civilization in Gravesend; of 'Chinese' Gordon who was sent to reorganize the defences of the river mouth and spent here probably the happiest years of a confused life; of Rosherville, a vision of refined pleasures in a chalk-pit which was vulgarized into a centre for shoddy entertainment. Apart from a statue of Pocahontas and the Thames forts there is nothing much to show for all this, although the remnants of an eighteenth-century town design—for the place was largely devastated by fire in 1727—have some interest. Beyond Gravesend the Dickens memories crowd in all the way to Rochester.

These attractions may not be sufficient to entice the traveller north of the road, and the appeal of quieter country and narrower lanes may prevail. Farther south the commuters have settled Longfield and Meopham—in more senses than one—but by skilled navigation their estates may be avoided. The escape route begins just beyond the point where a jungle of wire marks a major junction of the electric grid and, incongruously, the site of the Roman station of Vagniacae at Springhead. If the season is right one may see here a team of archaeologists exploring a site immediately adjoining the road.

To the south a road which soon shakes off its motorway origins ambles towards the tall battlemented tower of Southfleet Church and almost at once there is another surprise. Southfleet, which is within

view of the motor-road, is unspoilt—at least by the standards of the
South-east. Here is the ground-plan of a model community: cottages,
farm and school huddled companionably in the shadow of the church.
Not all the buildings are worthy but the row leading to the church
is charming. The village school still has a core of seventeenth-century
brick to mark the original foundation of Sir John Sedley. In the church,
which is better in general than in detail, the show-piece is an octagonal
font with panels carved effectively—and not so efficiently as to make
them too good for their modest setting—with bishop, grail, resurrection and a lively baptism of Christ. (The work is distinctive for all that
it lacks technical virtuosity, and one may note that the same craftsman
was at work not far away in Dickens's favourite church at Shorne.)

From Southfleet lanes go south-east around the modern estate of
Istead Rise, cross the Gravesend road, and pass through Nurstead—
but there is no village to pass, only a lonely church with the usual
Kentish tower, tall, square and corner-turreted, and Nurstead Court
in a small park, not revealing to the casual eye that here is the rare
survival of an early medieval hall-house. Thereafter the lane narrows
still further and twists and turns its way to Cobham.

Here surely was a minor objective of the Canterbury pilgrims, and
barely a mile off their route. The parish church achieved a rise in status
when John de Cobham attached to it in 1362 a college of five priests.
Later in the century the number was increased. The foundation enjoyed
a good reputation and had papal approval as a place of pilgrimage.
The founder greatly extended the church to make it fit for collegiate
use, adding aisles which make the nave an almost perfect square and
enriching the chancel with elegant sedilia for three officiating priests.

The modern pilgrim, who is less concerned with penance than with
the satisfaction of historical curiosity, goes to Cobham mainly to see
the array of brasses which pave the floor of the choir. Here is the finest
single collection of monumental brasses in the country, perhaps in the
world. They include John, *"foundeur de ceste place"* and several generations of his family. As works of art, as a record of history, and as a guide
to armour and costume, they are unsurpassed.

The priests of Cobham College carried out their duties for 175
years. When the future of such foundations was clearly foreshadowed
in Henry VIII's reign the brethren took the hint and surrendered the
house to the current successor of their founder, George Brooke, Lord
Cobham. It is he who is buried in front of the high altar in an aggressively magnificent tomb. Among the children who kneel in mourning
around the great central chest is the figure of William, the heir. In
1597 William put the half-ruined buildings of the college into repair
and endowed an almshouse for twenty poor people. This foundation
still continues, and visitors may see the charming buildings, rather like

an Oxford college in miniature with a central quadrangle and an open-raftered hall at the rear.

Literary pilgrims too come to Cobham for this is one of the principal Kentish centres for the worship of Charles Dickens. Just opposite the church is the Leather Bottle Inn, favoured by the Pickwick Club, and outside stands a sarsen stone on which one may still read the mystic words "BILST UM PSHI SM ARK". Barely three miles away to the north-east is Gadshill, where Dickens achieved his life's ambition when in 1856 he acquired the undistinguished "mansion of dull red brick, with a little weathercock-surmounted cupola on the roof . . . a large house, but one of broken fortunes", as he saw it in the context of *A Christmas Carol*, which was his last and favourite home.

Cobham is a tantalizing village, as full of good things as any in Kent but marred by some mean building—not all of it new—and by a lack of co-ordination. The high notes are admirably pitched but they are not sustained. There is a handsome town house at the west end of the main street—Owletts, a Restoration mansion now in National Trust hands—but the great house stands away in its park to the east and makes no discernible impact on the village. Cobham Hall, the home of Brookes and Darnleys, and now an international school for girls, is a mixture of styles from Tudor to Victorian—and even, thanks to contributions by the school, post-Second World War; the total impression, of warm red brick and onion-capped turrets, is Jacobean. The house is usually shown during school holidays. It is certainly worth seeing, but I prefer the park, with its fine timber a little decayed, and the pleasure gardens which a past Lady Darnley tricked out with temples, 'Neolithic' great-stone monuments and a grotto in the most delightfully inconsequential manner of the eighteenth century. Beyond the park lies Codham Great Wood which still extends as far as the motorway.

Keeping the main road away for a little longer, the road south from the drive of Cobham Hall turns east quickly and goes by gently undulating country through a chalk valley to Cuxton, a downland village which has recently become an outlier of the Medway towns and a commuter base. At the junction with the road through the Medway gap there is an exciting view of the great motorway bridge across the tidal Medway.

Here there is a straight choice between the Medway towns and the motorway. The motorway is very much quicker and in its first stage of considerable scenic interest, because in addition to the river-crossing there is a run through a deep cutting in the chalk with on the one hand the bulk of Fort Borstal, which looks like an Iron Age hill-fort and is one of the nineteenth-century defences of the Medway ports, on the other delightful wooded downs and valleys. However, the Canterbury pilgrims, even if they could have been offered the choice of another crossing, would surely have chosen to go through Rochester. In their day the city would have seemed livelier than it does today, for Rochester is going through a difficult phase, its trade declining and the battle with the internal-combustion engine by no means won.

Rochester is the classic example of a river-crossing settlement. The tidal river narrows here for the last time before spreading out into the wide and tricky waters of the estuary. There would have been a ferry here from the earliest times and a bridge came with the Roman road. The Roman town of Durobrivae was probably grafted on to a Belgic village. Then came the medieval stone bridge of eleven arches which was one of the wonders of its day. This lasted until 1856 when it was replaced by a strikingly unlovely structure which has only recently been improved by the addition of another carriageway downstream. Through all the centuries the history of Rochester has been that of the bridge. The vast and still splendid castle is meaningless except in the context of the river-crossing.

"Busy, beautiful Rochester, and none the less beautiful because busy," wrote Charles Harper in 1895. Poor Rochester is less than completely busy now and beautiful only in small parts. It is the saddest place I know in the South-east.

Whatever its future in industry and administration Rochester is potentially a major tourist centre. The antiquarian treasures are not all at present in good shape and their settings are often poor; but they exist. One day the attractions of ancient masonry and rich associations will be reinforced with lively and effective shops and a welcoming and invigorating atmosphere.

I wonder to what extent the city is inhibited by a sense of inferiority. It has always been bedevilled by comparisons with Canterbury. Canterbury was the cantonal capital of Roman Kent, the seat of the kings of Saxon Kent, the seat of the archbishop, the possessor of the shrine of Becket. The role of second-best is never enviable, but at least Rochester is second-, not third- or fourth-best. It has the second oldest foundation among English cathedrals, for Augustine was quick to see the strategic value of a bishop half-way along the road to London. The military importance of the castle was of major concern, so much so that, with two brief exceptions, it was always kept under direct royal control. Even in ruin the castle buildings are magnificent, and the twelfth-century keep has less than half a dozen peers in the whole country. The cathedral does not quite live up to its magnificent west front but it has one great masterpiece inside, the exquisite thirteenth-century doorway into the chapter house. The crypt too is not unworthy of comparison with that at Canterbury. The appeal of Rochester, however, is not comparative. In a straight fight Canterbury wins easily. Rochester's strength lies in its homeliness, in the small scale, the

Essex stream

Tile hanging in Surrey

(*below left*) New Town: Harlow (*below right*) Weatherboarding in Kent

absence of splendour and high drama. Walking in the precincts of
Canterbury one's heart is continually stirred by the soaring glory and
the heaven-seeking pinnacles of Bell Harry. Rochester's tower, a
twentieth-century recreation of the Norman original, is mildly comical
but most endearing.

There is comedy too, for the twentieth-century mind, in Rochester's
one great bid for a share of Canterbury's pilgrim-traffic. Every pilgrim
turned off from the route to visit the Cathedral Church of St Andrew,
but offerings were small and it was irksome for the monks to see all
that wealth going eastwards away from them. What they wanted was
a martyr-saint of their own. In 1201 they acquired one. A Scottish
master-baker, William of Perth, was on pilgrimage to Jerusalem. He
attended Rochester Cathedral and then went on his way. Next day he
was found murdered. He was a wealthy man and the roads were
infested with thieves. It is unkind, and probably unhistoric, to suspect
the monks. I do not think that they killed the poor man. They made
the most of his murder, however. To die whilst on pilgrimage was
clear evidence of sanctity. The prior gave William appropriately
splendid burial in the cathedral, set the process of canonization in
motion, and waited, not in vain, for the miracles to begin.

When I told the stories of St Thomas of Canterbury and St William
of Perth to a Danish visitor, he gave his opinion that a Scottish baker
had a better chance of possessing the true qualities of a saint than an
English archbishop. Whatever William's virtues the monks' enterprise
was rewarded; thereafter a little of the treasure passing along Watling
Street was left behind at the shrine of St William.

The latter-day saint of Rochester is Dickens. In this century such
pilgrims as have come this way most of them have been prompted by
a wish to identify for themselves the familiar scenes in the novels. It is
a pity that the demand for a national funeral took Dickens, when he
died at Gad's Hill, to Westminster Abbey; he would have lain snugly in
the cathedral and pilgrims would have had an appropriate objective.
As it is, they make do with following Mr Pickwick to 'The Bull' and
Miss Haversham to Restoration House, and they watch Pip in all his
sartorial splendour enduring his encounter with Tradd's boy. Of all the
great who came this way—Gundulf, King John, Henry VIII, Elizabeth,
Charles I and Charles II and James II—not a whisper endures, but on
the air of Rochester High Street one may still catch an echo of the
derisive and fictional "Don't know yah!" When Dickens came at last
to paint a full-length portrait of the city in *The Mystery of Edwin
Drood*, he chose, for some strange Freudian reason, to hide it under the
alias of Cloisterham. Dickens's last novel is in some ways his worst,
with all his sentimentality and florid writing indulged to excess, but
when, on the last day of his life, he sat down in his chalet in the garden

3

of Gad's Hill to describe the dawn of a Sunday morning in Rochester, he rose to unexpected heights of gay and shrewd eloquence. The passage came to an end, he laid down his pen, and there it rested.

In the grounds of Eastgate House, where an admirable museum occupies the building of Miss Twinkleton's school where Drood's insipid child-bride-to-be was educated, the tall wooden chalet given to Dickens by admirers and his own favourite workshop has been re-erected. On the way from the cathedral to Eastgate House one passes in the High Street the neat gabled box of Watts' Charity, where Dickens spent a fictional Christmas Eve with six poor travellers "being neither rogues or proctors" and made from the experience one of his most charming minor works.

Standing in Rochester High Street and facing east, before us lie, if not "deserts of vast eternity" at least the urban desert of Chatham and Gillingham, an area of unquestionable interest but one which I love not. Having got to Rochester, however, there is nothing for it but to grit the teeth and head eastwards, noting on the Rochester-Chatham boundary the big modern buildings of St Bartholomew's Hospital. This has tucked under its wing the tiny building of the original foundation by Gundulf, the first Norman Bishop of Rochester, builder of the original castle and a formidable prelate indeed. The Norman hospital consisted of a small infirmary hall to which was attached a minute apsidal chapel. It is still here, greatly restored and in use as the hospital church.

Until fairly recently the journey up the steep hill away from the Medway would have been enlivened with meditation about the Jezreelites and the Flying Roll upon which the Word of God was inscribed. Now Jezreel's Tower, in which five thousand of the elect were to shelter when the world moved to its inevitable destruction, has fallen to the demolisher, and nothing is left as a reminder of this exquisitely absurd and pathetic Victorian fantasy.

Instead the next tower which draws the eye is the tall typically Kentish tower of Rainham Church, and this is welcome not only for its fine soaring lines but because it is an earnest that the grip of the Medway towns is at last weakening. Beyond are the wide acres of the cherry orchards. Even here the only medieval sights are the towers, of Rainham, Hartlip and Newington. The Romans introduced cherries into Britain, but the ancestors of our own delicious dessert cherries came later, at the time when the Reformation was putting an end to the pilgrimages.

Here the old and tarnished nickname of Garden of England for once makes sense. For a few brief days in May these unexciting levels are transformed into a wonderland whose enchantment, perhaps because it is so transient, is renewed every year. The effect is strengthened by the contrast between the thick clusters of intensely white blossoms and the almost black trunks and branches. Like every other pleasure of the countryside, cherries are perpetually at risk. They have a very short season, so that the returns, although considerable—the price nowadays never drops below the 'luxury' level—are concentrated into a few weeks and thereafter the orchards, except for sheep-grazing, are unproductive. The pressures, economic and political, to turn to more consistently profitable crops, are considerable. And yet, Kent without cherries! The thought is not to be borne.

'Blossom Tours', so much favoured by motor-coach companies, seldom catch the cherry in flower. The blossom is matured and gone so quickly that it is impossible to plan a tour in advance. One must go out on impulse, obeying the singing in the blood which says that it is time, and hope to capture the moment as it flies. For those who miss the glory of the spring there is another, and a less regarded glory, in autumn. Few trees are more lovely in decline than the cherry. The long tapering leaves flame red and orange in the autumn sun, set against the darkness of the trees.

The best of these orchards—and they are bettered in only one parish in Kent—cluster around the parish churches of Hartlip and Newington. Indeed the 'picture-postcard' charm of Newington tower rising above the waves of blossom is familiar to thousands who have never seen the reality. Hartlip is slightly less well known and not less delightful. Apart from one or two timber-framed houses, and some remarkably comely new ones, there is nothing much in the village other than the church and the setting. The church has a pretty little angle-piscina of a kind which recurs in this part of Kent—in Borden and Bapchild for example —and the lean-to against the tower wall was the home, calculatedly uncomfortable, of an anchorite. Surely the pilgrims turned off the road here to gain merit by a gift to the filthy and verminous, but unquestionably holy, occupant.

Between Hartlip and Newington, on the main road, the pilgrims visited the shrine of another saint, Robert le Bouser. It was one of the chantry chapels which at one time marked the stages of all the main routes of England. At the Reformation the chantry was destroyed and the shrine vanished. It turned up later, having been smuggled into hiding to await better times, and was reassembled in Newington Church. St Robert's shrine is only one of the attractions of Newington Church. Beside the church path stands a big sarsen stone closely associated, as these alien boulders tend to be, with the Evil One. The Devil, it seems, braced himself against it when trying, as was his custom, to overturn the church tower. Among the fittings of the church, which is exceptionally well provided, prime place must be given to the font cover. The font itself is a plain octagon, and on it sits a towering structure of inlaid wood. It would be too much of a chore to lift this for every baptism, so two sides open like doors to give access to the consecrated water within.

Apart from the church and an ancient inn on Watling Street there is nothing to linger over in Newington. A big question-mark now hangs over the route. No such problems faced the medieval pilgrims. For them the way lay straight ahead down Keycol Hill and through Sittingbourne, their journey enlivened by visits to notable wayside chapels at either end of the town. (Indeed Sittingbourne is one of the few places which Chaucer mentions by name.) But Schamel and Swanstree chapels disappeared in the sixteenth century, and nothing of comparable appeal has appeared in Sittingbourne since that time! I am being unkind. There are many worse towns than Sittingbourne, even in Kent, and the new civic buildings are not only architecturally respectable but a useful addition to the life of the place. Nevertheless, after all those miles of Chatham and Gillingham, other pilgrims beside myself will have had enough of urban roads for a while, and will be ready for an untraditional diversion.

This escape route goes south at Newington for Stockbury. The peril of this kind of journey is that the siren delights by the way may be so insidious that the traveller may never arrive. Once beyond the orchard belt the chalk country tilts surprisingly and produces a landscape which for once in this mild country is almost dramatic. Because of the lie of these dry valleys there are few glimpses beyond the next rise and the enclosed intimacy of the views is most appealing. One of the steep banks, Queen Down Warren, is in the care of the county's Naturalists' Trust. It has always been renowned for the flowers, especially orchids, which carpet the slopes in early summer. To divert from our current diversion is surely permissible in order to come here, preferably at a sunny noon when the butterflies are busy enough to encourage the visitors to idle enjoyment. Access to nature reserves is commonly restricted, for the best of reasons; there is however a long tradition of free entry to Queen Down Warren, and visitors will respect the trust thus shown in their good sense and leave the plants, common and rare alike, where they belong.

The eastward view from the Warren is limited to the next ridge and beyond this the village of Stockbury occupies the next level, somewhat nondescriptly although it has the usual Kentish yeoman's house in the middle. The ancient settlement lies farther east where the chalk tilts sharply to the dual-carriage motor-road through Stockbury Vale. The church stands right on the edge and its fine flint tower—which demonstrates how effective this intractable material of the chalk downs can be when handled confidently—is a dominant feature of the scene in the valley. The building looks promising, but like so many in Kent Stockbury Church fell victim to the ruthlessness of Victorian restorers. Looking at the confusion and the inconsistencies left by those enthusiasts one cannot help cursing their self-confidence and consciousness of their own rectitude which led to so much irreparable destruction; yet their dilemma was as acute as our own. Most village churches, then as now, were in a state of advanced dilapidation, and there was a straight choice between restoration and total ruin. We might opt for ruin, and hide it under the cant name of 'redundancy'; the Victorians chose to restore, and in the process they did as much harm as the reformers and the iconoclasts of previous centuries. Stockbury Church, then, is a memorial to a great age of church building which enriched a modest rustic building with the sophistication of art, and to an age which knew better than its forefathers. We in our turn lack the faith of the one and the self-righteousness of the other.

From the churchyard one can see, in an admirable strategic position, a hump of earth rising up in front of the farmhouse and right on the edge of the ridge. This is the motte of a primitive Norman castle, hurried up in the crisis years which followed the Conquest and never, as others in Kent were, reconstructed in stone in the succeeding, more settled age. (At the far end of Stockbury Vale, where the escarpment of the downs slopes abruptly to the plain there is another castle of the same type on Thurnham Hill where the reconstruction took place, but time has reversed the process and the masonry has all but vanished from the original motte.) Church and fortified manor stand together as the type of an early settlement, but the illusion of a primitive community is shattered as much by the sophisticated pattern of field and orchard as by the traffic below, the concrete grandeur of the viaduct carrying the motorway across the valley, and the distant towers, spires and minarets of the industrial complex on Grain.

The essence of this North Kent landscape is contrast. The otherworldly beauty of the cherry orchards, the A2 polluting Newington Street and Sittingbourne, flower-strewn banks at Queen Down Warren, the tarmac carpet spread along Stockbury Vale—then across the valley the scene switches at once to the mild up-and-down charms of more orchards on the way to Bredgar. It is all unexciting but not unpleasing, highly cultivated and for once scientific husbandry goes hand in hand with good appearance. Only the occasional bungalow which was rushed up between the wars mars the scene. The rises are rounded and gentle, the 'bottoms' abrupt and dry, doubtless only in historic time for in pre-Roman Kent the water-table was higher and all these pretty V-shaped valleys had their streams. So by way of Deans Bottom—this, I suppose, does not commemorate the posterior of some venerable ruler of Rochester or Canterbury Chapter but the *dene* (valley) bottom—to Bredgar, which was a pretty village within living memory but has grown too much and too quickly for comfort. Bredgar is too far off Watling Street to draw any but the most dilatory or enterprising of pilgrims, although the college of priests established here in 1393—and represented now by a house called 'The Chantry'—might otherwise have been an attraction. The solid charms of the church attract today. It is a building showing plenty of flint, some fragments of a Norman predecessor, and an interior which links the medievalism of the structure and the more sober virtues of the eighteenth century in the hatchment boards and the barrel-organ. But one comes to Bredgar not so much for the village as for the wealth of houses which stand in the surrounding country. Any casually undertaken expedition is likely to reveal a couple, perhaps Swanton Court in sober and civilized brick and Bexon, a superb example of Kentish yeoman's house, timber-framed and thatched and clearly as good as ever after four centuries of use.

The motorway passes very near Bredgar, and Bredgar church-tower is conspicuous from it. A lane travels beside the motorway for a couple of miles and then turns to visit Milsted, a village which hides so modestly that only the sharpest observer will glimpse it as he hurtles along. Milsted is possibly the crown jewel of this unexplored and enchanting hinterland, a place which is happily free of tourist attractions but one which combines on a small scale all the elements which go to make a satisfactory downland village. Beside the crossroads is the classic juxtaposition of church and hall-house and across the way, behind a brick wall but not quite out of sight, is a singularly lovely house in timber and brick set in a discreetly perfect garden. One might be tempted to hoard these treasures, but there is probably no harm in offering to sharing them for they lie safely away from main roads and only the most dedicated and deserving of explorers will seek them out.

By now Sittingbourne has been safely bypassed, and one may return to Watling Street by way of a deep lane following the bed of a lost stream to Rodmersham Green and then past Rodmersham Church in its setting of orchards to Bapchild.

It is a characteristic of Watling Street, and one which is clearly marked here, that the ancient settlements avoid the line of the Roman road. Sittingbourne lies along it with the medieval church flush with the road, but the older settlement of Milton Regis—a royal manor in Saxon times—stands off to the north, and now comes Bapchild, just off the road on the south side, Tonge to the north, Teynham well to the north, Norton and Ospringe to the south. Only Stone church is close to the highway, and this, as we may discover, for a good 'reason. All these settlements were born, it would seem, of the early Saxons' distrust of the relics of Roman civilization, and it was not until well into medieval times that new communities began to spring up along the line of the road. These were stimulated by the opportunity to provide services to travellers on the busiest road in the country, especially after the murder of Becket, although most of the surviving buildings date— at least in outward appearance—from the later age of the stage-coach. All were in danger of being shaken to bits by heavy lorries until the motorway took some, but not all, of them away.

The little church of Bapchild, which displays one early Kentish characteristic in having the tower tucked into the south side in an almost transeptal position, was certainly close enough to the road to attract the attention of pilgrims and this may account for the exceptional richness of its detail. There is an unusual lavishness in the treatment of the arcading, and the little angle piscina, although like the one already seen at Hartlip, is most beautifully finished even to the carving of the rose of the outlet drain. Legend managed to link the name of Becket with a natural spring on the opposite side of the road and this 'watering' proved an attraction. It was in time encased in a little chapel, now vanished.

The waters of Becket's Well flow north-east and widen to form the millpond of Tonge Mill, which may have been the moat of a motte-and-bailey castle whose mound remains. Legend is at work here too, for Tonge, according to one tradition, was the seat of King Vortigern in the days of the first Saxon invasions and here Hengist's warriors smuggled swords into the goodwill feast and slaughtered their hosts. The whole story of the Saxon conquest is clouded in confusion and incontrovertible evidence is lacking, but it is a vivid tale which may have at least symbolic truth.

To the north, beyond the railway, lies one of the strangest and most empty tracts in Kent, between Milton Creek and Faversham Creek. There is a little revived industry at Conyer, as well as a sailing centre, but for the most part when the orchards come to and end the flat is given over to birds. Only a few tracks cross the levels to terminals of the lost ferries to Sheppey.

Watling Street here has little but its associations and its straightness to commend it, and the modern traveller is again tempted to frequent diversions, especially to the south where the old and new highways enclose an area of intensive fruit cultivation which is still of great visual and historic interest. There are fine houses everywhere, including a crop in Lynsted village—and a church here with notable Renaissance monuments—and an exceptionally fine and large magpie house at Provender, near Norton. This was the home of the Hugessons. The last female representative of this family took her name and fortune by marriage into the Knatchbull family of Mersham, afterwards Knatch-bull-Hugessons, and became grandmother-in-law of Jane Austen's favourite niece, Fanny Knight. To the north of Provender is Teynham,

the largest settlement hereabouts and one which has grown unbeauti-
fully around the railway station. Old Teynham is in orchard country
beyond the railway. Here stands a big, nobly-proportioned church in a
superb setting. Hartlip and Newington make a grand show of cherry
blossom, but to see the cherry at its most breath-taking one comes here
to the orchards of Teynham Court. Here, according to a persistent
tradition, cherries—that is the modern dessert cherry—were first established in the reign of Henry VIII, and here, appropriately enough, they
are seen at their finest. In the church a modern east window glows in
gorgeous reds and blues in a fine Nativity. (After writing these words I
was passing near Teynham in May 1973 and decided to photograph
once more the cherry blossom behind the church. The orchard had
been grubbed! Farmers have a hard life and productivity is all. But
Teynham's cherries were of national importance. As well might the
National Gallery grub its Rembrandts and plant a more profitable line
in pop art.)

This is an area, rare in this long-inhabited country, of lost villages.
Buckland-by-Faversham and Stone-next-Faversham appear on the
map, and both have nominal, but very small, populations, but they
defy identification on the ground. Buckland's church vanished long
ago. Four low walls in a field beside Watling Street, just opposite the
road to Lenham, are all that remains of Stone Church. This probably
became ruinous after the Reformation, when the decline of faith coincided with depopulation caused by the growth of sheep husbandry to
produce 'redundant' churches in many parts of England. The remains
have a slight melancholy picturesqueness, but they might otherwise
not attract notice. Recent archaeological study of the site has, however,
revealed that Stone has a startlingly long history. The medieval church
incorporates an earlier building and this, it would seem, a Christian
chapel of Roman times. If this is so, Stone may represent a place of
continuous Christian worship for thirteen hundred years, and the
decline of the place in Elizabeth's reign becomes even sadder.

A scattering of old houses marks the beginning of Ospringe, which
lies along Watling Street for a half-mile—although characteristically
the old village and church are to the south. Ospringe is usually identified with the Roman posting station of Durolevum and there have been
substantial Roman finds in the area. Some of these are housed in the
Maison Dieu, a stone and timber building in two parts separated by
Water Lane. This was part of a foundation, part hostel, part hospital,
established in 1234 for the benefit of travellers along the old road. Its
survival, when others declined with the end of the pilgrimages and
legislation against religious houses, is freakish but welcome, and in the
hands of the Department of the Environment the little building is well
cared for and attractive. It is not long since Water Lane was watery

indeed, at least in certain seasons, for the road was a bed of a stream which flows tentatively from the higher ground towards Sheldwich. This is a nailbourne, one of the rivers, particularly but not exclusively Kentish, which flow intermittently. They occur in chalk country and for long periods—including wet seasons—they remain dry; then, their underground reservoirs restocked, they will flow again. True men of Kent—the nailbournes occur only in East Kent—will claim that their active seasons are a presage of disaster, and there is never a lack of disasters to prove them right. Ospringe bourne is now tamed underground until it emerges in Faversham Creek.

Ospringe is within the borough of Faversham, both in local government terms and in reality for the town comes up to the main road and has done so for a long time. Yet, true to the traditions of Watling Street, it misses the town centre by half a mile. The original founders, applying unconsciously the principles of modern planning, planted their settlement away from the flow of traffic, with a wisdom from which their successors benefit.

In its origins Faversham was a port more than a highway town. The creek still brings enough tidal water from the Swale to preserve the illusion, but in the Middle Ages this winding waterway was the key to Faversham prosperity. The town was admitted to the Brotherhood of the Cinque Ports as a limb of Dover, and contributed its quota of ships for the king's business right up to the Armada. With maritime success came municipal independence, and Faversham gained its first charter in 1352 long before many proud south-eastern boroughs.

Although the town lay off Watling Street, pilgrims would certainly have turned off their route to visit the great Cluniac (later Benedictine) abbey of the Holy Saviour. This had been founded by King Stephen and at the end of that sad king's unhappy reign he was buried in the founder's position before the high altar. At the Dissolution the abbey suffered a more comprehensive destruction than most, the hostility of the commissioners being directed inexplicably against the royal tomb, and according to tradition the remains of Stephen and his queen were thrown in the creek. (The unmarked tomb in the parish church may be their second burial place.) The abbey was barely a memory when, in 1965, builders preparing the site of a new grammar school struck the foundations. Subsequent excavation revealed that the abbey church had been a building of phenomenal size, 370 feet long compared with Canterbury's 522 and Rochester's 305. Faversham Abbey possessed other relics besides those of the King, including, in common with many other of the major shrines of Christendom, a fragment of the True Cross. Stephen—a desperately inadequate king but a man of some personal quality—was not popular in death, but the building must have dominated the scene from the Roman road. Now, instead, there is the slim stone spire of the parish church, charmingly incongruous in this setting and in an essentially medieval town for it is a copy of Wren's St Dunstan's-in-the-East—baroque pretending, not too hard, to be Gothic.

The church is an exceedingly odd mixture of medieval and Georgian, fascinating but hardly admirable, and it possesses the finest set of choir stalls in Kent, equipped with misericords and carved arm-rests, an inheritance of the church's association with the Abbey of St Augustine in Canterbury. The immediate surroundings are pleasing, with late Georgian school buildings in mock-medieval stone and the original half-timbered hall of the grammar school. The red-brick brewery strikes no seriously discordant note, for it is only the present age which has found it incongruous to associate religion, education and industry.

In an age when most towns strive for a dull uniformity Faversham's record is outstandingly heartening. When I first came here twenty-five years ago it was a grubby place, rotting quietly away. Only a very discerning eye could detect the fine bone-structure under the shabby dress. Then Faversham—under the inspiration of a remarkable town clerk—took itself in hand and gave itself a hearty shake. Industry, not too much and that based largely on rural products, came to the town. The corporation adopted a policy of acquiring and restoring valuable but rundown houses in the heart of the town and produced in Court Street and Abbey Street the promise of as fine an urban road as Kent can show. The work still goes on, and a local society, outstanding for vision and practical enthusiasm, presses on with projects designed to reveal and preserve the past and to lay sound foundations for the future. There is much still to do. Abbey Street shows what imagination and good taste can achieve, yet there is still a lot of mess and unrealized architectural assets. The tightly-knit pattern of medieval roads is a challenge to planner and developer, and only vigilance prevents the town from being torn apart in an orgy of 'improvements'. Still, there are plenty of vigilantes in Faversham. Most important of all, the town keeps its scale. Growth is tightly controlled and contained within a small area, and Faversham remains a town and not an urban sprawl. It has won some balance, rare in the South-east, between commuters and local workers, and life goes on even after the morning trains have pulled out for London.

Among the revived houses of Court Street and Abbey Street is one, on the east side, which links in a mildly macabre way the pre- and post-Reformation story of Faversham. When the abbey was dissolved the land and buildings were bought by an enterprising businessman and mayor, Thomas Arden, and he made himself a house in part of the abbey gatehouse. Like some other tycoons, Arden probably neglected his wife in favour of his money-bags; at any rate she took a lover and the two conspired to murder Arden. After a few false attempts they achieved their aim and hid the body inefficiently in the abbey grounds. The crime was quickly traced to them and the lovers were condemned, the man to hanging, Mistress Arden—who was guilty of petty treason in killing her lord and master—to burning. The affair attracted attention beyond the bounds of the town, and an unknown playwright made it the subject of one of the earliest of domestic dramas. *Arden of Feversham*, still occasionally performed, is a curious blend of melodrama and knockabout comedy, and has enough local colour to encourage the belief that the writer came from these parts.

By Arden's day, the creek had begun to silt up and Faversham's prosperity no longer derived from its port. Instead the town turned to making gunpowder and built up a lasting reputation. Among the enterprises of the Faversham Society has been the recovery of one of the old factories from decay and the buildings are being restored as an industrial museum. We may look forward, after a century or so, to the launching of similar rescue operations to preserve fragments of the brewery and the canning factory.

Meanwhile modern pilgrims, with no True Cross to see nor chapel of St Crispin and Crispian—shoemaker saints who seem to have somehow got caught up in the Faversham story—in which to pray, must find satisfaction in the lesser shrines, including Davington Priory in a suburb to the west. This was a small house of Benedictine nuns, founded in the twelfth century, which somehow never prospered. Some of the conventual buildings are incorporated in the distinguished mansion on the site, and the nuns' church has survived intact. It is a notable, if austere, piece of very late Norman work.

On the way out of Faversham we, and the original pilgrims, should look in at the parish church of Preston, a village now separated from the town only by the railway track. This is an unexpectedly rich building with a group of canopied sedilia which are as fine as anything of the kind in Kent. The manor belonged to Christ Church, Canterbury, and the church doubtless benefited from the connection.

In front lie nine miles of Roman road, dead straight between visible points. Although there will inevitably be diversions, there is no reasonable alternative route to Canterbury, and so ancient and modern pilgrims step side by side all the way.

At first the route is dull. There is nothing much to see as far as Brenley Corner, where the motorway ends in a riot of flyovers and underpasses, continuing as Thanet Way, a three-lane road which in its day, not so long ago, was the last word in Kentish highways but which is now obsolescent. Watling Street goes forward until the houses of Boughton close in upon it.

This is Chaucer's Boghton Under Blee where the Canon and his Yeoman caught up with the pilgrims. They had seen Chaucer's party setting off in the morning from Ospringe, had liked the look of them— as who would not?—and ridden hard to catch them up. The Canon was looking out not only for congenial company but also for likely customers on whom to try his alchemical confidence-tricks. Unfortunately the yeoman was too frank about his master's technique and the canon "fledde away for verray sorwe and shame". No passage in *The Canterbury Tales* brings the mood of the pilgrimage so clearly through the centuries.

Chaucer's 'Blee' was the forest of Blean which covered a large part of East Kent. Like other wildernesses it was a haunt of outlaws and footpads, and the woodland was cleared a bowshot's length on either side of the highway as a protection for travellers. The ancient trees went long ago but the area is still heavily wooded with modern plantations, some of which come up to the road. Over to the north-east, in a nondescript area of coppices and haphazard bungalows which was once the heart of the forest, is the village of Blean—more correctly the Parish of St Cosmus and St Damian-in-the-Blean—with a church which, before the deterioration of the setting and an over-lavish restoration, must have been a most evocative woodland shrine.

So completely built up is the roadside of Boughton that one may imagine that, contrary to the usual practice, here is a village intimately associated with the Roman road. Not so. The ancient settlement is a mile south, in fine rolling country in which the church sits most effectively. Boughton Street is a later development when the promise of trade overcame a deep-seated distrust of the mysterious stone street made by giants or magicians. Today some medieval façades face the road, and there is probably more old fabric hidden behind the bland brick or plaster fronts of the eighteenth century. It is a neat village, or would be, were it not for the ceaseless flow of heavy traffic which threatens always to tear the heart out of Boughton. A bypass may come too late to save these unfussily civilized buildings.

Boughton Street ends at the foot of a long slow climb up Boughton Hill to Dunkirk. At the top church and school in sober Victorian stone face one another across the busy road. Both are associated through a bitter tragi-comedy with the big hotel on the crest of the hill. The hotel is called Sir William Courtenay and recalls not the ancient Kentish Courtenay—one of the greatest of medieval archbishops—but the lunatic who imposed himself dramatically and disastrously on the life of this quiet countryside in the 1830s.

The story of Thomas Thom, wine-merchant of Cornwall, alias Sir William Courtenay, Knight of Malta, has been told in full (in *Battle in Bossenden Wood*, 1961) and it is too complex to precis successfully here. The first act of the drama—this one pure comedy—was set in Canterbury; the second in Barming Asylum, to which the gallant knight had been consigned, in preference to Maidstone Gaol, when he was found guilty of perjury but insane; the last in and out of the villages of Boughton and Hernhill. Here the action was mainly tragic, not so much for Courtenay, who had at last found a cause upon which to fix his crazy energies, but for the depressed farm-labourers who took him for their messiah. The last scene of act three was played out in Bossenden Wood, a mile north of Dunkirk, when Courtenay was killed and his pathetic army scattered by the militia with bloodshed on both sides. The victims were buried in the pretty churchyard of Hernhill, below the hill. After the event early Victorian conscience stirred uneasily, if fitfully. Courtenay's followers had rallied to his tatty banner because of genuine social and economic grievances. The authorities saw in the affair evidence of the evils of ignorance and the decay of moral virtues. They built a church and a school at Dunkirk to combat these ills, but the labourers continued to starve.

A straggly village has grown up on the level ground around the church. A mile farther on, where the Gate Inn stands by the highway, the road dips and for the first time the towers of Canterbury appear below. Chaucer's pilgrims were too absorbed in the Canon's Yeoman's scandalous tale to notice, but in the age of faith this was a great moment in the pilgrimage. The high point of the cathedral was not Bell Harry Tower, which was built when the pilgrimages were almost at an end, but the massive Norman tower of Lanfranc's cathedral. This had a squat spire, rather like the modern spire at Rochester, and on it the gilded figure of an angel. At sight of the Angel Spire pilgrims fell to their knees in ecstasy and, rising, undertook the last miles of their journey with renewed zeal.

Road improvements have cut back the plantations of Blean Forest which here come up to the road. Watling Street now indulges in some un-Roman-road-like contortions as it descends the hill in a series of mild switchbacks to Harbledown. This is Chaucer's "litel toun . . . ycleped . . . Bobbe-up-and-down, Under the Blee, in Caunterbury weye", and a famous place in the Canterbury story. Its history is close linked with the hospital which the first Norman archbishop Lanfranc founded for 'lepers', that is for infectious diseases. This stood, and still stands, outside the city bounds and was a natural place of call for visitors coming into the city. After the murder of Becket the brethren of Harbledown moved in on the pilgrim business by acquiring relics of the saint. When Erasmus came on pilgrimage to Canterbury with his irascible friend John Colet, they stopped at St Nicholas's Hospital, Harbledown, where the master invited them, on payment, to kiss the martyr's shoe. Colet refused indignantly. Erasmus, who had absorbed the tolerance as well as the learning of the Renaissance, observed good-humouredly that the saint was still able to do good by ensuring a modest living for the brethren of St Nicholas's, and he cheerfully paid his dole.

Harbledown suffers more almost than any other village in Kent from a traffic problem. The road is narrow, steep and winding, and a very reasonable prohibition prevents car-parking. The modern pilgrim is therefore driven—quite literally—to pass Harbledown by. The village is too good to miss, however, and one should park in Canterbury and make a short return journey on foot. The village is built most pictur-esquely in terraces, with a great barn prominently at the foot of the hill and towers facing across the narrow way—for Harbledown has two churches. To be exact, it has a parish church and a chapel, the latter belonging to the hospital.

The hospital of St Nicholas stands on a bank high above the road, approached by a steep flight of steps. The domestic buildings, used as almshouses since early Victorian times, are agreeably rebuilt in a mildly Gothic manner. Lanfranc's chapel was remodelled, perhaps rebuilt, around the time of Becket's martyrdom and added to a century later. It is big by the standards of such buildings and delightfully light and uncluttered. There is a neat octagonal font—who, in this community of celibates, sick and infirm, was this meant for?—and a Norman arcade with amusing carving on the capital. The hospital had its own water-supply, a natural spring with beneficial mineral properties, and this is still there, enclosed in stone and with the Prince of Wales feathers in the keystone of the arch. This is inevitably associated with Edward the Black Prince, and he certainly knew Harbledown well from his journeys along Watling Street, sometimes *en route* for the wars in France, some-times visiting the chantry which he had endowed in the crypt of Christ Church. There is a nice story that, dying, he called for water from the well of Harbledown to cool his fever.

Modern pilgrims have a friendly welcome from the brethren of St Nicholas and are shown the treasures of the hospital. It is to be hoped that they will view them in Erasmus's friendly spirit, not with Colet's scorn, and will be as generous with their gifts as the former.

The hill out of Harbledown curves down past Regency and Victorian villas, and all at once there is Canterbury with the huge bulk of Christ Church Cathedral still dwarfing the rest of the city. The Roman road swept straight ahead here to the city gate, but the Saxon and medieval city was built across the symmetrical grids of the Roman streets and Saxon Watling Street bent left to enter Canterbury by the West Gate. Today the view has been opened up by Rheims Way, a new road which takes through-traffic across the water-meadows of the Stour and then along the line of the city walls. This road is among the most successful of post-war developments in Canterbury, partly because it spares the narrow medieval streets the worst effects of modern traffic, partly because it is itself a notable achievement which focuses attention on the river, the castle and the walls.

Rheims Way is for heavy lorries, not pilgrims—although pilgrims approaching in the fourth quarter of the twentieth century will be wise to get rid of their cars before they enter the walled city. Chaucer's pilgrims followed the country road past the village of St Dunstan's, with an awed look at St Dunstan's Church where Henry II prepared for his barefoot walk to the martyr's tomb. Then, through the brand-new arch of West Gate, rebuilt through the energies of Archbishop Simon of Sudbury who, as the pilgrims were sharply aware, had been beheaded by Wat Tyler's insurgents only a few years earlier, they probably separated, some to hasten at once to St Thomas's shrine, some to find refreshment or to fix up lodgings. Wealthy and distinguished travellers might expect hospitality in the guesten hall of the priory. Humble pilgrims sought a night's shelter in St Thomas's Hospital on the King's Bridge or one of the other charitable houses. Chaucer's friends, according to the apocryphal Tale of Beryn, put up at the 'Chequers of the Hope', an inn at the corner of Mercery Lane—and still there. Then they went along the lane, through a mean gate into the precincts—for the great Christ Church Gate was built much later— and reported to the Benedictine guide who would escort them through the nave, even then being transformed from Lanfranc's heavy Norman gloom to the sunshine glow of Henry Yevele's soaring English Gothic, to make their offerings at the many altars and finally, breathless with emotion, to view the jewel-encrusted wonders of the shrine.

Here one might leave them to return home, even the Good Wife of Bath perhaps chastened by the experience. There is neither space nor need for a detailed description of Canterbury, which, London only excepted, is the most written-about city in England. It might however be rewarding to consider briefly what Canterbury has to offer today's pilgrim to the vacant site of the shrine, who can expect neither mystical experience nor healing and who will not even be granted the visual delights of gold and gems. There is always the architecture, which the modern pilgrim will most likely appreciate better than his medieval counterpart. Despite the ravages of time the building is probably in better shape now than at any time in the past. It is certainly a more satisfying artistic entity. The transition from nave to choir is more effective than it was when the massive Romanesque nave joined the more lyrical French style of the choir. The matching western towers, even if one is a Victorian sham, produce a more harmonious effect than the uneasy mixture of Perpendicular and Norman which persisted into the nineteenth century. Above all, both physically and metaphorically,

Bell Harry Tower, which only the last and most disillusioned pilgrims saw completed, is the crowning glory of the great building. After the post-Reformation centuries of neglect and indifference, the cathedral is beautifully maintained. The Friends of Canterbury Cathedral, first and most active of such bodies, co-operate vigorously with the cathedral officers who, since Dean Bell set the standard, identify themselves with the building in a manner at once passionate and practical.

It was Bell too who conceived the idea, which in a sense looked back to medieval times, that the cathedral should be the centre of the artistic as well as the spiritual life of the diocese. Out of this came the Canterbury Festival, which produced, in *Murder in the Cathedral*, one major dramatic masterpiece as well as several other distinguished religious plays, and many memorable experiences of music and poetry. Today, in addition to the annual festival—at present a little less than enterprising—there is a year-long programme of artistic events in the cathedral. It was the presence of the cathedral, with its guarantee of a ceaseless flow of visitors to the city, which made possible the establishment in Canterbury of a municipal theatre, 'The Marlowe', named after the most famous of the city's sons; and it was the cathedral which was the decisive factor in the choice of Canterbury as the seat of the University of Kent. Here, too, plays, music and films enrich the life of a community which is far larger than that of the campus itself.

Other cities have comparable and better programmes of cultural events—although Canterbury must surely be the smallest to support such a variety of activities. Only Canterbury is *Mater Angliae*, and even if England no longer responds to the message of Becket or even that of Augustine, people are still, I think, sensitive to the cumulative experience of history which they find in a place in which so much has happened over so many years. The spirit of Canterbury is the sum total of Augustine, of Theodore and Hadrian—who by a calculated act of policy made the city one of the principal centres of education in Christendom, of Dunstan and Alphege, Lanfranc and Anselm, Courtenay, Cranmer, Juxon and William Temple. Even the most hard-pressed American tourist, doing Canterbury in two hours of a tight schedule, captures a little of this spirit in the echoing spaces of the crossing below Bell Harry, or in the flawless simplicity of the crypt beneath Becket's Crown.

Not long ago one of the city fathers declared, in defence of inner car parks if I remember correctly, that Canterbury was a shopping-centre or it was nothing. It is true that many East Kent residents find in the Canterbury supermarkets goods as good, or indifferent, as those in any other provincial town. It is not the shops, admirable as some of these are, which bring the world to Canterbury, in search of some indefinable experience distilled from a unique blend of beauty, antiquity and continuing history.

Thames Haven

Rochester Castle

Westmill, Hertfordshire

Yeoman's house, Bexon, Bredgar

3

Hop Country

THE visible symbol of Kent is the oast, and it is likely to remain so, even after every oast in the county has been turned into an expensive and slightly inconvenient residence. The homely building, to which the tilted white cone gives an endearingly tipsy air, has made its way deep into the affections, not only those of the Kentish-born. The hop too, although it may be grown as profitably in the red soil of Worcestershire and Herefordshire, is permanently identified in the public mind with Kent.

Of all the crops of the south country this alone has developed its own folklore and traditions; more than any other it has become a way of life. As I write these words in early September in my urban garden, my wife—a daughter of the hop gardens—has handed me an aromatic cone from the bine which she grows, for sound sentimental reasons, in memory of misty mornings and hot dusty days before the machine made hands obsolete.

For how long the hop has been king in Kent is not clear. The old rhyme

> Turkeys, heresy, hops and beer
> Came into England all in a year

is unhelpful, if it is not downright untrue. If the intention was to relate

the introduction to the Reformation this cannot be correct, for hops
were certainly used in brewing in the fifteenth century at least. Perhaps
the reference was to Lollardry, which would be more soundly historic.

The industry was sufficiently advanced by Queen Elizabeth's reign to
acquire its own textbook. *A Perfitte Platforme of a Hoppe Garden* is an
enchantingly written and exquisitely printed little book by Reynolde
Scot, issued in 1579. In it the author disposes of what were long-
established fallacies and lays down firm and well-argued guide-lines
for those who, having "beene trayned in the Open Fieldes to practyse
the Arte of Husbandrie with their Lymmes", now desire to "plant
Hoppes with effect". The basic language of today's hop-grower was
already current in 1579. Whenever the culture was introduced, it
probably came, like so much else in Kent, from Germany by way of
the Low Countries. Germany remains the principal source of the competition which, together with disease, makes this so precarious a crop.

Despite economic hazards, hops continue to claim a considerable
proportion of Kent's agricultural acreage. The trade has been helped
enormously by the setting up of the Hop Marketing Board, which by
fixing quotas and estimating demand has destroyed the old bugbear of
over-production, and has simplified the processes of selling. The board
and that invaluable middleman, the hop factor, have left the grower free
to concentrate on the essential work of production. Not even the Hop
Marketing Board can eliminate wilt or destroy the army of bugs which
descends on every garden as the bines grow.

Such economic and administrative considerations may not concern
the visitor to Kent, but they are vital to the survival of an industry on
which the pattern of this county depends. Without hops the landscape
would be infinitely less attractive, the passage of the seasons less
fascinating. The hop garden is good to look at in every stage of the
year. Only recently, I think, has the ordinary town-based observer
come to realize that the country does not shut down between October
and Easter. In some ways the winter months are the loveliest in Kent
when the fine bone-structure of the landscape is seen without its imped-
ing covering of leaves. In the thin winter sunshine the bare poles of the
hop garden stand like silver-grey skeletons and the complex pattern of
wires throws its grid over the bare earth. For me this is almost the
dearest of country sights, to be matched only by the winter sunset
against which the framework of the hop garden shows jet black. By its
texture and colour the hop-pole—now almost universally of chestnut—
provides an inexhaustible subject for the painter and the photographer.

In the winter too one may be able to witness the setting-out of a new
garden, the precise calculation which will produce the symmetrical
alleys and establish the position of each plant. This familiar pattern is
an innovation of late Victorian times. Before this, each plant occupied

a little artificial hill around which the poles were grouped. At harvest the poles were pulled and the whole garden dismantled. The poles were then stacked in 'wigwams' to await another season's setting-out. This practice is long discontinued, but each hop plant is still known as a 'hill'. The hop-garden is now built to last. The enormous strain of poles, wire and bines is borne by guy wires which are anchored deep underground to bulks of wood or concrete called deadmen. This complex structure will stand, barring accidents or a change in farming policy, for many years.

The first job of the new season is stringing. The once-familiar sight of a stiltman working aloft is now rare indeed, and mostly the stringer works from ground level, his ball of hairy hop-string carried in a satchel and running up his long pole through a metal pipe, so producing a continuous flow of string between wire and ground. Hop-stringing as practised at ploughing matches has acquired the status of a country sport, but I like to see it done in the realistic setting of the garden where the expert makes this difficult operation as seemingly effortless as a ballerina's movement as he passes without interruption along the alley.

Before weather has taken the brightness out of the string, one looks through a newly strung garden as if through a golden haze. The pattern changes at the next stage, when the rising strings are banded in at waist-height above each hill. The perennial plant is now growing, and hop-trainers, usually women, are busy at the back-breaking task of persuading each bine to grip and twine around its string. Thereafter the hops grow fast, almost visibly, as they fight their way towards the sun. Then, as the summer progresses, a soft fluffy burr appears and this gradually changes into the fine very pale green cones for which all this enterprise has been undertaken. They grow and hang in big clusters, a sight which brings great joy to every Kentishman and man of Kent.

As August moves towards September preparations are made for the harvest. Within the memory of all but the youngest, hop-picking was the great folk-festival of Kent. It was the occasion for yet another invasion of this much-invaded county, when thousands of Cockneys came down to the country for a working holiday, 'oppin'. For their reception, huts of wood, corrugated iron or brick had been roughly cleared of rubbish, and wagons met the hoppers' special at Paddock Wood or Tonbridge. Then for two or three weeks the village had to find some *modus vivendi* with their temporary, noisy, high-spirited and occasionally hot-tempered or larcenous neighbours. It was a situation which was always potentially explosive, but it was never dull. There was at least as much laughter as anger wherever the hoppers were to be found. The 'gay invaders', as C. Henry Warren called them in his exquisite book of reminiscence, *A Boy in Kent*, augmented the local work-force, for in every village in the hop country men, women and children dropped every other task to gather in the hop harvest. One may measure the authenticity of a man of Kent or a Kentishman not by his birth on one bank or the other of the Medway but by his nose. If his first remembered smell was of hops, caught as he lay in his pram beside the family bin, then he is the genuine article.

All this is memory now, kept alive by those who picked in sun and rain, and by the families sprung from the union of 'opper and villager in the light of the bonfires or as a by-product of post-hop-picking revelry; kept alive too by the principal brewers whose hop festivals, although inevitably an artificial creation, recapture some of the gaiety and good spirits of the past. The camaraderie of the hop garden has gone, destroyed for ever by the hop-picking machine. There is no profit in quarrelling with these huge and expensive monsters. They may not pick hops as cleanly as the old-time experts, but they pick them more cheaply. In any case the 'oppers themselves have been eliminated through affluence; they no longer need a cheap holiday in the country, and if they do condescend to return to the old haunts they come in their Rovers and Cortinas.

So the tallyman has joined the charcoal burner in limbo. A new and less picturesque ritual has replaced the old. The bines are cut and hauled complete by tractor to the machine shed where the cones are stripped off. There is still a little hand work in picking out the waste, before the green hops are packed loosely into pokes and carted off to the oast.

The heart of the whole operation is in the oast.

All over Kent, and in East Sussex and Surrey, the tapering roofs of oasts break the horizon, giving to the homely scene a little touch of fantasy. These small one-, two- or three-kiln oasts are all obsolete, converted or awaiting conversion into homes. They were the product of a small-farm economy in which every hop grower, however modest his output, held himself responsible for processing his own product. Today hop-farming is big-business. Economics dictate that the drying should be done in a few large centres, and improved transportation makes this easy to achieve. The new oast may not be as picturesque as the old—it need not be ugly—but it works on the same principles.

Old Reynolde Scot reserved the name 'oast' for the drying chamber, but it is now commonly used for the whole of the processing building: the gantry on which the pokes are stacked, the drying chamber itself, the cooling floor, and the pressing bay. The techniques have changed greatly, but each process has its counterpart in the past. 'Oast' is a word which is much older than hops; it was originally used for any form of drying kiln and only gradually became applied exclusively to the hop kiln. The term 'oast house' in popular usage is perhaps tautologous, unless it is applied to the whole building and not just to the kiln.

The familiar roundel was evolved at the end of the eighteenth century from older barn-type kilns which let the smoke escape, as in the medieval hall, from an opening in the roof. The improved oast was the creation of John Read of Horsmonden, who was an ingenious inventor with, among other devices, a stomach pump to his credit. He adapted the principle of the hot-house to hop-drying and after a long period of experiment produced a definitive oast at Teston in 1832 of which full details were published. The most characteristic of Kentish buildings has therefore been a feature of the scene for less than 150 years.

The hop may have escaped all the hazards of the long summer, wilt, mildew and canker, hop-fly and aphis, and all the other ills that it is heir to, but it will still have grown in vain if the hop drier is not master of his craft. This is the most delicate of all the processes of hop culture. If the hop is over-dried it may be scorched or become excessively fragile, or lacking in fragrance; if it is slack dried and so processed with an excess of moisture in it rot will set in and it will have to be discarded. It is the drier's task to produce sound hops by applying precisely the right temperature for the right length of time. As the process is continuous day and night the drier works under extreme pressure, snatching rest in brief catnaps and combating dehydration by drinking large quantities of weak beer and cider.

The drying floor is of open slats which are covered with 'hair', a thin loose-woven carpet of horsehair. On this the green hops are spread lightly and to a uniform depth so that the warm air will pass through them evenly. The white-painted cowl on top of the kiln, automatically set to the wind by its projecting vane, ensures an even draught and prevents rain from entering. So moisture is extracted until at the right moment the drier draws the hops out of the drying chamber and leaves them to cool. By this time the whole building reeks with the heady aroma of the hot hop, a smell which, more than all the perfumes of Arabia, has the power to evoke memories. It is not exactly a smell to like; it is not one which can be ignored.

When they have cooled long enough, but not so long that they absorb atmospheric moisture, the dried hops are pressed. They are loaded from above into a very tall sack called a 'pocket', into which they are introduced under pressure until the walls are hard. The pocket now stands more than man-high and weighs over one-and-a-half hundredweight. On its face are stencilled the name and farm of the producer and a serial number. Each pocket has a seam up its side, and from this the hop factor will take his sample, cutting out a small square of hop which will be tested and valued.

When all this has been done the garden is left empty, with a few stray scraps of unpicked cones blowing in the wind high up on the wires. These decay and drop, and the garden lies dormant under the frosts and snows of winter. Meanwhile, in the laboratories of Wye and

East Malling experiments continue to find new and more resistant varieties to set against the traditional Cobb's and Fuggle's and others evolved by Kentish growers in the great days of Victorian England.

This, in brief and very superficially, is the hop cycle in Kent, a process which has fascinated poets from Kit Smart to Victoria Sackville-West and which still, in these prosaic mechanized days, makes each journey into the hop country a voyage of discovery. So deeply committed is the county to hop cultivation, despite the effects of the Common Market and the rival demands of fruit and cereals, that a comprehensive visit would take the traveller to every corner of Kent. There is, however, I believe, something to be said for making this, for once, an intensive journey, and I therefore propose a shorter round than most and one in which we may linger and watch idly the activities of the hop garden.

One advantage of this course is that it will be possible to come to terms with a landscape which is less conventionally appealing than most of the south-eastern countryside. We shall leave for another day the downland gardens and those on sunny south-facing folds of the high Weald, and concentrate instead on the low and, at first glance, featureless plain which lies at a roughly uniform breadth of five miles between the facing slopes of greensand and wealden hills. Through the plain meander idly the Medway and its tributaries Teise and Beult, the one a stream with origins in the high sandstone country of the Sussex border, the other a purely Kentish and Wealden clay stream. It is a subtle landscape, sensitive to light and to weather, changing with the seasons more profoundly than most of Kent. It can look drab and completely unappealing one day; the next quite breath-takingly lovely.

The journey begins in what has become if not the capital, at least the clearing-house of Kentish hops. Paddock Wood is an entirely new village. Most places which have developed during the past century have grown out of an existing village, but there was nothing but the wood in Paddock Wood before the arrival of the railway. The main line was laid from Tonbridge to Ashford in 1842. It runs dead straight from Paddock Wood to Ashford, a rare phenomenon made possible both by the uniformly flat country and by the absence of such artificial obstacles as estates owned by wealthy and unco-operative gentry. Paddock Wood became the junction for a line running along the Medway valley to Maidstone—which still offers one of the prettiest rail journeys in the south country—and another following the Teise into the Weald and thence to Cranbrook and Hawkhurst. This latter has been long closed, but its course still makes an attractive subject for exploration. Paddock Wood station became the natural terminus of the hoppers' specials, from which they made their ways to farms in the central Weald. Since the war the place has developed an industrial area and has grown rapidly, without quite losing the curiously 'temporary' character of a place which is neither town nor village. It remained until recently a part of the civil parish of Brenchley and lacked an independent existence. It has acquired parish status only to lose it in the reorganization of the new Tunbridge Wells District. One gets some feeling of this dilemma in walking through its few streets. The shops form a minor marketing centre, but the place lacks a focus, unless it is the station. The big factory buildings beyond the line outbalance the residential area, and the church, which in an older community would be at the architectural if not the social hub of things, seems an afterthought—although quite a distinguished one. Here at the southern boundary there is just a hint of the village which it never was, with church, cricket ground and a beautifully-sited country school.

Many of the hoppers came out of Paddock Wood station and headed south-west, as we shall, to Five Oak Green, which was a busy centre of hop farming. There is still a magnificent group of roundels just back from the road, unusual in their black coats and with the gardens rising behind up the hill to Capel. Five Oak Green is still a hamlet of Capel parish, but it has vastly outgrown its parent without altogether losing its style. It has an important place in the Kentish hop story, for here beside the road is the Little Hoppers Hospital.

Hop growers have always depended to some extent on outside labour at the hop-picking season. The real mass invasion by hoppers began in the last quarter of the nineteenth century, and it brought with it a host of social, economic and moral problems. The farmers were not organized to deal with a sudden increase in population. Sanitation was minimal, accommodation was primitive to the point of savagery, pay was pitifully low. The blame could not be laid at anyone's door. It was not particularly the business of any authority to look after the temporary migrants. As for pay, the economics of hops were so precarious because of foreign competition that the most big-hearted of growers could not but cut his costs to the bone. So the hoppers had their working holiday, but lived in squalor with epidemic disease a constant and real hazard. They tended to find refuge from these unpleasant realities in the artificial heaven of the local, where their earnings made their way back to the brewers. Despite many recent closures there is still an unusually generous supply of pubs in the Weald, each retaining its memories of drunken and violent Saturday nights in hop-picking.

This was the situation when the Reverend Richard Wilson came to Paddock Wood in the hopping season of 1898. Having failed to get anyone to take seriously the idea of a hoppers' padre he had enlisted as a picker with a share in a bin worked by one of his London flock. In this first year his toil was varied only by a little primitive surgery—for there were countless minor injuries in the gardens—but Father Wilson had made his point; there was a place for a parson in the hop-gardens if he was prepared to work and not to preach. He came back the following year, and again and again, always concentrating his efforts on improving the physical lot of the pickers. Directly as a result of his work, legislation was introduced to fix minimum standards on the farms, and in time this was even implemented.

Father Wilson was not quite a pioneer. There had been missions to hoppers for about ten years before he went hopping. The difference was that the earlier missionaries based their enterprise on tracts and temperance. Father Wilson did not preach; he acted, and in consequence he was accepted by the hoppers as almost one of themselves—different of course because of his dog-collar but a man willing to share all the discomforts of the 'uts with them.

If Wilson had not been dedicated to the welfare of the hop-gardens at his first visit, his commitment was sealed soon afterwards. He encountered a woman picker carrying a bundle in which was wrapped the body of her dead child. It had died in the gardens and she was left to make, unaided, what arrangements she could for its burial. The incident determined the direction of Father Wilson's work for the rest of his life. Practical Christianity was to be the order, and nothing could be more practical than the care of the sick. Wilson took a cottage in Five Oak Green and equipped it with scrounged and borrowed beds. This was the Little Hoppers Hospital; and, with changed and gradually improved accommodation, it remained in operation for about ten hop-pickings. Then in 1910 the 'Rose and Crown' pub in Five Oak Green lost its licence. Wilson took a lease of the building and turned it into a permanent hospital. As he was a fervent teetotaler this act gave him particular pleasure, such as St Augustine's missionaries must have enjoyed when they 'converted' a pagan temple into a church. There was none of the clinical detachment of a 'real' hospital about the 'Rose and Crown', which the hoppers adopted as a kind of club house. It also served more conventionally as a mission-hall, and services were held inside as well as on the green and at farms.

During the First World War a fund was started, originally with money bequeathed to the mission by one of the voluntary workers who had been killed in action, to improve the 'Rose and Crown' and to make the new building into a war memorial. The money came in slowly, principally from the hoppers themselves who were never affluent, and the work was not completed until 1925. The old 'Rose and Crown' had stood back from the road behind a paved court. A new building was put up on the road-side, turning the court into a cloister. It consisted of an open-sided passage with pillars and a steep red-tiled roof, a distinctive and sightly building and one which had its uses as a foul-weather shelter. In two years Wilson was dead, and the makeshift hospital ward behind the 'Rose and Crown' was replaced as a memorial to him.

There are now no hoppers in Five Oak Green, and the Little Hoppers Hospital has lost its original occupation. It still stands, a most unusual and attractive building in an—on the whole—unattractive village, as a permanent reminder of the old hop-picking days and of a remarkable social experiment. It is perilously easy to sentimentalize about the hoppers. They were often—as George Orwell confessed in a lively essay—rogues and criminals, as dirty as they were dishonest, but they also had spirit and a generous fund of good humour. Their speech was richly laden with obscenities and bawdiness and yet it had in it a little of the rough music of folk poetry. If the locals rightly loathed them and locked up their movable valuables—and would have locked up their daughters too if they had been able—when the 'gay invaders' arrived, people like Father Wilson and the lively undergraduates of the Oxford Missions found in them a core of crude integrity.

While missions like Father Wilson's had greater or less success there is little evidence to suggest that the established church in most villages made any great impact on the invaders. Perhaps the parish church, like the superior inn, had a poster—albeit an invisible one—displayed, declaring 'No Hop-Pickers Served'. Five Oak Green, entirely a new village, is in Capel parish and its church is to the south, along the lane past the hop kilns. Quickly one is out of the 'towny' atmosphere of Five Oak Green and into a bit of genuine rural Kent. There are more orchards than hop gardens now, and in a few years I expect there will be more arable land than either. Capel itself is just the church, a farm and a few very good traditional cottages. The church, basically as simple as any in the county, has won a little fame recently with the restoration of wall paintings illustrating the story of St Thomas of Canterbury— the church is dedicated to him, and there is a tradition, without documentary evidence, that he preached here. These paintings are as faint and elusive as such ancient survivals tend to be. I much prefer the atmosphere of this little building, in which the centuries are one and the twelfth-century masons who raised these walls seem only just to have knocked off for their dinner break. It is very quiet here, a place for thinking in—and that is a rarity in Kent. Even the tractor working nearby is just a sound of the country, one with the blackbird and the wind in the hop-wires.

The slight rise on the road from Five Oak Green to Capel church is the beginning of the wealden hills and beyond the church the land is undulating all the way to Pembury and Tunbridge Wells. Our way however is farther westward at a modest elevation above the wealden plain. A quiet country lane passes through orchards and hop gardens,

with some woodland, and comes on to the major road from Five Oak
Green a little short of Crockhurst Street, a hamlet in the parish of
Tudeley. Tudeley itself, such as it is, lies just ahead at a crossing of roads.
Surprisingly, for this is very near to Tonbridge where there have been
massive residential and industrial developments, Tudeley is an authentic
village, small and inward-looking, and having that slightly smug air
which comes from the patronage of a great house. Just a little beyond
the village, off the road to Tonbridge, is the large and beautiful park of
Somerhill, which Turner painted, and the house in golden wealden
sandstone stands on a high point in a superb position. It belongs to that
great age of native architecture, before classical ideas got the upper
hand of English tradition, around the end of Queen Elizabeth's reign.
It was the seat of that Lord Clanricarde who ventured to marry the
most distinguished double-widow of the Queen's Court, Lady Essex,
formerly Lady Sidney, and the daughter of Sir Francis Walsingham,
who was the royal spy-master.

Somerhill came ultimately to the D'Avigdor-Goldsmids, who were
responsible for much of the resuscitation of Tudeley village and also
for as deeply moving a memorial as the southern counties can show. A
young daughter of the family was most tragically drowned in a sailing
accident. Marc Chagall was commissioned to design a new east window
in Tudeley church. The church stands unassumingly behind the farm-
yard with an oast for company. It seems the humblest of buildings,
with that charm which comes from a profound lack of pretension.
Enter, and there behind the high altar is the response of genius to
tragedy. The theme is the sea, eternally changing and changeless. The
restless blues are shot through with stronger reds. In analysis, these
colours are restrained, but this is not the initial impression which is
inevitably dictated by emotion. There are good examples of the revived
art of painted glass throughout the Home Counties, including the
cathedrals, but I know no place where its impact is as powerful as in
this homely building.

At the road junction in Tudeley, a lane goes downhill past the
D'Avigdor-Goldsmid's family graveyard towards the Medway, its
passage marked by the characteristic distorted shapes of pollarded
willows. This road crosses the river by Hartlake Bridge, an ugly concrete structure, and then goes through hop country—there is a fine oast
at Hartlake Farm—to Golden Green. This hamlet does not live up to
its name, being a rather nondescript community with some industry.
Across the fields to the north-west the tall mock-Gothic tower of
Hadlow Castle, an early nineteenth-century folly, makes a valuable
focal point in what is not an exciting landscape. Nearer at hand an
unusually large oast stands out of the flat plain. This is Faulkners Oast,
about whose future controversy rages; plans vary from demolition to

the establishment of a hop museum. The former fate is too grim to contemplate, the latter perhaps too good to be true.

The road goes eastwards back towards the river. On the way it crosses the Bourne, a minor tributary, a little short of which there are two notable houses, one in brick, the other an extravagant exercise in timber-framing. Then, with continual changes of direction, the road comes to what seems to be the village centre of East Peckham. East Peckham, a former centre of hop-picking, is one of the largest of Wealden villages, in population and area. It has grown considerably in recent years, linking what was once a group of scattered hamlets. The process has not been altogether happy, and East Peckham has become in plan neither town nor village—although a vigorous combination of new and old residents promises to achieve social unity. A few very charming cottages are caught up in the new developments. An unprepossessing church in early Victorian Gothic stands opposite the village school. That seems to the hurried visitor to be all about East Peckham. In fact the great house and the church are far away, on the greensand hills which terminate the flat Weald to the north. Roydon Hall is a big Henry VIII house in brick, massively altered in Victorian times. Neither the house nor the fine Tudor walled garden is shown. On higher ground, beyond the handsome Queen Anne block of Little Roydon, the old parish church crowns the hill. Dedicated, as old hill-top foundations tend to be, to St Michael, it gives from the churchyard or the lychgate one of the finest of wealden views, a wide flat expanse of orchard and hop-garden in which Hadlow tower stands out like a slim exclamation point.

There are famous hop-gardens all around. Just up the road is Mereworth, where C. Henry Warren's 'gay invaders', so entertainingly recalled in *A Boy in Kent*, stirred up the somnolent villagers; and beyond this is Wateringbury, the scene of George Orwell's unfortunate experiences with the hop-pickers. The other way the road goes straight towards the Medway until it is interrupted by the main Maidstone-Tunbridge Wells road. This followed left for a half-mile—there is a most handsome example of a wealden farmhouse of the eighteenth century on the left—brings us by a byroad to the Medway at Twyford. There are industrial buildings at Hampstead Lock, where one of the few 'cuts' of the Medway Navigation shortened the barge route by a mile.

The former hop-pickers and their families seem to have retained happy memories of Yalding, for they come on summer weekends in their hundreds to spend a day by the river in sight of the oasts and the hop-poles. One understands their point of view. It is an attractive scene—although less appealing when the Lees are black with cars and people. Fortunately only one area of the Lees—a wide strip of common land beside the river—is given over to parking, and the proceeds of this must make Yalding one of the most affluent of purely rural parishes. The sight of Twyford is the bridge, which is one of the four medieval bridges of the Medway, and a fine one in spite of having the parapet repaired in red brick. It is best seen from the lock upstream, or from river level—don't fall in, because the currents are tricky—where the fine pointed arches can be appreciated.

From Twyford Bridge there is a good view downstream, backed by the green wall of the greensand Yalding Hill. This used to have on top a specially fine and conspicuous oast, but this has recently undergone modernization and has lost its pretty white cones. Below the hill are the red roofs of Yalding, more oasts, and the mildly comical onion-capped tower of Yalding church.

Yalding is one of my personal favourites among Kentish villages. It possesses one of the essentials of all village designs—(visually; I am aware that it constitutes a traffic hazard, but there are other considerations beside that of the internal combustion engine) a closed view. The short, very handsome high street, so wide in proportion to its length that it might almost be called a square, is closed at one end by an incline of the road, at the other by the crossing of the river. Because of this one sees, undistracted, almost all the best of Yalding at a glance. Two very noble houses face one another across the street. One is a typical Queen Anne town-house, the other is the Court Lodge, an essentially rural building protected by a high wall. Across the head of the street is straddled Cleaves, tile-hung and cheerfully asymmetrical; here a Carolean merchant from London established a grammar school, reorganized out of existence earlier in this century. These, a little brick gaol-house, a great black barn, and a handful of cottages comprise the pleasing scene. The church just manages to peep over the roof of Hilborough House, but its body is quite hidden.

Yalding is a river village. As the name suggests, it was an early Saxon foundation, made possible by the river which gave access into the forest of the Weald. The village has grown up not on the Medway, which is a quarter-mile away, but on its tributary, the Beult, which is crossed, just beyond the high street, by a magnificent causeway-bridge in ragstone. The river is insignificant in normal weathers, but Yalding is notorious for its floods, and the medieval pessimist who built the bridge took it over the main stream and also its normally dry companions. It is an exceptionally fine structure, altered only in the middle where it has been widened to provide a passing place. The only point from which it can be seen adequately is the riverbank beyond the 'George' car park, but the sight should not be missed. Whoever built the bridges of the Medway valley, whether prior of Christ Church or woolmaster, gave Kent one of its most precious, and largely unregarded, possessions.

There are, including the tributaries, ten which probably date from the late fourteenth century when the boom in wool created a demand for improvements in communications. They are all still in use and have of course undergone many alterations, but all show the bold graceful sweep which marks all medieval stone bridges. One might spend a rewarding day on these alone, and indeed we shall see others before this journey is done.

In the next three miles hops and apples are slowly making way for wheat and barley, following the farming trend which promises to transform the Garden of England in the next few years. The oasts stick up in the flat landscapes like picturesque anachronisms. The scene is appealing, especially to those with time to come to terms with its unemphatic qualities. The first stage of the southward road is the hamlet of Benover which has, I believe, for its size the richest collection of wealden houses anywhere. Only one is of any size, but all are perfect of their kind and in excellent order. The big house comes first, set back on the right. Its black and white is so immaculate that one suspects a sham, but 'Normans' is a genuine timber-framed house, derelict for many years and now restored with due regard to its quality. After this come the village houses, timber-framed, tile-hung, weather-boarded, tiled and thatched running the full range of the minor domestic styles of the Weald. They are a most heartening sight and, if they are mostly no longer tied to the land as they once were, at least they are better cared for than at any earlier stage in their existence. The inn sign is a reminder that this road was on a pack-horse route in the heyday of Kentish wool. It was then a track through the forest. Now the woods have gone and even the little roadside thickets which once harboured primroses and blackberries are being grubbed in the interests of a greater acreage of arable. Next, I suppose, the little brooks which follow the lanes and drain the flat country will be piped and put underground, and then the kingfisher and the heron which still haunt this country will go into oblivion.

Collier Street is another hop-producing hamlet, extended along two miles of road, with the hops, the Cox's and the unbiquitous corn lying off on either side. Collier Street—the name recalls charcoal burners who were an indispensable element in the rural economy of medieval England and who, by a curious chance, lingered here right into the twentieth century—was carved out of Yalding and made into an ecclesiastical parish in Victorian times, to which the rather fine 'Early English' church bears witness. There are fine houses here too, although, unlike Benover, they are outnumbered by the mediocre and the bad. A handsome black-and-white house stands back a little beyond the church, and on a lane which loops around the back of the village through the hop-gardens there is a singularly good Georgian house in brick, showing how well the sophisticated town styles might be imported into the country.

Between Collier Street and Marden the main emphasis is still on fruit; indeed Marden itself is the site of the principal fruit show in the Southeast. The road crosses the little River Twist and just beyond there is a view of one of the most splendid of as-yet-unconverted oasts at Gatehouse Farm. Here a lane turns south to Marden, passing through a mini-industrial estate notable for the most enormous, still growing, and hideous, warehouses. These are impressive, but no preparation for the charms of Marden itself. So far the commuters have not settled here in large numbers, in marked contrast to other villages on the main railway line, but the future—especially a future shadowed by the Channel Tunnel—is most uncertain. Meanwhile here is a little wealden town which is still concerned more with its own affairs than those of the big city. Its shops serve rural needs; its pubs refresh rural workers, not refugees from the towns. The little square, which is merely a widening of the main road, is lined with houses whose appeal lies in their lack of pretensions. Weather-board, tile and brick offer variety, but no conflict, to the eye. The church is large and might look distinguished but for the absurd boarded cap on its sandstone tower. The church has good fourteenth-century tracery and modern glass.

The main road towards Maidstone is relatively dull, although enlivened by an occasional good house or oast. At Stile Bridge it joins a major road just before the bridge over the Beult, and then a narrow lane goes right. This soon joins another which goes right again, through attractive flat country, to a junction at Rabbit's Cross. Here is a superb example of the Kentish yeoman's house in a fine setting among trees. Like most others of its kind it has lost its central hall, open to the rafters, by the insertion of an upper floor, but the hall-house pattern is otherwise clearly preserved.

At this point the traveller has two options. He might turn north, following the line of a Roman road, and then take the first right turning to embark on an adventurous course on very narrow twisting lanes through astonishingly unsuburbanized country as far as Hawkenbury. The same point may be reached, less interestingly but also with fewer driving hazards, by turning the opposite (southern) way at Rabbit's Cross to Cross-at-Hand, crossing the Beult again by a medieval causeway bridge, then leaving the main road as soon as possible by another byway which recrosses the river at Hawkenbury Bridge—a medieval core with later trimmings—on the way to Hawkenbury. This is another hamlet of mixed good and indifferent houses, with one excellent timber-framed manor-house. From here an uneventful road follows the Beult valley to Headcorn.

Headcorn has been affected more than Marden by commuters and its local character has been a little compromised. It is a bustling community with shops of a more urban kind than Marden's and an air of being just the least bit better than its neighbours. I must confess that I loved Headcorn better before the commuters moved in, when it was more homely, and when it was the terminus of the Kent and East Sussex Railway, the most endearingly farcical of all rustic lines, with rolling-stock and social philosophy alike developed in the Emmett manner. But the branch line has gone, at least as far as Tenterden, and with it an essential part of Headcorn's heart. Instead we must be content with a venerable and impressive church and a group of notable half-timbered houses standing around it at the village's western end.

Having come so far upstream along the Beult, we ought to go a little farther to find the richest jewel of the valley. Following the main road eastward through Headcorn, and turning off it just where the turnpike, with a typical pike-keeper's cottage on a corner, swings south, we keep close to the railway for a mile or so and then cross under the line and pass through the orchards to Smarden. For some people, and I think that—despite the competition—I am one of them, this is the most perfect village of the Kentish Weald. 'Village' is not quite the word, because although Smarden has only parish status it has, like many of its neighbours, a complex pattern and a sophisticated air which marks it as townlike in character. This is derived from its history, for Smarden had a share in the prosperity of the Weald in the great days of Kentish broadcloth. This wealth, coming quickly, transformed the place and turned a humble forest 'den' into a community of prosperous weavers and farmers. The witness to all this is an astonishing collection of houses, mostly timbered, spacious and bearing, for all their traditional styles, an air of affluent well-being. Smarden grew up in the sixteenth century, and so its architecture, unlike that of, say, Tenterden, is free of alien elements. The builders of these hall-houses had never seen a London architect's pattern book and worked as their grandfathers had worked, but with less need to save pennies.

South of Smarden the country begins to rise towards the wealden hills, but our concern is still with the wealden plain, and we therefore come out of the village, crossing the Beult for the fifth and last time by the town bridge, a diminutive twin-arched stone structure, and quickly turn right for a half-mile and then left along a narrow lane which reaches the incredible height of one hundred feet. After this effort it declines to the main Headcorn road, crossing this on to another minor road. Here we cross over the lost railway track and go with many twists and turns to the hilltop village of Frittenden. Here is another place of old houses and new, a village of some style but strangely lacking the distinction of some of its wealden neighbours. From this high point lanes descend north and west towards Staplehurst.

Staplehurst is the principal commuter village of the Weald. The developers, held in check elsewhere, have here had their way, or at least a good part of it. Here too the development has taken place not apart from the old village but right in the middle of it. The results are visually rather dreadful. Socially the effects have been interesting. A traditional and very ancient community has had to come to terms with new neighbours who either acknowledged no traditions or subscribed to quite different ones. In anticipation one might have predicted total warfare between two factions. It has not been quite like that. Gradually a new society is emerging. The commuters may rush for their morning trains and not return until nightfall, but they are becoming excellent weekend countrymen. The original villagers benefit from the improved shops, the library, and the other blessings conferred by an enlarged population. They begin to achieve a *rapprochement* with the invaders and to recognize a common destiny. All seem to have in common a feeling for the wealden landscape and a determination that it shall not be further destroyed. Both sides take pride in the preservation of the ancient heart of the village, which still retains a good Georgian house or two, a fine range of timbered cottages and, on the point of the hill, a magnificent church. However much one regrets that so many good acres have been lost for ever under this heavy load of bricks and concrete, in Staplehurst there is a little hope to be taken for the future of the Weald, which will undoubtedly continue to grow but which need not on that account lose its true character.

At present the development of Staplehurst is contained within a comparatively small area, and to the west the new houses are quickly left behind. A lane ambles in the authentic wealden fashion, following ancient boundaries and the margins of farm-holdings in preference to pursuing an objective. The country is still low-lying, but not flat for at several points it rises beyond the hundred-foot contour. This is the watershed between Beult and Teise, and soon there is a gentle decline towards the latter stream. To the south the hills of the high Weald make a green wall, lofty by contrast but rarely going above three hundred feet.

The lane goes past Marden Thorn and heads for Marden, but just short of the village a lesser road turns left and crosses to the main Goudhurst road at Marden Beech. A lane opposite crosses the Twist and follows the Teise closely as far as the small hamlet of Claygate. By the way we pass the farm of Little Cheveney where there are some exceptionally handsome kilns, some square, the others the more familiar roundels. Then at Claygate a minor road keeps to the Teise valley through more orchard and hop country to Laddingford, where there are more oasts.

All through this journey we have been seeing oasts, all of them

Milsted village

Hop stringing

(*left*) Norman tower, Canterbury Cathedral
(*below*) Abbey Street, Faversham

looking roughly alike in general design. Among the individual features of these attractive buildings, one which attracts most attention is the vane projecting from the white cowl, the function of which is to turn the cowl by wind-power and so maintain the correct amount of draught. It is the Kentish tradition to display on the vane a small horse, rampant as it appears on the county arms, but incorrectly—in heraldic terms—painted black to make the best contrast with the white cowl. A collector might amuse himself by recording the variants of this theme. Along the Laddingford road someone—surely an immigrant homesick for the Antipodes—has set up a kangaroo. Near Staplehurst the horses are stolid Shires on all fours. At Collier Street one may see crows and pheasants, and also—a freakish fancy which does not quite ring true—a steam locomotive. An observant traveller might quickly add to this list.

Laddingford is a hop-growing hamlet in Yalding parish with nothing much to notice but the weatherboard pub. On the edge of the village the Teise, even at this last stage of its independent life not much more than a wide ditch, flows close to the road, and is then crossed by a lane—our route—heading for Beltring. Bridges lack interest when seen from above. If you risk a brief and harmless trespass in the roadside orchard you will find that here again is a medieval bridge, twin-arched and handsome.

Our route now takes us away from the Teise and across a very low ridge into the Medway valley with the river closing in on the right. We are approaching the climax of this journey and ahead are the myriad cowls of Beltring Hop Farm, the very centre of the industry and the custodian of hop traditions. The Whitbread farm at Beltring was the most famous and popular of all hop farms in the days of hand-picking. There were great scenes of industry here, and of revelry too on Saturday nights when the wayside inn—when I first knew the place it belonged, ironically, to a rival brewer—was overwhelmed by hoppers, genial, quarrelsome, maudlin. The hop-picking machine moved in, and a whole traditional way of life seemed to be doomed. Whitbreads decided that the old days should not be entirely forgotten. They inaugurated an annual hop festival, when hoppers and their families might come back to Kent and relive their memories. The hop festival is obviously an artificial creation. Hop-picking was much more than Saturday-night junketings with sing-songs, variety acts and good fellowship. It was also backache, rheumatism, mud and dust, hop-gout and hop-eye, low pay and starvation diet. Nevertheless it is natural that in retrospect the warm days and the full bins should be best remembered, and the hopper's heart should lift to the cry of "Pull no more bines". No one who cherishes this one true folk-tradition of the south country can grudge the old pickers their false nostalgia and rosy

5

memories, promoted so effectively and managed so professionally in the Beltring festival. Long may it survive to confound the realists and the management men who resent its blatant sentimentalism.

It is only a couple of miles from Beltring to Paddock Wood where the hoppers' 'specials', cold, comfortless, dirty, unlit, took the holiday-makers back, often by fantastically indirect routes, to the grey squalor of their London homes, there to await the time when they would return for another spell of 'oppin' dahn Kent-way.

4

Five Ports, Two Ancient Towns, and Some Limbs

WHILE the one unifying factor in the history of the Home Counties has been the influence of London, up to the last five hundred years an influence at least as powerful upon the south-eastern counties was the proximity of the continent of Europe. The story of Kent, and to a rather less extent of Sussex and Essex, has been one of invasions. The lemming flow of migrant peoples pressing always westwards moved across the land bridge and, when that link at last was broken, the narrow seas into the south-eastern tip of Britain. With each wave of invaders the character of the country and its people changed, newcomers ousting the sitting tenants, or assimilating them, or being absorbed by them. At last the Belgic settlers from Gaul established some degree of stability in the tribal kingdoms of Kent and Sussex. The once-fierce warriors moved out of the hills into lowland settlements, developing into farmers, traders and craftsmen. They offered little more than token resistance to the Roman legions in the Claudian invasion and settled down to a profitable enjoyment of the Roman peace.

To this time belong the first identifiable ports of South-east England. The base for the Roman invasion was a peninsula in the Wantsum, a wide deep-water channel between mainland Kent and Thanet. Here the legions set up their depot, with sheltered anchorage for their ships, and built their main supply road across country to the tribal capital of Durovernum (which was to become Canterbury) and so to London. Although their base at Richborough had the usual civilian appendages of all army posts, it was essentially a military port and probably remained a Portsmouth rather than a Southampton throughout the Roman stay. The civil port, although for reasons of strategy still firmly under army control, was farther west where the tall chalk cliffs were broken momentarily by the little River Dour. Dover offered a much less spacious and safe anchorage than Richborough, but the crossing to Gaul was short and this compensated for navigational hazards—these much reduced by the provision of stone light-houses on the heights on either side of the harbour. A new road linked the port with Watling Street at Durovernum. A third port developed westward again along the coast where the River Limen met the sea below steep greendsand cliffs. Portus Lemanis too was linked with the capital by a dead-straight road, and a loop road linked the three ports with one another.

This was the main pattern of communication with the Continental empire for over two centuries. Then in the third century cracks began to appear in the huge structure of Rome. Rival emperors struggled for power, and while the central administration was distracted a picturesque and enterprising rogue, Carausius, grabbed power in Gaul and Britain. Carausius was a sailor, which in those days usually meant a pirate, and his strategy was based on control of the Channel. For this he set up a chain of strong-points around the facing coasts of Gaul and Britain. The British line extended as far north as the Wash and south-west to Southampton Water. Then Carausius fell, murdered by his own lieutenant, and the coastal forts lapsed into disuse.

As Rome declined and her lines of communications with the Empire were shortened, barbarian wolves gathered to snap up the pieces. The coasts of Britain were subject to raids by Saxon war bands, and to counter these attacks the old decayed sea-forts of Carausius were put into repair and operated in conjunction with coastal naval patrols. The operation was under the control of an official with the picturesque title of Count of the Saxon Shore. It sounded splendid. The system probably worked, too, to the extent of postponing the inevitable. Then the Saxon tide swept over the land and the forts were abandoned, some of them for ever.

The Saxon Shore forts included existing forts at Richborough, which was strengthened with massive tall walls of flint and rubble, Dover and Lympne, and to the west new strong-points at Pevensey (Anderida) in a marshy estuary near the high chalk cliffs of the South Downs, and at Portchester on a promontory of the tangled coastline on the edge of Chichester Harbour. A fort at Reculver (Regulbium) commanded the junction of Thames and Wantsum, and another at Bradwell (Othona) stood at the mouth of the Blackwater in Essex.

Of all these Lympne fared worst in later ages. The Limen silted up and found a new outlet to the sea at Romney, and cliff movements tumbled the massive walls of the Roman fort down the hillside in confusion. They are still there, below the medieval fortified manor of the archdeacons of Canterbury at Lympne, flint and stone bonded indestructibly by Roman mortar, but too hopelessly muddled in ruin for their meaning to be read on the ground. Out of the steep footpath which reaches them grows Stone Street, a secondary road which still goes dead-straight except when it climbs the hill on the way to Canterbury.

Richborough had its scarred walls undermined by the River Stour in its wayward wanderings across the flats, but more than half remains to a good height, together with the stupendous earthworks and the vast concrete base of a central monument, put up when Goth and Vandal and Saxon were unknown to the glory of Rome and in honour of the conquest of Britain. Like Bradwell in Essex, the Roman fort was used as a base for the Christian conquest of pagan England, and the outline of Augustine's little church can still be seen in the turf of Richborough. The remains of Rutupiae, legionary depot, Saxon Shore fort and Christian springboard, however greatly ruined, still constitute one of the biggest and most evocative of the historic monuments of Britain.

Alone among the Saxon Shore depots Dover has retained a maritime function and this only by constant effort in resisting the effects of tide and silt. One Roman lighthouse remains to almost its full height within the medieval walls of Dover Castle, and the base of the other stands among the not less impressive Napoleonic fortifications on the Western Heights. The position of the Saxon Shore fort of Dubris was long a matter of contention among the pundits, but the puzzle was solved arbitrarily by the bulldozers which hit the ruins under the debris of medieval Dover, and there is a good hope that some of the remains may be preserved in situ.

Reculver was chosen as the site of an early Christian minster which was built within the Roman walls in the seventh century. Coastal erosion nibbled at the site until half the fort disappeared and the great church, extended from its Saxon original in the twelfth century and then dismantled, in one of the most blatant acts of educated vandalism in history, by a nineteenth-century vicar, stood right on the edge of the cliff. Here it stands, its romantic melancholy not quite dispelled by the twentieth-century vandalism of a big caravan camp.

The two western forts were taken into use by Norman warlords and their curtain walls were repaired as formidable coastal castles. The big castle of Pevensey still sits dwarfed in one corner of Anderida, and

Norman keep and church are mere minor intrusions in the huge rectangle of Roman Portchester.

Less remains above ground of Othona than of any other Saxon Shore fort in the Home Counties, but by a strange compensation Bradwell casts the strongest spell over the modern visitor, as we shall see hereafter.

The Jutish settlers of Kent in the fifth century were less inclined than some of their fellow-warriors from the German mainland to shun the remains of Roman civilization. They occupied Richborough, in which their king probably had a palace, until the silting of the Wantsum compelled them to abandon the old port. They established new settlements on either side of the mouth of the Channel, one on the accumulated sandy foreshore which grew into Sandwich, the other at Stonar on the Thanet shore. The port of Dover probably continued uninterrupted. Lympne port was unusable, and a new port grew up where the old mouth of the Limen had become a pebbly lagoon providing anchorage at Hythe. The Limen, or Rother, now reached the sea at Romney, and here new ports were established on the marshy shore as well as on the pebble ridge of Lydd where the eastward drift of the tides continually built up a new shoreline. Two islands in a shallow bay farther west became the ports of Rye and Winchelsea. Meanwhile, westward again where a small river flowing between high sandstone hills provided a sheltered inlet, a vigorous and enterprising tribe of Saxon invaders, the Hastingas, had established a base from which to control their semi-autonomous area of Sussex.

In the course of the next centuries these new ports built up a reputation based on trade and piracy and established by slow degrees a relationship with one another promoted by antipathy, distrust and common interests. From these improbable origins grew the uneasy and always precarious Brotherhood of the Cinque Ports. Like so many of the most influential English institutions the Cinque Ports were an evolutionary growth and they worked best when their functions were least precisely defined. By the time their practices had become codified and their privileges sanctioned by law the great days were almost over. The ports lingered on, sustained by tradition and by their own fierce pride in rights which no longer had much basis in reality.

Although the Cinque Ports formed a conferation of boroughs which is unique in England, their collective influence and importance were limited and so were their rights. For the most part they continued to act independently and solved their internal problems and pursued their individual interests without reference to the corporate authority of the brotherhood. The idea of the Cinque Ports has captured the historic imagination, and the relics of their great days are highly picturesque. In consequence a Cinque Port legend has grown up which is rather bigger and more romantic than the medieval realities of fishing and trading towns going about their business, occasionally responding—within carefully prescribed limits—to the call for service to the king, and asserting the very limited privileges by which they received payment for their national services.

In general their duties were limited to ship-service when the king or his officers needed to go abroad. This duty they shared in common with ports in other parts of the country, but as the five ports faced France, where the medieval kings had interests real and assumed, it was natural that their duties were arduous beyond the average. Their privileges were partly ceremonial, partly economic. They had the right of representation at the king's coronation when the Coronation Barons carried a canopy over the royal head. Of greater cash value was the right of 'den and strond' which allowed them to land at Yarmouth to dry their nets and to take charge of the judicial court at the annual Yarmouth herring fair.

These rights and duties, already in existence for an unknown period of time, were confirmed by a charter of King Edward I in 1278, which for the first time acknowledged formally the existence of a group of seven boroughs, with a common function and interests. (The original 'Cinque' Ports of Hastings, Romney, Hythe, Dover and Sandwich had been joined by the 'ancient towns' of Rye and Winchelsea in the twelfth century.) To these seven were added a large number of subordinate ports, some of them corporate members of the confederation, others occupying a minor role. In all thirty-nine towns and villages were at one time or another, and in varied degrees, involved in the enterprises of the Cinque Ports.

It was only to be expected that the ports should compete for precedence in the affairs of the brotherhood. Sandwich was arguably the most important in the early years of the ports. Dover had a record of continuous activity, and the Lord Warden of the Cinque Ports was traditionally also Constable of Dover Castle and had his headquarters there. Hastings argued its initiative in the affairs of the confederation, and most of the time this was conceded by the others. However, the ports were originally careful to hold their meetings in neutral territory. The seat of the Court of Shepway was traditionally on high ground above the port of West Hythe. The Court of Brodhull sat at the township of Brodhull, which seems to have been at or near Dymchurch. The Guestling took its name from a little village between Winchelsea and Hastings and the original meetings were probably held there. The functions of these latter organizations seem always to have been confused, but very roughly the Guestling was a meeting of the western (Sussex) ports; the Brodhull brought together the Kentish members. Nowadays the two are united, and the names corrupted, into the Brotherhood and Guestling of the Cinque Ports.

Such, in brief, was the Confederation of the Cinque Ports, an association, at first loose and informal, later governed by strict and rigid
regulations, of five ports, two ancient towns, eight corporate and
twenty-four non-corporate members, which were united by common
interests and by a common duty. Their national usefulness scarcely
survived the Hundred Years War, and they continued as a picturesque
anachronism, at once endearing and irritating in its absurdity. The
Lord Warden, who once had the tricky job of representing the king and
at the same time guarding the liberties of the ports, has long been a
national figure who adds this to a long list of historic and not-quite-
meaningless titles. Pitt, Wellington and Churchill held the office, and
the present Lord Warden is Sir Robert Menzies. Selected barons still
attend the coronation of the sovereign but they are no longer, after
certain unseemly incidents notably at the coronations of those rather
unseemly monarchs Charles II and George IV, entrusted with the
canopy. On these and other state occasions they wear their fine ceremonial dress. They serve to remind a forgetful nation of a past which,
if it was never as heroic and colourful as imagination paints it, was the
seed out of which we grow.

The fierce conservatism of the Cinque Ports has until recently
served to preserve their towns from the grosser aspects of development. They are still very well worth exploring for the relics of their
great days and for the ceremonies and rituals which persist with such
charming incongruity in these materialistic days.

So long as the Wantsum channel remained open, Sandwich held an
advantage over the other ports. The passage between Thanet and the
mainland was much preferred to the long haul around the North
Foreland, and Sandwich, sitting at the entry of the channel, was in a
commanding and profitable position. The pile-up of sand in the Downs,
to which Earl Godwin gave his name, helped for a time to protect the
port from the weather and made the anchorage attractive. There were
disadvantages. These amenities appealed to enemies as much as to
friends, and the Wantsum was greatly favoured by Danish raiders.
Indeed Sandwich was virtually a Danish port at one time and it was the
base for the final Danish conquest under Sweyn and Canute. The latter,
after his conversion to Christianity, took the priory of Christ Church,
Canterbury, especially under his protection and reinforced the connection between port and priory, and this association lasted throughout the
Middle Ages. A fair share of the profits of the port therefore flowed up
the Stour to Canterbury and helped to subsidize the unending building
and rebuilding of the cathedral.

It was probably the connection with Christ Church which determined Thomas Becket's choice of Sandwich as the port for his return
from exile in 1170. He had everything to fear from the civil authorities

but he was assured of the love of the monks of Christ Church. The port remained important for another century, but silt and sand combined in a slow and inevitable choking process. The Wantsum, badly silted, became too shallow to offer a sea-passage to Reculver and this process of decay was accelerated when landowners, notably the monks of the rival establishment of St Augustine's Abbey who owned Minster-in-Thanet, built flood barriers and reclaimed the bed of the channel. Its sea trade declining, Sandwich had a useful injection of royal aid when Edward III established a wool staple in the town in 1377. Decay set in again until by the beginning of Elizabeth's reign the town was more than half abandoned and falling into ruin. It was rescued by the arrival of Walloons, skilled artisans fleeing from the Spanish terror in the Netherlands, who made the place a centre for the manufacture of cloth. When Queen Elizabeth visited Sandwich in 1572 she found a town wonderfully revitalized, and not merely in an economic sense.

Today Sandwich stands again in a moment of crisis. The old town has survived better than any other of the Kentish Cinque Ports and it has avoided, or been shunned by, the kind of genteel artificiality which has taken over Rye. It has found a new source of economic stability in the development of massive industrial complexes across the river in Stonar. It has as yet failed to reconcile old and new. Above all it has not solved a traffic problem which threatens to solve itself by shaking the old town to bits. There is no secure future for Sandwich until the gigantic lorries are taken out of the narrow medieval streets. If this can be done soon Sandwich may become a better Rye, as beautiful in its buildings and more soundly based in twentieth-century realities. But it must be soon, or it will be too late.

Although much remains of the Roman buildings at Richborough, just outside the town, nothing is to be seen of Sandwich in its heyday. The Saxon and Danish town is buried under a medieval successor. From the Norman town survives one of the three churches of Sandwich, St Clement's, the oldest, largest, finest and the only one to continue its original function. St Clement's central tower was fairly new when Becket passed on his way to martyrdom. It is a fine structure, the four faces enlivened by round-arched blind arcading. Only the tower of New Romney rivals it in Kent. The rest of the Norman work has all but vanished through successive enlargements. St Clement's is a civic church with appropriate trappings and a perpetual air of occasion about it. It is out of the main flow of the town, which has no doubt contributed to its survival. The centre-piece of Sandwich is St Peter's—now sadly decayed and its future gravely in doubt—whose onion-capped tower dominates most views of the town. It is a building of no great distinction but visually is of the greatest importance. St Mary's, whose walls are daily threatened by juggernaut lorries, has better architectural features, although the loss of its tower gives it a curiously incomplete air.

These relics of medieval Sandwich are perhaps less notable than the remains of the town's defences. The town was never completely walled. The river marked one boundary, and along the others runs a high earthen bank and ditch. The circuit of this primitive defence makes a most enjoyable short walk. On the riverside are the two surviving gates: the Barbican, restored out of almost all recognition but highly picturesque, controlling entrance to a toll-bridge which still brings in a substantial daily revenue, and Fisher Gate, a tall gaunt stone arch rebuilt at the time of the town's revival in Elizabeth's reign.

It is not so much in these show-pieces as in the ordinary streets and alleys of Sandwich that the town can best be savoured. An unplanned stroll will reveal neat eighteenth-century façades and door-cases, Flemish rounded and stepped gables, bits of re-used medieval masonry, brick, timber-frame, freestone, rubble. Out on the Canterbury road and near to the boundary ditch is the fine stone house of Sir Roger Manwood, who founded a school here and who played a perilous and ultimately disastrous political and economic game in the reign of Elizabeth. Beyond the town ditch, is, to my mind, the best that Sandwich has to show, the hospital of St Bartholomew. Of the original thirteenth-century buildings only the chapel remains, but the present almshouses preserve the atmosphere of an inward-looking community. It is not certain whether the house was founded by Sir Henry de Sandwich, who was Warden of the Cinque Ports, but his tomb remains in what might seem to be the founder's position in the little chapel. Sir Henry lies on it in full mid-thirteenth century mail, an impressive figure.

Seven places—possibly eight—were associated with Sandwich in the Confederation. Only two, Fordwich and Deal, had corporate status. Fordwich, on the Stour below Canterbury, operated as the city's port and enjoyed unusual privileges for so small a place. Although never more than a village in population, it had its own mayor and corporation until 1883, and the town hall, tiny but completely equipped for the administration of civic affairs, remains beside the river. Like Sandwich Fordwich is today plagued with a traffic problem. Its main street is very narrow and sharply angled, yet heavy lorries have discovered that it provides a means of avoiding the notorious Canterbury bottlenecks and they thunder daily past the neat brick boxes of Fordwich's once delectable cottages.

Deal was of only minor importance in the Middle Ages. If it had a harbour this disappeared early, and the medieval village was well inland, where Upper Deal is now. Coastal Deal came into prominence when Henry VIII sited three of his new fortresses at Sandown, Deal and

Walmer, and prosperity followed as the Goodwins built up, making a large sheltered inshore anchorage. Deal men made a good living by piloting ships through the sands, rescuing those in trouble, and—perhaps—occasionally cashing in on a not-quite-accidental wreck. The town obtained a charter in 1699, by which time it had outgrown Sandwich, and as an incorporated member it exercised, belatedly, full rights in the Cinque Port organization. Although there have been great changes in Deal during the present century, some as the result of heavy shelling from France during the Second World War, enough remains to enable the visitor to read much of its history on the ground. The inland settlement still clusters around the Norman church of St Leonard's. Modern housing links this community with the larger one of Stuart and Georgian Deal beside the sea. Here are the symmetrically laid-out streets of a new town, some of whose original houses retain their memories of the great naval days, and a notable Georgian church. At the western end of the sea front the line of Victorian houses is broken by the massive squat walls of the castle, in which one can see most convincingly the design of Henry VIII's military engineers.

Of Sandwich's non-corporate limbs Stonar is historically of the first importance. The town stood on the Thanet shore of the Wantsum facing Sandwich and in Saxon times it constituted a potential rival. The traditional hostility between the towns was aggravated by Canute who, when confirming the rights of Christ Church in Sandwich, gave Stonar to St Augustine's Abbey. Thus to economic conflict was added conventual. Stonar lost most of the battles which followed, and the town met its ultimate disaster in a terrible flood in 1365. By the seventeenth century it had practically ceased to exist, and not a building remained when industrial development began with the making of munitions and other war supplies in the First World War.

Reculver was a member of Sandwich until the fourteenth century although after the Conquest it could not have amounted to much. Its decline was assured both by the closing of the Wantsum and by erosion. Sarre lasted rather longer. It was a place of some importance from early Saxon days, situated as it was on the promontory of Thanet at one of the crossings to the mainland. The ferry, operated for the benefit of the monks of Minster, did good business. But the little town depended entirely on the Wantsum and when this began to dry up the port came to an end. A bridge was built across to the mainland in 1485, and Sarre became merely a hamlet on the road to the Thanet towns. The population dwindled and the church fell into ruin. Today Sarre is noticed only by those travellers who break the journey to Margate to enjoy the hospitality of a celebrated inn.

Ramsgate became a member of Sandwich in the reign of Edward III. It never played a great part in Cinque Port affairs. In the Middle Ages a prosperous fishing village, with a fine church inland at St Lawrence to prove it, it came into its own with the popularity of sea-bathing at the beginning of the nineteenth century. Of this time there are some good terraces among later and less admirable holiday buildings, but architecturally the modern town is important for two major churches of the Gothic Revival.

All these towns are clearly involved in their parent port by common topographical interests. Sandwich, however, had one appendage for which there is no simple explanation. Brightlingsea is in Essex, on the tidal waters of the Colne. It is a town with obvious maritime interests, but how explain a connection with a port forty miles away by sea, in another county and with no common tradition or history? Its first appearance in Cinque Port records was not until 1442 when a charter confirmed its membership of Sandwich, but this specifically states that the association was "from antiquity". Whatever Brightlingsea got out of the partnership, there were advantages to Sandwich in having an outpost well on the way to the North Sea fishing grounds and the herring fair at Yarmouth. Brightlingsea today is an unexceptional small seaside town, with only the grand church as a reminder of former prosperity.

Last of Sandwich's non-corporate limbs, Walmer is now included in the borough of Deal. It was always subordinated to Deal, but acquired distinction when the Henry VIII coastal fortress was built there. This was later enlarged to make an official home for the Lord Warden of the Cinque Ports, and Walmer acquired an importance in the history of the Confederation out of proportion to its contribution. The little town, which has a number of pleasant narrow streets, retains a maritime connection by virtue of a lifeboat which is frequently in action over the Goodwins.

Of all the Cinque Ports Dover alone continues to make a good living from the sea. The natural harbour is poor. There is only a narrow gap in the chalk cliffs, through which an inconsiderable stream—the Dour— finds the sea. The usual hazards of eastward drift perpetually threaten to close the harbour-mouth with shingle. Only ceaseless hard work keeps the port operative. Yet Dover has one overwhelming advantage in the narrowness of the strait. It offers by far the shortest crossing to France, and this is important in days of air travel as it was when every voyage was an adventure which must be undertaken because half the king's realm lay overseas. So the piers have increased in number and scale and dredging keeps the openings clear—at a price.

The port played a great part in national history throughout the Middle Ages. Practically every king since the Conqueror passed through it, and pageantry was—and still is—a part of everyday life. The town's concern with commercial prosperity has often been at odds with the castle's regard for national security. There is something a little symbolic in the position of the castle, which stands aloof but dominant. The latent conflict between town and castle was sometimes embodied in the person of the Lord Warden, who was sworn to protect the liberties of the Cinque Ports but who, as Constable of Dover Castle, was often compelled to put national interests—and sometimes, admittedly, personal interests—first. He preferred to hold his court in the castle, where he could call upon the existing administrative machinery and make use of permanent buildings, instead of using the Court of Shepway which had only makeshift premises. The castle, being royal territory, was outside the jurisdiction of the Ports and the Warden often found this convenient, though the Ports did not. The practice, however advantageous to the Warden, was clearly contrary to Cinque Port law. After many protests a compromise was reached, and a Warden's Court was established outside the castle in St James's Church. This was conveniently placed and permanent, and it was within the Cinque Port liberties. Despite continuing objections and a record of abuses and corruption, the Court of St James's continued until 1855. The fine old church in which it was held was a landmark of Dover up to the Second World War. In the bombing and shelling to which Dover was subjected the church became damaged, and it collapsed suddenly, leaving only a picturesque fragment.

Dover was always an important member of the Confederation but, perhaps more than most, its interests lay outside. It was always prosperous, always busy, and did not need to call upon its neighbours for help in a crisis. Kings, bishops, armies, businessmen, pilgrims, all used the port and left some of their substance behind. The flow never ceased, and it still goes on endlessly. For the travellers a great medieval Warden, Hubert de Burgh, established the Maison Dieu for the hospitality of pilgrims, soldiers and other needy strangers. This great double hall, altered in centuries of use and misuse, is still the dominant building in the town and performs a civic function. Hubert de Burgh is one of the noblest names in Dover's story. In an age when honour and disinterestness were at a premium, he showed strength of purpose and loyalty, even to the deplorable King John. When the French King Louis besieged Dover in 1216 he pulled together the disunited and dispirited forces of the Cinque Ports, forced the king to raise the siege, and in the following year sent out the Ports' little ships to scatter and all-but demolish the French fleet in a brilliant action fought within sight of Dover. The purpose of the Warden in this was clear; the portsmen were inspired by loyalty but also by the prospect of profits, and in this, as in many subsequent actions, they made a good haul of ships and prisoners.

The geographical position which gave Dover its importance and prosperity as a port gave it also the greatest strategic importance. The portsmen might not love the castle but they could not ignore it. Then and now it bludgeons the observer with its strength and arrogance and majesty. It is arguably the most impressive castle in England and, except for the Tower of London, the one with the longest continuous active history. From the Conquest—and possibly before—until a very few years ago it had a resident garrison. Every century added to the fortifications until it became an extraordinary complex—not to say hotchpotch—of military styles, yet no castle looks at a distance more harmonious, more the result of evolutionary growth. It is full of memorable features: the earthen mound traditionally—and almost certainly —attributed to King Harold, the late Saxon church of St Mary whose beauty no injudicious restoration can quite destroy, the great keep of Henry II with its two exquisite late Norman chapels, the Constable's Gate, the chains of towers, the lofty walkways, the underground stores and communicating tunnels, all make a visit to Dover Castle an experience in strategy, history and aesthetics.

Nor are the Western Heights to be ignored, even though they do not offer as warm a welcome as the castle. Here, neglected, festooned with barbed wire, disfigured with admonitory notices, are military fortifications as impressive as can be seen anywhere in England. They date from the massive defence programme of the Napoleonic Wars and the mid-Victorian invasion scares. Unlike the medieval defensive works of pre-artillery days they avoid drawing attention to their strength, but the skill with which earthworks, concrete and brick are employed is evident. In this wilderness of disused army barracks and active penal establishments stands the Bredinstone. This is the base of the western pharos, twin to the Roman lighthouse on the castle mound, which was chosen in the seventeenth century as the site for the installation of the Lord Warden. This seems to have been a deliberate attempt, for obscure political purposes, to foist a new tradition on the Cinque Ports and to detract from the tradition of Shepway. It was only partly successful.

A visit to Dover today is a mixed experience. The castle and the western heights are magnificent. The Maison Dieu is a great hall. St Mary's church in the town has a noble Norman tower, and the civic paraphernalia is impressive. The newly restored chapel of St Edmund has atmosphere. There is a fine fragment of the priory of St Martin incorporated in the buildings of Dover College. For the rest—well, the town is busier than most, and a new traffic system has not solved its problems. Much is squalid and dull. Memories abound, but the present continually intrudes, not always with advantage. It is a town in which to revere the past, but only for people of a very special sort is it a town to love.

Associated with Dover in the Cinque Port organization were two corporate towns and seven non-corporate limbs. We met Faversham in Chapter 2; here it might be mentioned briefly that the borough had a confused existence in the Middle Ages because of the conflict of interests between the Cinque Ports, the abbey, and St Augustine's Abbey in Canterbury which owned the church. In one of the more spectacular of many rows the Abbot of Faversham found himself in gaol in Dover Castle for infringement of the Cinque Port liberties. Faversham, too, was the home and base-port of one of the most picturesque heroes, or villains, of the Cinque Ports, Henry Pay. 'Arripay' was active in the reign of Henry IV, when he and his squadron of Cinque Port ships were engaged in a variety of exploits, mostly of doubtful legality. His most brilliant exploit was the defeat of a French fleet which was operating off the Pembrokeshire coast in support of Owen Glendower. In this he appears in the role of gallant patriot; in others he was, in the best Cinque Port tradition, a pirate attacking whichever ships offered the highest profit. Sometimes these happened to belong to England's current official enemies. After a tempestuous career Arripay—the nickname was given by his Spanish opponents and hints at a blend of hostility and reluctant admiration with which they regarded him—came home to Faversham and died there in 1419. He is buried in the north transept of the parish church.

The other corporate member of Dover is Folkestone, which gained a charter, probably not its first, in 1311. The town's distinction came initially not from the port but from a convent founded by the saintly Princess Eanswythe, a granddaughter of Ethelbert and so in—as it were —the direct line of Christian inspiration from Augustine. The nunnery was built conspicuously on the high cliff and so attracted the attention of Danish raiders, so much that it never recovered. The house and the shrine of its founder disappeared. There was a sensation in 1885 when remains of a Saxon burial were discovered by excavation, and these were identified, with some conviction, as those of St Eanswythe. They were placed in a reliquary beside the high altar in the church, and Folkestone may therefore be unique among Kentish parish churches in possessing the relics of a saint. Below the cliffs on which the church stands was a modest harbour which made Folkestone the port of a fishing fleet. It remained a fishing town throughout the Middle Ages and performed its service in common with the rest of the Confederation, despite the havoc caused by the continual build-up of shingle. With its parent port of Dover it has continued to operate as a port for cross-Channel traffic. In the nineteenth century the town profited from the growing holiday trade and built itself a substantial reputation, unrivalled among resorts east of Eastbourne, for comfortable gentility. In this it was helped by the enterprise of Lord Radnor, lord of the manor, by whose inspiration the cliff top and face were developed into the Leas, a healthy and attractive promenade with hanging gardens. Recent developments have been less happy, and it seems possible that Folkestone, which long ago shed most of its medieval atmosphere, is now bent on sacrificing the Victorian and Edwardian trappings which were its principal charm.

The non-corporate limbs of Dover are a mixed bag. There was a group of Thanet members, which presumably followed the lead of Margate in preferring an association with Dover to the nearer port of Sandwich. Margate was an ancient port long associated with Dover; St John's, Goresend (or Goresdon), Woodchurch and St Peter's—all in the coastal area of Thanet—carried much less weight in Cinque Port affairs. They are all a little disappointing to visitors today. The history of Thanet is of enormous interest, but it is to be found in documents rather than on the ground. Apart from the churches, notably St John's and St Peter's, and the gatehouse of a fortified manor-house, 'Dent-de-Lion', surviving strangely among the modern housing of inland Margate, there is little to show of the Middle Ages; of the earlier period there is nothing. (I except from this the opposite shore of Thanet, facing the Wantsum, and the fascinating villages of Minster, Monkton and St Nicholas.) There were also two small members of Dover on the outskirts of Deal and belonging topographically to the port of Sandwich. These were Kingsdown, on the coast, and Ringwould inland. Neither seems to have made much mark. Both are worth a visit today. Ringwould keeps its village character intact and stands well on high ground overlooking the Downs; Kingsdown is almost a suburb of Walmer (and is included in the borough of Deal), but its little streets huddle attractively into the high cliffs, and here begins the best cliff walk in Kent to Dover by way of St Margaret's.

The next port westward is Hythe. The early story of this place is tied up with the vagaries of the Limen, an errant river which changed its course many times and made and marred the fortunes of many ports. Before the formation of Romney Marsh the river made its way through a wide marshy estuary below the line of the greensand cliffs in a course marked roughly today by the Royal Military Canal. It found the open sea a little beyond Lympne where in early Saxon times, if not before, there was a small fishing port at West Hythe. East of this was Hythe itself, where the cliffs came close to the sea, leaving a small haven fed by streams flowing from the high downland. The pattern of this country changed gradually over several centuries, through a combination of natural causes and man's activities. The ceaseless drift of shingle built up a wall of pebbles and sand between Dymchurch and Hythe, and the river brought its tribute of silt out of the Weald. To these natural processes was added, at some time unknown but possibly just before and during the Roman occupation, the construction of the

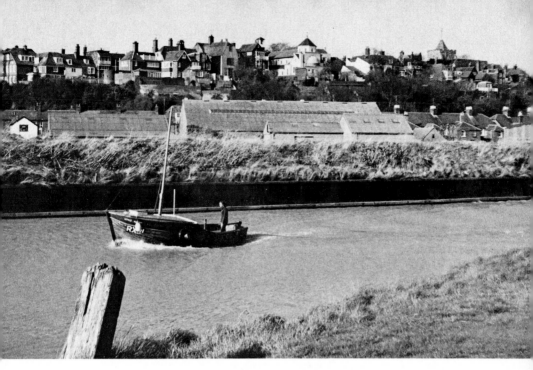

Rye from the River Rother

Laddingford Bridge

Beltring hop farm

Rhee Wall, an earthen barrage from Appledore to Romney. Under these influences the levels of Romney Marsh were built up between the Rhee Wall and the sandhills, and in the process the old course of the Limen was slowly filled in and the port of West Hythe became choked. Hythe survived longer because the shingle enclosed a lagoon in which ships might find shelter. At last the outlet to the sea was closed by shingle and Hythe's seaport days were over. Although, by energetic action and the employment of experts from Holland, the end was deferred by at least a century, in the reign of Charles I the shingle won its final victory. After two centuries of decay the town had a revival through the discovery, almost at the same time, of its virtues as a seaside resort and as a centre for military training.

Hythe was at its height as a port around the time of the Conquest. Later in the Middle Ages its position was somewhat anomalous. The town was within the manor of Saltwood and so lay under the control of the archbishop. Saltwood played a vital part in the quarrel between Henry II and Thomas Becket, and the castle was chosen as a base by the four knights before they moved on to Canterbury for the climax of the tragedy. Hythe achieved some degree of compromise over the management of its affairs. It was however dependent on the goodwill of the archbishop and his nominees until Cranmer surrendered the manor to Henry VIII; after that it had to contend with royal whims which were if anything less predictable than those of the primate. At last, in 1575, Queen Elizabeth gave Hythe a charter which granted the town the kind of municipal independence enjoyed by its peers among the Cinque Ports. In the same way Hythe suffered the ecclesiastical domination of Saltwood. It ranked as a chapelry of Saltwood Church until 1844 although from the thirteenth century it possessed one of the greatest church buildings in Kent.

No other building in the Cinque Ports—I leave out of account Dover Castle which existed in despite of the Ports—brings home to us the power and wealth of a leading Cinque Port in its heyday. An original Norman church was built into the cliffside above the harbour and this was extended in the twelfth century. Then the building was again expanded early in the thirteenth century, surely under the direction of someone who had seen what had been done at Canterbury thirty or forty years earlier. St Leonard's, Hythe, is a striking example of how inspiration can be stimulated by a difficult technical problem. The site was severely restricted. It was necessary to build right up to the eastern boundary. An essential part of the medieval ritual was the procession which passed around the church, always on consecrated ground. In order to provide a processional way at Hythe, the architect had to take it underneath the church and in consequence to raise the chancel high above the level of the nave. The result is a noble flight of steps

6

from lower to higher level, producing a soaring effect almost comparable to the matchless eastward rise of Christ Church, Canterbury. In devising this solution, the unknown designer could not have guessed that the processional way would become the 'crypt' and that it would be crammed with dispossessed bones from the overcrowded churchyard. To these, generations of sextons and vergers of Hythe have attached picturesque and spurious tales of battles long ago.

One may readily forget these absurdities in the contemplation of St Leonard's choir, rising in lyrical beauty out of the heavy sobriety of the nave. This is the purest Gothic manner, before on the one hand excessive ornamentation, on the other mechanical repetitiveness took charge. The arches, at once massive and graceful, soar confidently. The triple eastern lancets—renewed after war damage—spill light on to the cool grey-gold stone. Everything is restrained but by no means severe, its gravity relieved only in the elaborate arcades of the sedilia. Here for a brief moment in history the quarrels, the striving for precedence, the pettiness and the piracy of the Ports are forgotten, and portsmen and modern travellers are united in a rich experience aesthetic and spiritual.

Today there is little beside St Leonard's to remind us of Hythe's days as a port. There are remains of a medieval hospital, and some of the eighteenth-century frontages doubtless mask earlier work, but from the High Street northwards Hythe is essentially a small and in parts delightful Georgian town. Across the Royal Military Canal it becomes a Victorian resort built on the pebble ridge which was the old town's doom. Now, with the Small Arms School gone, this has become a relaxed, agreeable holiday-place for sober tastes and the population ages as more people wisely come here to retire. Less than any other of the head Ports does it hint at former maritime greatness.

Hythe has only one dependent limb, West Hythe at the foot of the steep cliffs below Lympne. It lost all importance as a port long ago. Of the original buildings only the church—doubtless the only building in stone—has survived and this in ruins. In these shattered fragments of wall there is a hint of former architectural sophistication, and the place has that air of attractive melancholy which clings to neglected old buildings. If St Mary's Church, West Hythe, were still roofed and in action its appeal would probably be less strong. Around it is nothing but the caravans of modern holiday-makers.

West Hythe is approached by a narrow lane which goes no farther as a motor-road. The road rising out of the marsh tackles the former cliffs steeply until it reaches the ridge at an historic point. This is the Shepway Cross, where a handsome modern stone cross marks the traditional site of the meetings of the Court of Shepway. It was an essential part of the Cinque Port tradition—one not always appreciated by the Warden—that they should meet on neutral territory and in no permanent building. A canvas town sprang up here for the meetings of the court and then vanished when the court rose.

Unlike the Brodhull and Guestling, which existed for internal matters, Shepway was the king's court which the portsmen attended by compulsion and at the Warden's demand. There they transacted not their own but the king's business, performing the civic duties which jurats of lesser places carried out in their hundred courts. Attendance was at once a recognition of their peculiar distinction and a chore which they might prefer to waive. Although the Warden swore, at the opening of every Shepway Court, to uphold the ancient liberties of the Ports, there were many occasions when his duty as the king's representative, or his self-interest, was in conflict with this undertaking.

Shepway was chosen as the site for the courts because it was neutral, being outside the territory of any of the ports, reasonably central, and well above the malarial swamp of the levels. It may have had some historical significance, now lost, as the administrative centre of Shepway Lathe, that mysterious archaic division of local government which was unique to Kent. Certainly the setting has a superb symbolic quality. Here at the foot of Shepway Cross is one of the great views of Kent, which today commands the whole of Romney Marsh. The ancient towns of Rye and Winchelsea are visible beyond the levels, and the dark bulk of the Fire Hills in the west hides the Port of Hastings.

Just along the road—and even nearer by footpath—is the archdeacon's manor of Lympne, its hall and fortified turrets open to the public, beside Lanfranc's fine church, and just below lie the scattered relics of the Saxon Shore fort of Lemanis.

Between Lympne and the Port of Romney stretches one of the strangest areas in England, the territory of the Liberty and Level of Romney Marsh. Romney Marsh is by common usage the name given to the whole of the flat country between Hythe and Rye which was recovered from the sea, but strictly it applies only to the eastern half, terminating at the Rhee Wall which is now indicated roughly by the main road from Appledore to New Romney. The observant traveller on this road, especially when afternoon winter sunshine throws revealing shadows, will notice a very slight difference in level in the fields to the south of the road. This phenomenon is best seen just beyond Old Romney. It is the ghost of the Rhee Wall, an embankment built to accelerate the recovery of the marsh. Here are the twenty-three manors which jointly accept responsibility for protection against the sea and for the administration of justice. Romney Marsh is unique in this respect, that it had, and in a real sense still has, a form of medieval administration found elsewhere only in municipal boroughs but here applied to a

purely rural area. There are no towns on Romney Marsh. The Port of
Romney is expressly excluded from the boundaries of the liberty.

Therefore, although the stories of Romney Marsh and the Port of
Romney are closely related, it is necessary here to avoid involvement
in the infinitely fascinating subject of the marsh and to concentrate
instead on the Cinque Port of Romney and its members.

Romney's history has been governed by the River Rother whose
waters provided its harbour and whose departure marked the effective
end of the port. In the early Middle Ages the river, which had originally found its principal outlet to the sea at Hythe, had flowed into a
wide shallow estuary of which one shore was formed by the Rhee
Wall. The western shore was less precisely defined, but it included the
high land of the Isle of Oxney, with a sea-water channel around it, and
the cliffs in Sussex crowned by the churches of Iden and Playden. To
the south a great shingle bank grew yearly at Dengeness and silt contributed by the river steadily formed the levels of Denge Marsh, out of
which rose the shingle ridge of Lydd. Long fingers of beach probed
towards one another to the south of Rye. By the twelfth century land
had been recovered from the sea to the west of the Rhee Wall, so that
the course of the Rother was dangerously diverted and had to make a
pronounced bend north-east to find an outlet beyond Romney. Romney Haven was almost landlocked by the rising shingle and sand
between Dengeness and Dymchurch.

This was the position of Romney in its great days. The early history
of the port is obscure, but it seems to have been a notable place in Saxon
times, sufficiently prominent to be chosen as a base for a savage Danish
raid up the Rother in 893. In the next century the town had a mint,
evidence of great prosperity and reputation. The port came violently
into prominence at the time of the Norman Conquest. The Normans,
who seem to have lost their Norse proficiency at sea, made a poor job
of the crossing and some of them landed at Romney, where the portsmen gave them a rough reception and then threw them back into the
sea. Almost the Conqueror's first act after the Battle of Hastings was to
march round to Romney to save his army's face by sacking the town.
But the port was too useful to be left in ruin. It was in the forefront of
Cinque Port activities during the frequent crossings of the channel in
Norman and Angevin times. By the end of Henry II's reign Romney
seemed set fair to play a leading part in history and to enjoy a long and
prosperous old age. But within a century the end was in sight. The
normal processes of silting and shingle-building were accelerated by
severe weather. In 1287 the end came dramatically. There was a terrible
storm. Two very high tides met the Rother waters in spate, the sea
defences were breached and Romney was flooded. When the storm
subsided and the waters at last ebbed, the men of Romney found that

their river had gone. The mouth of the Rother, between Romney and Lydd, had been blocked by shingle and silt and the river had been forced to find a new way to the sea past Rye. The blow was not immediately fatal. Like a stroke the storm left Romney a permanent invalid which lingered another century or two but only as a shadow of its vigorous self. Expensive attempts were made to connect the port with the river by means of a cut, but they failed.

The port died, but not the rights and privileges of a leading member of the Cinque Ports. In 1588 the call came to provide a ship against the Invincible Armada, and the call was not made in vain. No ships were to hand, so Romney hired one, fully equipped, and called upon Lydd and Old Romney to meet their ancient obligations by contributing to the cost. There followed a wrangle which continued long after King Philip's galleons had limped home and which indeed was never completely resolved.

Curiously Romney was slow in obtaining municipal independence. The manor belonged to the archbishop and what he had he held. It was not until the primate's territorial importance had waned after the Reformation that the town, which had made abortive attempts to get rid of its bailiff and elect a mayor, gained a charter from Queen Elizabeth in 1563.

After so long a history and so early an eclipse, it is not surprising that few signs of medieval New Romney are visible today. Indeed the most convincing evidence of the town's greatness is not the noble Norman church but the unique series of town and port records which have miraculously survived and provide a detailed story from the reign of Edward III.

The outward aspect of New Romney is that of a modestly prosperous town of the eighteenth century. Here and there it is clear that older work lies behind those sober façades, but the fronts are well mannered and symmetrical. A famous map of 1614 shows that the symmetry belonged to an earlier age, and a glance at a town plan and a thoughtful stroll around the streets brings home that this is a planned town built on the grid principle. There are three east-west roads, with regularly intersecting side streets. New Romney was indeed a New Town of the Middle Ages and a remarkable example of early town planning.

The medieval town had three parish churches, including in St Martin's, a minster which dated to the time of the original Christian missions. This venerable building, perhaps contemporary with the abbeys of Lyminge and Minster, was destroyed in 1551. St Laurence was founded later and was abandoned earlier. By the reign of Elizabeth, therefore, only one parish church was still functioning, the present parish church of St Nicholas. This splendid building, with its magnificent Norman tower, is a good example of the municipal church of a prosperous town. Its size is generous even for a large town, and it was used for many purposes besides worship. It was the original town hall and often the meeting place for the Brodhull of the Cinque Ports.

The curious flight of steps which leads *down* into St Nicholas church is a reminder of the disaster which destroyed New Romney. On top of the original level of the town lie many thousands of tons of silt swept into the town by the devastating storm and tide. The lane south past the church tower drops imperceptibly and then deteriorates into a track crossing the flats to the distant line of houses marking the present coast-line. The sea is now over a mile away, and standing where the ships tied up the magnitude of Romney's loss becomes sharply apparent.

Romney had one corporate member, Lydd, and four non-corporate limbs. Lydd is as fascinating a modern town as New Romney and one which preserves much of its individuality. It may not be too fanciful to attribute this to former insularity, for Lydd was an island in the mouth of the Rother. At first the pebble ridge was small, but it grew with the growth of the shingle bank and with the reclamation of the marsh, and Lydd is now, although small in population, very large in area, extending to the Sussex boundary, to Dungeness point and to the coastal strip of Greatstone. Like Romney the manor belonged to the archbishop, and the two towns were closely associated, not always to their mutual advantage. Lydd enjoyed its subordinate status, with comparably smaller responsibilities, especially when it became at least the economic equal of the head port after the destruction of New Romney's harbour.

Today much of Lydd's charm comes from the contrasts of ancient and modern. The compact little town is, like Romney, well laid out and offers a generally post-Reformation aspect. It embraced the modern world by welcoming an army camp, by giving its name to an explosive and a species of poultry, and lately by taking in an important cross-Channel airport. A great nuclear power station stands within the borough bounds—but at a comfortable distance from the town centre. At Dungeness is a bird-reserve with a world reputation. And all this has been done without loss of quality in the old town.

The best of the town is to be found in the diminutive high street and the tiny square just off it. Everything here is in scale, and everything is self-absorbed. Lydd has never set out to catch the tourist. Away from the central area is the Rype, a large open green across which the breezes whip smartly—and in winter there is no colder place in the South-east. The centrepiece of Lydd is the church, which is not as wide as New Romney's but quite remarkably long. The tower is in the Kent tradition of Canterbury, Ashford and Tenterden, very tall and slim with corner pinnacles; inside it is elegantly vaulted. Traces of a pre-Conquest original are revealed in the interior, and out of this little building has grown a nobly proportioned and very light hall, for me the most stately of all the fine churches of the Marsh. The sanctuary was wrecked by enemy action during the war, and the rebuilding, with its tall eastern lancets, has been done most discreetly.

Romney's minor limbs were Bromehill, Dengemarsh, Oswaldstone and Old Romney. Bromehill was a port on the Sussex boundary. The road from Lydd to Camber reaches the sea at Broomhill Sands, and the town was hereabouts. It seems to have been abandoned after the storm in 1287 and not a trace remains. There are lingering legends of a big town with several churches, and doubtless lonely travellers have heard church bells ringing by night, but there is no hard evidence. Dengemarsh and Oswaldstone were closely associated with Lydd, and were in effect limbs of that port. Nothing remains to be seen now. Old Romney was a port on the Rother up the estuary from New Romney. The 'Old' is a later addition and has no meaning of relative antiquity. Again there are stories of former greatness and the Ordnance Survey map indicates —with what authority?—the sites of two vanished churches. Today it is one of the smallest of Kentish villages and one of the most charming. The church, raised on a minute mound above the level, has no architectural pretensions but is perfect in its modest way, excellently maintained but carrying an air of extreme age. There can scarcely be a vertical anywhere. It makes a memorable picture from the main road; many a traveller has been tempted off his route for a closer inspection and has lost, once and for all, his heart to its intimate charms.

So, across Walland Marsh, the level to the west of the Rhee Wall, by way of Brookland with its celebrated candle-snuffer tower, to the Sussex boundary, and over the Guldeford Level to the River Rother in its current course and to the ancient town of Rye.

The careers of the two ancient towns of Rye and Winchelsea were always so closely associated that they cannot well be separated. Originally members of Hastings they had established a practical independence by the time of the Conquest and were in effect full members of the Confederation. Only universal familiarity with the old title prevented the ports from being redesignated Sept Ports. Hastings did not take kindly to the loss of its associates. When Richard I, on his way to the Holy Land, stopped in Sicily to sort out his sister's complicated affairs and catch up with his office work, he issued a charter confirming rights granted by his father to the men of 'Rya' and 'Winchenesell'. Hastings was very annoyed and lodged a complaint with the king (John, for Richard was too busy with his Crusade to bother further with such domestic matters). In vain. The ancient towns had broken their bonds and thereafter exercised full rights as Cinque Ports.

Rye had become established on its rocky peninsula in Saxon times. Winchelsea occupied lower ground on an island in the landlocked bay.

Where this had been is still a matter for dispute among the experts. Some favour a point near the golf course at Camber Sands, others the area below Pett in the shelter of the Fairlight Hills. The position was strategically good, geographically hazardous. The land suffered grievously from erosion and changes in level. Storm and the raids of enemies had reduced Winchelsea to a state almost of ruin when the famous storm and tides of 1287 which wrecked Romney swept over Winchelsea and literally wiped it off the map. Several years earlier the king, Edward I, had foreseen this disaster and had begun the planning of a new port on a more secure site to the north.

The storm which destroyed Winchelsea did some good to Rye. Previously the town had lain off the main trade routes of the Rother estuary. Now the river's main course flowed past the town, to the gratification of the portsmen. Thereafter Rye flourished exceedingly and earned a reputation for shrewd dealing, for gallant performance of the king's business, and for spectacular acts of open piracy. The town also suffered for its prominence. It became a target for French attacks, first in 1339 and later on three occasions during the Hundred Years War. In one of these raids, in 1377, the French added moral injury to physical by stealing the bells out of Rye church steeple. This incensed the men of Rye so bitterly that they sailed across the Channel two years later and stole them back, a colourful episode in a conflict which was on the whole one of purposeless destruction and human misery. (Memories last long in old towns like these. One of the modern events of the Rye year is Bonfire Night. It is associated now with Guy Fawkes Day, but the traditional form of the celebrations links them with more distant times and darker days when French seamen landed below the town and set their torches to Rye thatch.)

One result of these raids was that the town was walled. It already possessed a fortress on a high point, called, after a later owner, the Ypres Tower. This was now linked with the port's three gates, of which only one, the Land Gate, remains, by a fortified wall.

By Tudor times the Rother had got to work again changing the landscape. Silt once more combined with shingle to build up acres of land and the sea receded, leaving the town high and dry on its rock. In this crisis religious intolerance abroad, in the country which had done so much harm to Rye in the past, came to the rescue. Protestant refugees from the Huguenot persecutions which followed the Massacre of St Bartholomew flooded into the town, bringing with them skills in weaving and other specialist trades which gave new life to the decaying town. The process was repeated just over a century later when an influx of French artisans followed the revocation of the Edict of Nantes. Some Rye folk learned the new trades while others followed more traditional occupations of fishing and smuggling.

Fishing continues—smuggling too?—and the maritime connection is maintained by a host of amateur sailors who have adopted Rye Harbour as their own. Here among the sand dunes and in sight of one of the martello towers left over from the Napoleonic invasion scare there is a sense of leisured purposeful bustle which contrasts with the museum atmosphere of present-day Rye. For Rye, of all the Cinque Ports, has taken most readily to the role of tourist attraction, finding commercial profit in the picturesque relics of a stormy past. There is, happily, enough wealth to arrest decay without destroying the delicate patina of age which gives the lovely town its unique charm. It is unusual among the tourist towns of England in that it has no single major attraction. Even the noble and superbly sited parish church is matched by many others in less well-favoured places. Visitors come to Rye not to see the church or the Ypres Tower, or even to visit the admirable shops, but to walk the steep cobbled streets, to peer into enclosed alleys and gaze from the ramparts over the misty levels, and to savour an atmosphere which has no English parallel.

The route from Rye to new Winchelsea follows the military road which was part of Pitt's anti-invasion strategy in the Napoleonic wars. Its dead-straight dullness is enlivened by occasional brief glimpses, on the left, of the grey walls of Camber Castle. This most remote and most evocative of Henry VIII's coastal forts is currently under repair, from which it may emerge safe for another century, tidy and archaeologically emaculate, but with—perhaps—some loss of atmosphere. I like to think of Camber as I first knew it long ago, when there were no official custodians, few visitors and no residents but sheep and rabbits, and one could traverse its half-buried passages at some risk—willingly incurred —from falling stone.

At the end of the Military Road rises the steep cliff of Iham which in 1280 was selected as the site of a new town. Edward I, grim warrior and implacable enemy, was one of the great innovators of medieval England and the best town planner since the last Roman official went scuttling home from Rutupiae. His town of Winchelsea was conceived on a large scale and laid out with mathematical precision on the table-top of the high country which stretched westward to the old Cinque Port meeting-place at Guestling. Eight streets intersected at regular intervals enclosed 'quarters' which were each to be developed system-atically. In the central quarter of the eastern block stood a great church. This was a cruciform building in the short-lived Decorated style, enriched with much elegant naturalistic carving and with richly flowing tracery in the Kentish manner. The site of the town had been chosen by a master of warfare, and to its natural advantages of steep cliffs were added walls and three strong gates.

For a time, while the town arose quarter by quarter, Winchelsea prospered under the direction of the Alard family, who had come from old Winchelsea and who were equally distinguished in warfare, trade and piracy—and indeed these three were often indistinguishable. But Winchelsea's troubles were not over. The French arrived in 1377 and attacked the town savagely and were as savagely repelled. They came back in 1380 and did better—or worse—breaching the walls and burning houses, and left the town in ruins. Whether the French returned and administered the *coup de grâce* in 1448, as tradition asserts, is in doubt. By that time, in any case, the traditional pattern of decay had been re-established, for the sea which had destroyed old Winchelsea now abandoned the new town and left the port on dry ground. King Edward's great plan was never realized, the church of St Thomas of Canterbury remained without a nave, and the borough became in effect a village. Queen Elizabeth surely had her royal tongue in her cheek when, visiting the town in 1573 and enjoying hospitality of a ruinously generous kind, she called it 'Little London'.

Of all the seven head Ports Winchelsea alone lost the outward trappings of municipal greatness before the twentieth century. It has avoided the intrustion of the modern age better than any of them. Unlike Rye it takes no account of tourists and lives to itself, with no ambition but that of remaining beautiful in arrested decay. One hesitates to praise it too much for fear of sending more visitors to violate its calm. Yet its charms are so discreet and subtle that it will never attract a tithe of the money-spending hordes who flock to Rye. Its greatest appeal—and this is something which has not a majority attraction—is that of failure. Nothing brings home more keenly the gentle melancholy of Winchelsea than to leave the developed quarters by a quiet country lane, travel past peaceful pastures until the town is almost forgotten, and come suddenly upon the mouldering stones of New Gate where Edward's new town was planned to end on the landward side. To find a contrast to this experience one stands by the Strand Gate and looks down to where the heron-haunted waters of the Royal Military Canal mark the old shore line, and then one turns to the church where generations of Alards sleep in their gorgeous canopied tombs. Outside, above the makeshift porch in which the great church terminates are displayed proudly—but by this time ineffectually—the three lion-ships of the Cinque Ports.

The ancient towns had only one associated port, and that one a latecomer. Through "tides and burnings" Rye had come to such a depth of "waste and poverty" in the mid-fifteenth century that it was no longer capable of meeting its obligations for ship-service. In 1449, therefore, Tenterden was attached to the decayed port as a corporate member not, as had been done in other places in happier days, as a token of respect but as an act of charity. Rye then had a younger town, and one not depressed by enemy raids and the whims of the sea, to call upon for men and money. For its part Tenterden acquired status and a share of privileges.

It may seem strange that a hill-top town so obviously remote from the sea should play an important part in Cinque Port affairs. A glance at the map and a mental drowning of all land over fifty feet reveals that Tenterden had effective access to the sea. The low green whaleback of Oxney was an island indeed when the tidal Rother divided to enclose it in two wide arms. The re-establishment of the Rother as a considerable river makes sense of several topographical puzzles, including the medieval standing of the ville of Newenden and the building of a coastal defensive castle at Bodiam. Ships navigating the sea channel passed the narrows between Stone Point and Appledore, rounded the little church-crowned island of Ebony, and tied up at the small hythe of Tenterden port. The town supplemented its income from the wealden cloth trade with harbour dues and a modest interest in ship-building. When the port was at its zenith the harbour-master had a new house built, complete with docking facilities, a delectable building which, when the Smallhythe ship-building industry was scarcely a memory, became the home of the supreme British actress of her age, Ellen Terry. Even then sailing barges still reached Smallhythe bridge, but only by going right round Oxney for the channel to Ebony had become choked.

Tenterden had humble beginnings. It had been a 'den', a rough clearing in the wealden forest where swineherds employed by the abbey of Minster-in-Thanet grazed their pigs. (It was in fact the den of Tenet.) Minster Abbey did not survive the Danish raids, but the abbey's famous saint, the Saxon princess Mildred, still holds the dedication of the great church which is the centrepiece of modern Tenterden. The famous tower was added soon after the town became linked with Rye, and the mysterious saying that Tenterden Steeple caused the Goodwin Sands (or alternatively the decay of Sandwich haven) reflects obscurely the distrust of the old ports in the prosperity of this parvenu.

Now, when such suspicions have long disappeared, it is heartening to find, when so many of the ports and their associates are depressed, that Tenterden has found a viable twentieth-century way of life. It is the liveliest small town in Kent, well aware of the asset it possesses in the most beautiful High Street in the county, but not afraid of letting that asset earn its keep in contemporary terms. It has a remarkable range of shops, not all dedicated to the tourist trade. When the inevitable parking problem has been solved and the fine green verges of the wide street are free of their depressing ranks of cars, Tenterden will have rid itself of its one major defect and present us with that rare phenomenon, a town which is at one and the same time prosperous and lovely.

This westward tour of the Cinque Ports has come last to what has at most times been regarded as the senior partner. Hastings enjoys this distinction not by actual seniority, or by remaining active longer than the rest, or by occupying a central position, or by providing an administrative headquarters. It may derive from the favour of the Conqueror, or perhaps from the outstanding enterprise and ferocity of the inhabitants. Certainly Hastings men were feared greatly, and not only in foreign ports.

Like all the other ports Hastings suffered from the fickle affections of the sea. The original port seems to have been built near the White Rock where a considerable stream provided anchorage. This was over-whelmed by the sea, possibly not long before the Conquest. William took a personal interest in the town which he had used as a base for his operation against the English, and he established a new burgh under the shadow of his castle. This lay in the narrow trough between the West Cliff, on which the castle stands, and the East Cliff, along the banks of a small stream. The stream entered the sea just below the town and provided a haven for ships of the port. The town was well shel-tered between its twin hills, but the harbour was as vulnerable as any in the Confederation. Heavy seas brought shingle in a perpetual drift to choke the haven. The struggle to keep the mouth clear, and after-wards to build jetties out beyond the shingle-line, continued up to the last century, and there is still melancholy testimony to the victorious sea in the stumps of stone piers which stand battered below the East Cliff.

The mere loss of a harbour never deterred a Cinque Port from active interest in the brotherhood, and Hastings continued to emphasize its responsible position, including, it must be admitted, readiness to meet its obligations. Despite economic depression the port sent out its full quota in answer to the call for help against the Armada. Strangely—and the whole story of the Ports is one of anomalies—the premier port did not attain full borough status until Elizabeth granted a charter in the year of the Armada. In earlier years it had been inhibited by the interest of the sovereign and by foreign interference, because the castle was vested in the Counts d'Eu and the manor belonged—by an arrange-ment dating to the reign of Canute—to the Abbey of Fécamp in Normandy.

When the port finally died Hastings continued as a fishing com-munity, sustained by memories of past glories of which there were firm reminders in the meetings of the brotherhood and Guestling and the splendours of coronation ceremonial. Then, in the Regency, the town had a share of the prosperity enjoyed by its insignificant neighbour,

Brighton, with the growing passion for the sea and for sea-bathing. New houses and terraces on a grand scale carried the town westwards over the site of the original port, and in the course of the century came the planting of a new resort at St Leonard's. The process of growth continues, and of all the Ports Hastings alone plays a substantial part in modern commuterdom.

Hastings has so much to offer, as residence, holiday town and shopping centre, that it may be reasonable to complain that, in proportion to past importance, it has less to show of former greatness than any of the Ports except Hythe. For this one must blame a variety of causes, including enemy action in the Second World War, the pressure of traffic and of business interests, and even perhaps a certain insensitivity. The immediate surroundings of the old town and its two great churches are well kept, but it is difficult to bear or to forgive the treatment accorded to St Mary-in-the-Castle and its accompanying crescent, a charming Regency concept which has suffered a fate marginally worse than demolition. The fragmentary remains of the castle stand well on their isolated rock, and East Cliff invites two enchanting strolls over the sandy hills to Fairlight and Pett. In St Clement's, the civic church, there is an air of spaciousness and well-being at odds with the fortunes of the port when it was built, and it has notable fittings, especially a splendid font. It also displays one handsome reminder of the portsmen and their moments of greatness. When the Coronation Barons came back from the coronation of King George III they sacrificed the staves of the canopy which they had held, however unsteadily, above the monarch to make a silver candelabrum to hang in their church.

To Hastings were attached two corporate ports and six minor members. Seaford joined Hastings, rather as Tenterden had been attached to Rye, to provide a needed shot in the arm. This was an important place in pre-Conquest England and a prosperous port well into the Middle Ages, but for some reason, perhaps the influence of the great family of Warenne at Lewes, it did not play a formal part in the affairs of the Confederation. By the fourteenth century Seaford's great maritime days were over. Shingle blocked the harbour and the River Ouse was forced into a new channel from which it found fresh access to the sea at a point where later a New Haven was established. It was in fact an impoverished Seaford which was attached to Hastings by charter of Henry VIII in 1544, and the two unhappy ports shared the burden of ship-service between them.

There is little in the prosperous modern town and holiday resort of Seaford to recall the past. In Pevensey the past is ever present. To the visitor who is conscious of the roots from which this country has grown this is one of the most exciting places in England. The tall walls of Roman Anderida, the Norman castle dwarfed by them, the fine houses and the church, the misty fields happily veiling by distance the awful developments of Pevensey Bay, all evoke memories of a past continuously active and dramatic. It was probably by chance that the Conqueror made his landfall here. His navigation had been upset and he was doubtless aiming for Hastings. Nevertheless he used the Roman fort, which stood on a fair haven albeit with a marshy hinterland, as the site for one of his chain of strategic castles. The little port was associated early with Hastings and received a charter, perhaps not its first, in 1209. It was never a major contributor to the Confederation, limiting its commitment to a single ship. Pevensey suffered the fate of its neighbours through the drift of shingle, and now lies well inland.

Hastings acquired a curious collection of minor limbs. Bulverhythe was a place of some standing before the Conquest, and is now a western suburb of Hastings, almost entirely modern. Hydneye and Northeye were small ports, the one in marshy country beyond Pevensey and now a suburb of Eastbourne, the other higher up the little river which formed Pevensey haven. Petit Iham was at the western end of the ridge on which New Winchelsea was later built. All these were of small consequence in the affairs of the Ports. Hastings also had two very far-flung dependencies. Bekesbourne is east of Canterbury on the tiny Little Stour river. It was attached to Hastings by personal service, the manor being granted by Henry II to a shipmaster of Hastings, and paid service to the port—normally one ship or its cash equivalent—in succeeding reigns. Lastly Hastings drew hereditary service from the manor of Grench—now Grange—on the Medway estuary below Chatham, by virtue of an obligation incurred in 1284.

This long journey in time and around the coast of south-east England ends, therefore, not within sight of the sea, evoking brave thoughts of the little ships of the Cinque Ports seeing the king safely to his domains overseas, or fighting his battles, or indulging in casual piracy, but on the edge of a housing estate within the Borough of Gillingham, its drabness briefly enlivened by the slight remains of a chapel built by Sir John Philpot, a merchant-venturer of the days when the Ports were at their height of repute and prosperity in Richard II's reign.

5

The Iron Trail

EVEN by the modest standards of the South Country the hills of the Kentish Weald are not high, but they are not the less effective as viewpoints. On the precise crest of one such eminence, and closing the vista up the steep little high street, stands the parish church of Goudhurst. Nowadays most churches bar the tower door—if not the whole building—against vandals and legitimate pilgrims alike, but at Goudhurst the tower can on propitious days be ascended for the enjoyment of a singularly harmonious view.

This was the scene enjoyed by Richard Church when he did his firewatching duties here during the Second World War. Church, a fine poet and modest novelist whose true genius was for friendship, lived for many years, including those of the war, just below the hill to the north-east in a converted oast set in enchanting country. The view which he knew well and which we now look upon is essentially rural. Beyond the concentrated red roofs of the little town is open pasture, hop garden and orchard with, to the south, the darker greens of the forest plots of Bedgebury. Farm buildings and the conical caps of ubiquitous oasts show up everywhere, but it is, compared with much of Kent, quite empty country. Not a single road traverses the rectangle $4\frac{1}{2}$ by $2\frac{1}{2}$ miles whose corners are Goudhurst, Flimwell, Hawkhurst and Iden Green. Here, one may think, is a tract untouched by the intrusive housing and industry of the Kentish commuter belt.

This is true. Place-names on the map, however, hint at a very different scene in the past. Three Chimneys Farm and Furnace Farm, and perhaps Blackbush Wood, are reminders of the time, not far past in the scale of history, when this was the black country of England. If you had stood on Goudhurst tower, newly rebuilt, in 1640, you would have looked over a landscape of forest and coppice punctuated with the smoke and the glow of many furnaces, for Goudhurst is on the eastern fringe of the iron country of the Weald.

Iron was worked in this country from the dawn of history, and beyond. The existence of a good supply of a material so vital to the economy of Rome may have been a factor in Caesar's decision to invade Britain, and certainly the Romans exploited the industry during the centuries of the occupation. The same map which reveals the tell-tale farm-names around Goudhurst dating from the high summer of the industry shows too a suspiciously straight main road running roughly north and south with the village of Staplehurst stretched along it for a mile. A closer look shows that it continues, with minor interruptions, as minor road or footpath until it loses itself in the wide valley of the River Rother. This road, which joined the major highway of Watling Street at Durobrivae (Rochester) makes sense in Roman terms only if it is regarded as a miners' road which brought the products of the Wealden ironworks into the flow of civilization.

No doubt iron continued to be worked in a desultory fashion throughout the Dark Ages and the Middle Ages without making considerable inroads into either of the raw materials of ironstone and timber. The Roman roads decayed, and it was difficult to get iron out of the dense forest with its perilous tracks and its notorious mud. A powerful stimulus was needed to make iron an industry of national importance.

This came with the invention of gunpowder. War is a formidable partner of industry. When the demand for cannon became sufficiently vocal ironmasters were found in the Weald to supply it. Thereafter the industry fluctuated with the changes of national policy, booming with war and the threat of war, declining in the years of peace—although a secondary function developed with the emergence of the new rich whose country estates and town houses needed iron for grates and firebacks and railings.

For a closer look at the industry on the ground we must come down from Goudhurst tower and travel for three or four miles through the view to Horsmonden, a sizeable village in the orchard and hop country. The village has more to offer than is immediately apparent, but for the present we must forego the charms of the remote church set in parkland

Doorcase in Middle Street, Deal

(*below left*) The Land Gate, Winchelsea (*below right*) Shepway Cross

Lydd Church

and the memories of the Austens, a clothworking family who were ancestors of Jane, in favour of Furnace Pond. Past the Gun Inn—significant name—on the green is a narrow lane, leading eventually to Castle Hill and to spectacular views across the low Weald, which at a dip crosses a tiny stream. Just short of this a gate in the fence gives access in a few yards to a wide stretch of water, clearly artificial as the high barrage at the outflow indicates. Horsmonden Furnace worked most profitably during the Civil War when the owner, John Browne, who had been gunfounder to James I, played a somewhat ambivalent role, being courted by both sides. Furnace Pond provides a scene of considerable beauty, especially when visited, preferably early in the day before the anglers grow too thick upon the ground, either when the spring foliage is at its freshest or just before the first frosts send the gold and copper leaves flying. It needs a conscious effort of the imagination to recover the industrial origins of this enchanting place.

In addition to iron ore the Weald possessed two essential ingredients of the iron industry, fuel and power. The dense forest seemed to offer an inexhaustible supply of timber which could be turned into charcoal for the furnaces. Innumerable little streams, feeders of Rother, Cuckmere, Ouse and Adur, threaded the forest and these could be dammed to produce a head of water from which power might be harnessed.

The classic arrangement—nowhere now to be seen on the ground—was for the stream to be dammed at two points, producing a pair of ponds about half a mile apart. The upper water was the furnace pond, and this furnished power to work the big leather bellows which forced air into the heart of the fire. The heat melted the ore which was run off to form rough 'pigs' of crude iron. These were carted down below the second pond—the hammer pond—where the outflow of water was used to drive a trip-hammer which beat out the iron into workable units.

The pond at Horsmonden was a furnace pond, and there is no companion hammer pond. Most of the others which were once so plentiful in this country have now vanished. When the industry finally died—it had always been economically precarious, and the development of iron in the North Country, using coal instead of wood, produced too powerful a competitor—some of the ponds became silted up and gradually merged with their surroundings, some were adapted to provide power for corn mills or to make an ornamental lake in a landscape park, others were deliberately destroyed by breaching the barrage.

The few ponds scattered through Kent, Sussex and Surrey are not the sole heritage of the iron industry. In a sense we owe the whole landscape of the modern Weald to it. When the furnaces were lit at the end of the fifteenth century the Weald was still sparsely populated,

7

a country of few and vile roads, of inaccessible hamlets, a barrier between north and south which no one penetrated by choice. When Duke William won his decisive battle on a wealden hill in 1066 he did not press his advance on London by the direct route, but turned south again, followed the coast to Dover and then took the old Roman road. In his weakened state he would not risk the hazards of the forest journey. Later commanders followed his lead. It was iron which opened up the Weald, not so much by the destruction of timber as by the improvement of communications. As the ironmen hauled out their cannon with teams of oxen they widened and deepened the forest tracks, producing in the course of three centuries the sunken lanes, with their towering sandstone banks and their festoons of wild flowers, which are among the most admired features of the modern Weald. For centuries the roads remained notorious for their muddiness, but they made the forest passable, at least in the dry season, and they encouraged the growth of forest settlements—town-like rather than villages—at such places as Goudhurst in Kent, Lamberhurst right on the border, and Horam in Sussex.

Much of the original forest timber was destroyed in the first boom of the revived industry in early Tudor times. Critics of the ironmasters were not slow to complain about the destruction of the forest, and legislation made intermittent attempts to apply the brake. The good sense of the ironmasters themselves was more effective. They learnt to plant coppices of oak, chestnut and beech which could be harvested systematically and which would renew themselves over a cycle of a few years. Such timber was easier to cut and made better charcoal than the heavy old wood. Here and there in the Weald place-names— Colliers Green and Collier Street—show where the charcoal-burners or colliers—nomadic during the season—had their settlements. Many of these, practising one of the oldest of all rural crafts, survived the decline of the iron industry and there were a few about in the Weald up to the beginning of the Second World War.

The iron industry was the subject of one of the very earliest essays in the now-extensive literature of industrial archaeology. Although Ernest Straker's *Wealden Iron* was not published until 1931 much of the fieldwork was done around the close of the nineteenth century when it was still possible to find much evidence upon the ground which has now vanished. Combining topographical evidence with the evidence contained in archives he produced a remarkably complete survey of furnaces and forges and of the earlier bloomeries, together with reports on deposits of cinders and waste iron in remote woodlands. (*Wealden Iron*, long out of print and a costly collectors' item, was reprinted in 1969.) Invaluable as Straker's work is, there may perhaps be room now for a book which updates his topography and at the same time sets the industry against the social and political life of the times. *Wealden Iron* is a wonderful source book, but not even its most dedicated admirers would call it entertaining; yet the subject is rich in drama and humour, as Kipling showed when he put Master John Collins, ironmaster of Burwash, into *Puck of Pook's Hill*.

To reach Lamberhurst, the next stage in this journey—interrupted as soon as begun—a road leads due south from Horsmonden Green. Travellers who, like myself, rate the details of the journey above the achievement of a destination may make a diversion in a few hundred yards through a piece of delectable parkland around Horsmonden Church and its rectory. Rectory Park, a pleasing mansion of mixed dates which forms the centrepiece, was the home of the Smith-Marriotts, baronets, landowners and rectors whose church lies just beyond, where the land drops gently to the valley of the River Teise. A Smith-Marriott whose romantic temperament was matched with wealth once built a Gothic tower on a high point of the estate in memory of Sir Walter Scott, which a more realistic successor demolished. The landscape design of trees and water has lasted better and gives to the traveller on these public roads the illusion of progressing through his own park.

Horsmonden Church, remote from the village, is, like others in the Weald, more blessed in its setting and its general effect than interesting in detail. The golden sandstone looks well against the pattern of hop-gardens and ancient trees. Here lie Jane Austen's ancestors, industrious and successful makers of Kentish broadcloth.

These quiet, deep-cut lanes eventually work back to the Lamberhurst road which continues through orchards and coppiced woodlands to its junction with the London-Hastings trunk road on the outskirts of the little town. Just short of the junction, a lane leads left to the church which, in the manner of this country, stands aloof from the village with only the Georgian Court Lodge for company. Just beyond is the infant Teise, with footpaths exploring this mild and lovely country, on the one hand to Goudhurst Mill and the abandoned station on the old Hawkhurst railway, on the other to the high country signposted by the stone spire of Kilndown Church—a product of the high Gothic Revival which has its admirers—passing on the way the mansion of Finchcocks, built for a London merchant in 1725 and better fitted to a town setting than to this gentle wooded country.

Lamberhurst had its days of prosperity when the ironworks—the most famous in Kent—were at their most productive, and a revival when coaches heading for the newly realized seaside delights of Hastings rattled down the street to the Teise bridge. From this time survive some pleasant weatherboard and tile-hung houses and a notable inn beside the bridge. It is all quite harmonious and modern development has been held well in control, but the effect is largely negative; the place is inoffensive rather than exciting. So the modern traveller passes through without stopping, save for refreshment, no doubt to the relief of the residents. Before many years have passed there will be a bypass, and then it may be possible to discover the discreet charms of Lamberhurst in safety.

There are 'lions' in the neighbourhood. The nearest and the most notable lies just beyond the main street, where a long drive leads to Scotney Castle. Here the grounds are opened with generous frequency between spring and autumn by the National Trust.

A castle was built on low ground here in the reign of Richard II. It must have been somewhat of the pattern of Bodiam but smaller, and built for the same reason, as defence against deep French raids; just a screen wall circling an island in a lake with top-heavy machicolated towers at the corners and a central gatehouse. After a largely uneventful life this had become redundant and probably ruinous by the Tudor period, when a brick and tile house was built up against a solitary surviving stone turret. To this was added, in the next reign, a more spacious mansion with classical details. The effect was charming, but the site restricted further development and it was very damp.

This was the property which came in the 1830s into the possession of Edward Hussey. Hussey's passion was for the picturesque. The vogue of the Picturesque was at its height. Its apostle was William Gilpin, its satirist William Combe whose Doctor Syntax made agreeable fun of the fashion. Hussey resolved on a new house at Scotney and he commissioned the distinguished architect Anthony Salvin to design one. The site was on high ground overlooking the valley of the River Bewl, and the materials were quarried from the sandstone bank immediately below. This ensured that the new house would sit well in its surroundings, the golden stone weathering quickly to a grey-brown with deep ironstone stains in it; it also produced a precipitous cliff between house and valley. The purely functional quarry became a memorable feature of the garden, providing a superb terraced viewpoint at its head and a bold, quickly overgrown backcloth to the massed shrubs and trees.

There remained the old castle in its lake to which the eye was led inevitably from every point in the garden. It had all but one of the qualities for which the devotee of the picturesque craved; it was old, patterned with the delicate patina of the centuries, but it was insufficiently dilapidated. The line of tower, wall and roof was too perfect. So Hussey added one further element to his picture; he ruined his castle, taking off the roof of the hall and breaking up the too regular wall to produce a satisfyingly jagged edge. However much we may be tempted to mock so dedicated an addiction to a bygone fashion, we cannot but admit that he was right. The scene is almost unbearably picturesque, whether seen in the freshness of spring, framed with the massed blossoms of high summer, or—best of all—in the glow of a late autumn afternoon.

Scotney stayed in the Hussey family until 1970 when Christopher Hussey, an authority on domestic architecture and historian of the picturesque vogue, bequeathed the estate to the National Trust. The grounds had long been opened to the public by the Husseys, who were devoted supporters of the National Gardens Scheme, but now they may be visited regularly throughout the summer. Hordes take advantage of this opportunity, yet, such is the subtle design of the gardens, they are quickly swallowed up in its deep paths and the place never seems too crowded to disturb the kingfisher from his patrol along the Bewl or to tarnish the colours of the rhododendrons.

Back through Lamberhurst village, a narrow lane goes left steeply downhill towards the Sussex border. Immediately the landscape becomes enriched with massive wayside trees and long vistas across orchard and hop-garden. After about a mile a sign invites a visit to the gardens of Owl House.

After the century-old design of Scotney, this is a new landscape devised in the last few years under the inspiration of Maureen, Duchess of Dufferin and Ava. The house, pleasant in the wealden manner and of no special distinction, is not shown, but the gardens are opened in aid of a charity founded by the owner.

The gardens of Owl House have been carved out of woodland and imposed on farm pasture, and the process continues. The characteristic feature is a multitude of old roses, growing in great clusters up the trunks of old forest trees. Woodland walks, punctuated by vases and sculpture—the owl appropriately predominates—lead to shadowed pools or open rose gardens. It is all gentle and harmonious, but enough of surprise remains to keep the visitor always alert.

Beyond the approach to Owl House the road drops down past a wayside pond to a crossing of the River Teise near the county boundary. Here the entry into Kent is marked fittingly enough by a magnificent cluster of hop kilns. The river here is suspiciously straight, and suspicion is justified, for an artificial cut straightened out a kink in the Teise here in Henry VIII's reign to make a deep channel. This provided power for the most famous forge in Kent, which later became an even more famous furnace in the reign of William III. The future Queen Anne came here from Tunbridge Wells where she was taking the waters; she was accompanied by the Duke of Gloucester, and thereafter the ironworks were known as Gloucester Furnace. Gloucester Furnace enjoyed a certain notoriety—not unique—for supplying guns impartially to the Royal Navy and to her enemies.

Edward Hasted seems to be the source of the familiar story that the iron railings around St Paul's Cathedral were cast here. He also quotes the cost as £11,202 0s. 6d. Other ironworks in the Weald claim the same distinction, but without supporting evidence. Perhaps, because it was such a big job, they all had a share in the contract. What seems certain is that the most famous and elegant iron railings of the eighteenth century came out of the Weald.

Gloucester Furnace lay downstream from the road. Upstream the Teise flows through the noble parkland of Bayham Abbey, the seat of the Marquis Camden. The Pratt family, to whom the present owner belongs, acquired this land in 1714, and by this time the Bayham ironworks had ceased to operate. Furnace and forge lay in a classic relationship along the Teise and the ornamental water below the present house may have been remodelled from Bayham hammer pond.

Lord Montagu, who promoted the original forge, had acquired the lands of Bayham Abbey from Queen Elizabeth. Happily the site of the abbey itself did not commend itself to the ironmasters and so the medieval buildings, which would otherwise have been destroyed, or at least drastically pillaged for stone, were left to decay gently. By the age of Gothic romanticism they had reached a satisfactory state of ruin, and the Pratts built a house outside the broken walls in a style sufficiently archaic to satisfy their craving for a vaguely medieval mystery. To the chance which allowed industry to bypass the abbey and to the fashion which valued such relics of the past we owe the preservation of the finest monastic ruins in the south-east. Restored and tidied up by experts of the Department of the Environment, they are now open to visitors throughout the year.

Premonstratensian canons from two earlier houses in the south-east settled here in the early years of the thirteenth century, under the patronage of the Sackvilles from Buckhurst. The site, remote, wild, with a good supply of water, was ideal for a community which sought austerity and freedom from the distractions of the world, together with material self-sufficiency. Forest clearance, including the activities of the canons themselves, and the deliberate enhancement of the landscape by the Pratts, have transformed the scene, making it one of exceptional beauty, but the original settlers saw nothing of this. For them its principal attraction was its lack of comfort.

For modern visitors a new approach has been made from the Tunbridge Wells road, and this ends under the shadow of the Gothic house. The original entrance was from the north, where the ruins of a substantial gatehouse stand. This was altered by the eighteenth-century beautifiers to provide a pleasure-house and perhaps the bridge over the Teise was built at the same time, for the original course of the stream lay to the south. The first buildings were in the plainest Early English style, for the original Premonstratensians, like their monkish counterparts the Cistercians, eschewed ornament. This austerity did not last long, and within fifty years the eastern half of the church had been rebuilt in the rich Decorated manner with transepts, twin chapels set in each arm and soaring arches at the crossing. In the next century the nave was rebuilt too, but still on the narrow foundations of the original.

There are substantial remains of the church, enough to give a good impression of its splendour. The many-shafted columns of the crossing are very fine and so is the carving of corbels in the north transept. A vast tree grows across the eastern apse. Of the conventual buildings there is elaborate detail in the original south transept, which was remodelled as a book-room with elegant lockers.

On a sunny day Bayham is a sheltered spot in which to linger for an hour or two, enjoying the play of light on the pale gold sandstone of the broken walls.

There is attractive country to the south, threaded by narrow winding lanes which offer more interest than the rather dull main road to Wadhurst. It might be worth heading first for Frant, which is a village of character built casually around a big triangular green. Beyond is the great expanse of Eridge Park, the seat of the Nevills, Earls of Abergavenny. The Nevill badge is a bull, and a bull's head is to be seen on gateposts and estate cottages over a large area, often accompanied by an ornate capital A.

Eridge holds an important place in the story of Tunbridge Wells, for coming away from the house in 1606 and losing his way in the forest—he was doubtless drunk—Lord North stumbled upon a chalybeate spring and recognised the red stained banks which hinted at curative properties. Out of that chance discovery grew the largest town of the Kentish Weald and, despite some regrettable developments, the most elegant. Tunbridge Wells is a New Town. It grew literally from nothing, borrowing even its name from the ancient town which controlled a stategic crossing of the Medway a few miles to the north. It grew piecemeal, reflecting the fluctuating fortunes which accompany most inland spas. The original settlement clustered around the spring, where the chapel of King Charles the Martyr stood modestly—all puritanical brick outside, extravagantly baroque plaster within—at the head of the Pantiles. Regency and Victorian developments covered the 'mounts', Pleasant, Sion and Ephraim, but still the forest, in the shape of a rolling common out of which outcrops of sandstone thrust spectacularly, came right up to the heart of the town. More recent growth, stimulated by minor industry and major office development, have not damaged this most attractive feature which gives to Tunbridge Wells an individuality rare indeed among southern towns.

Eridge Park is private, but a public path, reached by a gate a short way beyond the green, crosses it to Eridge village. This passes midway a large and reedy lake, the furnace pond of a celebrated ironworks which was active in Queen Elizabeth's reign. It was presumably spared after the decline of the furnace because it provided a pleasing eye-catcher from the great house. There was also a hammer pond which has now gone, although the retaining bay is a feature of the walk through the park.

In the south-east corner of Eridge Park the land rises to a conspicuous wooded hill which is a major landmark of the border country. On the summit are the earth ramparts of an Iron Age hill-fort. Saxonbury continued in use after the Roman conquest. Like other strongpoints of the same period—High Rocks at Tunbridge Wells, Dry Hill near Edenbridge, and a string of greensand camps in Surrey—this may have been a refuge of forest settlers who were engaged in smelting ironstone.

Saxonbury is rather too much overgrown now to afford good views from the top, but from the edge of the wooded area the view opens up to afford tempting prospects deep into Sussex, with the spire of Rother-field church as a landmark in the middle distance. Even the most haphazard choice of direction will be rewarded by satisfactory dis-coveries scenic and antiquarian, but for the next stage in the quest for iron one takes the Wadhurst road which in about five miles from Frant Green leads to a little town—its sign establishes immediately the con-nection with iron—which has not yet surrendered its individuality. No tourist centre, Wadhurst exists very sensibly for itself and offers none of the conventional attractions to visitors. For the hunter after iron, however, there is one major relic in the church—the finest of all collections of iron grave-slabs. These pave the chancel floor, and there is an overflow in the churchyard. The principal family in these parts was that of Barlam whose home was Shoesmiths and who worked a profitable furnace at Scrag Oak. John Barlam was the ironmaster here during the Civil War and he has almost the handsomest of the Wad-hurst grave-slabs. The lovely tile-hung house at Scrag Oak perhaps dates from his day.

Scrag Oak is in the lightly populated country south of Wadhurst and is on the approach to Wadhurst Park, where a landscape park with a big ornamental lake in the valley is being developed as a country club and wild-life reserve.

The road out of Wadhurst goes east to Ticehurst, a finely placed village with a sandstone church on a high point. A short way along this main road, a lane goes south for Burwash, passing on the way the hamlet of Stonegate, with a Victorian church which for many years was the slightly incongruous setting for Andrew Young, parson, naturalist and poet of wild places.

The more direct route to Burwash goes east from Stonegate, but a rather more devious alternative which makes more of this quietly satisfying country goes towards Burwash Weald for two or three miles, crossing the inconspicuous River Rother, and then turns sharply east to gain the ridge at the head of Burwash Street.

Of all the towns and villages of the iron country Burwash—Burrish is a rough approximation of the local pronunciation—seems to me to have hung on best to its essential character, in spite of the increasing pressure of traffic along its single road. A singular harmony comes from these varied houses which ring most skilfully the changes on brick, tile and weatherboard. They vary greatly in size. The most splendid, on the south side towards the church, has an enriched door-frame with moulded plaster in the curved pediment. But the total effect of Burwash comes as much from the contribution of quite small houses as from this splendour.

In the church—massively restored and rebuilt but still effective—is the most famous of all the Wealden grave-slabs and the oldest, celebrated for its antiquity and for its associations with Kipling. On the wall of the south chapel is a rude cross in low relief with the inscription in Lombardic capitals "ORATE P'ANNEMA JHONE COLINS". The Collins family were ironmasters who worked Burwash Forge, which was on the Dudwell above Bateman's, and also Socknersh, nearer Etchingham, where this cross may have been cast. They also had interests at Lamberhurst, where Alexander Collins made the famous cut to serve the Lamberhurst Forge. A Joan Collins has not been identified but Jhone may well be a rendering of Johan; there was a John Collins at Burwash in Tudor times and this may be a memorial of his ancestor and namesake.

Readers of Kipling will remember that Panama Corner was a favoured haunt of the children in *Puck of Pook's Hill*. The spirit of Kipling still broods benevolently over Burwash, and rightly, for here he made his last home and most completely and finally found himself. His house, Bateman's, is found by following the lane downhill from the church and then turning right just before the bridge over the little Dudwell. At the end of the narrow lane the house makes an unforgettable impression, especially when the flat rays of autumn sunshine bring out the golden tones of the sandstone walls.

Kipling was living in Rottingdean in 1902. He was spiritually at low ebb. The influenza epidemic which came near to killing him had taken his daughter. He had, moreover, written himself out. His thoughts on India were all said; he had to find a new source of material or cease to write, and to a man of Kipling's driving energy the latter course was intolerable.

In this state Kipling and his wife went for a drive through Sussex and in a wealden valley found a small sandstone house, only recently recovered from decay. The effect was immediate. Kipling hastened to make "an honest woman" of this new mistress, and in the house and its setting he found just the inspiration for which he was searching. Out of Bateman's came the stories and poems of the 'English' Kipling, prompted by a most profound and intimate understanding of the land and its history. In return he restored the house and enriched it with the treasures of his travels around the world and enclosed it with a garden whose design was as much an original artistic creation as any of the poems.

Kipling died here in 1936 and on her death three years later Mrs Kipling left the house and gardens to the National Trust. In a real way it epitomizes the Trust's objectives, for it has a setting of great natural beauty, a historic and beautiful fabric, associations with a great man, and a garden in the pure English tradition. Bateman's is among the most popular of the smaller Trust properties, but no crowds can detract from the atmosphere of the house, which speaks so quietly and intimately to each visitor of its three centuries of history and of its restorer.

Who built the house and set the date 1634 above the door is unknown, but it is reasonable to assume that he was the ironmaster whose forge stood on the Dudwell upstream from Bateman's. The site of this can be reached—at least in theory, but the track is indistinct—by footpath from the house, and the path follows the Dudwell up to Willingford Bridge. This is Weland's Ford in the first of the 'Puck' stories. Pook's Hill is the modest rise of ground across the stream to the west of Bateman's, and other places may be reasonably well identified by those who know the stories well.

Immediately to the south of Bateman's the land rises steeply to provide some of the finest scenery in the Sussex Weald. Increasing acres of forest threaten to change its aspect in the future, probably not all for the better, but the summit of Brightling Down—at 646 feet the highest eminence in the south-eastern part of the Weald—is still open and on it stands the familiar landmark of Brightling Needle. This is one of the contributions to the landscape made by Squire John Fuller of Brightling.

It is no great deviation from the general theme to think about this picturesque character at this point, for the Fullers were important figures in the iron industry during the eighteenth century when their furnaces at Heathfield and Waldron produced many guns. John Fuller, Member of Parliament for Sussex and known variously—according to the whim or taste of the speaker—as 'Honest Jack', 'Jolly Jack' or 'Mad Jack', made little from iron himself, because the industry was fading by his day. His generous means came from less reputable sources which we need not go into here except to say that he opposed most vigorously the abolition of slavery. At this point in time one may forgive him much for his humour, his intermittent and selective social conscience, and his feeling for landscape and for romance. He is the sort of man around whom legends cling, some of them, sadly, incredible but all springing from the remembered reality of a richly colourful personality. Jack Fuller was in the grand tradition of English eccentricity and chronologically the last representative of that fine brotherhood in the eighteenth century. Better mannered than Mytton, more practical than Beckford, he was no fool and even his follies have point if looked at from the standpoint of his times.

One might say that Fuller's best memorial is not at Brightling but at Bodiam; he stopped the castle from being robbed for its stone by buying the ruins, thus ensuring that the most romantically beautiful of medieval castles should survive for our delight. Here at Brightling he built the sandstone wall which still stands in part along the seven-mile circuit of his estate; in this he was prompted not only by arrogance and the urge to flaunt his wealth but by the need to provide employment during a period of depression. He put up the obelisk on Brightling Down as an eye-catcher because it would look well—and it does. Nearby is an observatory with domed roof which demonstrates the scientific concerns of this many-sided man. In his park, exquisitely landscaped and still retaining much of its ornamental timber, stands an elegant classical temple.

Most famous of all his follies the Sugar Loaf stands on a high point just short of the main road at Woods Corner. The popular story of its provenance is so much in the spirit of the man that it may well be true. At dinner one night he declared that the spire of Dallington Church was visible from his house. A friend disagreed. In true eighteenth-century manner a wager followed. Next morning Fuller looked out of his window and discovered that he was wrong. No spire. So he built one, or more precisely he built the tip of one, exactly in line between Rose Hill and Dallington. The Sugar Loaf, which is hollow and contains a room big enough to have been lived in, is happily preserved as an 'ancient monument' or at least as a memorial to a fancy so grotesquely big as to be almost admirable.

As if such memorials were not enough, Jack Fuller is buried at Brightling churchyard in a monument which proclaims his extravagance and self-satisfaction. The great pyramid is hugely out of scale with everything else in the graveyard and threatens to outbid the church itself. Inside—so legend has it—Honest Jack sits perpetually at dinner, in evening dress and glass in hand. I wish one might believe a story which is so like all we know of this splendidly individual gentleman.

It is easy to make fun of Fuller. Here, however, is material for a full psychological study, for in his nature a conflict between opposing impulses raged perpetually. How much was due to his clerical origins?

How much to the early death of his parents? Did great wealth discourage him from exploiting his potential scientific talents, or did it allow him to indulge a natural dilletantism? The questions hang in the air.

Brightling village is on the watershed. To the north the wealden streams flow to the Rother. Southwards they run to join the tangle of waterways which drain Pevensey Level. One of these, an inconsiderable trickle coming out of the south-facing afforested slopes, provided power for the last of the Sussex ironmills.

To reach the Ashburnham sites, the road from Brightling drops steeply to the crossing of the Battle-Heathfield main road at Darwell Hole, rises again and then descends more gently to the tiny village of Penhurst. Here is that great rarity of the South-east, an unspoilt village, happily off the map and as yet undiscovered by commuters and tourists alike. Perhaps, anyway, the delights of Penhurst are too discreet to make a general appeal—a little church, a farm, a manor-house, all disposed artlessly beside a narrow and often muddy lane. In the church there is a cast-iron grave-slab from Ashburnham Furnace. The house, smaller than Bateman's but of the same golden-grey sandstone, was a dependency of the Ashburnham estate. Although it is utterly unassuming and, in strict aesthetic terms, a trifle wanting in proportion, this is a house which arouses in some beholders—myself foremost among them—the fiercest feelings of covetousness. If it was, as seems probable, a by-product of the iron industry, one forgives the ironmasters some of their single-minded concern with profits.

Their scene of operations lay just to the west, where the lane reaches its lowest point at the crossing of an inconspicuous stream. Here was the forge, and the road runs along the top of the bay of the hammer pond. The wall of the pond, long dry, is clearly visible. A public path leads agreeably up the valley to the site of the furnace and furnace pond, where the surviving cottage must have been part of the ironworks. The fires of Ashburnham finally went out in 1828.

Originally the works belonged to the Ashburnhams of Ashburnham Place. One of these, Sir John, is always known as 'the unfotrunate' because he allowed himself to be cheated of his fortune. In 1611 Sir John had to sell the Place, in Ashburnham hands since the Conquest, and also the ironworks which went to a William Relfe of Penhurst, but later members of the family bought back the mills in 1680. The big house had returned to the Ashburnhams earlier, thanks to the enterprise of Frances Holland who had married the unfortunate Sir John's son, another John. The mills did well in the early years of the eighteenth century, but they gradually faded out towards the end of that century.

Straker traced the track by which iron was hauled from Panningridge Furnace, above Ashburnham, and probably from Ashburnham itself. Instead of being taken downstream, as common sense and gravity would dictate, it was hauled uphill to the high point of the Penhurst road, then by woodland tracks to Mountfield Court and on to the Rother at Robertsbridge. Parts of the route can still be followed, but modern forestry and ploughing have confused the trail in places. Panningridge belonged to the Sidneys, which accounts for this lengthy haul to Robertsbridge where they owned the iron mill in the grounds of the former abbey. No such explanation holds for Ashburnham itself, but Straker points out that iron often went by way of Maidstone because in time of war the easier outlet by sea from Hastings was closed. A substantial part of the profits of iron must always have been lost in haulage costs.

The lane from Ashburnham Forge rises sharply and skirts the head of Ashburnham Park. The great house of the Ashburnhams, rebuilt after the Restoration of Charles II and no longer the home of this ancient family, is set in a designed and very beautiful landscape of the eighteenth century which most artfully simulates as it enhances nature. The serpentine lake which was an essential feature of the design cannot be seen from here; nor can the house and its attendant church. In the house, it is said, are relics of Charles I, whom John Ashburnham—son of the unfortunate Sir John—served on the scaffold.

To the west of Ashburnham a tangle of lanes—one of them sign-posted "Brownbread Street"—invite confusion. Indeed a very pleasant hour might be spent getting lost in this undulating country, in which wooded valleys threaded by tiny streams alternate with high open hills giving views to the South Downs. There are no objectives here, only the incidental pleasure of tile-hung farmhouses. Those in pursuit of the iron industry will eschew these mild delights and head north for the main road at Woods Corner, where Jack Fuller's Sugar Loaf caps the high point, and then turn west to Punnetts Town where a lane goes off left to Warbleton. Before this there is a turning to Rushlake Green in well-wooded country, perhaps the country of Kipling's "Old lost road through the woods". One road through the woods, a gentle bridleway, goes to Priory Farm on the site of a small house of Augustinian canons. This had moved, around the time of Henry V's French adventure, from Hastings and retained to the end its title of Hastings Priory. Very soon after the Dissolution the priory stream was damned and a furnace, later adapted to a forge, was established. This seems to have been connected with one of the most celebrated, and certainly the most tragic, of the Sussex ironmasters, Richard Woodman. Woodman's main scene of operations, however, was across the watershed in Warbleton parish.

The streams here all flow southwards to become the Cuckmere. There was a big furnace upstream, belonging to the Fullers. Wood-man's furnace is a little downstream of this; the site may be reached by footpath from Warbleton church. Woodman himself lived in the village, close by the church. Like many industrialists in other parts of the country he belonged to the reformed faith, and he was in trouble early in Mary's reign for speaking his mind too plainly to the pliant parson of Warbleton. When arrested, he argued vigorously with his accusers, not only on religious grounds. By imprisoning him, he said, they were upsetting the economy of the Weald and harming a hundred workmen who depended on him for employment. After a time he was released and sent home to Warbleton. In a year or two the sheriff's officers came for him again. A vivid first-person account in Foxe's *Book of Martyrs* tells what happened.

They had taken a man of mine, and two of my children, and kept them with them till their hour was appointed to come in; and then a little girl (one of my children) saw them come together, and came running in and cried, Mother, Mother, yonder come twenty men! I sitting in my bed, and making of shoe-thongs, heard the words, and suspected straightway that I was betrayed; I stirr'd out of my bed, and whipt on my hose, thinking to have gone out of the doors or ever they had been come. My wife being amazed at the child's words, looked out at the door and they were hard by. Then she clapped to the door, and barred it fast, even as I came out of my chamber into the hall, and so barred the other.

So there was a place in my house that was never found, into which place I went. And as soon as I was in, my wife opened the door, whereby incontinent they came, and asked for me, and she said I was not at home. Then they began to search. One looked up over the window, and espied a little loft, with three or four chests, and the way went in betwixt two of the chests, but there could no man perceive it. Then he asked my wife which was the way into it: here is a place that we have not sought yet. When she thought they would see it by one means or other, she said the way was into it out of a chamber they were in even now. So she sent them up, and cried, Away! away! Then I knew there was no remedy, but made the best shift for myself that I could. The place was boarded over, and fast nailed, and if I had come out that way that I went in, I must needs come amongst them all in the hall. Then I had no shift, but set my shoulders to the boards that were nailed to the rafters to keep out the rain, and brake them in pieces, which made a great noise; and they that were in the other chamber, seeking for the way into it, heard the noise, and looked out of a window, and spied me, and made an out-cry. But yet I got out, and leaped down, having no shoes on.

So I took down a lane that was full of sharp cinders, and they came running after, with a great cry, with their swords drawn, crying, Strike Him! strike him! Which words made me look back, and there was never one nigh me by an hundred feet and that was but one, for all the rest were a great way behind. And I turned about hastily to go my way, and stepped upon a sharp cinder with one foot, and saving of it I stepped into a great miry hole, and fell down withall, and ere ever I could arise and get

away, he was come in with me. His name is Parker the wild, as he is
counted in all Sussex. But if I had on my shoes, they had been like to have
gone away errandless, if there had been five hundred more, if I had caught
the plain ground once, to the which I had not a stone's cast. But it was
not God's will: for if it had, I should have escaped from them all, if there
had been ten thousand of them.

Woodman's trade had been, in a sense, his undoing, for the cinders
were doubtless from his own fires, spread out to form a causeway
across the marshy ground. Woodman was taken off to prison in
Lewes, from which he was delivered to the stake in 1557. He was
still a young man.

Warbleton is a pleasing little village. Its long, low-slung inn has a
sign which puns outrageously upon the village name. (There is a comparable pun at Heathfield where the name of the manor—Runtington—
has become Runt-in-Tun, and the jolliest of porkers emerges from a
barrel on its three-dimensional sign.) The church, placed most effectively above the meadows which slope westwards to the stream, is
notable for a high tower, adorned with grotesque heads, which is unusual
in this country of blunt spires and homely bellcotes. There is, appropriately, some excellent ironwork inside, which is by tradition
Woodman's work.

The natural lines of communication here run, like the rivers, north
and south, and to make the modest journey westward to Horam
involves many changes of direction. Horam itself is a sizeable place
grown around a road junction and stimulated by the arrival of the
railway in 1880. Despite its size Horam has not long enjoyed an independent existence, being an outlying hamlet of Waldron. In recent
years the village has become known as a centre for the making of
English wines and Merrydown wine now enjoys a healthy and deserved
reputation. The works are at Horam Manor and there is a showroom,
with an ancient press outside, on the main road.

Just behind the Merrydown factory, and approached by a hard
road which leads to a car park, is the beginning of the Horam nature
trail. The trail, created through the generosity of the landowner, and
provided very sensibly with two escape routes for those who find the
modest demands of the round trip too much for them, combines the
charms of a country stroll with the headier excitement of a detective
hunt on the scent of iron. The stream which charmingly provides the
direction of the walk is a feeder of the Cuckmere, and there is evidence
of iron everywhere, in the red rust stains in the banks, in the large mass
of discarded iron waste beside the upper pond, and in the obviously
artificial barrages which control the flow through the miniature valley.
The trail also affords the delights of many birds and flowers, the latter
at their best in spring. As with many nature trails the return route is an

anti-climax and those who tire before the end may console themselves with the thought that they have seen the best.

As the general direction of our journey is north-west it is in the spirit of this contrary country to begin by going south-west, leaving the main road at the May Garland Inn and heading for Chiddingly Gun Hill—the name and the inn sign are reminders of our quest—being left on the east. A bridle track along the road descends the valley to Stream Mill, where a shrunken millpond marks the site of an ancient furnace pond. Ahead is the stone spire of Chiddingly Church, but the lane characteristically avoids a direct approach. In the church there is a handsome monument to an Elizabethan Jefferay. The Jefferays lived at Chiddingly Place, where there are some remains among later buildings. They had interests in a furnace over towards Bexhill. Chiddingly Church contains, however, a reminder of a more famous family, for here is one of the familiar Pelham buckles. There are others in the neighbourhood, at East Hoathly, Crowhurst, Dallington and at Laughton, where the old home of the family rises above the windy levels of the Glynde.

The story of the Pelham buckle has, like most of the best historical anecdotes, been blown sky-high by the historians, but, like Alfred's cake and Canute's tide, it has an independent life of its own and will, I trust, go on being retold for ever.

Sir John Pelham was at Poitiers with the Black Prince. In the confusion of the battle he and other knights pressed around the French King John. It is not clear to whom the King, when he saw that the field was lost, surrendered his sword. Pelham claimed that the honour was his, but so did another Sussex knight, Roger de la Warre. The Prince of Wales resolved the squabble by taking over the royal prisoner himself, and he rewarded Pelham with the buckle from his sword-belt. It is this which, rendered formally in stone, appears in the fabric of the buildings where Pelham interests were strong.

Whatever the truth of this—and one must admit regretfully that the odds are against it—the Pelham family grew in wealth and influence through the later Middle Ages. In the Tudor period they invested in iron. Their principal furnace was at Waldron, on a tiny feeder of the Cuckmere half-way between Waldron village and Horam. This flourished until the beginning of the eighteenth century when the Pelhams sold out to the Fullers. By that time the family had higher social aspirations. In 1724 they had an elegant new mansion built at Stanmer, on the Downs outside Brighton, and in 1801 Pelham was created Earl of Chichester. The splendidly landscaped park at Stanmer is now public.

The way now lies north, although a diversion west by way of Halland—where the Pelhams had another mansion—and Terrible

Gatehouse, Bayham Abbey

'The War-Bill-in-Tun', Warbleton

Surviving forest tree, Sussex Weald

Down—an evocative name although one must discount legends of battle here—leads to Bentley Farm where there is a most attractive and important wild-fowl park. To the north of Chiddingly, however, more narrow lanes pass through coppices and over open heights to the main road at Blackboys. Thereafter an even greater confusion of ways, if pursued assiduously, leads to Buxted, an overgrown village at the gates of Buxted Park.

The great mansion of the Earls of Liverpool now has a high reputation as a health farm. Part of the therapy must surely lie in the influence of this park which is beautiful enough to exorcise the devils created by urban tensions and the pursuit of productivity. There are rights of way through this enchanted scene, through which passes the so-called Iron River, a tributary of the Ouse, which drains the southern slopes of Crowborough heights. The parish church is in the park, a pretty stone building with a shingled broach spire, not much less attractive now than when that fine topographical artist Frederick Griggs drew it for E. V. Lucas's *Highways and Byways* book.

At the entrance to the park, facing an elegant classical lodge, is Hog House, which is older than the mock castellated exterior would suggest. Ralph Hogge, who lived here or in an earlier house on the site, is persistently described as the man who "cast the first cannon that was cast in England".

A familiar rhyme claims that

> Master Huggett and his man John
> They did make the first cannon.

Huggett, whose name is preserved in Huggett's Furnace, a farm higher up one of the feeders of the Iron River, was probably Ralph Hogge and his "man John" was John Owen who was casting guns in the 1530s. But, according to Straker's researches, the credit for the first home-cast ordnance in England goes to a parson of Buxted, William Levett, who was turned out of his living during the years, so hazardous to clerics with a conscience, when the King was enforcing his supremacy in the Church. He was reinstated by Queen Mary and did not survive to adjust to further changes under Elizabeth. Hogge was presumably the craftsman who worked under Levett's sponsorship and inherited the business from him. He later described himself as "the Quenes Majesties gonnestone maker and gunfounder of yron unto her highness most honorable privie councell". Whoever was the pioneer, Hogge exhibited one essential quality of his age; he survived.

It is not clear where the historic casting took place. There was a furnace called Old Forge or Marshalls on a stream coming out of Ashdown Forest, in Maresfield parish but no great distance from Buxted. Then there was Huggett's Furnace which is favoured by

8

tradition, and Straker's own choice, Oldlands, an estate which belonged to Parson Levett. This is in the extreme north of Buxted parish and on the edge of the forest.

This last was an ancient iron-working site. Here, in 1844, a local parson with a taste for antiquarianism investigated for the first time the remains of Roman ironworks. The Reverend Edward Turner of Maresfield noticed that cinders turned up by workmen on some farm-land were mixed up with indisputably Roman pottery. He discovered that the site had been considerably disturbed but enough remained to show that iron had been worked here from the reign of Vespasian at least to that of Diocletian.

At this, as at all the other early sites, iron had been extracted without the help of water power. The ore was smelted in a hearth on which was built a mound of ore and charcoal enclosed in a crust of clay. Oxygen was fed to the fire in the heart of this 'pie' by small bellows which were poked through the crust on all sides. The heat was not sufficient to turn the iron to liquid, and so the 'bloomery' produced wrought iron which could be hammered by hand without further treatment.

This method was already in use when the Romans came to Britain, and it continued as the invariable practice until the end of the fifteenth century when the blast-furnace method, which produced cast iron, was introduced from the Continent.

Straker records the existence of ninety-three bloomeries in the Weald, most of them medieval but with a substantial number of Roman or pre-Roman sites. Their presence is betrayed by cinder, the debris of the bloomery hearths, which is different in form and texture from the refuse of the blast furnaces.

The Roman bloomery at Oldlands is on the edge of Ashdown Forest. This upland tract of open heath, plantation, thicket and bog has survived when most of the wealden forest has gone under the plough for a complex combination of reasons. The natural process of erosion was delayed when Edward III granted the forest to his son John of Lancaster. By this time the dense ancient forest had been opened up by felling and the resultant landscape of open rides and coverts was very suitable for hunting. John of Gaunt had a 'castle' or hunting lodge in the forest and, in spite of public duties which kept him on the move between France and the Scottish marches, he found time to chase the fallow deer and fly his goshawk. A more powerful factor in the preservation of the forest was the action of the Commoners who from the earliest times enjoyed rights of grazing and cutting. These rights were not in conflict with hunting, but when royal delight in the chase declined and Charles II, on his Restoration, granted the old Lancaster Park to the Earl of Bristol and the Earl at once began to enclose and clear the land for cultivation the Commoners reacted violently in defence of their rights. In the next two centuries there was sporadic warfare between landowners and Commoners, sometimes in the Courts, sometimes with more primitive weapons. At length, after an extended legal action between Earl de la Warr, of Buckhurst, and the Commoners—these included not only gentlemen of local standing but such formidable protagonists as the Earl Marshal of England—a settlement was reached in 1885 which placed the forest under the operation of the Commons Act, and a new Act created a Board of Conservators to control the forest. One effect of this, of which we are the beneficiaries, was that the public gained right of access to considerable areas of heathland. Today we can walk over ten square miles of fine country, with a freedom which can be found nowhere else in the south-east, enjoying the stimulus of noble views as well as the close-up study of wild nature, and this freedom was won a full ten years before the foundation of the National Trust.

The story of Ashdown Forest is told in an excellent book published by the Society of the Friends of the Forest in 1967. The text was by Garth Christian, who knew the area and its wild life intimately and wrote of it with deep affection.

Our iron trail leads south of the main forest mass through the village of Maresfield, a place of great importance in the heyday of the industry and one of considerable charm, could one for a few minutes ignore the traffic which flows ceaselessly round the sharp central bend. E. V. Lucas, writing long ago about the Eastbourne Road, pleaded for a bypass to save the soul of Maresfield and Uckfield. It is still awaited.

The road westward passes over Pilt Down, a name of awful joy to those who love to see the scholastically mighty brought low. Very sportingly the village pub has not changed its sign since the fraud was uncovered, and its skull—the reverse depicts a skin-clad savage at work—happily reminds the traveller of how the savants were fooled.

Here a lane goes off north-west to Fletching, where, on good authority, "the people . . . live by snapping and ketching". This was Simon de Montfort's land, and his army camped on the open heath here, in 1264, before moving south to meet the King's forces at Lewes. In the battle the Earl gave history one of its accelerating shoves but the Lord Edward reversed the movement in the following year at Evesham.

There is nothing of Earl Simon in Fletching today—although there is in the church a reminder of an abortive shove from a later century when a Fletching glover called Peter Dynot went off in support of Jack Cade. The village is homely and unexciting, the church notable only for its Norman tower which is almost a twin of Burwash's and for possessing, in a private chapel, the mortal remains of a great chronicler of mortality.

Edmund Gibbon, the historian of the decline and fall of Rome, was of Kentish origin, but his friend and patron was John Baker Holroyd who in 1769 bought the estate of Sheffield from Earl de la Warr. Gibbon often stayed in the Gothic mansion of Sheffield Park and watched the transformation of the wealden valley beyond its windows under the magic hand of 'Capability' Brown. Holroyd, who became Baron, later Earl of Sheffield, was a notable figure in his own right, a man who combined considerable political gifts with a genuine taste for scholarship, a considerate landlord and an efficient farmer. If his principal monument is the *Decline and Fall*, the lakes of Sheffield Park are no small memorial, and in both he achieved immortality by giving his patronage at the right moment to the right man.

Throughout the nineteenth century Sheffield Park was a typical, if especially admirable, example of the great art of landscape design. It underwent a second transformation in the early years of the twentieth century at the hands of a new owner, Arthur Soames. Soames enriched the classical design, which in Brown's manner concentrated on form at the expense of colour, by planting a rich variety of trees and shrubs, laying emphasis on the flowers of the latter, the foliage of the former. Sheffield today is a museum of trees, but a living museum which changes daily from the cool delicacy of spring to the blaze of autumn when maple and cypress burn with a splendour which is scarcely to be seen without tears.

The grand design of Sheffield Park includes four lakes. Two of these, around which the main interest is concentrated, are fed by springs arising near the house. These spill into the third and larger lake at the foot of the long vista; here a bridge crosses between third and fourth lakes giving access to the cricket ground where history was made in Victorian times when the third Earl promoted the visits of Test teams from Australia. The two big lakes were created by damming a stream which rises on high land in the forest a little below Wych Cross. By the time Capability Brown carried out his scheme this little stream had lost its industrial function. In Henry VIII's reign it had fed a large hammer pond to the north of Sheffield Green. (This can be reached by footpath from the green.) This forge worked in conjunction with a furnace at Sheffield Mill, which was on the Ouse where now the Bluebell Line comes to an end at Sheffield Park Station. (The line, operated by enthusiastic amateurs, runs north-west for seven miles or so through enchanting country to its terminus at Horsted Keynes.) The two Sheffield mills belonged to the Duke of Norfolk, the enterprising nobleman who played the power game most delicately throughout Henry VIII's reign. When he at last fell, the ironworks, with others in the Weald, was granted to the Lord Admiral, that attractive Tom Seymour who played for even higher stakes and lost his bet and his head. Straker quotes in full the inventory of Sheffield, detailing the contents of the forge, which was drawn up when the manor reverted to the King.

At Sheffield Park the big commuter sprawl of Haywards Heath is not far to the west, and to avoid this—although it is indeed very good as such places go, with a bright air and good shops—one goes north in the same direction as the Bluebell Line. At the crossing of the Ouse near Freshfield there is a surprising reminder that the shallow stream was navigable to this point, and indeed beyond. 'The Sloop' was a bargeman's pub on the Ouse Navigation.

Across the river the road rises through very charming country to Horsted Keynes, a village which, despite its attractions and its reasonable accessibility, has so far avoided the grosser aspects of commuterland. Behind the main block of the village rises the slim shingled spire of the church—with interesting monuments—from which footpaths lead west and north into the valley of a little tributary of the Ouse. Here was another furnace which was flourishing in the time of the Commonwealth and Restoration when it belonged to a formidable widow, Saphirah Lightmaker, who lived in the manor-house of Broadhurst, farther up the valley. She had the company in widowhood of her brother, Archbishop Leighton, formerly of Glasgow, who is buried in Horsted Keynes Church. The big lake may be the furnace pond, perhaps reconstructed as a landscape feature.

The road continues northwards, roughly parallel with the track of the abandoned railway, until it reaches a high ridge on which stands the village of West Hoathly. There have been developments here. They have, however, been confined to Sharpthorne below the ridge, and West Hoathly is unspoiled and arguably the loveliest place in the eastern Weald of Sussex. Part of its charm lies in its self-absorption. This is a village which lives to itself, not for tourists; even if it has at least one celebrated objective for visitors. This is the Priest's House, a property of the very enterprising Sussex Archaeologists Trust. The unassuming timber-framed cottage belonged to the Priory of St Pancras in Lewes. It is open regularly and is well worth a visit for its charm and for the little museum of Sussex bygones which it contains. Opposite the church is the manor-house, which is much more spectacular. It is a singularly fine example of wealden sandstone building, a little reminiscent of Bateman's and perhaps of much the same date.

West Hoathly is a place to linger in and to walk around. A longer walk goes south-west by way of Philpots to visit a beautiful wooded valley through which flows a small feeder of the Ouse. A shorter path, starting beside the manor-house, passes another iron site with a tiny pond. Nearby the sandstone outcrops dramatically.

For those who are carbound there is a very narrow but singularly delightful lane southwards out of West Hoathly. The views, confined by steep valleys, are limited but everything is exquisitely in scale. Too soon the lane dips steeply to a stream and then rises to the main road by the agricultural showground at Ardingly.

A mile up the road is the entrance to Wakehurst Place, a great estate with magnificent trees which the National Trust manages in co-operation with Kew Gardens. Woodland walks penetrate deep into the hinterland. Even if these are too demanding for some visitors there are delights nearer at hand where the late Tudor mansion is mirrored in a tree-girt lake.

Wakehurst was a house of a Sussex branch of the Culpepers, a family with considerable interest in iron. Sir Edward, who built Wakehurst, owned a furnace to the north at Tilgate in St Leonard's Forest and a forge as far away as Lamberhurst. The Wakehursts, who owned the estate before the Culpepers, may have been concerned with the Ardingly forge which stood on a headwater of the Ouse not far from Ardingly Church. The church itself, charmingly situated on the back lane to Balcombe, has brasses to Culpepers and a splendid brass to Richard and Elizabeth Wakehurst, who died in the reign of Henry VII.

The lane beyond the church to Balcombe is rewarding and glimpses of water give a promise of more relics of iron. These are not to be redeemed. The big lake is ornamental, and the altogether delightful little pool around which the road winds is a mill pond. The Balcombe furnace was at Strudgate, in wooded country to the north, and no remains are to be seen.

At Balcombe, a pleasant enough village but with no special interest, there are only a few yards of the main road before a lane turns west opposite the church. This rises to the Forest Ridge, in wooded country, and along the road are a few giants which have somehow escaped the general destruction of ancient timber in the Weald. (Farther east on this same road there are some even more fascinating specimens which, from centuries of lopping, have developed grotesque and disturbing features. Did Arthur Rackham pass this way in the years when he was drawing those not-quite-anthropomorphic trees of his?) Just short of this main road another lane turns off south and this, descending the ridge through most agreeable country, comes to Staplefield and then, by an underpass below the Brighton Road, to Slaugham. Before taking this, however, many travellers will wish to make a diversion north towards Handcross for a visit to the renowned gardens of Nymans.

Nymans was a house in the Gothic manner, vaguely ecclesiastical, whose fire-gutted ruins make the delightful focal point of a series of small linked gardens created over half a century. The estate was acquired by Ludwig Messel. He and his son Colonel Messel were dedicated gardeners and friends of gardeners, and the latter, among them Gertrude Jekyll and William Robinson, contributed ideas which the Messels realized. Colonel Messel died in 1954 and left the property to the National Trust, but the family, notably the Countess of Rosse, have maintained their interest and have continued to develop the gardens—for even so characteristic a memorial to Late Victorian and Edwardian taste cannot stand still. The essence of Nymans lies in its scale. The whole extent is only about thirty acres, but each area has its own enclosed character and the visitor moves quietly from one small surprise to the next, always satisfied but never overwhelmed. The scale is emphasized by the setting, for the gardens are set high, with views back into rolling woodland, in the depth of which glints the water of a restored furnace pond.

Back to Slaugham. This manor belonged to the Coverts, who flourished in the manner of 'new' Elizabethan families and then declined, leaving behind the remains of a Renaissance mansion. Footpaths cross the park, giving views of the fine ornamental lake. The Coverts built a chapel on to the parish church in 1613 and here are two memorials to earlier members of the family, including a showy piece of Tudor monumental sculpture portraying Richard Covert (1579), his two wives and fourteen children. Even better, the Easter Sepulchre is a monument to another Richard, this time with three wives, on which is a lively brass engraving of the Resurrection with sleeping soldiers in full armour of Henry VIII's reign.

Slaugham Church and the pretty cottages opposite originally stood within the walls of the park which stretched far on all sides, and the village street stops abruptly, only a bridleway crossing the former park to what was a parkside hamlet at Handcross. A half mile to the west of the church the lane passes along the bay of a sizeable pond, which provided power for a furnace belonging to the Coverts. Although by no means the finest surviving pond of the industry it is the most accessible. There is parking space at both sides, and one can walk along the water's edge, gaining, when there are not too many anglers about, good views of the lake and its inhabitants. The latter include an occasional great crested grebe. This is a good place too to examine the bay, a high earthen bank through which the outflow escapes in a narrow channel. The stream is one of several headwaters of the Ouse which join to form the artificial lake of Slaugham Place.

At Ashfold Crossways, beyond Slaugham, we are on another watershed. To the south-east the Ouse makes its hesitant path to Lewes. To the north, beyond the sandy miles of St Leonard's Forest, the 'sullen' Mole heads for the Downs and the Thames. West and south streams amalgamate around the great lake of Knepp Castle to form the Adur. All these streams made their contribution to iron, as did

Arun and Wey. There are many pond and pond sites to be found farther west, but time is running out and we must be limited to three related ponds which belong, by a freak of geology, to two different basins.

The village of Lower Beeding—it stands at about 330 feet compared with Upper Beeding in the Adur valley at 35 feet—has a road junction opposite the bold modern church. The southward turning quickly joins the busy London–Shoreham main road at the entrance drive of Leonardslee. Here, in late spring when rhododendron and azalea are at their most magnificent, the glorious gardens are opened to the public. The modern gardens are laid out on slopes below the house and they are all focused on a deep wooded valley in which a feeder of the Adur has been dammed to form a long serpentine lake. It looks like an ornamental water of the kind best loved by the eighteenth-century landscape artist, but it is in fact the Gosden furnace pond. There can scarcely be a more convincing example of how an industrial undertaking can be reclaimed to form a most beautiful feature in a landscape.

Gosden was originally worked in conjunction with the larger works in St Leonard's Forest to the north. To visit these it is necessary to go back to Ashfold Crossways and turn north-west on a lane which develops several hidden kinks. These take the road around and across the bays of two very big ponds, the biggest we have seen on this iron trail. (The road is narrow and busy, but it may be possible to park just before the first pond and after the second.) Most exceptionally the two are connected not in series but in parallel! Each is fed by a different stream and there is a very narrow watershed between them. The first, called Hammer Pond, served the forge, the second, Hawkins Pond, was the furnace pond.

These belonged, together with others in the forest, to the Duke of Norfolk. This was the duke—met at Sheffield—who played an important, and occasionally beneficent, part in the politics of the Reformation. He lost the game and his possessions when the Protestant faction triumphed, but recovered them again under Mary. His grandson was less fortunate. The fourth duke got into financial and political troubles and tried to bribe Queen Elizabeth with his wealden interests, but in vain; the Duke lost his head in 1572. The Queen then granted the ironworks to members of the Norfolk household, and control of the industry passed to three formidable Sussex magnates, Walter Covert of Slaugham, Edward Caryll whose estate was at Shipley, and Roger Gratwick of Sullington who had built the furnace at Gosden (Leonardslee). Straker unravels from the incomplete documentary evidence a story of violence which did not stop short of war between these men, and which was waged, in Romeo and Juliet fashion, by the servants of both sides. The wealthy Covert tried to bulldoze Gratwick out of his rights. Gratwick fought back and there were some savage affrays. In the end wealth told, and it seems likely that Gratwick lost his holdings in the industry.

These two ponds in St Leonard's Forest are the last reminders of iron to be met on this journey, as they are the largest and scenically perhaps the noblest. Each fills its narrow valley with trees running down to the water's edge.

So to Horsham. The capital of the West Sussex Weald saw the beginning of the iron industry and its decline. It took these changes calmly, and it has taken the inflow of commuters and the translation from coaching town to dormitory with comparable equanimity. Growth and a traffic problem have not quite taken from Horsham its charm and character. At a time when each town competes with its neighbour in the quest of uniformity the area around Carfax and the church and its causeway retain a rare and entirely admirable individuality. Long may it swim against the dismal urban current!

6

Family Fortunes in Kent and Surrey

THE public history of the South-east, as distinct from the private history of the numberless anonymous millions who worked the land and the mill, fed the furnaces and dug the chalk, is largely that of the great families. They were the links between local affairs and the business of the nation. They sat in Parliament. They dispensed justice. They built great houses and threw parks around them. Most—but not all—have gone, but they are remembered by their incursions into national history, by their monuments discreet and grandiose in their parish churches, above all by the marks they made upon the landscape which our own generation has not yet succeeded in obliterating.

Mowbray and Beauchamp and Valence have gone with the Plantagenets who ruled them, and only the names remain attached to the manors which felt the weight of their hands. Where they have gone we know not, but we know where Sidney is, and Sackville. The Braoses and the Warennes and the Clares have gone and their castles are in ruins. Petworth and Uppark have gone to the National Trust—and there are many less happy fates. There are dozens of names which awake no such echoes, people who were great only in their own parish; Darell and Twysden, Oxenden and Streatfield. Others, after centuries of respectable obscurity, flare suddenly into prominence. The Gibbons of Benenden produced Edmund and then returned to their dignified

nonentity. The Shelleys of Warnham had a past. Two of them were
rash enough to remain loyal to the fallen Richard II and died for it.
Their nephew married a daughter of the formidable Sir John Hawk-
wood and surely introduced some fiery spirit into the family. A little
of the blood of the old soldier of fortune lingered in the veins of proud
and stodgy eighteenth-century landowners and boiled up in Percy
Bysshe Shelley. (The Bysshes came from Worth in East Sussex.)

Some families seem to dominate local affairs and then disappear.
There were the Culpepers and the Colepeppers. They rarely made a
mark nationally, but by judicious marriages and shrewd enterprises
they held land from Hollingbourne in Kent to Wakehurst in Sussex.
They produced a herbalist and an adulterer. The rest are forgotten,
except by those who gaze on the splendid monuments in Goudhurst,
Hollingbourne and Aylesford churches.

There was an intricate network of intermarriages among the gentry.
The nobility looked, for the most part, beyond the county boundaries
for their wives and negotiated alliances with their peers. For this reason
local history refuses to remain local. The traveller who learns a trifle
of elementary heraldry finds the Sidney badge in Warwick and Ludlow, while Shelley's remote ancestor, whose cenotaph is in Essex, lies
in the cathedral in Florence.

The great houses of Norman Britain were sited for strategic reasons.
Control of the ports, the roads and the local population counted for
more than domestic amenities. In the South-east there was a chain of
fortresses between Dover in the east and Arundel commanding the
head of the estuary of the River Tarrent. Inland the Clare's castle at
Tonbridge stood at a key crossing of the Medway, Warenne's at
Reigate blocked a gap in the downs, and the royal castle of Guildford
held the Wey gap. North of the Thames the same pattern emerged
with Hertford Castle on the Lea, Berkhamsted straddled across an
important highway from the north-west, and Colchester at the head
of the tidal waters of the Colne. Of all these only Dover retained an
operational role, and Arundel successfully adapted to domestic life.
For the most part the great families destroyed themselves in the civil
wars or built anew on fresh sites. After the end of the Wars of the
Roses the property market flourished, and houses and land changed
hands frequently in the next century. Some of the buyers were those
who traced their line back optimistically to the Norman Conquest;
many were the new rich who had played the cloth market skilfully
and, after the Dissolution, bought monastic land profitably.

Stately-home visiting has become a national pastime born of the
mobility of the population and the impoverishment—comparatively—
of the aristocracy. It is a game, I must confess, which I play with no
great enthusiasm. The settings of the great show houses are invariably

magnificent. The architecture is often splendid. Too often the multi-tudinous family portraits merge before one's sated eyes and become one single vacuous likeness. To my untrained mind one tallboy is much like another. Above all I cannot become reconciled to the guided tour; the enjoyment of a work of art is a highly personal thing, requiring quiet communion with one's soul, and the conditions inevitably deny this.

Yet it would be sad to reject today's opportunities. A few great houses, like Blenheim and Penshurst, have been opened to the public through all the centuries, but never before have so many come within our reach. There are matchless facilities for comparison, for exploring the changing way of life of generations, and for wandering in the fascinating byways of genealogy.

Here, therefore, is a leisurely journey through South-east England, picking up here and there the threads of family histories as they are evoked by the sight of a dignified Georgian façade or deep-red Tudor brick.

We might start in east Kent. The coast was rarely popular before the nineteenth century, and so we may leave the shingle beaches of Deal and Walmer with only a brief glimpse of Robert Bridges, poet laureate to be, spending an affluent childhood at Roselands, Walmer, before his mother's remarriage took him off to Rochdale. He was of an old Thanet family from St Nicholas with a pedigree leading to an Elizabethan rector of Harbledown.

Bridges, sometimes spelt with a 'y', is a common name in east Kent. A family of Brydges, who married with Egertons, produced Sir Egerton Brydges of Wootton, between Canterbury and Folkestone, who earned a modest reputation as a poet and romancer before moving to Lee Priory at Ickham and going into publishing. His Lee Abbey Press served the cause of literary scholarship; perhaps more importantly it foreshadowed the private presses which reformed the art of printing at the end of the nineteenth century. Sir Egerton also dabbled in genealogy and encouraged his elder brother Edward to make a bid for the vacant barony of Chandos. (Handel's patron of Canon's Park had been a Brydges.) The action failed, not without grave suspicion of falsifying evidence falling on Sir Egerton. A modern age might classify him as ass rather than rogue, but a man nevertheless of good taste and scholarship. Lee Priory has gone now, but Sir Egerton's second home at Denton Court is still to be seen, with its very charming garden and the parish church tucked snugly under the wing of the old house.

More Bridges appear at Goodnestone, a tiny and very neat village near the Kentish coalfields. The whole village, including a largely rebuilt church, shows evidence of the benavolent tyranny of the

Bridges. Their house has a rather severe façade staring out over the beautiful park. The family came here early in George I's reign. Brook Bridges—the first name was repeated in each succeeding generation—moved here from Midblesex and rebuilt the house. (His elder brother went into Northamptonshire, and his son wrote the classic history of that county.) One Brook after another inherited Goodnestone and served Kent with undistinguished devotion. Then, at the end of the eighteenth century, the family had an encounter, which perhaps they did not recognize, with genius. A Brook Bridges who died in 1791 had a family of six, including two Brooks. (The eldest died before he could inherit and his brother William hastily adopted the time-honoured name.) One of the girls, Elizabeth, married a neighbouring gentleman, one who rented a minor manor house at Rowling in the same parish, named Edward Austen. Through Edward, his sister Jane came to Goodnestone, observing, analysing and assessing the company with her matchlessly critical eye.

The Austens came originally from the Weald of Kent, but the branch to which Jane belonged were in Hampshire when Edward became involved in the affairs of a Kentish estate. On the far side of Canterbury from Goodnestone a family called Knight owned a hand-some residence at Godmersham in the Stour valley. They were child-less, and their search for an heir led them to cousins and to Edward Austen. They adopted him, he changed his name to Knight, and in due course he inherited Godmersham Place. Jane visited him here often, feeding whatever maternal feelings she possessed with his daughter Fanny who was the favourite of all her nieces. At Godmer-sham she lived inside one of her own novels, so perfectly does the house, its setting, and the intricate pattern of social visiting with neighbouring houses, mirror her most favoured themes. The letters she wrote from here, full of the idle gossip of a rather trivial round but livened with characteristic flashes of shrewd malice, are the rough stones out of which the polished novels were built.

Through the generosity of the present owner, there are opportunities for a close look at Godmersham Place where the gardens are open on several occasions during the summer. An early visit, when the drifts of daffodils are at their freshest, is memorable. The house is one's dream country seat, not too big, intimate rather than imposing, and put with exquisite precision into its landscape setting. The gardens retain the landscape concept of their origin. They are artfully informal, with green alleys leading the eye to a classical summer-house, and the soft swell of Godmersham Down beyond.

Fanny Knight, like her father, married locally and, unlike him, into a higher rank. She became the second wife of Sir Edward Knatchbull of Mersham Hatch and the mother of the first Lord Brabourne. The

Knatchbulls had been prominent in Kentish affairs from the reign of Henry VII when Richard Knatchbull bought the estate of Mersham Hatch, a few miles east of Ashford. His descendant Sir Norton Knatchbull was a Sheriff of Kent and a local benefactor through the foundation of the free grammar school in Ashford. (The schoolroom still stands in the enclosed churchyard which is the most attractive part of that not very prepossessing town.) Norton became a recurrent forename in the family from his day. His nephew Norton earned a modest reputation for biblical scholarship at the time of the Restoration, and another Norton, elder brother of the present Lord Brabourne, died in action in the Second World War. Fanny Knight's husband was the son of an Edward Knatchbull who married Mary Hugessen of Provender, the lovely house at Norton near Faversham, and later members of the family added her name to theirs. The Knatchbulls had, as a matter of course, represented either Kent or Hythe in Parliament, but Fanny's Edward was, I believe, the first to play an active part in government. Prior to the passing of the Reform Bill he was what would now be called a 'Tory rebel', occupying an independent position on reform and helping to bring about the downfall of Wellington's ministry. In Peel's ministry he accepted the post of paymaster and showed impressive abilities, and when Peel returned to power in 1841 he held the same office with distinction. His second son Edward followed him into politics, although he seems not to have inherited his father's skills. Although he held ministerial office, his posthumous reputation rests more on the stories which he wrote for the delectation of his large family. These fairy-tales were published in a large number of volumes and, although both verbose and laboriously fanciful, they have acquired a certain period charm.

It was a Sir Wyndham Knatchbull, who adapted the family name to Knatchbull-Wyndham, who decided to rebuild the old house of Mersham Hatch. Early in the 1760s he had talks with Robert Adam about his scheme, but he was dead and succeeded by his cousin Sir Edward Knatchbull by the time the work was done. Mersham is not in Adam's finest manner. Its classicism is a little severe, as if the architect's dour Scottish nature was to the fore. It is a big house, comprising a central block with pillared portico balanced by matching wings. The long brick façade is relieved only by the central steps and porch and by large niches with statuary. If the house is impressive rather than beautiful, the emparked setting is magnificent, with many noble trees towards the road and long views to the backcloth of the downs.

The present Lord Brabourne, who introduced another thread into the complex tapestry of the family history when he married Lady Patricia Mountbatten, moved out of the Hatch and lives now in a smaller house in the neighbourhood. The fate of great houses is always in the balance when the family leaves, but Mersham Hatch found a new destiny when it was leased by the Caldecott Community, an organization dedicated to helping children suffering from the contemporary diseases of broken homes and social deprivation. At the Hatch these children live as members of a big family and find there security and affection and, to use words which may have lost their meaning in general currency but not here, moral purpose. The house itself, with its superbly proportioned rooms, its gracious fittings and its fine pictures—where else, I wonder, do deprived children dine in an Adam hall with a Canaletto looking down on them?—is an important factor in the effective work of this remarkable organization.

The fortunes of the Knatchbulls were closely involved with those of Ashford, a small town which survived well into the nineteenth century on the strength of its market where fat Romney Marsh sheep changed hands profitably. Ashford was transformed by the arrival of the railway line from London to Folkestone and Dover and by the establishment of locomotive engineering works. As these declined, other industries kept up the spread of the town, which also became a major commuter centre as well as a recipient of London's overspill. These developments have not, in environmental terms, been very happy. Ashford has become big but not great; it is a place where people live and work but not yet a fully integrated community. Growth goes on, accentuating the human problems, and over the town lies already the shadow of the Tunnel.

Two great estates hem in Ashford on its western side. To the north beechwoods of a surpassing beauty clothe the downs above Eastwell Park, but the house, home of Moyles and Finches, has gone and only the grandiose mock-Jacobean gatehouse astounds the traveller on the Faversham road. A marvellous story belongs to Tudor Eastwell. This has been retold often and has recently formed the subject of more than one novel, but it is worth recalling. Sir Thomas Moyle, in the reign of Henry VIII, noticed that one of the craftsmen working on his new house sat apart from his fellows, reading. This was unusual, and still more unusual that he read Horace in Latin. Sir Thomas gained the old man's confidence and discovered that his employee was—or claimed to be—a natural son of King Richard III. On the eve of Bosworth Field he had been summoned to the King, who told him of the relationship and promised him recognition if the battle went well. If not, he was to seek the safety of obscurity. Considering the number of pretenders during Henry VII's reign he had been lucky enough to remain anonymous and safe. Sir Thomas kept his secret, but saw that he was buried as Richard Plantagenet. The full story has sufficient circumstantial detail to compel belief.

The chapel where one of the last of the Plantagenets was buried stood in the park, beside the ancient track of the Pilgrims Way. In the eighteenth century the park was beautified by the creation of a large ornamental lake. All is now in ruin. The church, damaged and neglected during the Second World War, fell down, and the monuments of Moyles and Finches, some of them of outstanding quality, have been taken into sanctuary in the Victoria and Albert Museum. The great lake is reeded up and its elegant bridge is much decayed. A mild melancholy hangs over the place. Nothing remains to recall the stormy career of Sir Heneage Finch in the Civil War and Commonwealth, or the gentle romanticism of Ann Finch, Countess of Winchilsea, who, in the full day of the Augustan Age, looked, not at "nature to advantage dress'd" but at flowers and trees, and who wrote verse which foreshadowed the Romantics.

Godinton never enjoyed the social standing of Eastwell in its great days, but its fate has been happier. It has remained a home and has become a notable show-place. The medieval estate passed from Godintons to Champneys, from Champneys to Goldwells. The male line of Goldwells died out, and Godinton went as the marriage portion of Joan Goldwell to Thomas Toke of Westbere. Nicholas Toke remodelled the house in James I's reign, retaining the medieval hall but adding greatly to the original building in the high-spirited, charming and not over-tasteful manner of the times. The parkland setting was developed by later Tokes.

The Earl of Thanet's mansion at Hothfield has been destroyed, and so has the Dering house at Pluckley. This latter, which was most regrettably lost by fire twenty years ago, was a very sad loss indeed, for it was architecturally the equal of Godinton and its family history was more distinguished. The Derings were among the oldest of Kentish families, and they served the county faithfully through the centuries while succeeding in avoiding national prominence. The exception to this admirable rule was Sir Edward Dering who, like other country gentlemen of the time, found himself reluctantly forced to take sides in the debate between King and Parliament. By inclination a moderate Parliamentarian, by breeding a royalist, his middle line was favoured by neither party. The Parliament put him briefly in the Tower. The King accepted his troop of cavalry but distressed him by his gross opportunism. There was no place for the uncompromisingly honest man in the Civil War situation, and Dering escaped back into private life on payment of a substantial fine. With the loss of Surrenden Dering, visitors must seek for the family's story in Pluckley church, where there is a Dering chapel complete with faked memorial brasses devised by Sir Edward in happier times. The family is remembered too in this and neighbouring villages by 'lucky' Dering windows—double-

Burwash

Wakehurst Manor

arched—which were the distinguishing feature of estate cottages built by the eccentric Sir Cholmeley Dering in the nineteenth century.

Pluckley is built right on the greensand ridge which from here to the Surrey border and beyond affords a continuously extensive, and at times monotonous, view across the Weald. The range is on the whole a little lower than the parallel ridge of the North Downs. In striking contrast to the Downs, which were without permanent settlements in Saxon times, the greensand has a series of ancient settlements right on the ridge. A traveller on the narrow and often attractive lanes in the low Weald cannot fail to observe the succession of spires and towers from a succession of old churches. Pluckley's spire is a landmark and Egerton's tower—almost the finest of the characteristic Kentish type—is the most familiar eye-catcher in central Kent. Next along the ridge comes Boughton Malherbe where the regularity of the view is varied by a long spur to the west. Within the shelter of this arm nestles the manor house, accompanied only by the church and the pretty Victorian schoolhouse. It is a typical Kentish group and remarkably pleasing at first glance. A closer look reveals that the house is only a fragment of a large Tudor mansion in Kentish rag and brick. The house suffered in the bad days of the 1920s when many of its fittings were sold to America.

This was the home of the Wottons, a family which over the period of rather more than a century played a conspicuous part in diplomatic life. How a Kentish family of country gentlemen, who only occasionally aspired to knighthood and who had to wait for James I to grant the modest distinction of a barony, gained the expertise for their delicate role, or the cosmopolitanism to enjoy it, is a mystery. They came of London merchant stock. The founder of their fortunes was a draper and Lord Mayor of London in the year of Agincourt. The manor of Boughton came to him by marriage, and this remained the family house. This Nicholas Wotton was grandfather to the first two Wottons to acquire national fame. Edward was knighted by Henry VIII, and he served the king in various roles, notably—and most profitably—as Treasurer of Calais. The post kept him out of England a great deal; it may have denied him higher promotion, but it probably enabled him to escape deep involvement in the power struggles which followed the king's death. Edward died in 1551 and is commemorated by a brass in Boughton Church. His brother Nicholas had a more spectacular career. He entered the Church and held various livings in Kent, but his interests lay in secular rather than religious affairs. He came into public view during the negotiations over the marriage of Anne of Cleves, and despite the failure of the marriage he retained the King's confidence and was given the job of breaking to the Duke of Cleves the news that King Henry did not care for his 'Flanders mare'. Meanwhile the greater monasteries had been dissolved, and Nicholas was appointed the first Dean of Canterbury. To this was added, two years later, the Deanery of York. So Wotton became responsible simultaneously for control of the two greatest chapters in England. The responsibility does not seem to have burdened him, and he continued active in embassies abroad. He was ambassador to France when Edward VI died, and he managed the transition to the new regime with his customary delicacy. Again, when Elizabeth succeeded, he kept his balance and his status. Refusing promotion within the Church—he could probably have been archbishop if his ambitions lay that way—he kept at his diplomatic tasks, returning home only to die. Nicholas Wotton was a man of the new age in his balanced view, his moderation and his shrewdness. His monument was the first major addition to Canterbury Cathedral since the Reformation. It is symbolic of the age in its classical grandeur and restraint. Symbolically too the Dean kneels with his back to the site of St Thomas's shrine, his mind occupied with intellectual problems rather than prayer.

Sir Edward Wotton's son Thomas is the 'unsuccessful' member of the family. Promotion evaded him in his ambitious younger days. Edward VI promised him a knighthood, but the King died too soon and Mary revoked the order and put him in prison for his protestantism. Under Elizabeth he returned to prominence in local affairs, but experience seems to have destroyed his taste for power. When Queen Elizabeth stayed at Boughton in 1573 he refused her offer of the accolade, and he remained a country gentleman, absorbed in his duties as justice and sheriff and in the promotion of religion. He was buried at Boughton and in the church there is a most striking portrait monument to him.

Thomas's son, another Edward, had all the ambition which his father lacked. Elizabeth used him for embassies to Scotland and France and he struggled hard to win her favour. He had to wait until the accession of James. The Scottish king liked his brand of obsequiousness and created him Baron Wotton of Marley.

Thomas Wotton had been twice married. By his second wife, a member of the Finch family, he had a son who brought the most lasting distinction to Boughton. This was Henry Wotton, in whom the family taste for scholarship and skill in diplomacy were allied to deep sensitivity. He spent much time abroad, discovering the wonders of Italy and carrying out delicate missions for his master the Earl of Essex. The fall of the Earl ruined his political hopes, and he stayed abroad until the Queen died. James I gave him appointments as ambassador to Venice and the Netherlands. The wit which endeared him to his friends and enemies damaged his career. His definition of an ambassador as "an honest man sent to lie abroad for the good of his

country" came to the King's ears, and James had only a Scottish sense
of humour. Sir Henry was lucky to suffer nothing worse than the
loss of royal favour. He was lucky too that, at his lowest financial
ebb, the lucrative post of Provost of Eton fell vacant, and he won the
appointment in the face of opposition from such formidable rivals as
Francis Bacon. Thereafter his was a pleasant, relaxed life of scholarship,
scientific experiment and the company of the young. There was,
moreover, as Isaak Walton points out, the possibilities of escape from
the cares of office to a summer evening's fishing in the Thames. Of all
the Kentish worthies, Sir Henry Wotton comes down to the present
most clearly, as a charming, humorous, worldly man, a fine poet and
a cultured gentleman.

One other Wotton calls for notice. The second Baron Wotton had a
daughter, Catherine, who became his heir. She inherited a good share
of the family enterprise and love of travel. After a brief marriage to
Lord Stanhope, she had a lively widowhood before marrying a Dutch
nobleman, John Kerchhoven, who was in England on embassy from
the Prince of Orange. She returned to Holland with him, as governess
to the young Princess Royal, and she stayed on at court, exercising
a powerful influence over the Princess. During the Civil War she took
part in the continuous plotting to reinstate the monarchy, to which
she contributed her own ingenuity as well as substantial funds. This
did not prevent her from visiting England during the Commonwealth;
not surprisingly she was arrested, and all the Wotton diplomacy was
needed to get her out of this dilemma. Her Dutch husband died shortly
before the Restoration, and she returned home to a third marriage. At
last she had a husband to match her enterprise. This was Daniel O'Neill,
soldier of fortune and the first Irishman to play a considerable part in
English affairs. He was approaching the close of an adventurous life,
which had included battles, intrigue and an escape from the Tower
dressed as a woman, when he met Catherine. After the battle of
Worcester he had escaped abroad, and here he encountered Catherine
at the court of the Princess Royal, being involved with her in royalist
plots. By the time of their marriage he had at last reaped the reward of
his work. Charles II showed unusual generosity to the Irishman whom
he called "as honest a man as ever lived". Daniel died in 1664 and was
buried at Boughton in a splendid monument. This has been dismantled, but three very handsome lions from it are still to be seen in
the church. Catherine survived him for three years. What a woman
she must have been, vivacious, adventurous, interfering, mercenary,
yet faithful to a cause. There is room here for a full-length biography,
or a magnificent historical novel.

A few miles west of Boughton Malherbe the view opens up again
from the small village of East Sutton. The slope of the ridge is laid

out as landscape design providing a noble setting for East Sutton Park, the great Tudor mansion of the Filmers. Few houses can have a finer position, with the Weald spread out like a carpet. The house is now a penal establishment for girl offenders, and one cannot doubt that the influence of so noble a house is a powerful agent of rehabilitation. The house came to the Filmers by purchase early in the seventeenth century when Sir Edward Filmer bought it from his wife's brother. Sir Edward is remembered by a superb brass in East Sutton Church, which is almost the last great example of this art. He and his wife Elizabeth stand side by side in attitudes of not too serious devotion, while beneath are ranged their nine sons and eight daughters. This masterly work is signed Edward Marshall, presumably the famous monumental sculptor.

Sir Edward's son Robert was a passionate royalist, and as a result the house was cruelly treated by the forces of Parliament on many occasions and Sir Robert himself suffered imprisonment. Sir Robert was a political theorist of an extreme reactionary kind, who occupied his time with a long and laboured refutation of Hobbes' doctrine of social compact. This circulated among his friends but was not published until 1680 when it was received with derision. Poor Filmer in life was no match for Hobbes, and from his grave he saw his beloved *Patriarcha* savaged by Locke.

Next along the ridge, past Sutton Valence and Chart Sutton, comes Boughton Monchelsea where fallow deer graze below the steep slopes and the big, grossly-restored church commands a magnificent view. The church almost obscures Boughton Monchelsea Place, a sober Tudor mansion (open to the public during the summer) which demonstrates how effective a building stone Kentish rag can be. This was built by Robert Rudston. Rudston had spent his boyhood at Boughton Malherbe Place, as his mother had married the Treasurer of Calais, Sir Edward Wotton. He later reinforced the connection with his neighbour by marrying Ann Wotton. Robert Rudston was a friend of the younger Thomas Wyatt, and friendship, if not political conviction, prompted him to join the Kentish insurrection. He was arrested and sent to the Tower, but Queen Mary had one of her intermittent fits of clemency—or perhaps Rudston was considered harmless—and he was reprieved. He was allowed to redeem his Kentish estates, which were forfeit through his treason, and he returned to Boughton. His later life was uneventful, and the house saw nothing further of national affairs.

Boughton and Linton are linked by a footpath—part of a longer ridge track which, with some breaks, crosses half the county—which here runs just behind the escarpment. This crosses the drive of Linton Place, a huge white monster of a house which was the home of Sir Horace Mann, Horace Walpole's friend. The view from the ridge is superb. Walpole said, splendidly, that Mann had "all Kent for his garden" and the swaggering phrase is almost true. The estate passed at the end of the century to Horatio Mann who has an honoured place in the story of Kent cricket.

After Linton the ridge, which has run unbroken for so long, begins to turn towards the north at the Medway gap. The traveller is forced either into the valley towards Hunton, where Campbell-Bannerman, briefly Prime Minister, had his estate, or towards Maidstone. Here the big park of the Mote, formerly the seat of Lord Romney, belongs to the town. The landscaping is very fine, but the late eighteenth-century mansion, now a Cheshire Home, is rather too gaunt for beauty.

It is sad that, in a county so rich in towns of character, the county town should seem so lacking in quality. It took over the principal administration from Canterbury very early, but never acquired that elusive quality which marks the true county town. Despite the bustle of Week Street, and the occasional ceremonial splendour—diminished since it ceased to be a garrison town—Maidstone is mostly a workaday town, dedicated to making money. This it seems to do very well, and in keeping up with the commercial Joneses the face of the town is transformed with multi-storey shop- and office-blocks which, if their design is not offensive, are as anonymous as those of any other booming town. Travellers trapped in its formidable traffic system may be forgiven if they do not know where they are, for as prosperity comes in individuality flies away. Only here and there, among the seventeenth- and eighteenth-century façades of Earl Street, the precariously surviving medieval frontages in Bank Street, or the incomparable ragstone group of church, palace and college which bear witness to the beneficent influence of the archbishops, old Maidstone shows its quality.

The biggest visual surprise of the Maidstone area can only be appreciated on foot, or by boat. A mile below Maidstone the grey walls of Allington Castle rise almost out of the Medway in a scene of almost unbearably picturesque beauty. This is so much the dream castle come true that one looks instinctively for the plasterboard and paint of a stage set. Instinct is partly right. Allington is a genuine castle, or at least a fortified manor house, of the fourteenth century, crenellated to defend the head of the tidal river against the threat of French raids. By the end of the nineteenth century the castle had become a farmhouse and the defences were down. The ruins were bought by Sir Martin Conway, a romantic and a lover of the spirit of chivalry. Conway restored and rebuilt and re-created the old building, making it just a little better than new.

Allington was the home of the Tudor Wyatts. Sir Henry Wyatt bought the estate in 1492 when he was one of Henry VII's privy councillors and a man of improving fortunes. He had backed Henry against Richard III and had suffered for it, being racked and imprisoned in the Tower. The nicest of all Wyatt stories is of doubtful authenticity, but it has a sufficient ring of truth to be worth retelling. While Henry was in the Tower and on prisoners' rations—which is to say, largely unfed—he was kept alive by a cat which brought him a daily pigeon. Thereafter Wyatt "would ever make much of cats". I don't know if there is a castle cat today, but the Allington pigeons—red and reputedly of Italian origin—are familiar to every modern visitor.

Sir Henry lived long enough to see his son Thomas established at court and then in peril because of his involvement with Anne Boleyn. The Wyatts and the Boleyns were close friends, and Thomas did not hide his familiarity with Anne even from the King. He survived when many others of the court suffered, perhaps because he was too useful to be sacrificed. Thomas Wyatt was a typical man of the Renaissance. He was good at manly sports and equally at home in the courtly arts of music and verse. Yet, while he could sing and dance and pay a pretty compliment with the best of the courtiers, he also showed great skill and patience in complicated foreign missions. He probably had no deep spiritual convictions and readily took his share of the material profits of the Reformation, the rich estate of Boxley Abbey. His poetry shows however that he was a man of his time in the blending of intellectual and physical passions. Of all the verse poured out in the artificial atmosphere of the court his more than any other bridges the centuries, because he writes like a man.

Sir Thomas married early in life. His wife was a Brooke of Cobham, and they had a son named after his father. Thomas the younger was barely of age when his father died and he inherited the great Kentish estates. He was scarcely ready for this responsibility, and he seems to have behaved wildly, joining the poet Earl of Surrey's gang of hooligans and getting into trouble with the law. Later he found an outlet for his energies in the French wars. By the accession of Mary he was ready to settle down. The news of the proposed marriage between the Queen and the King of Spain disturbed him profoundly and he was provoked into leading a revolt of Kentishmen against the Spanish match. Despite Wyatt's personal courage and energy the gamble failed and he died for it. He was only thirty-three. In another twenty years his energy, harnessed by experience, might have been invaluable to Queen Elizabeth.

Mary was a strange mixture of generosity and bitterness. She showed no grudge against the Wyatt family. The estates were automatically forfeit but she restored them to Sir Thomas's heir George. He continued to live at Boxley Abbey, occupying himself in writing a biography of Anne Boleyn and in the defence of his father's reputation. George Wyatt married a Finch of Eastwell, and in the next generation

the adventurous Wyatts had their last fling. George's son Francis was
a pioneer in the settlement of America. In 1621 he went out to James-
town as Governor of Virginia. During the next four years he laid
sound foundations for the young colony and saw many hundreds of
new settlers established. Despite conflicts with the Indians the colony
flourished and the colonials acknowledged that this was due to Sir
Francis's wisdom and good judgement. When George Wyatt died in
1625 Sir Francis returned home to manage his Kentish estates, but he
went back to Virginia for a second term fourteen years later. It was
a sadly different colony which he found, divided by conflicting interests.
The pioneering days were over temporarily, and Wyatt could not
cope with the meaner spirit which now prevailed. He returned to
Kent in 1642, only to die.

Francis's home was at Boxley. A comfortable house had been built
among the ruins of the great Cistercian abbey, and the family preferred
this to the more Spartan amenities of Allington. Today Boxley Abbey
is still a private house. The great barn of the abbey is conspicuous from
the motorway, but of the wealthy abbey little else survives, only a few
broken walls and the chapel-at-the-gate, now a cottage. The despised
castle has found a new function in recent years. It belongs to the
Carmelite Friars of Aylesford, who use it as a retreat and conference
centre, and visitors are welcomed daily. The warmth of the welcome
is unfeigned, and the castle, with its great hall and galleries, filled with
art treasures of many countries and centuries, is shown most generously.
It is good to see an old building fulfilling a genuine modern purpose,
and at Allington there can be no doubt. The relaxed and friendly
atmosphere creeps in upon the visitor, whether conference delegate,
concert-goer, weekend student, or rubber-neck, and no one comes
away unmoved by the experience.

Upstream from Maidstone there is a glimpse at Teston of Barham
Court, white and remote above the road. This had a place of honour
in the story of the fight against the slave trade when Sir Charles and
Lady Middleton supported their vicar James Ramsey in his work which
laid the foundations on which Wilberforce built. Farther along the road
is Wateringbury with the tall brick walls of Wateringbury Place
rising behind the church. (If the gardens are open in the summer, don't
miss them, because they offer a close view of the dignified Queen Anne
mansion and the gardens themselves, with sunken rose garden and
water garden, are extremely pleasing.) This was the home of the Style
family, and Oliver Style occupies the eye-catching place in the church.

Wateringbury Place is a nice example of eighteenth-century economy
and restraint. Next along the road comes an eighteenth-century extra-
vaganza. Mereworth Castle is the supreme expression of Palladianism
in the South-east. Here in the cold and foggy greensand country of

Kent rises an Italian villa, domed, pillared, colour-washed. It should look absurd. It is entirely delightful.

Mereworth Castle is evidence of the power and the arrogance of the wealthy eighteenth-century gentleman. Wateringbury Place was barely sixteen years old when John Fane decided to rebuild the family house at Mereworth. The village, the church and the manor house huddled together companionably in the valley of a tiny stream. Fane's ideas did not include this typical feudal group. The confidence bred in the eighteenth-century aristocrat was in him strengthened by experience on military service with Marlborough. Such a man did not scruple to move the village down the road, leaving the site clear for his new mansion. The church followed twenty years later. This is why Mereworth today does not look like a Kentish village, which mostly look as if they had grown out of the soil, like mushrooms, in pleasing lack of order. As for the church, it is a gorgeous Tuscan temple picked up in the City of London and dropped down among the hop-gardens.

Where the village had stood Fane's architect Colen Campbell built a careful copy of Palladio's celebrated villa at Vicenza. Although it was called a castle, and it occupied a moated platform, it was in fact a palace, or at least a pleasure-dome, in which, as John Newman says in his admirable Penguin *Buildings of Britain* volume, Fane "indulged his fancy". One readily, at this stage in time, forgives him the ruthlessness out of which came this lovely fantasy. The setting is appropriate in its blend of grandeur and intimacy. The approach-drive strode over the hill where West Malling airfield now blocks the way, bringing be-wigged visitors by coach from the old London Road. They passed between handsome lodge-houses and so over a bridge to the flight of steps leading to the grand colonnade. This was flanked by elegant pavilions. Behind the palace the hill was planted with fine trees, among which stood stone temples. A central avenue led the eye southwards to a high point crowned most satisfyingly by a grand Ionic arch.

All this remains. The house—no longer open to the public—is in beautiful order and so are the lodges—but a new road to Tonbridge cuts them off from the drive. The temples are roofless and decayed, and crudely-painted notices threaten the trespasser with a horrid fate. The great archway stands beside the old road, now a narrow twisting lane, most appealing in its desolation but disfigured by barbed wire. One of Fane's contemporaries might have found in the sight material for a neat essay on the transitoriness of worldly greatness.

The road past Mereworth Church continues as a narrow lane with, on the right, a very handsome house of about 1660, Yotes Court, on the left Dukes Place, a rambling half-timbered structure reputedly a Commandery of the Knights of St John. The road then takes to the hills. Below the ridge is Oxenhoath, a curious Victorian house on an ancient site, surrounded by the remains of a noble park. Then beyond the valley of the Bourne another big estate occupies the slope of the hills. This is Fairlawne, the home of the Vanes. Sir Henry Vane came originally from Hadlow. He improved a modest fortune by judicious manœuvrings at court and so was enabled to buy not only Fairlawne but Raby and other big estates in County Durham. He was a royalist who changed sides after the fall of Strafford, but never gained the full confidence of Parliament. His son, another Henry, was an early convert to puritanism. Unhappy in the England of Charles I he sought religious freedom in New England. He was there for two years, joining, not altogether successfully, in the politics of the colony. On his return home he took public office without compromising his religious scruples, but in the conflict between Charles and his Parliament there was no doubt where Sir Henry's sympathies lay. After the King's trial, in which he took no part, he supported the Commonwealth vigorously, particularly in the development of the navy. He distrusted Cromwell's ambition, however, and rightly. He was constantly in trouble with authority during the Protectorate and by the Restoration his fortunes were at their lowest. In spite of this he was excluded from the Act of Indemnity and put on trial for treason. Sir Harry knew that enemies had determined on his death, and he therefore used the trial as a stage on which to declare his belief in the sovereignty of parliament. Even the worst of his opponents admired his resolution and the indifference with which he went to the scaffold. He was buried at Shipbourne. In the gardens of Fairlawne, opened during the summer by the present owner, there is a 'haunted walk' of Sir Harry Vane, and indeed no one would have more right to return to a world which denied him an outlet for genuine talents.

Later Vanes, while retaining Fairlawne, tended to prefer their Durham estates. Sir Henry's second son was created Lord Barnard by William III, and a younger son occupied Fairlawne. This was the father of the unfortunate William Vane who married a scandalous widow, Lady Ann Douglas. Fairlawne was a changed place during the reign of 'Lady Fanny'. She gambled her husband's fortune away and entertained her guests with detailed accounts of his marital inadequacies: her personal morals may be deduced from the "Memoirs of a Lady of Quality" which she is said to have written and persuaded Smollet to insert into *Peregrine Pickle*.

Viscount Vane's steward in the days before his disastrous marriage was a man named Smart, and his son Christopher was born at Fairlawne in 1722. He went to live on the Vane's northern estate at Raby while he was still a boy, but Kit Smart never forgot his childhood in Kent. At the height of his powers he wrote a delightfully mannered but technically precise description of hop-culture in Augustan blank verse, and in the days of his madness images of his Kentish days crept into the confused and magnificent responses of *Jubilate Agno*. But Kit Smart's story belongs properly to London, to Grub Street, Bedlam and the King's Bench Prison.

Fairlawne, today better known for racehorses than for either Harry Vane or Kit Smart, looks a modest house from the road, for the mass of it lies to the rear, but the grand avenue spills over beyond the modern road and another continues behind the house as far as the Plaxtol road. The park, traversed by a public path, is very fine. There are Vanes in Shipbourne Church, farther down the road, although the church, rebuilt in Viscount Vane's day under the direction of Gibbs, was replaced late in Victorian times. The first Lord Barnard, who was fortunate in dying before Lady Fanny brought disgrace upon the house, sits here in baroque splendour.

A track almost facing the drive to Fairlawne leads across the fields to Ightham Mote, the finest medieval moated house in the South-east. Happily the fortunes of the Selbys and later owners were never sufficient to support the rebuilding or updating of their archaic house. This is just below the greensand ridge. Next, and lying back from the escarpment, comes the greatest house in our journey. Knole is a legend as much as a house. In its vastness and its complexity it seems, as Virginia Woolf said, "a town rather than a house", or like a natural growth rising from the ground. No architect's name survives, and one does not willingly accept that these towers and courts found their expression on a drawing-board. Surely someone planted the seed of Knole.

The cold facts of history record that the estate was bought by Archbishop Thomas Bourchier in 1456, and that he rebuilt the house and his successors added to it. Then it fell, as attractive and rich houses were wont to do, into the hands of Henry VIII, who added his contribution. In 1566 it came, by the Queen's gift, to Sir Thomas Sackville, and the long and mutually profitable association of Knole and the Sackvilles began.

The story of the house has been told most beautifully and lovingly by Victoria Sackville-West, who was born here, and it would be absurd to repeat and impossible to add to her account. Here one may perhaps pick out here and there a pearl or a ruby from the necklace of the house, indulging one's personal delight in the wisdom or the eccentricity of its owners.

There is the first Sackville of Knole, Elizabeth's elder statesman and her cousin by virtue of the marriage of his grandfather to Margaret Boleyn, Elizabeth's mother's aunt. Sir Thomas had been a poet in his younger days, and Knole and poetry always went together. He and a friend had collaborated in the first formal classical tragedy in English— *Gorboduc*—a work of unreadable frigidity but a landmark of literary history. He was also the leading contributor to *A Mirror for Magistrates*, a long and uniformly gloomy examination of the vanity of human greatness. Here his melancholy is matched with sombre eloquence. Even such sober diversions were put aside when Sir Thomas became involved in affairs of state. He became Elizabeth's Lord High Treasurer and a leading figure in her council of state, universally accepted, in that age of jealous place-seeking, for his integrity and disinterestedness. He was created Baron Buckhurst—named from his Sussex estate—and in James's reign Earl of Dorset. In his time Knole acquired the general appearance which it bears now.

The Sackvilles tended to alternate between wise and foolish. The third earl was foolish. He made one mistake which he lived to regret, by marrying a great heiress. The temptation was strong. He was by nature a gambler and a spendthrift, and the fortune carefully built up by Sir Thomas's father would not last for ever. But Anne Clifford was a match for any man. Her father had been Earl of Cumberland, owning vast estates in the North and having in his own country almost royal status. Lady Anne inherited when she was fifteen, but through legal complications her inheritance was delayed, and in the meantime the young girl was under pressure from her kinsfolk, her husband and her king to surrender her rights or—her husband's best hope—turn them into hard cash to subsidize his gambling. She stood firm in face of this formidable opposition. Richard Sackville did not hesitate to put her life in peril or use their infant daughter as an instrument of blackmail. Her response was unvaried: she "would never part with Westmorland". The story of the battle is told in Lady Anne's own diary, edited by Victoria Sackville-West, which paints an unstudied self-portrait of the stubborn, cantankerous and infinitely courageous woman in her lone fight. She was undefeated when Sackville died at the age of thirty-five, worn out by dissipation and, perhaps, by exasperation. Lady Anne Clifford lived to be eighty-six. She wore out another husband, and finished her life, "all passion spent", as a superb manager of great estates, a benefactor, and the ruler of six northern castles.

Richard was succeeded by two 'good' Sackvilles and then came the sixth Earl of Dorset, another wicked one and the gayest of the lot. This was Charles, called Charles I by Nell Gwyn to distinguish him from Charles II. Both enjoyed her favours to the full. Charles lived through five reigns and the Commonwealth, married three times "withouten other company" as Chaucer might have put it. He lived brilliantly, wrote some very fair poetry, played a part in the revolution which brought Dutch William to the throne, and died sadly, diseased and senile. It is best to remember him as Kneller painted him in the portrait which hangs at Knole. Here he is handsome, splendid, humorous, obviously enjoying every drop that he squeezed out of life.

After Charles the Sackvilles became Dukes and serious. That is until the third Duke, John Frederick, a spectacularly handsome man as Gainsborough's portrait shows. He was one of the cricketing Sackvilles to whom the game owed much both for his patronage and his performance. Nearly all the family had been patrons of the arts. The third Duke's enthusiasm was for ballet, and he brought back to Knole a notable addition to the treasures of the house, an Italian dancer named Giannetta Baccelli. Her life-size figure, delightfully nude, is the most surprising and not the least pleasing of the attractions which Knole offers the modern visitor.

The male line of the Sackvilles failed with the death, at twenty-one, of the fourth Duke, a pretty boy who was at Harrow with Byron and who died in a hunting accident. Knole passed to Lady Elizabeth Sackville who married John West, Earl de la Warr, and so the family continued as Sackville-West. Victoria Sackville-West was born at Knole, and so was her cousin, Edward the novelist, and the literary tradition of the house continued. Victoria at length went with her husband to live at Sissinghurst where they created the famous gardens which are among the modern glories of the Weald. In doing so she was in a sense returning to a family home, for the first Sackville of Knole, the Lord Treasurer, had married Cicely Baker, daughter of Sir John Baker who lived at Sissinghurst Castle and who enjoyed notoriety as a persecutor of heretics in Mary's reign. It is a happy chance that the persistent memory at Sissinghurst is that of Vita and not Bloody Jack Baker.

The setting of Knole changed as the house changed. To the original deer park of archbishops and kings were added the formal gardens of Tudor and Stuart times; then in the eighteenth century the deer park was beautified in the grand landscape manner. Lovely as the house is, for me the glory of Knole is the park, which, unlike the house, remains in private hands but which is opened generously and freely to the public. At every season and in all weathers it is beautiful and deeply rewarding to the visitor.

The drive of Knole leaves the main Hastings road on what are now almost the outskirts of Sevenoaks, among the grey stone of Sevenoaks School and opposite the handsome church. Here the road is lined with attractive houses, Georgian and earlier. For the rest Sevenoaks is mainly a modern town, one of the first to accept the role of commuter-town and still one of the most successful. It takes its prosperity for granted and the big houses with their immaculate and colourful gardens come right up to the centre of the town. For most of the residents the most important building is not Knole but the railway station.

Knole stands on high ground rising to more than 650 feet. Penshurst Park at its highest point is not half that and the house itself lies low in the Medway plain. The position is typical of a medieval manor house which chooses a discreet and unostentatious site. Although it was originally without defences the position lent itself to them, and in fact defensive walls were added within the first half century. This substantial building grew under a variety of owners, notably the Duke of Bedford who dominated politics after the premature death of Henry V. The house was transformed in Elizabethan times and again early in the nineteenth century. The resultant house ought to look a hotchpotch, but time and the local sandstone have given the whole a satisfying patina.

Like Knole, Penshurst had run through a great many owners before it found its family in Tudor times. The Sidneys traced their line back to a Sir William who came from Anjou with Henry II. It was not until 1552, when another Sir William settled in the medieval house, that they reached Penshurst. He died shortly after and was buried in the Sidney Chapel of the parish church, in a handsome stone chest which remains. He was succeeded by his son Henry who sought to strengthen the family fortunes by marriage with Mary, daughter of John Dudley, Earl of Warwick and later Duke of Northumberland, the most powerful and sinister influence on the young King Edward VI. Sir Henry was involved in the disastrous attempt to give the crown to Lady Jane Grey and he was lucky to escape the fate which came to the principals in that affair. During the next reign, however, he was helped by the connection with his brother-in-law, Robert Dudley, Earl of Leicester, the rising star of the Elizabethan age. Sidney played an effective part in public affairs, notably as President of the Council of Wales. His headquarters were in Ludlow, which is why his most famous son went to school at Shrewsbury.

Philip Sidney was born in the year when his father inherited Penshurst. Sir Henry had been forgiven by Queen Mary, to the extent that the Sidney baby had as godfather the King Consort himself and was named after him. Philip grew up to be an influential figure at court. His posthumous reputation is coloured by an heroic death and a dying gesture of that grand unstudied kind which was part of the essence of the Elizabethan age. To his contemporaries he was the pattern of Englishmen, "the observed of all observers", the man who touched many things and turned them all to gold. He was at once courtier, statesman, scholar, poet and soldier. As a young man of twenty he had been commissioned by his father to oversee the improvements to Penshurst Place, and the Elizabethan rebuilding is in a very real sense his work. Sir Philip was buried in St Paul's, in a funeral ceremony of such magnificence as has rarely been granted to kings, and his memorial at Penshurst is the house itself.

Philip left only a daughter who married the Earl of Portland and died without a family. Penshurst passed to the second son, Robert, who was created by James I successively Baron Sidney, Viscount Lisle and lastly Earl of Leicester. His son, another Robert, became the second Earl of Leicester, and he married Dorothy Percy, daughter of the Earl of Northumberland, and they became the parents of celebrated children. Of these, the eldest succeeded as earl. The third son Philip became Colonel of the Buffs and enjoyed notoriety as the reputed father of the unhappy Duke of Monmouth. A fourth son, Henry, became Earl of Romney, and earned the title at King Charles II's court of 'Terror to Husbands'. A daughter, Dorothy, married the Earl of Sunderland and attracted the attentions, not altogether desired, of Edmund Waller, who celebrated the charms of his 'Saccharissa' in elegant verses.

The most notable Sidney of this generation however was the family rebel, Algernon, a dedicated republican in whom the literary genius of the Sidneys found an outlet in political pamphlets expressed in powerful and deeply-felt prose. Algernon survived the Restoration but was implicated, perhaps unjustly, in the Rye House Plot and executed in 1682. Controversy has not yet died over his career, but he is arguably the greatest of the family after Philip. His body was brought back to Penshurst for burial.

Meanwhile the family went on, strengthening its alliances by marriage with wealthy local families like the Colepeppers of Kent and the Pelhams of Sussex and with great families at the heart of national affairs like the Cecils. The earldom was extinguished, but Lisles—later De L'Isles—continued, and the present owner of Penshurst, Viscount de L'Isle, VC, KG, distinguished both for public service and for involvement in local affairs, is named after his greatest ancestor Philip Sidney.

Penshurst is almost as charming a village as can be found in southeast England and shows throughout the influence of the great house. This is evident in Leicester Square, the tiny courtyard in front of the churchyard, with a top-heavy, timber-framed gatehouse flanked by black-and-white cottages which are delightful phoneys of mid-Victorian origin. The village was largely renewed between 1850 and the end of the century in the fashion for archaism which transformed other parts of this country, notably the neighbouring village of Leigh. Only the stuffiest of purists would complain. Certainly the genuinely old buildings, like the rectory, seem perfectly at ease in this company.

From Penshurst it is a pleasant short drive through the upper valley of the Medway to the county boundary at Groombridge. Here is another delightful village and a tiny one. Across Kent Water, in Sussex, a new Groombridge has grown up, but here on the Kent side there is no discordant note. A little triangular green has on one side a paved walk lined with tile-hung cottages of characteristic wealden type. Opposite the line is more irregular but not less pleasing. The third side is occupied by the church and the park.

Groombridge Place was originally a moated and defensive manor house. This was rebuilt just before the Restoration, and the setting was emparked and provided with a large ornamental water in the next century. The three stages of this development are clearly to be seen on the ground.

The manor was bought early in the fourteenth century by Thomas Waller and the house remained with this family for more than two hundred years. Thomas's grandson fought at Agincourt and was lucky enough to capture one of the most valuable of the French nobles, Charles, Duke of Orleans, the most famous poet of his age and the king's cousin. It is probably untrue that Orleans spent his exile at Groombridge, as he was too politically important to be risked in such a remote place. A contemporary painting shows him writing in the Tower of London. Waller however seems to have done well out of his exploit and to have rebuilt the house with the profits. He continued to serve with distinction both in action and in diplomacy. From him were descended a long line of Wallers, including Edmund Waller the poet and his cousins Sir Hardress Waller, the regicide, and Sir William Waller, one of the most efficient of Cromwell's generals.

But by their time Groombridge had passed out of the family. George Waller married Mary Hardress and their son Hardress was born at Groombridge. The estate soon afterwards passed to the Sackvilles who sold it in 1618 to a prosperous official of James I's court, John Packer. Packer was a royalist and a hater of Spain. When the Prince of Wales went off with his friend the Duke of Buckingham on a harebrained trip to Spain to woo the Infanta, Packer, in common with most Englishmen who remembered the Armada and cherished traditions of the fires of Smithfield, was appalled. The Spanish match failed and Packer and England rejoiced. Packer expressed his satisfaction in a practical way. He pulled down the old church at Groombridge and replaced it with a building in a deliberately archaic style. In modest brick the exterior is not striking. The interior is most pleasing, having the manner and the scale of a minor college chapel. Above the porch appear the Prince of Wales' feathers and Packer's dedicatory inscription—recut—"For Prince Charles' happy return from Spain". Despite this admirable gesture Packer was a lukewarm supporter of Charles during the Civil War and as a result was rather roughly treated by both parties. He died in 1649 and was succeeded at Groombridge by a younger son Philip. Philip was a man of the new age, a lawyer and a scientist. He was one of the founding fellows of the Royal Society, in company with his friend John Evelyn, who was his guest at Groom-bridge. Around the time of the Restoration he decided to rebuild the old house. To Evelyn's distress he chose not to use a healthier site on the slope but to rebuild within the original moat. It might have been a damp position but it is one of considerable beauty and the house is surpassingly lovely. It is not over large and although it favours the restrained good taste of Restoration buildings it is satisfied with a slightly old-fashioned ground-plan. The garden design is sometimes attributed, probably wrongly, to Evelyn. All in all Groombridge is one of the rarer delights of these south-eastern counties. Happily a public footpath from the green passes near enough to give satisfying views of the house, the park and the moat.

While we are on the Sussex border we might go westward for a few miles to pick up more memories of the Sackvilles at Withyham. This was their home before Sir Thomas went to Knole, and it has remained their home manor to the present. They came here around the beginning of the thirteenth century when Jordan Sackville married a Sussex heiress, Ela de Den. These were the founders of the abbey of Bayham at Lamberhurst, and they and their descendants were buried in the abbey until the reign of Richard III. Then in 1488 Humphrey Sackville was buried at Withyham, and this has been the family sepulchre ever since.

The Sackville home was Buckhurst, a very large house in its time standing in an enormous park carved out of the wealden forest. It was always a favourite with the Dorsets, and when the dukedom was extinguished with the death of the fourth Duke in 1815 the estate passed to Earl de la Warr, and the senior branch chose Backhurst in preference to Knole. The old house has gone now, all but a melancholy tower which can just be seen among the trees.

In a corner of Buckhurst Park stands the little parish church of Withyham. It stands well on a bluff above the road, but looks homely rather than impressive. The north-eastern chapel below which genera-tions of Sackvilles lie has however the finest collection of monumental sculpture in any English village church. Among more restrained tributes there are four major works of art. The chapel is dominated by a huge altar-tomb with life-size figures in white marble. On the chest reclines Thomas Sackville, son of the fifth Earl. He was a younger brother of the disreputable Charles. His parents must have contrasted his fate, dying at thirteen, with that of his brother, who was by that time well set upon a career of debauchery. They commissioned the finest sculptor of the day, Caius Cibber—father of the egregious Colley —to design his memorial. Cibber put the brothers and sisters, including Charles, around the base as weepers, while the Earl and Countess kneel over their young son. It is an extravagant—in every sense: it cost £350—essay in baroque, yet it remains strangely moving.

Linton Park

A garden pavilion at Mereworth Castle

Cibber's work makes an effective contrast to the three superb wall memorials behind it. On the left (as one faces) is the most nearly conventional of them, the memorial to the third Duke, designed by Nollekens. The gay Duke, his scandals forgotten, or at least forgiven, is shown in portrait relief, surrounded by mourning cherubs suitably naked. Next comes the third Duke's widow, long suffering Arabella who tried marriage a second time and outlived the Duke by twenty-six years. She, poor woman, does not appear at all. Chantry chose to show her already in her urn, beside which kneel the draped figures of her daughters. The flowing lines convey resignation rather than bitter grief. The latter is shown by Flaxman in the third monument. This is in memory of the young fourth Duke who was killed at twenty-one. He is shown in a small medallion below which sits his mother— Arabella again. The apparatus of grief is in the conventional neo-classical manner, but there is nothing conventional about the stillness, more affecting than any passion of grief, of the dominant figure. A marvellous work.

Buckhurst stood on the edge of Ashdown Forest, and to the west the array of great houses is interrupted by the forest. The next main group will be found on the North Downs in Surrey, and to reach them one must travel northwards towards Edenbridge passing near Hever where the old manor of the Boleyns was restored and trans-formed by the Astors in the early years of the century. Just before reaching Edenbridge there is a westward turning towards Lingfield, leading through quiet pretty country among the head waters of the Eden. Just off the road is the site of Sterborough Castle, a small fortified manor of the Cobhams marked now only by its moat. Here lived a formidable warrior, Sir Reginald Cobham who fought at Crecy and Poitiers and died miserably in the Black Death. His descendant, another Reginald, married a daughter of another warrior, Lord Bardolf who was at Agincourt, and they founded a college of priests at Lingfield. While we are so near it will be worth making the diversion to this pleasant town to see the remaining building—the Guestenhouse—of the college and the very fine tomb of the founders in the parish church.

A little to the north of Lingfield a road passes the drive of Crowhurst Place, the moated hall of the Gaynesfords. This is out of sight from the road but a footpath passes near. The spectacular half-timbered gatehouse on the road is a fantasy added after the First World War. Purists under-standably don't like this, but I find it a welcome highnote in a slightly dull route. The Gaynesfords are buried in Crowhurst Church, farther along the road, which is better known for its great churchyard yew, hollow and as big within as a rather small room, and for one of the most elaborate of wealden iron slabs.

It might be tempting to continue north through Limpsfield for a glimpse of Titsey Place below the Downs, but the house is changed and very private and so is the magnificent park. This was the home of the Greshams, who rebuilt the older house in 1775, in the process destroying the medieval church, and laid out the landscape garden. The situation is most beautiful, with the hills rising behind to above 800 feet and forming a huge natural amphitheatre. But prohibitive notices adorn every entrance, and we had better head farther west.

This route passes through Bletchingley, a former rotten borough and still, despite traffic on the A25, a very attractive village. Here was a Norman castle of the Clares, long ago destroyed. Later owners, notably Sir Robert Clayton, are remembered in the church. Sir Robert, whose monument fills the church in the grotesque baroque manner of the late seventeenth century, was a 'character'. John Evelyn, not the man to tolerate fools, records with some satisfaction how Clayton received the manor of Bletchingley in settlement of Lord Peterborough's debts. He called him, without irony, "this Prince of Citizens", and admired the liberality with which he carried out his duties as Lord Mayor of London. Clayton lived at Marden Park, to the north in the parish of Woldingham, where he built a house—now gone—and transformed the bare landscape with exotic trees.

As one goes down into Redhill on the main A25 road the eye is distracted from the general dreariness of the town by a swell of fine green downland beyond. This, it is clear even at this distance, is a landscaped park, its trees cunningly disposed to simulate nature and beating nature at her job. Set like a slightly inferior stone in this noble setting is a white mansion. The park is really the best of Gatton and it is very good. Here the ancient trackway of the Pilgrims Way climbs almost to the crown of the downs.

Gatton is famous, and was notorious, as one of the most spectacularly corrupt of pocket boroughs. It enjoyed borough status from the middle of the fifteenth century, yet less than a century later there was only one elector, Sir Roger Copley, who nominated and voted in two Members of Parliament. The Copleys were recusants after the accession of Elizabeth, and their political influence thereafter had to be used discreetly, but the scandal remained. When the Reform Act was passed in 1832 there were twenty-three houses in the parish. In grief for the loss of his power the lord of the manor placed a memorial urn in the 'town hall', a delightfully absurd open temple in the park.

Gatton Place ran through a great many owners after the Copleys until, late in Victorian times, it came to Lord Monson who began the rebuilding of the house. The work was later completed by Colman, of mustard fame. The buildings are now a school, and many subsidiary buildings, not all of them equally happy in design, spread across the park. The most conspicuous, and surprising, part of the house is the great pillared portico which looks as if it were part of some grandiose neo-classical design from the Augustan Age and which dates from 1891.

The park is of course private, although public paths cross it. One of these goes to the parish church, a humble building which Lord Monson took and transformed into a museum of art by importing woodwork and other treasures from Belgium and France. It is a freak but a pleasing one.

By continuing up the hill past Gatton and then dropping down Reigate Hill it is possible to cut out Redhill and to arrive instead in the pretty, over-busy high street of Reigate. Of the castle of the Warennes only earthworks remain. The Augustinian Priory was acquired at the dissolution by the Howards and made into a fine house, just behind the high street. This came by inheritance to the second Lord Howard of Effingham who commanded the sea forces of England against the Armada. He is buried in Reigate Church.

Modern Reigate, which includes the railway settlement of Redhill, suffers from traffic. Help is on the way, and it will not be long before travellers to and from Brighton will be trapped on the new motorway. The M25, taking the east-west traffic away from the streets, will not come as quickly. When it does Reigate may discover its potential as one of the most attractive of Home-Counties inland towns, with shops to match the individuality of the houses and with marvellous lungs available, by courtesy of the National Trust, on the Downs above the town. It will never rank high as a tourist centre and this is all to the good. Reigate is for the Reigatians.

The road from Reigate to Dorking has little to commend it other than the views to the downs which culminate in the noble spur of Box Hill. Through the Mole gap there are some minor houses of interest, notably Juniper Hall which was still quite new when it became the home of refugees from the terror of the French Revolution, among them Talleyrand and M. d'Arblay who had the distinction of marrying Fanny Burney. Across the valley from Juniper Hall is the green rise of Norbury Park, a richly wooded estate on the side of Fetcham Down. A rewarding network of public paths have been established here which give glimpses of the eighteenth-century mansion and offer the chance of a stroll beside the River Mole in one of its most engaging reaches. The river, could one follow it so far, would lead to Stoke d'Abernon with its celebrated brasses and its eighteenth-century manor house, from which a diversion might be made to Esher and Claremont, most famous of Surrey estates with memories of Vanbrugh, Clive, Capability Brown and Queen Victoria. This is worth a long journey for the sake of the superb landscape design, one of Capability Brown's happiest concepts and one preserved for us by the National Trust.

This, however, is a long way off our route, and one ought perhaps to forego the pleasures of the Mole and go through Dorking, a town almost as attractive and of as great a potential as Reigate, on to Wotton. Here was the home of the Evelyn family and the birthplace of the diarist. The house, of which little survives from Evelyn's time, is now the staff college of the National Fire Service. Footpaths heading for the delights of Friday Street and Leith Hill pass through the park, giving some impression of the landscape improvements devised by Evelyn which anticipate in some ways the more elaborate schemes of the next century.

The Evelyns came to Wotton at the beginning of the seventeenth century, and many are buried in the parish church which stands in a highly picturesque situation to the north. Motorists grinding up the steep narrow hill on the A25 are usually too preoccupied to notice it. The tower is of the kind one finds in the fortress churches of the Welsh Marches. Here it looks more than a little odd, but certainly not un-attractive. The building sits snugly into the sandstone hill and looks across to the wooded slopes of Ranmore Common, making one of the least spoiled landscape pictures of the commuter belt. It has changed amazingly little in the fifty years I have known it.

This surely is a happy resting place for John Evelyn, who was one of the first Englishmen to analyse scientifically his reactions to natural beauty. He represents one aspect of the England of Charles II as Pepys represents another. His mind ranged widely and to every interest he brought a clear critical brain. As an efficient and conscientious civil servant he spent much time in travelling the south-eastern counties and the diary records faithfully duties performed and buildings and gardens assessed. He was too admirable a man to be lovable, as we love Pepys while deploring his naughtiness; the diarists are alike in their dedication to work and in their practical good sense. It is appro-priate that, among the baroque extravagances of his kinsfolk, Evelyn lies at Wotton under a plain grave slab. He was essentially a grave man.

From Wotton it is best to abandon the A25—never the most com-fortable of roads—in favour of the downs and a narrow twisting lane to Polesden Lacy. This, one of the most popular, and charming, of National Trust properties, is too familiar to call for detailed comment here. The manor passed through many hands, including those of Admiral Geary and Sheridan, gayest and most improvident of drama-tists, before coming at the beginning of the twentieth century to the Hon Ronald Fulke-Greville. The house, originally a Regency villa, was burnt, altered and extended many times until the Grevilles trans-formed it into a monument to Edwardian prosperity, elegance and taste. So it remains, for on Mrs Greville's death in 1942 the house passed to the Trust and time stopped.

The house is filled with fine art treasures, evidence of the owners' discrimination and their friendship with the King, the Czar and many others, for the Grevilles were at the hub of Edwardian society. The gardens are equally a work of art, the long terrace completed by Sheridan giving glorious views over the wooded hills of Ranmore, a walled garden, and gracious lawns set about with vases and sculpture.

A lane from Polesden Lacy gains the main road at Great Bookham. I remember this road from Leatherhead to Guildford as a quiet lane, wooded, dotted with pretty villages, and disturbed by the rare occasional phenomenon of a motor car. Now it is a highway, the villages have lost their individuality, and the houses of prosperous commuters fill the gaps between them. Here the popular, and profoundly mistaken, idea of Surrey, as one single huge commuter estate, seems to have come true. We pass through Effingham, which gave its name to the destroyer of the Invincible Armada but has nothing to show of him; East Horsley, which has astonishing things to show of the activities of a romantic Victorian magnate; and East Clandon. Between these two the fine park of Hatchlands lies to the north. The refined and restrained Palladian mansion, with interior decoration by Adam, was the surprising home of 'Old Dreadnaught' himself, Admiral Boscawen, who was the most thoroughly professional of the professional sailors of the mid-eighteenth century. His performance in the wars against France in India and the West Indies was always unspectacular and sound, and spoiled only by the incompetence of colleagues. It was the experience of folly and irresolution which prompted him to order the court-martial and to authorize the execution of Admiral Byng. This tough and businesslike old fighting sailor spent his prize money on Hatchlands and delighted in seeing it made unfussy and shipshape. It is now in the care of the National Trust.

The Trust is also custodian of the next estate along the road, at West Clandon. Here is the classic example of the Palladian manner in South-east England. Less extravagant than Mereworth it depends for its effect on pure proportion. The result is a little severe for some tastes, at least as regards the exterior. By contrast the interior is warm and gracious, especially since the Trust completed their recent restoration and brought back the noble rooms to something like their original decorative state.

Clandon Park was the seat of the Onslow family who gained property in Surrey by marriage early in Elizabeth's reign. Their new house was commissioned by Thomas, second Lord Onslow, the architect being an Italian, Giacomo Leoni. The house was completed around 1730 and the park was laid out under the direction of Capability Brown forty years later. The Onslows were conscientious politicians, if no more, and several members of the family became Speakers of the House of Commons. There was also a naval tradition in the family, while one maverick member took to music and enjoyed a modest reputation as a composer in nineteenth-century France.

One oddity of Clandon Park is that it ignores rather pointedly the village of West Clandon and is approached by a mile-long drive from Merrow. Merrow too is the traditional burial place of the Onslows, although their church was substantially rebuilt in the Victorian age.

At Merrow the tide of Guildford's houses laps almost at the walls of the village church, and travellers who wish to avoid on this journey the lively, enterprising but overlarge town may be inclined to turn off here. To the north the pretty River Wey and its accompanying navigation make a big loop around the parkland of the most famous private house in Surrey, Sutton Place. This superb mansion, built for Sir Richard Weston, a courtier of Henry VIII, in the height of fashion, red brick and terracotta, is now in the best of hands but its perfections are not normally to be seen. This journey through the great houses of Kent and Surrey must therefore conclude elsewhere, and not unworthily. The road south-east from Merrow Church—the A25 again— leads by way of Newlands Corner, with its magnificent views to the Weald, back to Albury where another road runs below the high ridge of St Martha's Hill to Shalford, following the valley of the pretty Tillingbourne. From Shalford one may cross to the Wey valley and then, just short of Godalming, turn westwards on the road to Compton. There is an enormous temptation here to go straight on to Compton Church, perhaps the most interesting in Surrey and in some ecclesiologists' 'top twenty' for the whole country. But half-way to Compton a drive goes off north to Loseley, and here is the climax of the journey.

Loseley House is only a single surviving wing of a much greater house, but it gives no impression of incompleteness. No great house has a more perfect harmony of the whole and its parts, and it sits in its park as if it grew there. Unlike so many Elizabethan houses it is a grave, restrained building with more of the intellectual Renaissance than the exuberance of the Elizabethan age about it. Contrary to the fashion of the time, too, it is built not in brick but in stone, boldly set off by white blocks of toughened chalk. The stone, it is said, came from Waverley Abbey, the first of all Cistercian houses in England, whose ruins adorn a picturesque wooded reach of the River Wey not far from here. It would certainly have been in the spirit of the time for Sir William More to have raided this convenient quarry for his new house. Sir William's son George added to the house when he inherited in 1600.

It would annoy Sir George More, a conscientious public servant and the friends of kings, to know that he is best remembered today because of the injudicious marriage of his daughter Ann. Ann More was sent to London, following the custom of the time, to be brought up in the household of Sir Thomas Egerton, the Lord Keeper. Sir Thomas's son had taken part in the Earl of Essex's spectacular raid on Cadiz in 1596 and with him went his friend John Donne. (Another of the adventurers on this exploit was Henry Wotton of Boughton Malherbe.) After this excitement the two young men returned to London and Donne was employed as one of the Lord Keeper's secretaries. Some time during Donne's employment he and Ann fell in love. They were separated when Lady Egerton died in 1600 and Ann had to go home to Loseley. She was back in London a year later; the lovers met secretly, and as secretly married.

It was unwise. Sir George More was a wealthy and important man. He had reasonable plans for his daughter and these did not include marriage to a poor and clever poet. When Donne at length screwed up his courage and confessed the good knight was very angry. He pressed successfully both for Donne's imprisonment and for his dismissal from the Lord Keeper's service. The poet summarized the position briefly and gloomily: "John Donne: Ann Donne: Undone." However, Donne had good friends as well as enemies, and after long persuasion Sir George relented, and Ann and her penniless husband were reunited, to enjoy a marriage of rare beauty which ended with Ann's death in childbed after sixteen years of happiness.

It is tempting to dismiss Sir George as the heavy father of melodrama. He was indeed a man of varied attainments, intelligent, articulate and shrewd. Both Elizabeth and James I valued his judgement. He ruled Loseley well. The proper marriage of his children was obviously important to him, and obviously, according to custom, it was his right to choose their husbands. He looked for something a great deal more suitable than a clever adventurer for his third daughter.

The male lines of the Mores, jeopardized by the death of all but one of Sir George's sons, died out in James II's reign, and Loseley passed by marriage to Sir Thomas Molyneux. The Molyneux family adopted the name of More-Molyneux, and the house has remained in the family to the present. The owner, Mr J. R. More-Molyneux, opens the house most generously to the public, and a visit is a most memorable experience. Here is a great house which is also clearly a home, its treasures valued and understood, a house in which history is, as we have seen at Knole and Penshurst, a continuing process.

7

Silly Sussex

SILLY Sussex is a term which has been long in use to convey the kind of affectionate derision, entirely devoid of malice, which one reserves for an object intimately known and much loved. At no time, I think, has it been designed to impute folly of the Gotham sort, half stupid, half cunning, which traditionally marks the English rustic. In origin the term surely has a totally different meaning.

Silly is one of those words which have suffered the process of deterioration which attacks all languages, the process which changes 'presently' from 'at once' to 'some time or other'. Silly is in its uncorrupted state *selig* by which our Sussex Saxons meant 'holy' or 'blessed'. In time the concept, common to all unsophisticated communities, that the mentally retarded are especially under God's care, worked upon the word and produced the idea of one in whom stupidity is next to godliness. In more artificial societies the holiness is lost and only silliness remains.

It may seem strange to outsiders—although men of Sussex will see no cause for surprise—that Sussex should be singled out for holy simplicity. The Kingdom of the South Saxons was in no great hurry to embrace Christianity. This, however, was more the result of geography than of original sin. The whole history of the southern counties has been governed by the phenomenon of the Weald, a very long, substantially wide tract of dense forest which lay between an inhabitable coastal strip and the accessible downland to the north. The Weald effectively prevented communication between north and south for many centuries and right into the Middle Ages it was a formidable barrier, as much for its deep mire as for the denseness of the woodland. Of the original Saxon settlers only the Hastingas who occupied the extreme south-eastern territory, and they not certainly, made inroads into the forest and made contact with their neighbours to north and east. The lowlands farther west were eminently suitable for settlement, especially by tribes with experience in cultivating heavy soils, but those who lived there had to reconcile themselves to isolation. Their only visitors would come by sea.

There is a remarkable episode in the story of Wilfrid, the first saint of Sussex. Coming back in the year 666 from the land of the Franks, where he had sought consecration to his office as Bishop of York, the young priest—he was only thirty-two—was driven off course by a violent storm and washed up on the shore of Sussex. Wilfrid and his party looked for shelter and were set upon out of the wild darkness by savages urged on by a pagan priest. These Saxons lived by shipwreck and the bishop seemed their natural prey. A lucky stone killed the high priest, and after a brief skirmish Wilfrid and his followers managed to escape. It was an incident which stuck in his mind and had important consequences.

Wilfrid is the first great figure in the history of Christian Sussex. He is certainly almost the most fascinating character among the English missionaries, if not quite the most lovable. In him differing impulses warred constantly. He had a gift for awaking strong emotions in friends and enemies. No one seems ever to have been neutral about Wilfrid. Even Theodore, the organizing Archbishop of Canterbury who seems to have been the first great management man in English history, lapsed momentarily—but with far-reaching results—when confronted with the phenomenon of Wilfrid.

The future apostle to the South Saxons was a Northumbrian, born into a kingdom barely emerging from paganism and with the Roman doctrines of Augustine's lieutenant Paulinus weakened by contact with the single-minded dedication of Aidan, who brought to Lindisfarne the severe rites of Celtic Christianity.

Wilfrid adhered all his life to the Roman idea. This gave direction to his work and at the same time made him powerful enemies in the North. He did not help himself. Tact has seldom been a prominent characteristic of saints, or of North Countrymen, and it was not tactful of Wilfrid to encourage the Northumbrian Queen Ethelthrid to leave her husband, Wilfrid's own patron, and found the abbey of Ely. He was not worldly-wise in antagonizing the King's new wife, to whom his love of ritual and the splendid standard of living which he considered appropriate to a great prince of the Church were repugnant.

At this crisis in Wilfrid's life Archbishop Theodore appeared. In his view Wilfrid, as head of the Church throughout the North, had too much to do. It is a pity that Theodore chose to divide the huge northern diocese—a very reasonable act—without telling him, and worse that he consecrated the newly created bishops in Wilfrid's own cathedral. Failing to get justice from an aloof archbishop and an antagonistic king, Wilfrid decided to appeal to the Pope. In days of appallingly hazardous journeys he was already a seasoned traveller. He had been in Europe several times before and had made friends—and enemies. One of the latter got to hear of his new journey and set up an ambush for him. He escaped by a coincidence which—but for the consequences —was pure farce. A Mercian bishop Winfrid happened to be travelling at the same time, and the ambush caught the wrong man. Meanwhile Wilfrid made a leisurely way to Rome and gained the Pope's support for his cause. Unfortunately when he got back home the Northumbrian king would have no regard for the Pope's judgement and accused Wilfrid of buying it. Instead of finding himself reinstated the bishop found himself in gaol. There he stayed for the best part of the year before the King had second thoughts and let him go.

There seemed no future for Wilfrid in the hostile North, and so he travelled south into Mercia. Here he found the kingdom in the hands of a kinsman of his Northumbrian enemy, and so he went on again to Wessex, where once more the enmity of the North pursued him. In despair he moved to the least hospitable part of the country where fifteen years earlier he had been shipwrecked. So, almost by accident, began the mission to Sussex.

Wilfrid was not the first Christian to come here. The King, Ethelwalch, had already been baptized, converted, as King Ethelbert of Kent had been, through the influence of his queen. There was even a minster in the land, a tiny monastic community governed by a missionary from Ireland, which—if the romantic story is true—was established on an arm of the sea called Bosenham. The King welcomed Wilfrid and gave him land on the extreme tip of his kingdom, a shingly peninsula called Seal Island or Selsey. There he set up his minster. (He does not seem to have attempted to make contact with the Irish monks of Bosenham, who followed the Celtic rule which he disliked.)

The story of Wilfrid's mission, as told by Bede and by his own follower Eddi—the 'Eddi of Manhood End' in Kipling's charming poem—is convincing in its very homeliness. He found the pagan Sussexans deep sunk in despair. Their morale was low and their economy in ruin. They starved in a plentiful land, and when they could no longer bear their sufferings they jumped off the cliffs or walked into the sea. So, before he taught them the Gospel, Wilfrid taught them to fish. The symbolism probably appealed to him.

It is not surprising that the South Saxons were inclined to listen to a man who fed them, and who taught them a skill by which they might continue to eat and gain independence. The success of his mission was well founded, and he made sure of it by a miracle—or by the good luck which had escaped him so often in the past. Just at the moment of baptism of a crowd of converts the long drought which had exacerbated the sufferings of the pagans broke, and Wilfrid was rewarded with a symbolic double harvest of souls and corn.

The mission to Sussex lasted less than five years. Then Wilfrid left for Wessex, having been a party to a political and military coup by which Cadwalla gained that throne; and shortly afterwards he returned, through the good offices of Archbishop Theodore, to his native Northumbria. There were still more than twenty years of conflict before him, including yet another journey to Rome—at the age of seventy—to seek the Pope's support in a grievous dispute with the King. He seems never to have returned to Sussex, whose conversion he probably regarded as an incident in a life dedicated to greater matters.

There is a South Country sequel to a story which belongs largely to the North. Wilfrid was buried in his own minster at Ripon, in a setting where he had enjoyed what little calm a stormy career had allowed him. Fifty years after his death Archbishop Odo claimed his relics for Canterbury. There is no evidence that the angry old man protested from the tomb against an action so profoundly contrary to his own wish. Apart from a youthful visit to the city he had had no joy of Canterbury in his lifetime, but Canterbury, the arch collector of holy relics, had him now.

Wilfrid's best memorial is his life story told by his priest Eddi and the few vivid pages in Bede. His career was one of failure as much as achievement, but his lasting appeal comes from a personality full of strong contradictions. He must have been a difficult man—one sympathizes with King Aldfrid and even more with Theodore—but he was never dull.

In Sussex his work endured. A great cathedral grew up at Selsey and from this centre the Gospel was taken into the darkest corners of Sussex. The see endured until 1075 when it was transferred to Chichester, a larger and more convenient place and the seat of temporal government since Roman times. It went none too soon. The long south-pointing finger of Selsey was subjected to the force of the tides and was already badly eroded. By the sixteenth century old Selsey was entirely beneath the sea. Of the famous cathedral a few stones alone may remain, built into the war memorial in the new holiday town. They have the characteristic interlaced sculpture of Anglian art, and it is just possible to believe that they were carved under the inspiration of Wilfrid.

As to modern Selsey, reactions must be an individual matter. Plenty of visitors go for the bathing and for sailing in the creeks of Chichester harbour. The inland country, the Hundred of Manhood, is not to all tastes. It is flat and fertile—where it has not been required to grow bungalows rather than wheat. Occasionally, in certain weathers, it can be most beautiful. One catches a breath of the past most effectively on the edge of the wide ruined harbour of Pagham. The eastern shore of this expanse of saltings, rich in waders, is overgrown with caravans; the west, around Church Norton, is still largely deserted. Here the parish church of medieval Selsey stood on a bluff above the harbour. The western three-quarters were dismantled in 1865 and the materials re-used in the building of New Selsey church. The tiny choir was left standing in a situation at once charming and melancholy. Although the fabric dates only from the thirteenth century, it is known as St Wilfrid's Chapel. Inside, someone had the happy notion of putting up, in a fine illuminated copy, Kipling's verses about Eddi's ministry to the beasts which capture the atmosphere of the seemingly remote place.

There is nothing of Wilfrid in Chichester. This is where King Ethelwalch presumably had his palace—unless he occupied the half-ruined Roman palace at Fishbourne, so excitingly rediscovered and restored in recent years. There must surely have been a church here in Saxon times, but the great ecclesiastical days of Chichester began when Selsey was abandoned shortly after the Conquest. The Norman cathedral was begun before the end of the eleventh century and went on, interrupted by fire, for a hundred years. The great influence upon the fortunes of Chichester in the Middle Ages was the cult of St Richard. St Richard was another of the saints of Sussex who belonged to another county, but unlike Wilfrid Richard gave his best and his last years to Sussex.

Richard came from Droitwich in Worcestershire. He was born at about the time that Chichester Cathedral was being reconsecrated after the great fire of 1187. His early career was fairly conventional. As a younger son of a landed family he had no inescapable temporal duties and so he became a clerk and studied widely at Oxford and abroad in France and Italy. He rose to be Chancellor of the University of Oxford and later Chancellor of Canterbury under Archbishop Edmund. In 1244 King Henry III proposed to appoint to the vacant see of Chichester a disreputable courtier called Robert Passelew. The archbishop protested and there was a splendid row. The archbishop favoured Richard and consecrated him bishop in 1245. The king retaliated by confiscating the temporal property of Chichester and subjected the new bishop to petty and major irritations and indignities. These continued even after the Pope had confirmed Richard's appointment. He seems to have borne the persecution well, helped by a remarkable lack of interest in his personal comfort. In an age of growing wealth in the Church he remained an ascetic and persistent returner of good for evil. It must have been maddening for the King.

In 1253 Richard preached a Crusade, and he was in Dover, organizing the spiritual side of the campaign, when he was taken ill and died in the maison dieu of that port. He was taken back to Chichester and buried in the chapel of St Thomas—which he had himself rededicated to include the name of his old master St Edmund of Canterbury. Miracles promptly took place at his tomb and he was canonized nine years after his death. In 1276 his remains were translated, in the presence of King Edward I, to a magnificent shrine behind the high altar— in the same position as St Thomas's shrine at Canterbury—and this became an object of pilgrimage. At the Reformation Cromwell, being conscious of the "superstition and a certain kind of idolatry" associated with the shrine, not to mention the richness of its jewels and gold, ordered its complete destruction. The site is in the most beautiful part of this very lovely and strangely undervalued cathedral, in the Retro-Choir where the Norman arcades damaged in the 1187 fire blossom into the elegant slim-columned piers and triforia of a brand-new architectural style.

To St Richard it is tempting to add another man who did great work in Chichester and who enriched the cathedral not only with stone and sculpture but with his spirit and who, if the Anglican order went in for saints, would surely qualify for canonization. George Bell came to Chichester from Canterbury where he had been one of the greatest deans since that office was created after the Dissolution. In his tough humorous reign he made Chichester Cathedral an outstanding centre for artistic effort and a place which spoke clearly to its diocese. When he died in 1958 he was taken back to Canterbury for burial, but he has a superb memorial in Chichester in the very beautiful choir-screen, built originally in the fifteenth century. This had been dismantled in Victorian times and the pieces stowed in the bell tower. It was restored to its original position in memory of Bishop Bell and of his medieval predecessor Bishop Arundel who had been responsible for the original screen.

Much of the outstanding modern additions to the cathedral came shortly after Bell's death, but are to be traced directly or indirectly to his inspiration. These include the refitting of St Mary Magdalene Chapel in 1961 with lovely stonework and the superb altar painting by Graham Sutherland, the pulpit of 1966, and John Piper's deeply moving tapestries over the high altar of the same year. These—which may disturb some visitors brought up in a milder school of religious

art and which indeed ought to disturb everyone—are in the tradition
of a building which has always been changing and incorporating new
concepts. The Piper tapestries touch the viewer in just the same way as
the two magnificent twelfth-century reliefs illustrating the story of the
raising of Lazarus. (The legend that these came from Old Selsey
cathedral must reluctantly be dismissed.) Each is a major work of art
of its century and each seems completely at home in an anachronistic
setting.

It has been in a sense anachronistic to my plan to visit the Norman
cathedral at all, for Selig Sussex is Saxon Sussex, and, rich as are the
remains of Roman and medieval Chichester, there is little in the modern
city to remind the visitor of the Saxon kingdom and of the continual
and ultimately futile struggle to retain independence of the powerful
neighbouring kingdom of Wessex. Travellers, however dedicated to
the theme of this chapter, will however not reject an interlude in a
city which is careful of its heritage from the past and conscious of its
present function as a centre of commercial and artistic life. The cathedral is the city's central jewel, but there are other fine stones, some of
them not a generation old.

The Roman road westward out of Chichester, which passes the
magnificent and evocative remains of Fishbourne, palace of the Vice-
roy of Roman Sussex, touches the head of the creek on which stands
Bosenham, where the exiled Irish monk had his minster in Wilfrid's
time. Bosenham is Bosham ('Bos'm' in the Sussex tongue), a place of
great antiquity and no less great significance today for those who sail
the tidal waters of Chichester Harbour.

If the story of Dicul the Irishman is true—and there is no reason to
believe otherwise—then Bosham is the earliest known Christian site
in Sussex. (Of course there was probably a Christian chapel in Roman
Chichester, and one day a lucky chance may disclose a private chapel
in one of the numerous Roman villas, as was discovered so excitingly
at Lullingstone in Kent.) The site had the makings of a good port,
before tide and silt produced the wilderness of shallows and saltings
which is modern Chichester Harbour, and the place was strikingly
prosperous by the Norman Conquest—on the evidence of Domesday
Book. The minster flourished. The manor belonged to the archbishop
and was transferred—there is a very nice and improbable story about
this—to Earl Godwin in the reign of King Edward the Confessor.
Another legend associates it with Canute, and certainly Bosham was
just the place in which to demonstrate the limited powers of the
monarchy over the tide. This is a legend, and a happy one. It is history
that Harold Godwinsson sailed from Bosham on that fateful voyage—
whether deliberate or accidental is one of the unsolved mysteries of
history—which took him to Duke William's court in Normandy,

and the Bayeux Tapestry shows him setting out in all the vigour of his young manhood.

This was Saxon Bosham, and there is solid supporting evidence in the wonderful church which dominates the view from the harbour. Holy Trinity, Bosham, is one of those rare churches which retains to the full its atmosphere of a remote past without sacrifice of modern relevance. It is so old that the early English lancets of the enlarged chancel seem new, yet it carries its thousand years with dignity. The present building was perhaps a rebuilding, or a substantial expansion, of the original minster carried out by Canute or possibly with some of the wealth of the Godwin family. The tower, capped with a later broach spire, belongs to the late Saxon manner, and the chancel arch is surely the most sophisticated piece of Saxon construction extant in the South. The walls are characteristically tall and thin; Saxon masons built with exuberant confidence and faith, and their work was so often destroyed in favour of Norman solidarity and strength that this faith was seldom put to the test of the centuries. In Bosham it has stood well.

Local tradition, although it can seldom be proved right, is often supported by the discoveries of archaeology. There was for example the legend that the headquarters of the Roman invasion force was near Bosham. Legend fixed on the wrong site, but the archaeologists found Fishbourne. In Bosham church it has always been said that Canute's child daughter was buried in the choir. The tomb pointed out as hers was fourteenth-century, but during restoration in mid-Victorian times a stone coffin was discovered nearby containing a child's bones. There was no evidence to identify the remains, but one could hardly blame Bosham for having them reinterred in the name of a Danish princess.

There has been some unworthy development inland, but creekside Bosham is still enchanting, not less so for the constant movement— when the tide is right—of sailing men and women. Some lovely flint cottages come right to the tideline, and Quay Meadow, a diminutive green patch on the point, is safe in the hands of the National Trust.

While in this far west of Sussex it is worth picking up a few more memories of Saxon times, especially as these are to be found in very beautiful and largely unspoilt country. Almost due north of Bosham the South Downs are disturbed in their steady east-west march and swing southwards in a spectacular loop around the valley of the Lavant. The rounded top of Bow Hill is peppered with big round barrows from the Bronze Age. Many such burial mounds are damaged by ploughing or stand in unworthy settings; here on this high point, with Chichester Harbour lying below like a map and the Isle of Wight clear to the south-west, one sees how good an eye these remote ancestors had for landscape and for an evocative setting. The escarpment of the downs below is covered with a dense grove of ancient yews. This is Kingley Vale, where tradition has been busy again, placing here a great battle of Saxons and Danes. According to the Anglo-Saxon Chronicle the men of Chichester routed a Danish war band in 895, and this may be the seed of the story. A place to visit, whatever the truth behind the legend. A track descends the far side of the Bow Hill spur to the pretty village of Stoughton. Near here, according to yet another tradition, Wilfrid's patron Ethelwalch was killed in battle against Wessex, and the same tradition—tradition is never very sound on archaeology—buries him in one of the Bow Hill barrows. The church of Stoughton must have been built when the legend of Kingley Vale was still fresh. It is tall and slim in the Saxon manner and may have been built very close to the date of the Conquest. There is a tall chancel arch, handsome in its austerity, to which we shall find parallels elsewhere on this journey.

The tiny stream which flows through Stoughton village becomes the Ems and goes south-west to form the county boundary at Emsworth. On the eastern side of Bow Hill the river Lavant leads south through a gap in the downs between the facing—and in altitude almost identical—heights of Bow Hill and the Trundle. At West Dean a fine downland area of West Dean Park has been transformed in the most imaginative way by the formation of an open-air museum. Here buildings which have become redundant in their original settings— the first for example was displaced by a reservoir—are re-erected in attractive country. The enterprise grows yearly and already makes an objective for a rewarding day's outing. Below this is Singleton, possibly the prettiest of all these delightful villages in spite of the main-road traffic. Here is Sussex downland flint used to best effect in a clutch of delectable cottages. Above these rises the sturdy Saxon tower of St John's church. The body of the church was renewed late in the twelfth century, and the whole building carries its years most graciously.

The country around Singleton is dominated equally by the racecourse of Goodwood and the hill-top fort of the Trundle, a Neolithic camp enlarged and re-used by Iron Age tribesmen, a place of assembly in later ages, and now the site of a radar station. There are fine views to Chichester and the sea. Within the compass of the earth ramparts are the broken walls of a medieval chapel to St Roche.

Here there is a choice of ways. One may follow the Lavant to its source near East Dean and then continue east by way of Up Waltham where, snug above the road, sits a church which exhibits unchanged— except in detail—all the qualities of the building put up by the Normans in the early days of their occupation, to where Stane Street strides across the high down on its relentless way to London. There are good things on this route, others as good on the south-eastern roads which

Sir Robert Clayton in Bletchingley Church

Sackville monuments at Withyham

St Wilfrid's Chapel, Selsey

Polesden Lacey

cross the downs to Boxgrove and its noble priory church. The Saxon trail leads north, however, to the valley of the Western Rother, the loveliest of Sussex streams, which hangs on to its charms in face of drastic changes which come from improvement of the western trunk road. Here one might seek out Chithurst, which has a church in a circular churchyard—the broadest of hints at a pre-Christian origin—and Woolbeding, where the church, set prettily near the big house, shows Saxon pilaster work in its tall nave. The '-ings' hereabouts denote early settlements of Saxon families, tempted so far inland by the waterway.

The Rother goes from here through the centre of Midhurst and then across the lovely green expanse of Cowdray Park. The urban centre can be avoided by way of Easebourne, where there are remains of a house of Benedictine nuns, to pick up the river again at Selham. The pretty village has as its central attraction a church with a most astonishing chancel arch. The lines are those of Saxon work as we saw it at Stoughton, but the capitals have been decorated with extravagant ornament, interlaced ropes and twining dragons. It is all highly dramatic and clearly Saxon in its imagery.

Here one might avoid Petworth—a fascinating place whose history lies well outside the theme of this journey, one too with a dreadful traffic problem and an even more dreadful threat of a drastic solution of its troubles—by going south-east across the Chichester main road and skirting the wooded expanse of Burton Park. The lane passes the foot of Burton Pond, a landscaped lake formed out of one of the ponds of the iron industry, and comes by way of Coates to Fittleworth. Just to the east the Arun, near its confluence with the Rother, is crossed by the most celebrated of medieval Sussex bridges at Stopham. Near the river is another church with Saxon work, notably in two fine doorways. The church is full of memorials to Barttelots who owned the manor from the Conquest and lived in Stopham House from the reign of Henry V. A lovely place this with the mild, slow river, the comely stone bridge, and quietly satisfying parkland.

At Pulborough, Stane Street, which crossed the downs as a fine clear track, has become a motor road and remains almost to the county boundary as the main road to London. Just south of Pulborough—a pretty place before modern traffic got to work on it and still attractive in parts—there was a Roman staging post at Hardham on the old road of which a few fragments remain. There is also a most interesting church, built not much, if at all, later than the Conquest. The Roman buildings were substantially robbed for its fabric. It is notable for one of the most complete systems of wall paintings surviving in England, carried out in mid-twelfth century and even in its faded state a powerful reminder that the medieval church was the poor man's Bible. Along the road are thin remains of a priory of Augustinian canons which died before Henry VIII's Commissioners could get at it.

For more Saxon work one crosses the Arun and goes east and south, past the fine park in which stands Parham, almost the loveliest of all Tudor mansions in the south, through Storrington to Sullington, a very small settlement tucked under the flank of Kithurst Hill. All the down country to the south is of the greatest interest. One of the innumerable downland trackways—the exploration of all of them might occupy a moderately energetic man for the leisure hours of a lifetime—comes down here after crossing from Burpham, near Arundel. (The *burh* of the place-name was a strong-point established by King Alfred as part of his strategy in the Danish wars, and the raised table of his work can still be seen towards the river.) This track goes over Harrow Hill. This was occupied by successive tribes of prehistoric times, and the superstitious Saxon settlers in the valley named it *hearg* (holy) to placate the ancient ghosts who haunted it. At Sullington the church shows the typical long-and-short work of pre-Conquest masons beside a primitive round-headed doorway.

It is now main road all the way to Steyning, with the high downs almost unbroken on the right and with Chanctonbury Ring, the most familiar of all Sussex sights and the best loved, marking the half-way stage of the journey.

At Steyning, neat little modern town, former port and rotten borough, we pick up the tracks of another Sussex saint, possibly not the most saintly but by a long way the nicest of them all. Cuthman's story is told with so much circumstantial detail that no reasonable person would doubt its truth, but the dating is difficult. It has been suggested that Cuthman might have been one of the brethren of Dicul's minster at Bosham and therefore a contemporary of Wilfrid. Alternatively he may have come from the West Country and learned his Christianity in Avalon. He had the authentic innocence and practical good sense of the early saints; he was concerned with goodness rather than dogma. As a boy he kept his father's sheep well without interrupting his spiritual exercises; he used to draw a circle around them on the ground with his crook and the sheep dutifully stayed within this invisible boundary. Unfortunately his father died and Cuthman was hard put to support, in the words of one authority, "his decrepit mother". He therefore set out, in fairy-tale fashion, to seek his fortune, pulling the old lady in a homemade wheelbarrow. In Sussex the rope broke. He repaired it with twigs. The yokels jeered at him, and in uncharacteristic anger he called up a downpour of rain to spoil their hay-making. However, the locals had been right. You can't pull a wheelbarrow with twigs. They broke; Cuthman took the hint, and settled down on this spot. It was Steyning, where the River Adur turns before passing through a gap in the downs. His first care was for his mother, for whom he built a little cottage. Then he turned to the Lord's needs and built a wooden church, helped in certain technical difficulties by a mysterious stranger who turned out to be the Lord Himself. Cuthman spent the rest of his life in Steyning, teaching and performing miracles, always, one may assume, with modesty and good humour. A good saint. No wonder Christopher Fry fell in love with him and made out of his story the enchanting play *The Boy with a Cart*.

Cuthman was buried in his own church. The place where he settled became a town and a port at the head of the tidal Adur, a far bigger river than the muddy lazy stream of today. It was favoured by the kings of Wessex and had a palace and a mint. According to some sources, contradicted by others, King Ethelwulf was buried here in 853. His younger son later succeeded to the throne of Wessex as Alfred the Great. A stone coffin lid in the church is said to be his, or Cuthman's or somebody's. By Alfred's time Cuthman's timber church must have been replaced. It was rebuilt again when Edward the Confessor granted the manor to his favourite Norman abbey of Fécamp, together with Rye and other places in Sussex, in whose ownership it stayed until the abolition of the alien monasteries in the reign of Henry V. This pre-Conquest Norman church was itself rebuilt a century later in the grand style of late Norman work, and the nave of this building remains.

The Conqueror, when confirming the grant of Steyning to Fécamp Abbey, gave neighbouring land to one of his most reliable followers, William de Braose, who built the great castle of Bramber as one of the five strategic strongholds of Sussex. Each of these, together with one other at Chichester, was made the central point of an administrative division known as a rape (comparable to the Kentish lathe and as obscure in origin and precise meaning) which the Normans probably took over from an existing system; the boundary between the rapes of Bramber and Lewes was the traditional division between East and West Sussex and is still the boundary between the two administrative counties. On a ledge below the downs at Edburton one can still trace the earthworks of a motte-and-bailey castle which stood precisely on the boundary and presumably had some administrative function.

This, however, is to anticipate, for the present route must cross the downs by a high road to take in almost the most celebrated of Saxon relics in Sussex. The road from Steyning to Sompting follows an ancient track and has only recently, and regrettably, been adopted by motor traffic. It is a fine scenic route with wide views, more particularly to the west where the ramparts of Cissbury dominate the scene. This finest of the Sussex hill-forts takes its name, as does Chichester, from Cissa, son of Aella, the formidable war-leader who conquered Sussex and became its first Saxon king. It may have been used, like Pevensey, as a last stand by the British forces and have been, as we know Pevensey was, the scene of appalling slaughter. North of the bold open ramparts of Cissbury Ring, there is an unfamiliar view of the beech-ring of Chanctonbury. Then the narrow road tilts downwards and passes beside Sompting Church.

Everyone must have seen a picture of Sompting's 'helm'. The tall slim tower is topped by a most curious quadruple gable, an ingenious rather than an attractive device which is said to have its counterpart, perhaps its prototype, in the Rhineland. The tower is a textbook of Saxon architecture in its height, in the narrow walls, in the slim flat strips which bisect each face in imitation of timber-framing, in the triangular-headed and twin-light windows, and the long-and-short masonry at the angles. It is a demonstration of the Saxon builder's confidence, and its survival is his proud vindication. The tower arch giving access to the nave has ornamental capitals like a more sober version of the work at Selham. There seems to have been an altar in the tower, which may have been, as in other Saxon churches, the original nave; this would have made the tower arch into a chancel arch with a small apsidal sanctuary to the east. If this were so, the exterior must have presented a most comical top-heavy appearance.

There is a number of most attractive carved stones let into the walls of the later church, and these may perhaps have come from a demolished Saxon chancel. They have characteristic Saxon scroll and interlaced ornaments.

The church west of the tower was rebuilt late in the Norman period, probably at the expense of the wealthy order of Knights Templar who owned land here and who were granted the church in 1154. They extended the building eastwards and provided it with a large double chapel to the north. On the south, in a position which does not quite correspond to the conventional transept, they built their own chapel, a square nave with a very small sanctuary. Both north and south additions are of considerable beauty. They are austere by the standards of late Norman work and reflect no doubt the outlook of the as-yet-uncorrupted order. When the Templars fell at the beginning of the fourteenth century, either condemned justly for their Satanism or 'framed' by enemies jealous of their great wealth, Sompting passed to the rival order of Knights Hospitaller, who added another chapel against the north wall of the tower and nave, for reasons which remain obscure; but when this order in turn was dissolved the new chapel fell into ruin while the much older work remained.

The problems of medieval church architecture are not to all tastes, but at Sompting they are so curious, so much tied up with the activities of the military orders of priest-knights which sprang from the great debate of the Crusades, so productive of fine building and ornament, that the layman may here find as rich a reward as the expert. Sompting Church is a building as beautiful as it is intriguing.

Modern Sompting is neither. The narrow downland road ends in a scurry of traffic and a rash of modern housing, from which the quickest escape route is by a narrow lane leading back almost to the starting-point at Steyning. This may seem an illogical course, but this country beside the ambling Adur is too good to be missed. It starts in fine style with a glimpse of Carpenter's superb neo-Gothic chapel of Lancing School which is enough to get any traveller a-tiptoe with excitement. (Lancing seems to be named after another of King Aella's sons, Wlencing, who shared in the murderous conquest of Sussex.) The narrow lane then wanders inland, passing two entirely charming little villages at Coombes and Botolphs with diminutive churches, both of which have surviving Saxon fragments and plain chancel arches. Eventually this lane arrives at Bramber, and the route passes through the pretty village. (Its charms are a little marred by development and by its popularity with tourists come to see the scanty remains of Braose's, castle, St Mary's, and—most of all—the absurd and splendidly evocative Victorian museum.) Over the Adur bridge there is a mile or two of main road northwards before a lane turns right to follow the foot of the downs all the way to the Brighton Road at Pyecombe. This, if it has no obvious Saxon interest, has other offerings in plenty, especially some superb views of the steep escarpment of the chalk. After Edburton and Fulking the scene is dominated by the deep grassy combe of the Devils Dyke—which looks much better at this range than close to—and then there are the rich wooded hills of Newtimber, in National Trust care, on the right and the bold spur of Wolstonbury Hill ahead. This, because it thrusts forward from the line of the downs, gives perhaps the finest view in the South Downs with a command of the whole of the Sussex Weald from Blackdown to Ashdown Forest. All this and an Iron Age hill-fort too.

After this it is difficult to avoid anticlimax, but fortunately Clayton is near. The village is small—a pub, a few houses, and the rich comedy of a railway tunnel entrance masquerading as a castle—but the back-cloth of the downs, capped by Jack and Jill, best loved of all Sussex windmills, is grand and just below is little Clayton Church. Here, surely, is one of Kipling's "little lost down churches". It looks humble, a short tall nave, a tiny chancel, a wooden bellcote. Go inside and there is a shock. Clayton has its wall paintings intact. Like those at Hardham, they were probably painted in the twelfth century under the influence of Lewes Priory. Clayton belonged to St Pancras's Priory founded by William de Warenne and the daughter house of Cluny where there was the most notable school of painting in Normandy. The Cluniac order was devoted to elaborate ritual with its accompaniment of rich vestments, colour and all the aesthetic ancillaries of worship, and something of this rubbed off on to the little remote church under the downs. In the age of the iconoclasts these vigorous illustrations of the Judgement went to ground under a layer of whitewash, from which they emerged, faded, battered but intact late in the nineteenth century.

The wet plaster on which the pictures were painted was applied to walls which were already about a hundred years old. The tall nave betrays its Saxon origin, and so does the beautifully austere chancel arch. After the sculptured extravagance of a building like Selham this is severely plain, and the present may be the first age since it was raised to value this noble simplicity above the lush ornamentation of later centuries.

The lane past Clayton Church follows the course of the downs below Ditchling Beacon, highest of the eastern downs, past Westmeston and Plumpton, under Mount Harry where Simon de Montfort's army grouped at dawn on 14th May 1264 before descending to catch the King's forces by surprise and to win what, but for the sequel, might have been one of the major battles of our history. Lewes is one of the most interesting of English towns and, but for a traffic problem of formidable proportions, one of the most delightful. If not a Roman town it was certainly a Saxon burh. Its situation, trapped between high hills and itself rising to a considerable height above the river-crossing, makes it an obvious site for a strong defensive point, especially if one visualizes a wide tidal Ouse flowing up to the walls. Viewed from above, from the heights of Cliffe Hill, or from the levels below, the dramatic position of the town, with its Norman keep capping the highest point, is immediately apparent.

What one sees in Lewes today is a medieval town which spilled over its walls in the sixteenth century and had a drastic face-lift in the eighteenth. Of the Saxon town there are, doubtfully, the earthworks in the north corner of the wall. It is just possible, too, that the Normans based their defensive system on existing mounds. Would this perhaps account for the most enigmatic feature of Lewes Castle, the double motte? In addition to the very tall mound on which stands the shell-keep there is a smaller and obscured motte called the Brack Mount. Between the two lies the bailey which is now represented largely by a bowling green, one surely in an unrivalled romantic position. In the extreme angle of the town wall, beyond Brack Mount, the churchyard of St John-sub-Castra occupies an obviously artificial platform. The church is of the nineteenth century, but it contains one unique relic. This appears to have been the chancel arch of a Saxon church, and on it is inscribed a Latin record of one Magnus, a Danish prince who became a hermit here. The historical imagination leaps on this fragment of the remote past, to turn it into a romance of warfare, worldly power and renunciation.

Here, unfortunately, is no place for a detailed exploration of a town which, for me, is second only to Canterbury for interest among south-eastern towns. The pitiably ravished walls of Warenne's great priory of St Pancras, the graves of the founder and his wife—the discovery of which is one of the great romances of British archaeology—the lovely houses in the town and its suburbs of Cliffe, Southover and Malling, the many churches, all demand close and loving examinations. Here is time only for a brief visit to South Malling in the valley north of the town, where, according to ancient tradition, a minster was founded by Wilfrid's king of Wessex, Cadwalla. This, if it existed, was refounded as a college of priests by Archbishop Theobald, who was Becket's mentor, and the archbishop's palace, now reduced to a bit of wall, was the scene of one episode in the murder of Thomas. Seventh- and twelfth-century stories alike are clouded in unreality.

The way now lies down river, by the road hugging the downs on the eastern shore of the lost estuary. This leads, by way of villages tucked modestly into the hill, cement factories and modern housing estates, to the one-time port of Seaford. Here is a memory, and a macabre one, of another Sussex saint and the most obscure one of all. Of Lewine (or Lewinna) nothing at all would be known but for an extraordinary—by modern standards—episode in the eleventh century. There is a story that Lewine was converted by Wilfrid and after-wards fell victim to a pagan Saxon, but there is neither record nor convincing legend to reveal the details. However she died, she became a virgin-martyr and was enshrined in a Sussex church. Here legend ends and documentary evidence takes over. There was a monk of St Winoc's Abbey at Berg in Flanders who earned himself a reputation in the mid-eleventh century as a collector of holy relics. This Balger came to England in 1038, met King Edward the Confessor, and was encouraged by him to collect the remains of St Oswald and take them back to his abbey. He came back twenty years later and landed at a place called Zefort. Inland from the port Balger discovered a minster and learnt that it was the honoured burial place of the holy martyr Lewine. This brought Balger's collector's instincts to the fore and he attempted to negotiate a deal with the resident priest. The offer was not well received. Balger therefore decided that he must steal what he could not buy, and, encouraged, as he said, by a dream in which the virgin announced—surely this was out of character—that she was willing to go along with him, he smuggled her bones out of the church. He sent them to Flanders in the care of a colleague, while he stayed behind to demonstrate his innocence. The bones were duly added to the holy museum of St Winoc's.

The story is so detailed and so horrid, as related by a monk of Balger's abbey, that its truth cannot be questioned. It is however anachronistic to shudder. By the standards of his day the relic-hunter was in his rights in cheating and lying his way to success.

Where did all this happen? Only guesswork can supply an answer. The minster was presumably near Seaford, and it was dedicated to St Andrew. Is it coincidence that there is a St Andrew's Church near Seaford, and that this is a building which was standing in 1058 when Balger came this way? At the end of a lane up into the hills—it continues as a track which crosses the downs through delightful scenery and descends to the valley at Firle—stands the ancient settlement of Bishopstone. The church of St Andrew dominates the head of this enclosed valley. For me this is one of the supremely beautiful small churches in England. The bishops' influence (for the manor belonged to the bishops of Chichester) may have ensured that this would be a handsome building. One can only assume that the bishops lost interest, and therefore there were no important changes after the thirteenth century. So in this retired place survives a church which is basically Saxon, enlarged in the twelfth century by the addition of a tower and a north aisle, and extended in the time of King John into an exquisite small sanctuary. All these stages of the building represent the best qualities of their periods, and the different styles blend miraculously. In few old churches can one feel, as here, the weight of the centuries and the relevance of their message.

The Saxon work is probably earlier by a century or more than most of the buildings we have so far seen, and it has all the familiar characteristics: daring height and slimness of walls, massive rough-hewn stones at the corners. The south-western chapel, which is also the porch, is especially lovely; there was an altar centrally in the east wall, lit by a little window, and the door into the nave was set unobtrusively at the western extremity. Above the entrance, in which a Norman doorway was later inserted, is a sundial on which is engraved the name of Eadric, a Saxon patron of the church.

This may have been Lewine's church. She could hardly have had a more perfect setting. But, remembering Balger's rapacious hands, one hopes that it was not this lovely building that he defiled.

This eastern end of the long wall of the South Downs shows the chalk hills not at their highest but at their most characteristic. It is good to look up at the escarpment from the Weald, but the downs can be known only on foot—or on horseback. The track from Bishopstone to Firle and from Firle by way of Alfriston and Windover Hill to Jevington and Eastbourne offers as rewarding a walk as these southern counties, which cannot compete with wilder northern lands, can afford. It is changing country. The downs extolled by Georgian poets have gone, transformed by the effects of ploughing, by the decline in sheep grazing which radically altered the quality of the famous downland turf, and by the virtual extinction of rabbits through myxomatosis. (They have come back, but in such reduced numbers that the balance of nature has not been restored.) The chalk now grows barley rather than grass, and there are gliders as well as orchids. The air is as exhilarating as ever it was, and the lark is as vociferous.

A few crops of houses have appeared on the high ground—happily not many except in the hinterland of the coastal towns—but in general the downs are uninhabited, as they have been from Saxon times. The climate was wetter when prehistoric tribes occupied the tableland, but by the decline of Roman Britain the water level had sunk and the downs remained waterless until the invention of deep-bore wells. The villages still keep to the Saxon pattern of valley settlements, linked by modern roads around the edge of the high down and by ancient track-ways across the top. So, as we have seen, Bishopstone is linked by track with Firle, Firle with Alfriston, Wilmington with Jevington, West Dean with Friston. The list might be extended indefinitely.

The motor road, less adventurously, leaves Seaford and crosses the lower levels of the downs to drop into the Cuckmere valley at Exceat, a lost medieval village. Beyond the river modern plantations have changed the downland, somewhat to its scenic detriment, and in the heart of the woodland an old village, West Dean, huddles in its narrow valley. There are few villages in this part of the country which have survived so well. The houses have been renewed, or refaced, but the pattern cannot have changed much since this was a manor of the Saxon kings. Here, according to Asser, who wrote a contemporary account of King Alfred's career, he first met the only English king to be called 'Great'. Of Alfred's Dean there is nothing now to be seen. The Norman church probably occupies the site of a Saxon original, and the priest's cottage was replaced in stone and flint when the church was a century old. This example of medieval domestic building, rare in Sussex, remains beside the church gate.

The main road climbs up Exceat Hill, giving views back to the extraordinary meanders of the Cuckmere in its last miles to the sea, and arrives at Friston, another pretty village with a picture-postcard church and fine coastal National Trust land nearby. Here a road turns north to pass through a narrow dry valley to Jevington. Most of the ages of history and prehistory have made their contribution to this scene. The Saxons provided the church, in a lovely setting under the hill, but later generations of builders have obliterated all except some masonry in the tower. The spectacular carving, now reset but origin-ally perhaps a grave slab, which shows Christ harrowing Hell, seems to belong to the century after the Conquest and to betray a Norse influence.

The Jevington valley leads to Polegate, where one might follow the downs briefly westwards again. If the light is right, there are good views of the Long Man of Wilmington from the road. This is the only ancient chalk hill-figure in the south-eastern counties, and even the antiquity of this is in doubt. As usual with these huge works of art, mystery breeds controversy, and there is an abundance of theories about the Long Man, his date and his purpose. Some of these are intriguing, a few comical. Like the other giant, at Cerne in Dorset, he is naked, but less aggressively so, and may have some significance as a fertility figure. Like all the other old chalk carvings, he stands among relics of prehistory, long barrows and field systems. Like the Cerne Giant, he towers above a medieval religious house. From all this disparate evidence the visitor, in the absence of a firm line from the pundits, will draw his own conclusions. One thing is plain. Whoever cut this figure had a keen eye for landscape; the steep green face on which the Long Man stands is perfectly suited to displaying him. Whether he is pagan or Christian, god or pilgrim, he is a most memorable addition to the downland scene, and we must be grateful to his unknown creator.

Here the way lies northwards in the Cuckmere valley to a lonely church at Arlington. This, as the name suggests, is a Saxon settlement where the Earl at last lay down his sword and put up his roof-tree beside the river. The site was old in his day, for Romanized Britons had been here first and had buried their dead on the site which the Saxons chose for their church. They used materials from the Roman buildings for this, and these remain together with additions from at least two later ages.

The Cuckmere leads up to Dicker, where the handsome and admirably kept remains of Michelham Priory offer medieval and later attractions, and beyond this is Hellingly. The big mental hospital looms forbiddingly, but it is worth making a brief visit to the church which, like the one we saw at Chithurst, stands in a round churchyard and, by implication, occupies a pagan religious site. Hereafter it is plain driving, through pleasantly unspectacular country, to the forest ridge at Mayfield and to memories of another Sussex saint.

In a jolly song Arthur Beckett, one of the most dedicated lovers of this county, declared: "Oh, Wilfrid was a Sussex man, a Sussex man was he. . . ." As we have seen, he wasn't. In fact, with the possible exception of Lewine—and heaven knows where *she* came from—the Sussex saints all came from somewhere else. This is no discredit to them, or to Sussex. Their association with the county was by choice, not by the chance of birth. Dunstan came from Glastonbury—however fiercely Hilaire Belloc might deny it—and his greatest exploits were there, and at Canterbury, and wherever King Edgar held his court. His connections with Mayfield may be slight, but they have not deterred an admirable artist from depicting him on the village sign. Here he performs his most celebrated feat, pulling the Devil's nose. He used his red-hot goldsmith's tongs for the job and the Devil, understandably, jumped eight miles and eased his scorched proboscis in a spring at Tunbridge Wells—hence the chalybeate waters.

By the time Dunstan came to Mayfield he was Archbishop of Canterbury and in effect Chancellor of England, and he probably had no time to exercise his undoubted skills as a goldsmith. He built himself a house in Mayfield, which became a palace of the archbishops for the next four hundred years. The buildings, partly of the late thirteenth century, are now a convent school. They may offer only the faintest reminder of their great founder, but the buildings are impressive and the village, packed tight on a narrow high ridge, is most delightful.

Dunstan was nearest among the Sussex saints to Wilfrid, for he too was the statesman priest and the kingmaker, but he had more tact than Wilfrid and greater worldly wisdom. He held the kingdom together by sheer force of character until the unspeakable Ethelred and his murderous mother dismissed him and ushered in the age of 'Danegeld'. It is not easy to share his enthusiasm for monastic reform, and he evokes respect and admiration more than affection. It is heartening, however, to meet his sturdy forthright figure among the dark oakwoods of the Weald.

This journey through Saxon Sussex is almost over. There remains one church and one saint, the latter attached to the county by the slenderest of threads. A wide tract of forest country in the central Weald is called St Leonard's Forest. The modern plantations, east of Horsham, are the merest hint at the vast acreage which once supported pigs, deer, charcoal-burners and outlaws. And who was St Leonard? He was not a Sussex man. He wasn't even English. He was a Frankish nobleman of the sixth century and a prominent figure at the court of Clovis I. From this he turned in revulsion and became a hermit in the great forest of Limoges. He founded an abbey in the forest which afterwards took his name as dedication. His experience of life among the wealthy made him a friend of the poor and the helpless, especially prisoners. He spent his energies in their defence, and after death he became the patron saint of captives.

Leonard therefore was a forest saint. The Sussex forest seems to have taken its name from a chapel dedicated to him which stood near the big hammer pond outside Horsham. Belloc, who always sponsored improbabilities with all the might of his exuberant dogmatism, claimed that Leonard was himself the hermit of this forest chapel and a native of the Sussex woods.

Belloc also extolled the beauty of the forest. He might—it is unlikely, for he was not one to be subdued by vulgar realities—be a little less enthusiastic about the present-day scene. There are of course delightful moments, but the woodlands are largely enclosed and minor haphazard developments have destroyed their continuity. The most splendid scenery is associated with the two great ponds on the southern boundary of the shrunken forest.

Once the forest tracts spread across northern Sussex, St Leonard's merging with Tilgate, Tilgate with Worth, Worth with Ashdown. In a corner of one of these woodland wastes stood, and still stands, a church, one of the most remote, most ancient and memorable buildings in this commuter country. Worth is not two miles from Crawley New Town and within earshot of Gatwick, but it belongs to another, and for some people a more pleasing, world.

St Nicholas Church, Worth, is the most complete Saxon church in Sussex and in its scale almost the most impressive pre-Conquest church extant. The origins of the building are obscure, and it is not known under whose patronage it was designed with a lavishness which would have been notable anywhere and which seems extraordinary in a small forest clearing. It was built around the middle of the tenth century, in the lull between the two principal Danish invasions. Dunstan was in Canterbury, and the precarious Saxon monarchy had achieved temporary stability. In this eye of the storm Worth church arose. Miraculously—for the manor belonged to the Warennes of Lewes, compulsive Norman builders—it was left alone in succeeding centuries, and there were only minor alterations, such as the insertion of some larger windows in the thirteenth century, until the nineteenth century. Doubtless restoration was overdue by that time, but the Victorians as usual could not leave well alone. They took down a homely shingled spire which rose, in a mildly absurd way, out of the north transept and replaced it with an incongruous essay in mock Early English. The big window in the south transept came at this time, and the timber porch followed. Inappropriate as these additions are, one must be thankful that the restorers stopped there.

These minor excrescences apart, at Worth we have a large Saxon church with wide nave, narrow chancel and two unmatched transepts. Because of the small windows the building is dark, but this adds mystery to the grandeur of the design. As usual the Saxon work is lofty, and the height relieves the heaviness of the masonry, for the sandstone is cut in characteristically huge bulks. Five tall arches dominate the interior: north and south doors (the former now blocked), entrances to the two transepts, and between them the majestic chancel arch. The weight of the centuries has flattened this slightly but without reducing its splendour.

Buildings which have attained a great age, and especially those which have kept the same function throughout the centuries, achieve an emotional as well as a physical patina. The accumulated spiritual aura of all those generations of worshippers works upon the visitor, disarming critical judgement. If one can escape briefly from the spell, intellect will confirm instinct in acknowledging that at Worth we have a church of most rare beauty. This is not a matter of detail—the little twin-light windows are charming but that is quite another matter—but of scale and proportion. There is a noble inevitability which neither Victorian irrelevances nor alien—but very fine—fittings can interrupt.

Happily the tide of commuterdom, whose waves pile up against the railway line at Three Bridges, has not reached Worth. The church is in remote country still, sufficiently wooded to encourage the illusion that the forest lies all around. The setting ensures that shock of surprise which is essential to all satisfactory historical exploration. It preserves too the illusion that here time has stood still, and that Worth is a lonely sanctuary of Selig Sussex.

8

A South Country Waterway

WATER was the first highway. From the moment that an observant man noticed that a fallen tree floated and would bear his weight, the rivers provided him with his simplest and cheapest transport through country which was either densely overgrown or deeply boggy. There were drawbacks. In the hot season the river might dry up, in wet it became dangerously swollen. Even when climatic conditions were for once without extremes there would be shallows on which a boat could ground, and holes in which a careless navigator might drown.

The Romans had an answer for this, as for most purely practical problems. Their command of engineering skills and of unlimited labour enabled them to put nature in a strait-jacket, building highways across mountains, carrying water over the parched plain, and cutting waterways which would not dry up. Their Fossdyke still plays a part in the communications system of Lincolnshire.

The secret of the canal was lost, along with other skills of Rome. Engineering in the Dark Ages was confined to war. Alfred caught the Danes napping by diverting the River Lea, but that great man never had time to consider how a similar strategy might benefit a country at peace. The rivers continued to be a major means of communication, competing easily with the muddy tracks which, in places not blessed with the decaying remains of Roman roads, served as high-ways. There were snags. Water was also a major source of power, and every river had its chain of mills, each using water power and passing it downstream to its neighbour. To keep a head of water strong enough to turn a wheel the mill needed to impede the flow with a weir. Watermen going up or downstream were faced with a slow and difficult, and potentially dangerous, operation when they passed through a gap temporarily opened in the weir. They also had to endure the hostility of the miller whose water was 'stolen' by the passing boat.

The situation was aggravated by the growth of prosperity in the later Middle Ages. More raw materials and manufactured goods had to be carried across country, and for most of them water transport was obviously most suitable, if the rivers could be relied upon. The pressure of necessity coincided with the beginnings of a spirit of scientific inquiry, and perhaps also with curiosity about the achieve-ments of the classical past. The first canal since Roman times was cut in Devon early in Elizabeth's reign. This was an independent channel, but for the most part the promoters of navigation schemes were concerned with improving existing rivers. The Medway, which was capable of playing a vital part in the iron industry of the Weald, was an obvious case in point, and promoters could claim patriotism as well as self-interest, for were they not facilitating the supply of ord-nance for use against enemies of the Crown? However, attempts at improvements early in the seventeenth century all failed. The cause of inland waterways received a boost as a result of the Civil Wars. The wars brought home very sharply the need for better communica-tions. Some of the Royalist exiles found their way to the Low Countries, and saw what experts could do with water. When the King came home from his travels he brought with him several enthusiastic converts to the canal creed.

Meanwhile Parliament had been having its own ideas. As early as 1641 a Bill to join the Wey and the Arun by a canal was debated and rejected. Ten years later another attempt, on a less ambitious scale, succeeded and in 1653 work began on the Wey Navigation which would bring barge traffic from the Thames to Guildford. Despite appalling growing pains the scheme was carried out. A similar scheme for the Medway was approved by the Restoration Parliament, but for reasons most probably of finance this came to nothing. The South-east had to wait until 1740 for another attempt to open up the water-ways to barge traffic. This again concerned the Medway, and plans to improve the channel up to Forest Row were agreed. The scheme was over-ambitious and in fact the improvements never got farther upstream than Tonbridge. These developments were concurrent with improvements which had at last come to the roads, and navigations and turnpikes grew side by side to their mutual benefit.

The great age of the canal was still to come. The initial impetus for this came from the industrial expansion of the Midlands and North, and the Home Counties were involved mainly as recipients. Under the stimulus of the great Duke of Bridgewater, backed by the technical genius of Brindley, a network of new waterways spread across the Midland counties, linked with the capital by the Grand Junction Canal (which we meet briefly on another journey). Canal enthusiasm became canal mania, and fantastic schemes which had no basis in commercial viability were peddled around and even undertaken. In this mood of unguarded optimism the Wey and Arun project of 1641 was brought up again and this time adopted. The River Arun was already navigable to beyond Pulborough, and the grand design was completed with the opening of the canal link between the Arun and Portsmouth in 1823. A Grand Imperial Ship Canal, designed to provide deep water from Deptford to Portsmouth by way of the Mole valley at Dorking—alternative routes were also suggested—happily foundered. Even earlier than this, the elder John Rennie had proposed, in 1810, a Grand Southern Canal. This would go west of Tonbridge along the Eden valley, across the upper Mole, through the Sussex Weald, and join the Arun above Arundel. As if this were not enough there would also be a Weald of Kent Canal to Rye, with a branch to the North Kent coast at Herne Bay, links with the Ouse and Adur in Sussex, and one to the Thames by way of the Mole valley. Even without these grandiose concepts the South-east, although by no means as generously provided as more northerly parts of the country, had by this time completed its quota of canals and navigations. Already the rattle of trucks along the Surrey Iron Railway was sounding, for those who could hear, the knell of all these costly and beneficial undertakings.

The canals had a strategic as well as a commercial role. In times of Continental wars the Channel coast was always in hazard. We have seen (in Chapter 5) to what extraordinary efforts the ironmasters were driven to take their produce northwards through the muddy Weald of Sussex when southern waterways offered easy transit to the Channel ports. Northern waterways which offered safe passage to the Thames had obvious national benefits to offer. (Maybe in 1940 we might have been glad of the Grand Imperial Ship Canal or even the Grand Southern Canal.)

One by one the canals and navigations of southern England went out of business through the competition of the railways. In their search for easy gradients the latter often adopted an almost identical course to the canals, so making their competition particularly apparent.

Hardham Church

Worth Church

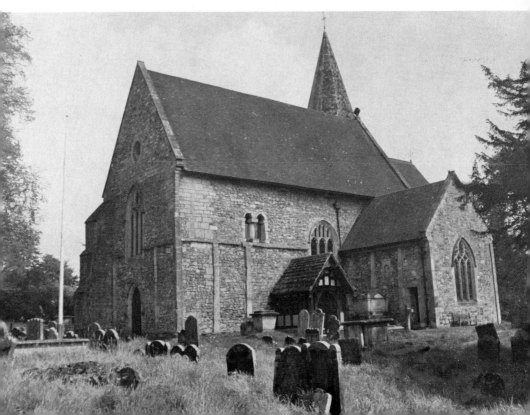

(*above left*) Saxon window, Worth Church (*above right*) Templar's chapel,
Sompting

Guildford Guildhall

The Portsmouth-Arundel, which had never been really successful, died first, in 1847, and the Wey and Arun followed in 1871. The navigations lasted longer. The Earl of Egremont's cherished Rother Navigation was the first to go, although it continued in theoretical existence, but without water, until 1936. The Arun took its last tolls in 1889; the river is still potentially of commercial value, but passage north of Ford is blocked by a low fixed railway bridge. At last only the Wey Navigation remained. It continued to do modest business well into the twentieth century, and then, in 1964, it was passed to the National Trust. Its commercial life is probably over, but it faces an active future as one of the richest environmental amenities of the Surrey commuter belt.

This half-forgotten waterway across southern England would make a most effective long-distance footpath, if only the complex problems of access to the central canal section could be overcome. It would have, for idle walkers at least, one advantage over the more spectacular Pennine Way and Cleveland Way; all the gradients would be easy and at its highest it would not take the walker above the 200-foot contour. What it lacked in drama it would amply make up in peacefulness, for it would take the traveller right across one of the most densely populated parts of England with, for the most part, only distant glimpses of houses. It would, moreover, insulate him from the ceaseless traffic of the main roads.

Thanks to the activities of the navigation engineers, and to the National Trust which preserves their work, there is no problem about the first third of the walk. The towpath is intact and freely accessible for the full course of the Wey Navigation from Weybridge to Godalming. Similarly the Arun towpath can be followed for most of the way from Bury to the sea. In between lie the tangled, overgrown and silted miles of the Wey and Arun Canal (currently attracting the attention of a preservation society). This could be the most rewarding part of the journey, passing as it does through the rich and beautiful country of the Surrey-Sussex border. At present, however, the canal bank can be followed—at least legitimately—for only a mile or two at a time, and the walk would deteriorate into a frustrating shuttle between footpath, farm track and minor road. It would be worth trying, at least in parts, but the achievement of the complete through route must depend upon the effective collaboration of national and local authorities, voluntary associations and, most vital of all, the landowners.

While this Wey-Arun Way remains a dream, one must make do with a less exciting road journey which, if it is pursued discreetly, may surprise those whose acquaintance with Surrey and Sussex is confined to the Portsmouth road and Brighton front.

12

The real problem is where to start. Not that there is any doubt about the route. Historically, and in present-day reality, the Wey Navigation begins at the mouth of the river just north of the town centre of Weybridge. No one would dispute the fact. What is in question is whether one would want to endure the congested roads of this ceaselessly active area, unable to escape, as can the walker and the navigator, on the cool green reaches of the river. Those who find outer suburbia especially hard to bear might skip the first few miles and pick up the threads of the journey on the Portsmouth Road at Wisley Common. For hardier souls the start is around the packed, but superior, houses of Thameside between Weybridge and Walton, whence the navigation makes its way under the main road just to the west of the hub of Weybridge.

Weybridge is, surprisingly, very much more interesting than it seems at first glance. Under every commuter town lies buried the village from which it grew, but most commonly the detritus lies too deep for penetration without an archaeologist's spade. Weybridge's bone structure is fine—to vary the image—and it shows through the mess and clutter and the, for the most part, third-rate architectural thinking of the present century. Although only an inn or two and a few good houses remain from the eighteenth century, and nothing shows above ground of the great royal palace of Oatlands, and of the succeeding and no less lavish mansion of the 'grand old Duke of York' very little, the story of the town and its great residents is told most effectively in the admirable local museum, a model of its kind.

At Weybridge the seventeenth-century navvies cut a new channel, leaving the River Wey to wander unfettered around the base of St George's Hill. The scene is so encumbered now that it is difficult to see the scene through the eyes of Richard Weston of Sutton Place and his fellow investors in the navigation, much less through those of the Iron Age tribesmen who raised the earth banks of the fort crowning the hill. Today St George's carries its burden of houses as well as a golf course and its tactical value may not be apparent. Wipe the scene clean of all buildings, and the hill emerges as a most effective eminence commanding the peninsula between Wey, Thames and Mole; the faded ramparts assume meaning, whether as a tribal refuge or as a base for offensive action against a passing enemy. Beneath the hill, and trapped on the island between Wey and navigation, is another reminder of the ruthless passage of time, the remains of Brooklands where the early history of motor-racing was written in oil and blood.

A little to the west of Brooklands the Wey Navigation parts company with its offspring, the Basingstoke Canal, which was completed in 1794 and which creates, in the manner of canals, a narrow band of green through the densely packed area of Woking. At this point neither navigation nor canal is accessible except on foot—or by boat—and road travellers must take them on trust. By road the route is neither clear nor attractive. The best that can be done is to leave Weybridge by the road running between St George's Hill and Brooklands, following the Wey valley, and when this ends veer east and then south, passing one of the characteristics ponds of the Surrey heathland, to reach the Portsmouth Road at a point overlooking—if it wasn't for the trees in between—the River Mole. The Portsmouth Road, although certainly busy, is attractive here as it crosses Ockham Common and passes Balder Mere, another and a more accessible road. At its busiest and most congested Surrey is constantly redeeming itself with these patches of sandy woodland, often unfenced and open to walkers and riders, which afford welcome relief from urban pressures.

At the next right turn, our route goes north and so do the many motorists bound for the delights of Wisley. Just off the main road the Royal Horticultural Society have taken advantage of the Wey, here making one of its characteristic loops and depositing alluvium on top of the sand, and have established a magnificent series of experimental and show gardens. Those who have been wise enough to join the society may enter free; others may on most days pay for this inestimable privilege. The gardens, although of great scientific interest and importance, have not the clinical atmosphere of the laboratory. They are gardens in the great English tradition; that is, they rate architecture above horticulture. Each enclosed area has its master design, dictated by landscape considerations, into which the fine details of individual plants are fitted with enormous skill. Because the emphasis is on design the gardens are beautiful at every season; one may have a preference for spring bulbs or for the fantasy of gigantic dahlias, but the gardens are above such personal considerations.

Wisley Common is perhaps best seen in spring and autumn, when the foliage is thin and not of a uniform greenness. The village is so small as to be passed almost without notice, but individual cottages deserve attention. Last of all comes the tiny church which is late Norman work at its humblest, too unimportant to attract the worst attentions of the restorers and consequently still keeping its patina of age. The lane bends here and just beyond crosses the navigation at a point which displays its charms most effectively. Pub, bridge and lock are in their classic positions, and the water, green and cool on the hottest and bluest of days, invites closer acquaintance. If time does not press, the three-mile towpath walk up to Newark would be rewarding, especially if a friend can be persuaded to pick you up at the other end. At the half-way point the River Wey comes alongside and river and navigation march together until, just before Newark, they divide and the river splits into a confusing multitude of streams.

If time is important, the hour's walk can be transformed, at great loss of enjoyment, into five minutes of driving along the narrow twisting lane to Pyrford, where a busier road takes over. There should anyway be time for a short walk to Pyrford Church which is perched high above the road on a little sandy bluff. This would be my choice for the prettiest small village church in Surrey. Its architectural detail is marginally richer than Wisley's, of about the same age, and its situation is greatly appealing.

Pyrford belonged to the Augustinian Priory of Newark, and the little church looks down to the ruins of its parent on the river bank. This is a perfect textbook site for a monastery, secluded, austere—in medieval times, amply supplied with water, and with a useful connection with the economic realities of secular life in a nearby mill. What remains above ground is mostly from the eastern half of the priory church. It yields little of its secrets to the casual visitor, but the grey crumbled walls are exceedingly picturesque in this watery setting. Newark is presumably the New Work, new, that is, late in the twelfth century when the canons first moved here from an earlier settlement.

Newark Priory, although so near Pyrford, is in Send parish and the village is two miles along a lane which keeps close contact with the navigation for most of the way. We are still well within the influence of the big commuter conurbations and Woking, a heathside village now monstrously swollen by the railway into a sizeable town which can scarcely seem beautiful save to those who call it home, is just across the river. Send still manages to retain some of its village character, aided by proximity to the river. (All riverside places enjoy an unfair advantage over their earthbound neighbours.) While we are so near, we might risk a foray across the Wey—beyond the navigation—to visit the original parish church of Woking which stands right on the river and is literally the last building in the parish. Some pretty houses survive near it. The church is larger than those we have seen so far on this journey, and it even has the distinction—comparatively rare in Surrey —of a battlemented tower. A very plain Norman doorway in the tower still retains its original door, complete with elegant ironwork. Like most of the oldest surviving ironwork in this country—there is a fine example at Staplehurst in Kent—this has a Norse feeling in its elaborate dragon-like curlicues and half moons, as if Thor himself had beaten them on his subterranean anvil.

We should be well advised not to press farther north into the expensive commuter estates, and, although I could spend a pleasant day on foot between river and navigation, getting a kind of scenic bonus from the very nearness of the urban mass to this most peaceful scene, we must get on, for the journey is scarcely begun. Where the main road makes a sharp turn over the navigation at Send a minor road goes almost due south in company with the stream. After a mile and more a drive off the road gives approach to Send church, as remote from its village, and from most other houses, as possible. It is a pretty riverside scene and the building has some antiquarian interest, but for me the charm of Send church is in direct ratio to its remoteness. The pressures on land in the Guildford area are enormous, yet here a little scrap of rural Surrey survives miraculously. For how long? Its very existence constitutes a challenge to the developer, who may even now be calling for his bulldozer.

The threat to our peace becomes reality in the next mile, for the lane past Send Grove dumps us helplessly on the Portsmouth Road. We may choose a temporary respite in another mile and turn right across the traffic through Burpham, now a suburb of Guildford. There is a sudden return to Arcadia at the bridge where water-meadows stretch to the wooded belt sheltering Sutton Place from the vulgar gaze.

Sutton is not for visitors, but it is a house to recall in our present context, for here was the genesis of the Wey Navigation. The great brick and terracotta mansion was built in Henry VIII's reign by Sir Richard Weston. Sir Richard's son was one of the gay young men of the court and with some of his friends paid for his gaiety with his life when Anne Boleyn fell. Despite this nominal treason the house was not confiscated—it must not have appealed to the King's aesthetic sense or even to his cupidity—and it passed in time to another Sir Richard in Charles I's reign. Sutton Park, as you may readily see, is half encompassed by the river, and it was regularly inundated in the wet season. Sir Richard was one of the modern men of his time, with a taste for technology. He travelled in the Low Countries and studied the way the Flemings controlled their rivers with locks. These devices, by which the water was impounded within walls, unlike the primitive flash locks which simply provided a temporary passage through a weir, were already in limited use on the Thames. Sir Richard experimented with a pound lock on his own river and when the results proved satisfactory he put up a scheme to make the Wey navigable. Then the Civil War broke out and Sir Richard, a Royalist and a Papist too, was in trouble and had to escape the country. When the King's cause was irretrievably lost, he negotiated his return to Sutton. In 1650 he revived his Wey Navigation scheme, through the intermediary of Guildford Corporation, and an Act was duly passed in the following year. Sir Richard was the principal shareholder and the most energetic protagonist of the scheme. Unfortunately one of his partners, an Ironside officer named Pitson, was either incompetent or a rogue, and Weston found himself in financial straits and died before he could sort out his affairs. The resulting legal wrangles went on for years, long after the navigation had been completed. Sir Richard Weston may perhaps be regarded as the first martyr to the cause of inland waterways, but not the last. In addition to his canal work, he was a pioneer of scientific farming, a notable theorist of the rotation of crops and a successful practitioner of his theories. In this way he found a use for talents which, as a Catholic, he was unable to exercise in the normal activities of his class, by service to Parliament and the shire. Had Sir Richard lived he would surely have become a foundation member of the Royal Society and in the company of his peers would have found the satisfaction which just eluded him at Sutton.

In his work Sir Richard had the support, and sometimes the hindrance, of Guildford, and the town was a principal beneficiary of his navigation scheme. Now, after indulging in a flourish of curves as if to demonstrate its freedom from the Weston bonds, the River Wey doubles back upon itself and rejoins the navigation, and the united stream enters the built-up area of the town. Here we cannot pursue it, except on foot, and we must therefore head southwards past Stoke Park, most agreeable of urban open spaces, to the head of the most celebrated, and still perhaps the finest, high street in south-east England.

Kingston may possess its coronation stone, on which the last seven Saxon kings—before the Danish conquest—were crowned, but Guildford has always been the county town and the centre for the administration of justice. This is not perhaps as great a distinction as it might be in some other counties. Surrey was a slow starter. The poor soil, mostly either chalk down, sand or clay, did not attract the more selective of Saxon settlers, and so the county grew slowly and remained poor. It may never have been a full kingdom of Saxon England, staying under the domination of one or another of its prosperous and politically active neighbours. Guildford however was clearly designed by nature for an important role. The narrow gap in the downs through which the Wey flowed gave it strategic importance, and the river enriched the surrounding meadows. There was probably a settlement of some kind from the earliest times. The later Saxon kings held the manor. William the Conqueror retained it among the towns reserved to the Crown, for obvious reasons; it offered a perfect site for one of the ring of castles which were to surround his capital. An earlier motte must have been thrown up here very soon after the Conquest. Indeed, there was probably some fortification before this, for that wily old strategist, Earl Godwin, had an interest in the place, and he would not have left it undefended.

The original earthen motte was later reinforced with a shell keep, but Guildford Castle was drastically updated by Henry II, who built the surviving stone keep and so effectively commanded the Wey gap. The castle however lost its strategic role fairly soon. It saw action during John's war with the invading French, but that was really its first and last military adventure. The stresses of the kingdom were felt elsewhere, and Guildford Castle deteriorated into being first a minor royal fortress and palace, then the county gaol. It had, however, served its purpose in establishing the town beyond its gates, and the town flourished as the castle decayed. It acquired useful patrons, like the Mores of Loseley who worshipped at St Nicholas by Guildford Town Bridge and in due time lay to rest there, and the Westons of Sutton who favoured Holy Trinity at the top of the town. Then there was George Abbot, who was born here and in the days of his greatness as Primate of All England remembered his home town and gave it its finest building.

Prosperity has not deserted Guildford. It is as bright and lively a town as can be found. Perhaps it has lost some of its characteristic style in recent years, under the dreadful disease of levelling down which attacks every urban community. Vigorous efforts have been made to eliminate the town's personality, and they have not been altogether unsuccessful. Still it survives, its shops a little more interesting than any of its neighbours, its modern buildings not quite as bad as some. It has that precious rarity among southern English towns, an active live theatre dedicated to the memory of the most dearly loved of actresses, Yvonne Arnaud—who lies in the churchyard of St Martha's high on the sandy ridge above the town. It has—and this is still its most valued possession—the river. To this must be added such trifles as a new cathedral and a university, as well as many miles of undistinguished and expensive houses. All in all, a town to be reckoned with.

Apart from a mention in King Alfred's will, Guildford's first emergence from anonymity is associated with one of the most grisly episodes in Saxon history. When Harold Harefoot, Canute's unworthy son, was on the throne, Alfred, who was the elder son of Ethelred the Unready by his second wife Emma and consequently Harold's half-brother, entered England to visit his mother in Winchester. The Anglo-Saxon Chronicle puts the blame for what followed squarely on to Earl Godwin. At Guildford Godwin set upon Alfred and his Norman followers, decimated the band and took the prince off to Ely where he was blinded and finally murdered. The whole story is mysterious. Was the attack unprovoked, or was Alfred making a bid for power in the confusion which followed the death of Canute? He would hardly have made a worse job of kingship than Harold and his horrible brother Harthacanute. Godwin was presumably backing what he thought would be the winning side, or more reputably he was giving his support to the king elected by the Great Council according to law; anyway he was activated by a lifelong dislike of Normans. Whether or not the story is literally true, it lay behind the antipathy which Edward the Confessor, Alfred's younger brother, always felt for his great earl, and which helped to push him ever farther into the Norman camp. One might thus even say that one of the seeds of the Norman Conquest was sown in Guildford.

Of Saxon Guildford only a few stones remain in the tower of St Mary's, the cramped church in the middle of the town. The tower was retained when the church was rebuilt at about the time of the remodelling of the castle, and the new building was wrapped around its sturdy walls with their typical flat pilasters. Chapels were added later in the Middle Ages as the town prospered, to produce the complex building which survives. There were two other medieval parish churches: 'High Church', which is Holy Trinity, and 'Low Church' just beyond the bridge, which is St Nicholas. Holy Trinity was substantially rebuilt in the eighteenth century in a not very exciting style. It served as the cathedral of the new diocese until the new cathedral was built. St Nicholas belongs to the late nineteenth century, except for the very attractive chantry chapel of the Mores of Loseley.

Except perhaps for St Mary's the churches of Guildford—and I include the cathedral—are not of the first interest. The castle too, slighted not by enemies but by indifference and misuse, has neither the romantic history nor the grandeur of Dover or Rochester. The castle gardens make a welcome splash of colour in the middle of the busy town, but the buildings are mainly of interest to the informed antiquarian. The visual highlights of Guildford are not here but in the High Street, in which there are three marked accents at different levels of the steep highway. At the top, near Holy Trinity, is the flat stone façade of the grammar school, a foundation of Henry VII's reign to which Edward VI added an endowment and thereby, rather half-heartedly, gave it a royal title. Below this, and on the opposite side almost facing Holy Trinity, is Abbot's hospital, by far the finest building in the town. Below this again is the splendidly ostentatious town hall, its overhang, cupola and enormous projecting clock altogether dominating the scene. We may not admire it all critically, but this is what we remember most about Guildford.

George Abbot was born in Guildford in Queen Elizabeth's reign. For a provincial family of no great wealth or standing the Abbots did remarkably well. George's eldest brother Robert became Master of Balliol and Bishop of Salisbury, and Maurice was knighted by James I and became Lord Mayor of London and Governor of the East India Company in the vital years of its growth, while George himself rose, despite a profound and unpopular Calvinism, to be Archbishop of Canterbury. His was a stormy career, if one so uniformly gloomy could be said to produce anything as dynamic as a storm. Not a conventionally attractive character, Abbot's happiest moments are associated with his native town, in his deep and lasting love for his parents and in the gift which he made to the town largely as a memorial to them. In 1619, when his public life was entering a new and difficult phase, he took time off to lay the foundation stone of the Hospital of the Holy Trinity, for a master, twelve brethren and eight sisters, which he built at his own cost and endowed richly. Abbot was not as self-consciously a prince of the Church as some of his predecessors on the throne of St Augustine, but here at least was a truly princely gift. In the private suite which he provided for himself he spent perhaps the most rewarding years of a not conspicuously happy life.

Abbot modelled his foundation on the hospital, also dedicated to the Holy Trinity, founded at Croydon by Whitgift, his predecessor at Canterbury, and the layout at Guildford follows the Croydon pattern closely. Abbot's Hospital was however on an altogether more lavish scale. Where Whitgift is homely Abbot is in architectural terms positively spectacular. The four octagonal towers of the gatehouse, with their onion caps, might belong to one of the great mansions of the Elizabethan age or to an Oxford college. Any suggestion of worldly extravagance, so alien to the spirit of the old puritan, is denied by the fine and unobtrusive craftsmanship of the rich red brickwork and the good taste of all the detail of windows and doorframes. Abbot's hospital continues its good work today, and the quadrangle, hall and chapel of the foundation offer a miraculous haven of quiet in the heart of the modern town.

The Wey makes no great visual impact as it flows through the northern part of the town below Stag Hill on which the cathedral sits. It emerges into view at the foot of the High Street where the theatre contributes effectively to the riverside scene. The wharf has been tidied up in recent years, with a little loss of authenticity, but the massive crane operated by a treadmill housed in the adjacent weatherboard shed still hints at a commercial activity which has long departed.

Beyond Guildford the river passes between two parallel main roads, and there is here a choice of routes. The westerly road, heading for Godalming, has the advantage of giving access to St Catherine's Hill, the easterly heads in the right direction for the Wey and Arun Canal. It would certainly be a pity to miss St Catherine's, which gives a fine bird's-eye view of the river as it passes through the deep cleft in the North Downs. A short chalky track leads off the road to the hilltop on which stand the battered remains of St Catherine's Chapel. The Pilgrims Way crosses the river just below and mounts the opposite hill to the chapel of St Martha. The existence of these two ancient buildings on the trackway are arguments in support of those who believe that the Way was precisely what its romantic Victorian name suggests, a major pilgrim route of medieval England. The matter remains unproven. St Martha's at any rate seems to have been a very ancient foundation, and the early Christian missionaries had a fancy for hilltop shrines, especially those associated with anything as mysterious as a prehistoric trackway. The beginnings of St Catherine's are obscure. The chapel was already old when the rector of St Nicholas, Guildford, restored or rebuilt it early in the fourteenth century. The roofless remains are substantial but not very informative. The chapel is tall in proportion to height and width, and it seems to have had, like the nearby church of Compton, an upper storey which was perhaps provided to house some precious relic.

South of St Catherine's, road and river head for Godalming where the navigation, extended from Guildford in 1763, comes to an end. The official notice of this extension—reproduced in B. A. L. Vine's valuable *London's Lost Route to the Sea* (1965)—shows that the traffic was in heavy goods like timber and coal, as well as "woollen rags and other kinds of manure". Beyond Godalming the Wey, unfettered by locks, wanders in a series of big loops from its source across the Hampshire border, passing the English mother house of the Cistercian Order at Waverley and many delectable villages. This, however, is departing too far from our brief, for the route to the English Channel goes steadily south as the Wey swings westward.

For the Wey and Arun Canal one takes the Shalford road out of Guildford, crossing the water-meadows of Wey and Tillingbourne on which the greatest of the Surrey fairs was held. It would be pleasant to believe that Bunyan, who has a connection with the parish, was thinking of Shalford when he wrote his terrible description of Vanity Fair, but like most speculations about the Pilgrims Way hard evidence is lacking. The best thing in Shalford today is a very handsome watermill on the Tillingbourne, which now belongs to the National Trust.

A little south of this a road goes left towards Albury and another west to Godalming, and then the southward road crosses a small waterway. This is the Wey and Arun Canal, fresh from its parting with the Wey Navigation, and for the next four miles it passes not far away from the road between Bramley on the west bank and Wonersh on the east.

Wonersh is associated with one of the staunchest opponents of the canal enterprise, Lord Grantley of Wonersh Park. Lord Grantley was in fact one of the original supporters of the Bill, but when he found that the canal would pass through his own land he had a sudden change of mind. One may sympathize with the poor man, for the canal was destined to cut his park neatly down the middle, and there was no practicable alternative route. His demands for compensation were perhaps extortionate; the compensation was paid however, and the noble lord, reconciled to his fate, played his full ceremonial part at the opening of the canal in 1816.

There is a curious sequel. Just thirty years after the great September celebrations which launched the Wey and Arun an Act was passed to build a railway along the same course as the canal and offering the earlier enterprise the most direct competition. The scheme was opposed most bitterly—by Lord Grantley, the third Baron this time and not less vigorous in defence of his own than his father. He failed, the railway was built and the canal ruined. When the canal was finally abandoned Lord Grantley objected again, this time to having to fill in the channel across his estate.

The valley has now almost disappeared under houses and the railway has gone the way of the canal; perhaps even more completely, for the canal is still partly in water—and efforts are being made to revive it— while the embankment of the railway only occasionally appears in the landscape. At Rushett Common, where the first road since Bramley leaves the main road, there are glimpses of both canal and railway, companionable in their mutual ruin.

This piece of country, where the canal faced its major challenge as it climbed to the watershed between the valleys of Wey and Arun, is one of the loveliest in this journey. Often border country produces the finest from both partners, and here, where Surrey approaches Sussex, its beauty is most richly satisfying, not less because it is quiet and unspectacular. The altitudes are inconsiderable, the main road rising only to 229 feet, but on either side the wooded hills rise quite steeply. This is the country of the lower greensand, the companion ridge which marches very roughly parallel to the chalk of the North Downs. Normally the chalk is the dominant partner, although in Surrey the highest land is reserved for the greensand which reaches its climax to the east in Leith Hill. The nearer spurs of the ridge are more modest but still, in a relative sense, impressive. To the west the green, heavily-wooded swell conceals the earth ramparts of Hascombe Hill while over to the east is Holmbury Hill with an almost bald summit. These are both hill-forts of the Iron Age, perhaps refuges for tribesmen engaged in extracting iron from the forest below the ridge. Nearer at hand, at a lower level but more immediately attractive, is Winterfold Heath, where new forests give way occasionally to typical Surrey heathland with long views into the Weald. Here are some of the characteristic hollow ways of the greensand, deep-cut tracks sometimes converted to modern byways, more often offering the walker a memorable stroll. If Surrey has some of the most densely populated country in the south, here by contrast houses lie very thin on the ground and one may walk for half a day without seeing another human being.

One simple basic necessity of a canal is in short supply in the high country—water. However skilfully the bargeman may operate, he inevitably squanders water on his passage through the locks and this must be replenished. Not far from the summit of the canal the engineers constructed a reservoir, linking it with the canal by two miles of leat. Their work was eased because there was already a pond in being at Vachery. Indeed there had been a hammer pond here from the sixteenth century in the heyday of the iron industry. This was south of the present Vachery House in Cranleigh parish, and was made by damming the winding wealden stream which still drains the country just west of Stane Street. This, however, was abandoned in Elizabeth's reign, and was probably out of water by the early eighteenth century. However, the owner of Vachery House made himself an ornamental water in the fashion of the times, and this the canal company leased, strengthening the bay and raising the banks to provide a good flow of water even in the dry season.

Vachery Pond is still an important feature of the Surrey Weald, especially when seen from the heights of Winterfold Heath or Coney-hurst Hill. It is worth a visit, for those willing to walk, because al-though the park is private a public track goes right around it, passing the pond at its outflow. The track starts just east of the built-up area of Cranleigh and the round trip takes in also the fringe of Baynards Park where Sir George More, whom we met at Loseley (Chapter 6), built a mansion to rival the principal family seat. (In fact he built on to an earlier house which was associated with that most attractive of all Tudor women, Margaret Roper, and here, according to a persistent tradition, she preserved the severed head of her saintly father, Sir Thomas More, until it could find a final resting-place in the family vault in Canterbury.)

Large as Vachery Pond is, it was never fully successful in keeping traffic moving on the canal. Major errors had been made in the initial surveying of the canal, and it was always vulnerable in the dry season—and subject to severe flooding in the wet. After some years of unsatis-factory working two windmills were built to pump water back to the upper levels. Even these were not sufficient and the mills, extremely costly to erect, lasted barely twenty years. Even without the competi-tion of the railways, the Wey and Arun Canal did poor business except when a wet—but not too wet—season allowed the traffic to flow freely.

From our diversion to Vachery Pond we return to the canal as it crosses the watershed and begins its quicker descent towards the Arun. Just outside Cranleigh to the west a minor road goes left and this converges on the canal which it touches at the junction with the main Horsham-Guildford road. Here contact is lost again as the canal continues west and we are forced south on the main road. At Alfold Crossways however, another minor road turns towards the channel which it reaches a little beyond Lakers Green at the inn—'The Compasses'—which played an important part in the early history of the canal. The lane goes on parallel with the canal and crosses its dry bed on the edge of Sidney Wood, and then goes on to Dunsfold. Having come so far, one should go on to see this extremely charming village with its wide common, varied cottages—which offer a quick summary of all the mannerisms, materials and styles of South Country domestic architecture, and the remote and beautiful church. There are those who would say that in the 'folds'—Dunsfold, Alfold, Chiddingfold—the best of Surrey villages are to be found, and I would not deny this. There is something sharply appealing about places which have survived the onslaught of industry, as we have discovered in the iron country. Here, in these rich wooded valleys of the Sussex border, is the site of a glass industry which flourished through the later Middle Ages. (The fascinating story is told in full detail in G. H. Kenyon, *Glass Industry of the Weald*, 1967.)

However we have come too far off the route and must return to Sidney Wood. Here the canal builders faced their biggest challenge in taking the canal down a steep slope, engineering a series of considerable curves and losing altitude through a succession of eight locks. The work was done clumsily enough, so that the maximum difficulty was given to the barges with the maximum loss of water. Much of the channel can be seen on foot in Sidney Wood, which is traversed by several public paths, and except in very wet weather the bed is dry. For those who are sensitive to the charm of ruins, this is a place charged with a peculiar nostalgia, for all that the canal was both a materialistic and an unsuccessful commercial venture. And even if these long-abandoned channels, ruined locks and overgrown towpaths speak no message from the past, the scenery is enchanting and the walk rewarding in aesthetic as well as archaeological terms.

In the woods one may easily stray across the county boundary. To continue the route, we backtrack past Lakers Green. Here the official opening ceremony of the canal took place in September 1816, with drinks at 'The Compasses' followed by a ceremonial cruise down the canal to Guildford. We cannot emulate the latter, but refreshment may still be had at the inn which owed its existence to the canal and has long outlived its begetter. At Alfold Crossways we follow a secondary road south to Alfold. The village is small and has its share of attractive cottages, as well as a pretty, homely church just back from the road. Such a village rarely qualifies, thank goodness, for much of a mention in the guidebooks and most travellers keep moving. For me much of the delight of the Alfolds of this world is their low key; in not striving for fame and distinction they achieve something at least as precious, harmony and self-sufficiency. "If these delights thy mind may move", stop in Alfold and stroll along its single back lane or sample the quiet pleasures of its field tracks to capture a fleeting whiff of the authentic Surrey. Then in half a mile Surrey gives place to Sussex, and the road continues through Loxwood to cross the canal once again just outside the village.

The scene is changing again. The high hills of the greensand are left behind and, although there are sufficient differences in level to forestall any accusation of flatness, there are no real eminences this side of the wall of the South Downs. The Weald sustains its reputation for woodland, but much open country provides variety. Over to the west the irregular country around Plaistow is the home of Sussex marble, a limestone richly encrusted with shells—there is a comparable phenomenon in the green sand far to the east at Bethersden in Kent. The worked product—it takes a good polish—may be seen in local churches, and the unfinished stone is used to surface old paths. To the south lies a broad bank of wealden clay, which is still rich in oak trees.

The main road south will lead quickly to the end of the canal at Newbridge, but it keeps well away from the channel and for the most part lacks interest. It will be better to leave the road in Loxwood village and travel two or three miles eastward to the first turning right. This lane, narrow and steep, quickly reaches the canal bank, here taken over by a little stream, at Drungewick. The moated manor house is a reminder of an age when canals were unknown. The stream, which has come out of the 'fold' country and which has lost the brick aquaduct which carried the canal across its course, is here at the last stage of its independence and in the next mile it enters the Arun.

The Arun—originally the Tarrant but renamed in deference to the town and the great castle on its banks—is the major river of West Sussex. In its origin it is an iron stream, for several of its many feeders flow out of St Leonard's Forest and they provide water for the great hammer ponds outside Horsham. Another of the headwaters delighted —for he was always fascinated by streams—the infant Shelley, whose birthplace was Warnham Court on the western side of the town. The Arun has taken tribute of its upper feeders by the time it crosses Stane Street, and when it reaches the canal near Gibbon's Mill it is a sizeable stream. For the next five miles the canal utilized the course of the river and borrowed its water. In time of spate the generosity of the stream was embarrassing, and the Wey and Arun Canal, whose enemy for half the year was drought, was in the other months liable to be engulfed by the exuberant floodwaters of its lively young neighbour.

None of this country of the upper Arun is easily accessible either by road or on foot, and one must be content to follow the lane past

Drungewick back to the main road and thence uneventfully to New-bridge.

The Arun had been navigable up to Newbridge for a good thirty years before the Wey and Arun Canal completed the link with the Thames. As for the 'New' bridge, this was so called early in the seventeenth century and in the typical English way was the oldest bridge within a very wide radius. When the canal came here its wharf was already a going concern, especially in the transport of iron and timber. The completion of the canal brought the wharf further into prominence. It had a warehouse and an inn, as well as a full-time officer to superintend the traffic.

Of all this busyness little remains. The warehouse still stands, but the canal has decayed. (A big notice proclaiming "Wey and Arun Canal Restoration" promises well.) The last tolls were taken in 1888. The pub has moved away. Meanwhile, across the bridge passes an endless flow, for this is the A272, a valued relief route to the west. Anyone who stops here to indulge in a melancholy reflection on the mutability of human fortune does so at his peril.

The upper stages of the Arun Navigation flow well away from roads, and one must for the most part take them on trust because they are inaccessible. Where navigation and river part company the canal is mostly out of water while the river flows unfettered in a series of loops. A new footpath here would open up a rewarding area of quietly charming country.

Road-bound motorists must turn from these delights and follow the westward road to Wisborough Green. Here is a good place to stop, with such attractions as pubs, a wealth of good houses and a green on which cricket is played. There could scarcely be a more comprehensive summary of all the essential ingredients of a Sussex village. The church, standing apart on a little knoll, has an appropriate individuality, its Norman and later elements blended to produce a building at once charming and full of character. The dedication—most unusually—is to St Peter ad Vincula (St Peter in Chains), like the chapel in the Tower of London. There is a little of the siren in Wisborough Green: pause for a brief rest here and you may find your halt extended to include a meal, and if the local team is playing late into a summer evening there may be nothing for it but to stay the night. There could be far worse fates.

The next stage of the journey is highly enjoyable but mostly irrelevant. The road out of Wisborough Green, and its first turning left, take the traveller away from the river and from thoughts of commercial traffic, into high wooded country, along lanes at times positively steep and always narrow, always lovely and in spring and autumn breath-taking with their soft and richly varied tones. From this

enchantment we descend to the realities of the bustling Pulborough
road at Fittleworth, where there is little time for anything but the next
traffic problem.

Despite its traffic Fittleworth is a very charming village, rich in
fine cottages. The best of the village is off our route, to the south at
Lower Fittleworth where the prettiest of Sussex streams, the Rother,
flows under an old stone bridge, and west where the Petworth road
skirts a high breezy common. The village makes a base for exploring
some of the finest Sussex country: the villages of the Rother valley,
Bignor's Roman villa and the course of Stane Street across Bignor Hill,
Burton and its great pond, and not far away the park and palace of
Petworth. All beautiful, memorable and, sadly, not much to the purpose of this journey. So, turning away from these delights we go east
along the main road until it reaches our watery objective at one of its
most celebrated points, Stopham Bridge (see Chapter 7). The loveliest
and perhaps the oldest bridge in Sussex proved an obstacle to barge
traffic. For more than thirty years the low arches prevented full exploitation of the navigation. When the new Wey and Arun Canal
increased the potential of the waterway, pressure to improve the flow
of traffic increased and in 1822 the central arch of the fourteenth-
century bridge was rebuilt at a higher level. (The same thing happened
to medieval bridges on all the navigable rivers, as anyone familiar
with, for example, Aylesford and Teston on the Medway will know.)
Familiarity has taken away some of the incongruity of this change,
but Stopham lost some of the perfection of its line in the remodelling.
It is still a singularly fine structure, especially when viewed from downstream. A little farther along the road, there is a track across the meadow
to the river at the point where it is joined by the last stage of the Rother
Navigation, here running dead straight while the River Rother goes
into an exuberant loop before it reaches the parent river.

Of all the enterprises stimulated by the canal craze the Rother
Navigation was surely the least promising. Canals served industry,
and, even by Sussex standards, the Rother valley was not industrial.
The project was the inspiration of one of the greatest of Sussex landowners, George Wyndham, third Earl of Egremont, whose home was
at Petworth. Egremont was a man of enormous wealth, and he had the
style and the sense to spend it effectively. The Petworth which we
visit today was largely of his making, for he laid the foundations of its
art collection which dominates the interior of the house and he introduced reforms in husbandry for which the estate was famous. An
energetic, generous and resourceful man, contemptuous of convention,
a patron of art with a flair for recognizing genius, he gave Turner the
freedom of his estates, with notable results. He saw canals not as a
source of even more wealth but as a contribution to the well being of

Newark Priory

Wey-Arun Canal

his county. With this in mind he backed the Wey and Arun Canal with influence and money, and when this was done he launched single-handed a scheme to make the Rother navigable to Midhurst. The enormous cost of the scheme, which included eight locks, three wharfs and a basin at Midhurst, was borne exclusively by the Earl, and he used his own direct labour. This was a novelty and one which was greatly appreciated in the locality. Usually the heavy work of cutting the new waterways was undertaken by imported labourers, the navvies, whose rough language and behaviour made life a hell for residents to whom these high spirits were an unwelcome novelty. Egremont's own farm labourers took on this work as a well-paid extra, and if they swore and got drunk they at least did it like true men of Sussex. No wonder Sussex loved the great Earl and readily forgave him his sexual adventures and the eccentricity which prompted him to install his favourite mistress at Petworth, postponing his marriage to her until, apparently, all affection was spent.

The Rother has reverted to a pretty but insignificant stream, and of the work of Egremont's amateur navvies little remains. The cuts which reduced the length of the river mostly survive in water, notable near South Ambersham, but of the locks and wharfs scarcely a shadow remains. The navigation never made a profit, but that was not in the noble earl's mind when he launched his enterprise. His reward lay in the benefit which this new lifeline conferred on his neighbours and tenants, as the navigation opened up new markets for them.

At Stopham Bridge the Arun, whose course for several miles has been southerly with only minor deviations, swings east in the biggest of all its loops. The main road follows the river for the best part of three miles right into the centre of Pulborough before it turns south again and works its way back past Greatham Bridge. The floor of the valley is only a few feet above sea level here and is obviously vulnerable to flooding. To the engineers of the Arun Navigation this presented a problem which called for a drastic answer.

Before seeking the solution however, we should take time off to look at Pulborough, which is a little town of quite exceptional charm and interest. The Roman Stane Street crossed the river here, encouraging the development of a Romanized British settlement. The site was so attractive and rich in amenities that the Saxons, who normally preferred to avoid the works of their predecessors, could not resist it. The medieval village grew, adding a fine stone bridge and some big houses. In the coaching age the emphasis shifted from Stane Street to the east-west road, and Pulborough acquired its quota of staging inns. Modern developments have been kinder here than in many Sussex towns. The water-meadows have effectively limited growth to the south, and the town consequently comes to an abrupt halt, almost as if it were a seaside resort. For once the visual delights are general rather than particular, although the church is attractive in detail as well as in setting, and Old Place and New Place merit a closer look. Park Mound, which lies beyond Old Place and is accessible by track, is a big defensive earth-work superbly placed above the Rother and looking down to the Stopham crossing, probably a Norman motte and this perhaps utilizing an older mound.

Pulborough was the biggest place on the upper Avon Navigation. It had road links and local industry, notably quarried stone, for which water offered the most satisfactory form of transportation. The wharf there was kept busy. There remained the problem of the tortuous river loop. In 1789 the Avon Navigation Company took the bold step of beginning a tunnel through the hill at Coldwaltham to bypass the Pulborough loop. This was finished in the following year. The Hardham Tunnel did not bear comparison with the much longer canal tunnels farther north, but it was by far the most ambitious undertaking in the Wey-Arun scheme.

The cut was started just beyond the point where the Arun turned north-east towards Greatham Bridge. Here the land rises steadily and the tunnel entered the hill and continued NNE for less than a quarter mile, emerging beyond Stane Street close to Hardham Mill, where the Rother enters the Arun. Bargemen had to navigate through the tunnel by 'legging' along the walls or pushing the roof, as there was no towpath. Unfortunately the original engineers were less than ambitious, and they made the tunnel too low and too narrow, so effectively preventing the growth of traffic, and bigger and more profitable craft continued to make the longer trip through Pulborough.

In 1859 the Mid-Sussex railway was built right over the top of the Hardham Tunnel. As the canal declined and maintenance work ceased, this became a potential hazard, and at the end of the century the railway company had the tunnel filled in to roof level.

Coming out of Pulborough by the Arundel road, past the ancient and lovely church of St Botolph (Chapter 7), there is a track right almost opposite the entrance to Hardham Priory which crosses the railway and comes out almost at the lost tunnel. Just over to the left, between railway and river, is all that remains of a Roman staging post on Stane Street. The railway has cut through the site, leaving only one corner exposed. The stage was established where the road crossed the river—the next on Stane Street is at Alfoldean where there was a crossing of the upper Arun—and a branch road went off into the rich corn country of East Sussex.

In the next mile the road passes through Coldwaltham village, which suffers from traffic and is not of the first interest, and then, on the edge of the village, a road goes left over the Hardham cut, crossing the Arun at Greatham Bridge. To the south, reached by a footpath which starts near the bridge, is the flat watery expanse of Amberley Wild Brooks. No place could quite live up to so enchanting a name, but the Wild Brooks—'wild' refers not to the savage aspect of the place but to the Weald—have a highly individual character. These four square miles bounded on one side by the Arun, on the other by the rising ground of Greatham Common and Parham Park, are an admirable habitat for wildfowl, for the area is crossed and recrossed not with wild brooks but with very tame drainage channels. They are most rewardingly visited in winter.

The road from Greatham Bridge continues east to the village, where there is a turning opposite the church leading across the common. Then, when the South Downs come fully into view, displaying almost their most attractive full-face aspect, another road turns westward again to Amberley.

Amberley is of the river but not on it. It played no part in the navigation and gained no particular benefits from it. The village grew up along a low ridge raised above the flood level which in early times must have been a peninsula. The later taming of the river changed its aspect and now, except in the wettest seasons, Amberley stands aloof and self-absorbed on its little hill. It would be, I suppose, on most people's shortlist for the title of prettiest Sussex village, but it encourages neither the competitive spirit nor the visitors attracted by its fair reputation.

Amberley was a manor of the bishops of Chichester, and from an early date an episcopal manor house stood beside the church. During the Hundred Years War, when French raids along the south coast and up the river estuaries became more frequent and violent, the bishop got approval to fortifying his house, which he substantially rebuilt and strengthened with walls and a gatehouse. Lest this seem an inappropriate activity for a man of peace, it must be remembered that bishops had secular as well as spiritual responsibilities, and Bishop Rede held his land at Amberley of the king and was charged with its safe keeping from the king's enemies. There are many parallels to his crenellating Amberley, including the archbishop's castle at Saltwood and the archdeacon's at Lympne, both fortified in this same period. Amberley was never put to the test, and its outlines were softened in the sixteenth century when it passed into lay hands and new apartments appropriate to a peaceful age were added. One can best capture its medieval aspect from below the ridge, where the embattled walls show well.

Amberley Castle stands immediately next to the church. If a natural disaster, or a sudden outbreak of 'redundancy', destroyed all the ancient parish churches except Amberley, here would remain an epitome of what had been lost. This is not to say that here is a building of

outstanding merit; it is a typical building, illustrating, most clearly
the evolutionary growth of the English parish church, to which each
succeeding century adds something characteristic of itself. The original
church was replaced late in the Norman period by one fit for a bishop,
with a grand chancel arch enriched with sophisticated formal decoration. The next age substituted a sanctuary with three slim lancets, and
a west tower followed in the reign of Edward I. When the castle was
being fortified, the church was refurbished and a new doorway inserted. So the process continued, with the late Victorian Age contributing an exquisite window by Robert Anning Bell.

If the village has no outstanding house it has far fewer unworthy
cottages than the average. Styles and materials are pleasantly varied,
with a generous sprinkling of flint—for we are near the chalk—and
thatch.

Isaak Walton commends—it is not clear whether this is from personal experience—"Amerley trout". The river life of Amberley is
centred on the main road bridge and its attendant inn, and the weekend
scene is filled with fishermen; but whether they find trout I know not.

The Arun gap is by far the finest river scene in the South Downs.
To the east the downs are open pasture and arable tricked out with
spinneys, shelter belts and rings which contribute effectively to the
rounded slopes. On the western bank the wooded hills of Arundel
Park are dark and strange. In the mile-wide gap the Arun twists
fantastically, with navigation cuts across the biggest loops. Presumably
through difficulty in negotiating towing rights with the Dukes of
Norfolk, there is no towpath here and barges had to sail or pole though.

It is not possible to explore the gap fully by road. A lane beside
Houghton Bridge peters out at North Stoke. To reach South Stoke
one must go through Arundel and up the lane past the park through
Offham. A good alternative to this unsatisfactory journey is to abandon
a car at Houghton and walk downriver along the bank, making the
return trip by entering the park at Swanbourne Lake and heading for
the riverside gate near Houghton village. This is scenically rewarding
and varied, for the outward trek is almost on one level, while the return
rises to the wooded crown of the park, a steady climb of 400 feet.

By car, the road is followed across the Arun at Houghton Bridge
and through the single street of Houghton, where there are some pretty
cottages and a plain church, up to the big crossroads and roundabout
at Whiteways Lodge. Opposite, there are tracks through Houghton
Forest rising to the open top of the downs at Bignor Hill; one passes
through a not very distinct causeway camp of a Neolithic tribe of the
down country, accompanied by later burial mounds, just before the
summit is reached. The forest has a place in later history, for here
young Charles II, on his long journey from the battlefield of Worcester,

almost literally bumped into the Governor of Arundel Castle. Charles was a great deal less alarmed than his escort. They descended the hill and spent the night in Amberley Castle before going on to Shoreham to take ship for France.

Despite the aggressive roundabout and the traffic, Whiteways is an agreeable high point, and a large car park makes a useful base for walks through Arundel Park and the woodlands. Straight ahead a very beautiful woodland road descends to Fairmile Botton, but our way lies south around the park wall, dropping steadily all the way to Arundel High Street.

By this approach the unique quality of Arundel is not fully appreciated. The approach from the east is more effective, as one comes up to the Arun Bridge. Better still is the view from downstream on the towpath, where the profile of the town on its hill is oddly unreal as if it were the creation of some romantic landscape painter of the French School.

This impression is not altogether uncalculated. The two principal elements in the scene are essential the work of art, not evolution. What one sees of the great Norman castle belongs to the romantic revival of Gothic. The church which disputes with the castle for dominance in the landscape is mid-Victorian Gothic, the deliberate evocation of an unfinished French cathedral. Neither building quite stands up to critical analysis, but neither invites it; they are meant to be seen as a whole in their setting. In evening sunlight they can seem almost unbearably lovely.

Arundel was made by nature to be a major defensive site. It sits in the neck of the Arun gap with tidal water to the sea five miles away. The land rises steeply from the river bank to a ledge from which a fortress can command the land and sea approaches. In any strategy based on command of the Channel its value is obvious. William the Conqueror saw it as a vital link in his chain of south-coast strongpoints and he gave the Honour of Arundel to Roger of Montgomery, a Breton baron and one of his most reliable lieutenants. Here he threw up a typical motte with double bailey which was later reinforced with walls and a stone shell-keep. Roger's son, Robert de Belleme, inherited. All the worst Norman characteristics, treachery, self-seeking, cruelty, were concentrated in this one man, together with great personal courage and intelligence. He played an individual power game against Rufus and Henry I and eventually lost. So the honour returned to the Crown, and passed later to the Fitzalans, Earls of Sussex, who held it right down to the reign of Elizabeth. It then descended to Thomas Howard, Duke of Norfolk, whose descendant, the premier Duke and Earl Marshal of England, holds it today. The medieval castle survived until the seventeenth century, when Norfolk held it for the king in the Civil War. Sir William Waller took it after a short siege during which his artillery reduced it almost to ruin.

By 1644 Arundel Castle had been well and truly 'slighted', in common with most of the other castles which had attracted the attention of the forces of Parliament. Most of them remained in ruins, awaiting the coming of an age which would find their desolation romantically beautiful. Arundel was rebuilt. The Howards clung persistently to their traditional home. The eleventh Duke, a genial eccentric, rebuilt the ruins in what the early nineteenth century, under the spell of Sir Walter Scott's medievalism, considered an appropriate castellated manner. Arundel owes much to the eleventh Duke, known to his contemporaries—and a nickname is a sure sign of affection—as 'Jockey of Norfolk'. He was a huge, clumsy, blundering man, not too nice in his personal habits—the servants took advantage of his bouts of inebriation to wash him down, for, sober, he objected strongly to cleanliness—but strong-minded and uncompromisingly honest. A convinced Whig, he hated kings and was a personal friend of the Prince Regent. Despite his rough manner he was a patron of the arts and one of the sponsors of the classic history of Sussex. The Duke died in the year of Waterloo and in him Arundel lost some of its authentic local colour. At the end of the century, when the builders were again busy restoring and extending the castle, the work was done more correctly and was much less entertaining.

Like Windsor, Arundel today is a castle which is also a palace and a home. Like Windsor too, it reveals beneath all the trappings of a fake medievalism the fine bone-structure of the genuine. From a high point in the castle one looks down on the original motte and bailey, and reads into the scene all the vicissitudes of nine centuries.

The priory which Earl Roger founded under the wing of the castle in the early years of Norman rule did not survive. In its place the celebrated Richard Fitzalan established a college of priests, and he rebuilt the parish church during Richard II's reign in a slightly archaic style and on a scale appropriate to the importance of a great nobleman. This remains, although overshadowed by the neighbouring Catholic church of St Philip Neri. The parish church has one curious feature. It is cut right across the middle by a solid wall. Fitzalans and Howards were buried in the chancel of the church over a period of five centuries. The Howards have mostly been Catholics and traditional leaders of the Catholic community in England. 'Jockey of Norfolk' himself was a Protestant, as befitted his radicalism. Henry, the fourteenth Duke, grew up a not very convinced Anglican, then returned to the old faith and became more Catholic than the Catholics. His successor went one better. In 1877 he took on all the might of the Established Church in a lawsuit over ownership of Arundel Church chancel and at length judgment was given in his favour. Thereafter it became the private property of the dukes.

The nave, transepts and central tower were remodelled to provide all the needs of the parish, while the chancel became a chapel dedicated to the memory of the Fitzalans and their successors. There are some splendid sepulchral memorials and brasses.

The fifteenth Duke, while his legal battle for the Fitzalan Chapel was still going on, put in hand the building of the Catholic chapel just across the road from the parish church, employing as his architect a man named Hansom who won lasting fame by inventing a new form of public transport, the Hansom cab.

The town, which is tilted downhill, has some attractive houses of varied styles. One or two of the shops are outstandingly good, and there is a bright, brisk air about the place. Down by the bridge, where there are a few featureless remains of a maison dieu contemporary with the church, a holiday spirit prevails. It is a good town to visit, to see the church and the chapel and to do the round of the castle. Best of all, there is the park to walk in. This was created, about the time of Waterloo, when the most famous age of landscape design was over, and its naturalism is rather less self-conscious than some of the more celebrated examples of the art. Apart from the lake few of the conventions of landscaping are present, and the designer made his effects by skilful disposition and massing of timber and by leading the eye discreetly and inevitably to the glorious 'Gothic' improbabilities of the castle profile. Nor did he forget that on the gloomiest days the southern horizon would be bright with the thin line of the sea. This wonderful tract of woodland and glade, created for the delight of a duke, is here for our pleasure by the generosity of his descendant. Even if, as I did once, you visit Arundel on the one day in the year when His Grace, to preserve his legal rights, closes the park to the public, all is not lost; a public path crosses the finest part of it, and in walking it you reinforce *your* rights.

In common with other south-eastern rivers the Arun has been affected by the eastward drift of shingle. In early times it flowed eastward after leaving the gap through the downs, eventually joining the Adur. Then, as the mouth of the Adur was closed by shingle, forcing the river to flow east to find another way to the sea, the Arun turned west, making a number of mouths which successively became blocked. At last it found its present outlet at Littlehampton. All these changes of course had not encouraged shipping, although Arundel had been a port of sorts at least from Norman times. An energetic earl of Henry VIII's reign made enormous improvements to the channel and built up banks in an effort to reduce flooding. For the next three centuries the town enjoyed a fair degree of prosperity as a port.

The river flows with strong tides from Arundel to the sea. All the way it is remote from roads and is crossed only once, at Littlehampton. (It is possible to walk all the way along the bank.) A minor road leaves the outskirts of Arundel and goes uneventfully to Climping and so by main road to Littlehampton and the river mouth. On the way there are slight remains of an Augustinian priory and a charming Norman church at Tortington, another pretty and most interesting church at Ford, and a medieval church at Climping. When the Climping road reaches the main coastal road, it crosses straight over first as a public road, then as a bridle track, right to the coast at the ancient manor of Atherington. Littlehampton itself has grown rather too quickly in recent years, but it has style if no individual features of distinction.

Here, I suppose, this journey from Thames to Channel should end. We ought perhaps to find a more notable conclusion to a long and often beautiful trek than this mild and unexciting port and watering-place, and the activities of the nineteenth-century canal builders offer an alternative conclusion.

In 1817 a Bill was placed before Parliament to make a canal between Ford and Portsmouth. The scheme had the formidable support of Lord Egremont and other noblemen, and the Bill passed briskly through its stages. The Portsmouth and Arundel Navigation Company was formed and work began in the following year. On the surface this seemed a straightforward operation. The land between Ford and Chichester Harbour is among the flattest in Sussex, a rich corn-growing plain nowhere rising beyond thirty feet above sea level. In practice difficulties emerged. A great many small streams—called rifes—drain the plain, and these had to be crossed on costly aqueducts. As for the sea-water channels, as fast as they were dredged the tides replaced the mud. The Portsmouth and Arundel was by far the most expensive canal venture in the South-east and the least successful.

The promoters had, figuratively at least, missed the boat. Their motivations were largely political. The long wars with Napoleon had made coastal trading difficult, and beyond the memory of the promoters there had been wars and threats of war. The prospect of a waterway linking London and Portsmouth, always free from enemy attack, was enormously attractive. Napoleon finally fell in 1815. In 1817 the Portsmouth and Arundel Act was passed. The promoters could not be expected to foresee that the danger had past. But habits died hard, and no hostile acts put pressures on traders to change them. No one in fact really wanted the new canal. Only the cut up to Chichester, an afterthought, paid its way. The main canal was virtually dead by the middle of the century, although it lingered on in theory until the 1890s when the company was at last liquidated.

This very expensive error may still be traced upon the ground, and its exploration makes an enjoyable introduction to a part of Sussex which is attractive, fertile and well away from the normal tourist routes. It is a journey which is best made on foot, because, although much of the channel is now barely a shadow across the fields, the towpath has for the most part survived as a pedestrian right of way. If the walk is impracticable, however, a journey by car can be made which will take in the more attractive villages and pick up the canal here and there.

The canal began half a mile south of Ford railway bridge—originally a wooden bridge on rollers which could be run back along the line to leave the river clear—close to the attractive Saxon and Norman parish church. The church stands away from the road to which it is linked by canal and path. The towpath goes almost due west over the road to Yapton, which by car one reaches along two sides of the triangle of which the canal forms the third. A fine and most interesting church stands away to the north. The canal here runs parallel to the road through the village, and then strikes off west again, skirting the village of Barnham. The modern village has grown up along the road, but the old settlement, with church, manor and great barn, is close to the canal, and it makes a pretty group.

Here road and canal part company, the former heading north-west through the overgrown village of Eastergate and then south through Westergate and Woodgate. The canal is crossed half-way along the main Bognor road, and then a turning at Shrimpney takes us around the perimeter of the seaside town. At the next cross, in North Bersted, a main road goes north across the canal again to Merston. Here yet another minor road heads towards the canal and then runs parallel with it past a very plain, small thirteenth-century church. Road and canal converge beyond this point, and for the next two miles they run side by side. At North Mundham there are some good houses and a fine church just south of the road. This is much of an age with Merston but strikingly different in scale and detail. At North Mundham the canal is for a short space in water.

Next along the route comes Hunston, and beyond it is possible to continue to the point where the canal beyond Birdham disappears into the muddy waters of Chichester Harbour. We may, however, feel that enough is enough, and that a more satisfactory end to the journey can be sought by heading north at Hunston, for here the Chichester Canal, still wet and still to a modest degree in business, leads off. Following it, either on foot or by way of the Chichester bypass, we find the end of our journey from the Thames at Southgate Basin, well inside the city and within sight of the heart-lifting cathedral spire.

9

Chiltern Circuit

BY a freak of history the Chilterns have become associated in the popular imagination with political expediency. There is no legal process by which a Member of Parliament can resign his seat, but if he occupies a position under the Crown his seat is automatically forfeit. By a tradition dating to the seventeenth century the reluctant M.P. applies for the Stewardship of the Chiltern Hundreds.

It is coincidental that the three hundreds of Stoke, Desborough and Burnham, with the surrounding country, have for the past three centuries been the favoured country of many politicians—and a few poets. In the Tudor Age politicians and public servants like Rich and Petre found it convenient to live in Essex. In the succeeding age the fashion changed to Buckinghamshire, which offered rustic seclusion coupled with tolerably good communications. One cannot travel far in these still-delightful lanes without disturbing the shade of some Georgian orator or Victorian legislator. A ghost hunt of this kind provides a convenient excuse for the exploration of the Chiltern beechwoods and, alas, the Chiltern housing estates.

With the exception of southern Hertfordshire, no Home County has suffered more from developers than Buckinghamshire. For this very reason the contrast between the ruined and the unspoilt is the sharper. When the last gash in the chalk is passed, the beechwoods enclose the traveller with a singular benison. To risk a generalization, no Home Counties country town has been more drastically ruined than High Wycombe; but there is no more lovely and peaceful country in the Home Counties than the Hambledon valley, less than ten miles away. Here, in an exaggerated fashion, is the familiar contrast of these counties.

Even in the devastated areas pockets remain. Roughly speaking a line drawn between Chesham, Amersham, High Wycombe and Marlow leaves largely spoilt country to the east, unspoilt to the west. There are many exceptions, and more may develop. One wonders what the effect of the M40 motorway will be. It has already taken some of the pressure off Beaconsfield and Wycombe, but will it produce more commuter estates farther west, around Stokenchurch or even beyond the escarpment of the hills so cruelly scarred by the new road?

While such speculations must occupy the planners and the conservationists, both alerted to the dangers, the visitor enjoys—perhaps selfishly—the delights to hand, notably a handful of villages of quite remarkable perfection, the best maintained footpaths in the Home Counties if not the whole country, and the matchless beauty and peace of beechwoods growing on chalk. Here one may stumble upon a stockbroker's retreat rather than the woodman's hut which I knew as a child, but these changes somehow serve to reinforce the fundamental changelessness of this Chiltern country.

The Chiltern circuit in search of politicians and poets may reasonably start beside the Thames at Eton, which watched over the youth of both sorts. It would produce an intolerably long catalogue to attempt a comprehensive list. Poets suffered the genial brutality of Keate. Statesmen snatched a little wisdom from contact with Wotton. The little town, shadowed by the castle across the river, has recaptured some of its former charm since the Thames bridge was closed to motor-traffic. Antique shops and restaurants flourish quietly beyond the walls of the college, and the river still offers a little of the peace which it afforded Wotton and Isaak Walton.

Alas, between us and the first poet and statesman lie the massed defences of Slough, which must somehow be breached. Slough is a subject for the sociologist rather than the topographer. As a study in environment it is fascinating, a melting-pot of races and classes. Of history it has none—although it is busy a-making. Of architecture—chacun á son gout. Let us grit our teeth and get through quickly.

On the northern side the town relinquishes its grip suddenly and the elegant suburbanism of Stoke appears. Stoke Poges church, off the road to the west, can be found easily by following the American number plates of innumerable cars, for this modestly charming building has become, incongruously, one of the major shrines of the modern

world. Incongruously, and perhaps even mistakenly, for there is some
support for the theory that Gray was thinking not of Stoke but of
Upton, the old parish of Slough. No matter. The pilgrims have kept
Stoke Poges charming, while Upton has been swallowed up. And
from the churchyard one may see, if not "lowing herds", at least green
fields and woods and the peaceful memorial gardens nearby.

We might reasonably have started this chapter with Gray, who is
associated strongly with Eton, although modern taste tends, rightly,
to reject the spurious poeticisms of the "Distant Prospect". It is sometimes difficult to take Gray seriously as a poet; the "Elegy" is so familiar
as to defy critical assessment, and the odes are almost grotesquely dated.
At Stoke Poges we are close to the best of Gray, the odd unworldly
scholar, endearingly naive in everyday affairs, a devoted son, not less
attractive for being just a little comical.

There is something mildly funny about the Gray memorial at Stoke
Poges, put up by a descendant of William Penn and just out of scale
with its surroundings. It must be among the least 'important' of
National Trust properties, but one sees the point of preserving for the
future an object so illustrative of the bad taste of its time. The immediate surroundings are most appealing, and it is to be hoped that even
the most hurried of pilgrims will spare a moment from contemplation
of the grave of Gray and his mother to look at the gentle landscape and
to think of the other great of Stoke, the Penns and that most savage and
eloquent of Jacobean lawyers Coke.

Beyond Stoke Poges the dullness of the main road towards Gerrards
Cross is interrupted by one of those open commons which are a
welcome characteristic of south-eastern Buckinghamshire. They are as
unlike the Chiltern chalk as the northern commons of Surrey are unlike
the North Downs. On the edge of Stoke Common a lane meanders off
left, partly rural, partly developed, to the village of Hedgerley, which
is the first taste of what this country can offer. For a few moments
London seems far away. Hedgerley was a manor of the Bulstrode
family who made their mark on Buckinghamshire over several generations and who gave their name to the great park which stretches from
Hedgerley Green to the Oxford road. This is still a fine example of
landscape design, despite the erosion of its eastern edge by the new
housing of Gerrards Cross. On the edge of the park too the low ramparts of a large plateau camp of the Iron Age stand surprisingly among
the villas.

In the Middle Ages the Chiltern country was the poor relation of the
Buckinghamshire family, for its thin flinty soil could not compete
with the alluvium to the north. The Bulstrodes of Hedgerley were
among those Chiltern gentlemen who saw that this country, which
grew poor corn, would grow good grass and fine specimen trees, and

so created the Chiltern feature which is second only to its beeches, the parkland.

Bulstrode was a centre of political activity and influence over a long period, one of those places, like Cliveden in a later age, which becomes by a mixture of chance and personality the focus of aspiring politicians. Between the Bulstrodes and the Bendincks came Judge Jeffreys, an incongruous intrusion perhaps but no mean political influence in his day, a great lawyer and by no means as black as he has been painted— but I should not have cared to see him from the wrong side of the dock.

The most notable of the political Bulstrodes was a descendant on the female side. Bulstrode Whitelocke was the son of a judge of Charles I's reign who married Elizabeth Bulstrode of Hedgerley. The father owned property in Fawley, a village in splendid Chiltern country right on the Oxfordshire border north of Henley. Judge Whitelocke trod a delicate path between King and Parliament in the early stages of Charles's reign, and he was fortunate to die before the conflict reached flash-point. His son spent almost his whole life in the conflict. Bulstrode was always a moderating influence, although he had strong provocation from Prince Rupert, who sacked his house at Fawley early in the war. He carefully avoided extremes, to the extent of keeping away from the King's trial and execution. It was perhaps for this reason that he escaped the royal vengeance after the Restoration. Charles II dismissed him as one of those who "were rather carried away with the torrent than swam with the stream", which was a comfort to him although less than justice to his influence. He was allowed to end his life quietly in retirement on his estate. Like his father he was buried at Fawley.

Bulstrode Whitelocke lived at a time which made greater demands upon him than it was his nature to meet. William Bendinck was one who matched the challenge of his age. He was fortunate in the success of his master, William of Orange, but his share in that success was earned by ability as well as integrity. He was possibly the most competent of those who came to England to find a place in the court of William III and certainly the most honest. That was why he was so heartily disliked by the English. It is one thing to tolerate competence and honesty in one's own countrymen; such qualities are quite intolerable in a foreigner.

Bendinck made his English home at Bulstrode, and this became the seat of his descendants, the Dukes of Portland, until the fourth Duke transferred his affections to Welbeck Abbey. In the time of the second Duke the house was a centre of cultural activity, not from any inclination of the Duke but because of his duchess. Margaret, daughter of Pope's patron the Earl of Oxford and the "noble, lovely little Peggy" of Prior's presumptuous eulogy, survived her husband by twenty-three years and presided over the refined gaieties of Bulstrode until she was seventy. Bulstrode was a more colourful and probably a happier place in her reign than under her son, the third Duke, who twice became Prime Minister because, while not the most able man, he was the least offensive. To the advantage of great wealth he added honesty and, a rarer quality among eighteenth-century Whigs, a capacity for hard and detailed work. It was sad that he was forced back to the Premiership in old age and sickness. He muddled, or at least permitted others to muddle, the management of the war with Napoleon, and his one political talent—the reconciliation of opponents—failed him in the case of Canning and Castlereagh. The ministers fought their duel, Portland resigned and he was dead within the month. It is happier to think of him at Bulstrode, enjoying music with his friends and debating the affairs of the nation, quietly and rationally, with Fox and Burke.

It is possible to gain closer acquaintance with this mild and pleasing parkland by following a public path which crosses the park from Gerrards Cross to Hedgerley. His Grace's entrance was on the Oxford Road, and almost opposite this a very narrow lane promises more rustic delights to the motorist. These are not fully redeemed. After two miles the fields and woods give place abruptly to the urban sprawl of Chalfont St Peter, the once-charming centre of which stands on the main road following the valley of the Misbourne.

When the present is unlovely one has to make do with memories. This is Quaker country. The names of Penn, Penington and Ellwood call up memories of the finest days of the Society of Friends, when, misunderstood and persecuted, they laid foundations of fellowship and integrity on which the movement was built.

The Peningtons came to Chalfont St Peter around 1635. Isaac Penington was a London merchant and, like many of his kind, a rigid Puritan. Although he owned land in Buckinghamshire, business and a fondness for public affairs kept him for most of the time in London, where he was successively alderman, sheriff and Lord Mayor. He was also an aggressive representative of the city in Parliament. He was from the beginning a bitter opponent of Laud—at Chalfont he was in trouble on Sundays for refusing to follow the Laudian ritual—and it no doubt gave him great satisfaction when, as Lieutenant of the Tower, he was responsible for the arrangements for the Archbishop's execution. He was also a commissioner for the trial of King Charles I and, although not technically assenting in his execution, he was always regarded as one of the regicides. At the Restoration he was arrested and died in prison in the Tower.

This stern old puritan managed to produce—however joylessly— one of the first and most attractive of the Quakers. The younger Isaac Penington suffered in an acute form from the uncertainties of young manhood. Rejecting the rigid code of his father, he was not attracted to the Anglican creed and he drifted uncertainly through the crisis years of the Civil War and the Commonwealth. Then, in the early 1650s, he met a remarkable Kentishwoman, the widow of Sir William Springett. She too had rejected puritanism and, despite the incumbrance of a ten-year-old daughter Gulielma, had taken to the gay life. They married in 1654 and soon afterwards Isaac became involved with the Quakers of Berkshire. He and his wife quickly joined the society, to the fury of old Isaac Penington, who however relented sufficiently to give his son a house in Chalfont. This house, the Grange, became a major centre of Quaker activity as well as a very happy home.

The Restoration which brought disaster to the elder Penington was unfortunate for his son. The Quakers were principal objects of persecution in the early years of Charles II's reign, and Penington was in and out of gaol during the next seven years. While he was in this plight he suffered the loss of his house, which, as the property of his father, was forfeit when the old man was convicted of regicide. Undeterred, Mary Penington bought another house outside Amersham, and here they lived after Isaac's release from prison. Meanwhile Mrs Penington had bought land at Jordans, in the neighbouring parish of Chalfont St Giles, which was intended for the use of the Friends.

One of the Peningtons' friends at Chalfont was Thomas Ellwood. He had known Mrs Penington in the days of her early widowhood when neither had any knowledge of Quakers. Meeting her again in Buckinghamshire he was attracted by the relaxed and peaceful air of the household and he soon followed then into the society. Like Penington he suffered imprisonment on several occasions. While in London, he was persuaded to call upon a poor blind poet who was living in retirement. This was Milton. Ellwood visited him daily to read to him and to talk. This interlude ended when Ellwood was once more put in prison. On his release he retired to Buckinghamshire as a member of the Penington household. While he was there he took a "little box at Giles Chalfont" for Milton's use, and the poet came here while the Great Plague was at its height in London. Ellwood read the manuscript of *Paradise Lost* here and dropped a hint which resulted in the composition of *Paradise Regained*.

Although Ellwood is remembered best because of his friends Milton, Penn and Penington—and what a glory such friendships were!—he was a fascinating and admirable person in his own right, a considerable intellectual and controversialist, and with a strong vein of Quaker integrity. After his father's death he acquired a house, Hunger Hill, at Amersham, and this was his home for the rest of a long life. He died there at the age of seventy-four and was buried at Jordans. His autobiography, which contains attractive impressions of Milton and Penington, was published posthumously.

These Quaker memories have taken us beyond Chalfont St Peter. Our journey lies along the main road for two long miles and then west into the village of Chalfont St Giles—village no more, although the core of the old community is still evident around the church. Milton's 'little box' is beyond this, a very pretty cottage, as neat and unassuming as a Quaker daughter. Some Milton relics are preserved inside. The commuter tide has washed close to this spot. Farther on the country returns briefly, to be succeeded by more housing at Jordans. At a road junction beyond this stands Mrs Penington's little meeting house.

No number of pilgrims can destroy the atmosphere of Jordans Meeting House. The little building, put up in 1688, is utterly without architectural pretensions, and it, and the tiny plot of land on which it stands, have the beauty of perfect simplicity. Few places can be more moving or for more elusive reasons. I am no more a Quaker than a Brahmin, but I am under its spell. The soaring spires of cathedrals, the towers and the trumpets of castles, are far away, and here is only the still small voice, insistent beneath the buzz of passing traffic.

Although the spirit of Jordans is to do with the relationship of God and man, not with the cult of personality, inevitably the memory which endures most here is of Penn. William Penn is the strongest, the most colourful and historically the most influential of all the early Quakers. He had long ago revolted against the bluff parental tyranny of Admiral Penn and had received the traditional Quaker baptism by imprisonment when, around 1688, he encountered the Buckingham-shire Friends. Other spells in gaol followed, although Penn had the advantage, not of his own seeking, of friends in high places as well as considerable personal wealth.

Penn found in Buckinghamshire the perfect wife for a man of his temperament and aspirations. She was Gulielma Maria Springett, stepdaughter of Isaac Penington and consequently in the heart of the Quaker community. Their twenty-two years of marriage were among the most exquisitely happy in history, strengthened as well as saddened by the death of four of their seven children and by the delinquency of a surviving son. Until her death in 1694 Gulielma shared his adventures in America and the foundation of the free society of Pennsylvania—named in honour of William's father the admiral—his struggles to establish religious tolerance in the England of James II, and the hazardous days of the Revolution during which Penn's acknowledged friendship with the deposed King brought him within hailing distance of a charge of treason. During their early married life they lived just over the border in Rickmansworth, moving to Sussex in 1677. Guli-elma was buried at Jordans, and there William too lay after his death in 1718. There too were buried his second wife and several Penn

Newbridge

(*above left*) Lodge gates, Great Hampden (*above right*) Waller monument,
Beaconsfield

Fingest Church

children and grandchildren. Penn had never lived in Buckinghamshire and his activities had ranged far in this country and in America, yet it is with the little plot of ground at Jordans more than any other single place that the founder of the first free community in modern history is identified. A man who avoided extremes, a gentleman with a gentleman's feeling for style, Jordans suits him well and the plain headstones in the Jordans turf are as much physical memorial as he needs and would wish.

Penn's son Thomas strengthened the Buckinghamshire connection by buying the estate of Stoke Park at Stoke Poges, and broke the association with Jordans by being buried in the church there. His son rebuilt the house and put up the Gray memorial in a corner of his park.

To the west of Jordans, on a high point to which the tide of commuterdom has not quite crept, stands the parish church of Penn. Here are notable monuments, principally brasses to the family which took its name from the village. It would be satisfying to identify them with the ancestors of the founder of Pennsylvania, and Penn himself did not hesitate to do just this when he was writing his father's epitaph. No connection has however been found between the two Penns. This should not deter travellers from making the journey here; the church is worth a visit for its own sake and for the memorial to an infant grandson of William Penn, and the byways coming off the ridge run through still-delightful country. One of these drops down past a wooded National Trust property—a memorial to another Quaker of the Cadbury family—before becoming entangled in the new urban growth of Beaconsfield. This is, in fact, rather good as modern towns go, but travellers looking for the twin pleasures of fine country and historic associations will continue to the centre of Beaconsfield on the Oxford Road. Here modern growth has been held successfully in check—for how long?—and there is a spacious air about the wide high street with its coaching inns. The motorway which has won for Beaconsfield a little respite passes to the south across the former estate of Edmund Waller. We came across the origins of the Waller family on the borders of Kent and Sussex, but Edmund, the most famous but not the most admirable member, belongs largely to the Chilterns. He was born at Coleshill, a plain village towards Amersham, and died at Beaconsfield. His tomb is in the churchyard. Waller wrote one incomparable lyric—"Go Lovely Rose"—and much which is forgotten because its conventions had not enough either of passion or of eloquence.

A far greater name than Waller's belongs to Beaconsfield. This was the last home of Edmund Burke and he is buried in the church. Among all the time-servers and cynics of eighteenth-century politics here is the honest man, resting quietly and undemonstratively in his adopted county.

Burke's association with Buckinghamshire began in 1768 when he was approaching forty. In that year he bought an estate called Gregories —long vanished; it was in the now-built-up area towards the station. It was a gamble for a man with no great personal fortune and one which he may, for financial reasons, have often regretted. He did not regret his choice of country. The part of the country gentleman suited him very well. He lived in modest style and took a keen, and characteristically practical, interest in farming, to which he applied the newest techniques of his day. In all the stormy passages of his life, when he was at the height of his powers and when condemned and slandered, Gregories was his refuge and a place for renewal, and here he wrote his pamphlets, eloquent, wise and sometimes wrong-headed, on the great domestic and world issues of his time.

One of the happiest episodes in a life not overfull of happiness— except in the company of his friends—belongs to this country. His was no theoretical anger over the plight of victims of the revolutionary terror in France. In 1796 he persuaded the government to support him in a scheme to provide a school for children of the refugees. This was established in Penn, and Burke spent all the time he could spare from public business frolicking with the French children in their formal military dress.

When Burke died at Gregories in 1797 his friends claimed him for Westminster Abbey, but he had taken care to forestall this by arranging to be buried in Beaconsfield. This was done with dignity among the mourning of his peers. The memorial tablet in the church is suitably modest, for Burke's flamboyance was directed towards his causes, not himself.

At Beaconsfield the traveller is in some difficulties. To the west lies the urban sprawl of High Wycombe, which must be faced some time but not now. Southwards we shall come too soon to the end of the Chiltern circuit. Back north to Amersham, therefore, where the very agreeable high street is worth visiting for its own sake and for memories of the Peningtons and their Quaker brethren. The main road follows the Misbourne valley—very pleasantly in spite of the traffic— past the fine estate of Shardeloes where the stream has been widened to make a characteristic ornamental water between road and house. Here a footpath offers a pleasant stroll through the informally designed landscape to Little Missenden. Shardeloes belonged to the Tyrwhitt Drakes, one of whom had a brilliant brief career as explorer, archaeologist and naturalist in the Holy Land in mid-Victorian times.

An alternative route would be to go north from Amersham towards Chesham, but instead of entering the bright but overgrown town turn east along the Chess valley to Chenies. Here in a village of almost unbearable perfection is the manor house of the Russells in warm Tudor brick, beside the chapel in which the family lie buried. Froude is out of fashion now, but his essay on the Russell monuments at Chenies is still required reading for all who come this way.

Just beyond Chenies the Chess, still the clearest and prettiest chalk stream in the Home Counties, marks the boundary with Hertfordshire, and, beyond, a tangle of narrow lanes give welcome respite from the main-road traffic. By Latimer and Flaunden and White Hill the way passes through country which has miraculously evaded exploitation. Then comes Berkhamsted, where road, rail and canal aim together at the Midlands, and where, one might say, the Norman Conquest begun at Hastings came to a formal conclusion when the Atheling and the Saxon earls submitted. Here the Conqueror threw up one of the first of his earth castles. Later this was reinforced with masonry, but time, weather and stone-plunderers have undone the work so that at Berk-hamsted one can see as well as anywhere just what the ground plan of a motte-and-bailey castle was like. The ruins are just beside the railway station, and a road beyond this climbs quickly into splendid Chiltern country at Berkhamsted Common. This big horseshoe re-entrant pro-vides the foreground to Ashridge Park, where the philosophy of Con-servatism was long debated in the Bonar Law College, now superseded in Wyatt's Gothic fantasy of Ashridge House by the trendier doctrines of management. The Chiltern air which elsewhere provided solace to retired and relaxation to resting politicians here offered a headier bouquet to aspiring statesmen. Much of the estate, but not the house, belongs to the National Trust, and there are ample opportunities for walking on the breezy commons and among the more sophisticated scenes of the park. Here too is the tall pillar commemorating the Duke of Bridgewater whose Grand Union Canal cuts boldly through the plain of Aylesbury below.

Good things come in large helpings in this area. Just below the hill on the north-east is the pretty River Gade, flowing down to enliven the urban scene of Hemel Hempstead New Town. On the opposite side of the Ashridge spur is Aldbury, another singularly perfect village, and to the north-west the chalk comes to an abrupt and splendid climax in Ivinghoe Beacon. Heights are relative. At 700 feet the Beacon Hill looks from the vale as impressive as the Wrekin.

This northern thrust has taken us to the farthest edge of the Chilterns, and our proper course lies far to the south and west. One must therefore backtrack to Amersham, or take a difficult course through the tangled lanes between Tring and Great Missenden. All the valleys run south-east to the Chess, and the lanes consequently deflect the traveller from this southern course. However, by one means or another, we get back to the Misbourne valley and to Little Missenden. The village is most happily bypassed by the main road and it is quiet as well as exceedingly pretty—too pretty indeed to have as its resident worthy the disre-putable Dr Bates of the Hell Fire Club. (But we shall come upon him and his cronies later.)

The Misbourne, never a big stream although an important con-tributor to the landscape, is small at Little Missenden, and at Great Missenden it is not much more than a trickle through the park of Missenden Abbey. The abbey, a Gothic mansion on the site of a house of Augustinian canons, is now a residential conference centre where delegates may be distracted from, or inspired to, study by the enchant-ing landscape setting.

Great Missenden is a small town with charms of its own, but its distinction lies in its position at the entrance to one of the finest parts of the Chilterns. Between here and Princes Risborough the chalk hills and the beechwoods are almost unblemished. Until the escarpment is reached there are no far-ranging views and none is needed, for the immediate prospects are deeply satisfying. The hills are folded gently one on another, each with its characteristic crest of trees. Villages are few and are confined to the 'bottoms', where water—scarce on the chalk—could be had. The lanes are fitful and wayward, wandering in apparent aimlessness, or coming to an unexpected end. For a taste of typical Chiltern country one might go first to Little Hampden, where there is a tiny hamlet and church at the end of the tarmacked road, which fades out on the common and then reappears a mile farther on. Such casual behaviour, maddening if one has made a wrong decision at the road junction and is in a hurry, is delightful to the leisured traveller who cares not where he gets so long as the way is agreeable. And this is certainly agreeable country, to be savoured for its intimacy and friendliness and for its avoidance of the dramatic and the merely picturesque alike.

In the heart of this country is the most celebrated village of the Chilterns, with a name familiar to English-speaking people all over the world, among them many who not only have never visited the Chiltern country but have never heard of it. Great Hampden gave its name to one of the legendary figures of history, and John Hampden, a sturdy middle-of-the-road English gentleman became, despite himself, a symbol to his own and succeeding ages of resistance to oppression.

The lane out of Great Missenden rises steadily and beautifully with views to the billowing chalk hills to the north. Just before Hampden Bottom there are two jolly little 'pepper-box' lodges framing a green vista at the beginning of the two-mile-long drive to Hampden House. The house itself is not in view from this point, and indeed it avoids attention from most angles. Only to the north does the so-called Queen's Gap offer a handsome view. The road cuts across the park, and one may well end up by missing Great Hampden altogether, for church and house huddle together among trees and the village itself, at Hampden Row, hardly exists—just an inn and a handful of cottages. After the anticipation this may seem anticlimax, and many pilgrims may go away disappointed. Great Hampden is one of those elusive places which are not to be hurried. An American-style tourist visit is more than usually meaningless. One must potter about, taking in the mood of this quiet country and extending delicate tentacles to establish contact with the genius of the place.

In this relaxed situation one may perhaps tune in to John Hampden of Great Hampden, gentleman, Member of Parliament for the Borough of Wendover in the County of Buckingham. In an age of quick promotion and easy ennoblement his simple style is notable; Hampden was more concerned with honour than with honours. He came, like Cromwell, to whom he was distantly related, of good country stock with deep roots in the soil of Buckinghamshire. Men of that sort are not prone to extreme positions; they are slow to provocation, but they do not care to be pushed. Very early in Charles's reign he allied himself with the opposition, showing great unwillingness to meet the King's demand for a loan. In 1635 a crisis was reached with the writ for ship money. Buckinghamshire's share of this was assessed at £4,500, of which Hampden, a man of some property, was required to find something around £20. He held land in Stoke Mandeville, assessed for tax at twenty shillings, and it was over this sum that Hampden stuck. It was not, in terms of his wealth, a great deal of money. As Burke said later, when another principle of unjust taxation was in debate, "Would twenty shillings have ruined Mr Hampden's fortune?" Refusing to pay precipitated a legal wrangle which lasted for years; Hampden lost his case and won a substantial moral victory. Thereafter he was an acknowledged leader in Parliament, the more so because he made no show of his opinions but behaved with a quiet gravity which was far more impressive than bluster. Slowly and inevitably he rose to prominence in the struggle with the King. He was one of the five 'birds' who flew from the House before the King came to arrest them, and this action of the King, according to Clarenden, tipped Hampden into uncompromising hostility. He soon set about raising a regiment of 'green coats' in his county and trained them for action. "When he first drew his sword he threw away the scabbard," said Clarenden. It is a fine symbolic phrase but not literally true. His own performance in the early stages of the war was not spectacular, and he spent much energy trying to put sense into the Earl of Essex's erratic strategy. While his forces were deployed in a muddled fashion in the low country below the western ridge of the Chilterns, Prince Rupert made one of his characteristic lightning attacks. Rupert withdrew, and Hampden rallied a small force and chased after him towards Oxford. Rupert turned and destroyed his pursuers. Hampden was badly wounded and rode off the field to the little town of Thame, where he had been at school. Here he collapsed. He lay dying for several days. It was said that the King offered to send him his own surgeon. Charles, who had moments of perspicacity, probably saw that any hope of a reconciliation with Parliament lay with popular moderates like Hampden. However Hampden's wound was mortal, and he died at Thame. He was taken home to Great Hampden and buried in the church which nestles against the great house.

Strangely, in view of his wealth and popularity, no monument was put up immediately to his memory. It was left to a descendant, Lord Trevor, to set up a tablet a century later. The Hampdens continued to exercise influence in and beyond Buckinghamshire. John's son Richard was in a way as remarkable a man as his father, although his career was without the colourful elements which made John Hampden memorable. Richard played the country squire to perfection, and also served in Parliament with Cromwell. He survived the Restoration without loss of prestige, and represented his father's old constituency of Wendover in Charles II's reign. He was a firm opponent of James and a leading supporter of William of Orange, under whom he served as Chancellor of the Exchequer. Like his father he had no use for public honours and refused a peerage from William III with a decision equal to John Hampden's. His life was saddened by the disastrous career of his son, another John, who had become involved, innocently or not, with the Rye House conspirators and only escaped their fate at the cost of his own dignity and self-respect. He struggled back into public life but ineffectually, and at last, a year after his father's death, he finally abandoned the fight and killed himself.

It is a sad story to set against those of the other Hampdens. There is however no sadness at Great Hampden, even if a gentle melancholy pervades the church. The house, greatly altered since the seventeenth century and not open, turns its back to the church, and there is little to see but some tall chimneys. The district is heavily wooded, so that it is difficult to realize that this is in fact one of the high points of the Chilterns (over 700 feet between the house and the inn). The mysterious earthwork called Grim's Ditch, which makes an intermittent appearance throughout the county and seems to have been a linear earthwork, perhaps from the time of Mercia's dominance of Saxon England, runs through the park and then, taking an abrupt turn, crosses the lane a mile west of Hampden Row.

From Great Hampden it is not much more than four miles due north to Chequers. It is to be hoped that every Prime Minister, of whatever party, picks up on the south wind something of the sturdy independent spirit of the old Buckinghamshire squire.

Chequers has been the Prime Minister's official country house since 1921. Sir Arthur Lee decided to give up his home for this laudable purpose during the war, retaining only the right of his and his wife's tenancy. In 1921 he realized that this compromise would not work, and he made an outright gift of Chequers to a trust which would administer the house on behalf of the nation.

There is a singular appropriateness about Chequers. It is essentially an English house. The roots are deep in the Middle Ages and, as such roots tend to be, they are muddled. The present house is, roughly speaking, Elizabethan, which means that it is built in a style which derives more from native tradition than foreign example. A century later it would have been more elegant but it would have belonged to a Continental manner. In its early days the house played only a modest part in national affairs through the Hawtreys and the Crokes, holders of minor offices under the Crown. The connections with Cromwell are indirect; the Protector's daughter Frances married, as her second husband, Sir John Russell, a West Country knight, and one of their sons married the Chequers heiress. (Through this marriage the house acquired its famous collection of Cromwell relics.) The setting rather than the history of Chequers fits it for its national role. Here surely is the mainstream English house in typical English country, not looking out boldly across the Aylesbury plain but enclosed in hills which turn the house in upon itself. A place this for meditation, and, one hopes, for decisions reached without distraction.

Certainly there is no distraction from the general public. The most famous house in the Chilterns is not a show house. The hazards of public life in the post-war world have meant a great tightening of security. However, attempts to close a public footpath which passed perilously near the house were happily frustrated; the right to walk through the country is a part of the continuity of history for which Chequers stands. Walkers may therefore still get a glimpse of dark-red Tudor brick in a bower of trees and rounded hills. Motorist must make do with a glance up the long drive from the Aylesbury road.

To the south of Hampden there is slightly nondescript country of woodland, open hills and some disturbingly ill-conceived new communities. There are some of these on the route through Speen to Bradenham, a confusing tangle of roads which involves Grim's Ditch again on the high wooded ground above the latter village. Then the road drops sharply through the woods before skirting the green of an astonishingly unspoilt, perfect village.

Some of the hazards that threaten this over-pressurized countryside are absent from Bradenham, for much of the village and its surroundings came into the care of the National Trust in 1956. This is not one of the show properties. The manor house is not open to the public, and visitors enjoy no special privileges in access to the fields and woods, and this is as it should be. This is not the extrovert kind of scenery which thrives on mass appreciation. It is, rather, country which lives for itself and its own affairs, and the intruder must tread lightly.

The charm of Bradenham is the sum of its parts. Individually they are not of the first importance. The church has a south door from the earliest Norman period, or just possibly earlier, but otherwise is not of high architectural interest. The manor house nearby is a modest dwelling, and the cottages, charming in total, are not separately distinguished. Yet Bradenham has the essential village quality. When a distant traveller thinks of home it is such a place as this that comes into his mind's eye.

The memory which remains alive in Bradenham is that of the Disraelis. The elder, Isaac D'Israeli—his son got rid of the apostrophe—came to live in the manor house in 1829 and stayed for the rest of his life. His son Benjamin was twenty-five when this became the family home, and so the Buckinghamshire countryside can hardly claim to have played a formative part in his growth. He loved this country, however, and recalled it at the very end of his life in his last novel *Endymion*.

The elder D'Israeli was a rather surprising figure to find playing the country squire. He belonged by blood to Spanish Jewry, by inclination to the literary world of London. For most of his life he pursued a desultory career as a miscellaneous writer, writing poetry well enough to attract Scott and achieving popularity with a collection of anecdotes called *Curiosities of Literature*. Only at the time of his move to Buckinghamshire did he really find his personal talent for history. Perhaps the Chiltern air persuaded him to choose the reign of Charles I and the character of Hampden. Country life suited him. He lived at Bradenham for close on twenty years and died at eighty-two. He is buried in the church. By that time his son was on the way to dominance of the Conservative Party and was negotiating for the purchase of a mansion over in the next valley.

In 1848 Disraeli was leader of the party and owner of Hughenden: a remarkable 'double'. The earlier years had been more difficult. The English distrusted flamboyance as much as they did intelligence. They might read *Vivian Grey* and chuckle at its brilliant audacity, but this did not make them wish to hand over power to the author. In 1832 Disraeli stood for High Wycombe. In an exuberant speech delivered from the porch of the 'Red Lion' he predicted that he would be at the head, his opponent at the tail, of the poll. He was wrong. Only in 1837 and then on the unfamiliar ground of Maidstone did he succeed in convincing the electorate that he was not too clever for his own good. He came back before the Buckinghamshire voters in 1847. By this time he had achieved political respectability, though not political mediocrity, and he represented the county for the rest of his stay in the Commons. Some of the most famous of his speeches were delivered to Chiltern audiences; I hope they appreciated the wit.

However Disraeli had no wish to make of Hughenden another Bulstrode Park. He played the political game in Westminster. The country was for relaxation and for the company of Mary Ann, whose fortune had enabled him to buy the modest Georgian estate. He enjoyed the countryside as he enjoyed power and the friendship of royalty, with the same frank and unconcealed delight. Although certainly no nature mystic he got deep satisfaction out of drives through the hills and identifying himself with them. At the end Buckinghamshire won the struggle in his contrary nature; he rejected his rightful place in the Abbey in favour of burial as a private person in the little church beside his house at Hughenden, not far from the De Montfort monuments which he fondly, and mistakenly, connected with the great pioneer of Parliament.

The Queen Empress came down to Hughenden and erected a memorial tablet whose text, "Kings love him that speaketh right", would have given him a wry smile.

One need not possess a strong vein of reverence to enjoy a visit to Hughenden. The associations are there to be savoured, but equally one may delight in the woodland scenes which gave Dizzy such satisfaction. The house and estate were vested in a trust which in 1947 handed them to the National Trust. The house, which was almost rebuilt from its Georgian original by Disraeli, is shown regularly, and there are pleasant walks in the park. The church is of interest not only for the Disraeli associations but also to collectors of historical curiosities, for the De Montfort monuments which are mostly fakes put up by a sixteenth-century gentleman desirous of ancestors.

There seems no alternative now to going through High Wycombe. This is the largest town after Slough in Buckinghamshire and almost as ugly. It is harder to bear. Slough never had any advantages, while High Wycombe was blessed with a lovely setting in a fold of the hills with the pretty River Wye flowing through the valley. Within my memory it was a brisk market town and a centre for furniture making, which was then almost a cottage industry. The beech woods, in which woodmen lived in conditions of extreme simplicity, huddled all around the town. Intensive development of the industry, together with the intensification of traffic along the Oxford Road and the adoption of the area by London commuters, has wrought a massive change and hardly one for the better. Recent redevelopment of the central area has, with the best of intentions, confused the pattern of the old market centre whose town hall and market house were the hub of the community.

However this is not a study in town planning but an exploration of political and poetical Buckinghamshire, and we may therefore grit our teeth and persist along the Oxford Road westwards. The town at last relinquishes its grip, and there is a brief respite in open country before West Wycombe.

There was much public debate in 1929 when the Royal Society of Arts bought much of West Wycombe village. The Depression was beginning to bite, and many citizens could see better uses for money than the resuscitation of a row of old and almost derelict cottages. After restoration, the society passed the houses to the National Trust. This was an imaginative enterprise, somewhat in advance of its time, which would have been more effective if traffic could have been diverted from the village. Nearly forty years of lorries, each year bigger and faster, have shaken the place most pitiably. The motorway, passing well to the south, has perhaps come a decade or so too late.

This is nevertheless a village of almost unique interest. The completeness of its survival comes from the influence of the great house and of the unusual continuity of tenure. This is Dashwood territory, marked by the gates to the park on the one side, by the extraordinary church perched high on the other.

Although the church is clearly a Dashwood eccentricity, its position is traditional and hints at the existence of an ancient settlement. Hilltop churches—and this replaces an earlier building on the same site—are nearly always of very early Christian origin and often point to an earlier pagan shrine. The bold earthworks around the church are those of an Iron Age hill-fort in a typical position on a spur of the Chilterns. Without going all the way with H. J. Massingham in his theories about the nature of Dashwood's religious revival (in his wholly delightful and provocative book *Chiltern Country*), one may readily see how the antiquity of the site prompted the noble lord to replace a medieval church with a building more appropriate to his own tastes and to the grandeur of the position. Here at any rate, for whatever reason, is one of the memorable sights of the Chilterns, the classical hall, tower and gleaming ball withdrawn from the hustle of the road below. Modern traffic and, one suspects, Christian ethics were alike matters of indifference to its designer.

Against this church and the infantile-vicious exploits of the Hell Fire Club, West Wycombe Park might be set in the Dashwood scales. Worthy burghers and honest developers of the twentieth century produced the sprawl of High Wycombe. The profligate rake of the eighteenth century set at the head of the Wye valley an exquisite work of art composed of house, water, trees, lawns and temples, which abides as a source of joy and refreshment. Which party is best deserving of our gratitude and the gratitude of our children's children?

In fact Dashwood is a man to whom legend has done much less than justice. In an age of cynicism he seems to have had rather more than the conventional share of principles. He was probably more effectively politically when he was in opposition to Walpole; when, under Bute and North, he held office he was a great deal less successful. A fundamental weakness in elementary arithmetic made him a less than completely successful Chancellor of the Exchequer. A better critic than creator, in fact, may be fair comment. Perhaps he was too intelligent to make a good eighteenth-century politician. His contempt for the accepted social standards of the time may have driven him into the excesses of the Hell Fire Club, and one may argue forever about the activities of this body and about what truth there is in the popular picture of the Monks of Medmenham. At worst Dashwood is saner than most of his rivals in the great age of English eccentricity. Does it really matter? He gave us West Wycombe. His descendant Sir John Dashwood confirmed this gift to posterity by passing the estate to the National Trust, and the family, most happily, still live there. We have therefore the best of worlds in West Wycombe; corporate ownership which ensures the future of the house and its surroundings, and the personal involvement of a family for whom every detail has a meaning which transcends history and aesthetics.

At West Wycombe, although ears and noses confirm that we are on the Oxford Road, we are not far from what for me is the most characteristic as well as the most lovely of Chiltern valleys. This may be approached more directly by the first southward turning on the main road, but to savour the valley to the full it is better to continue west beyond Stokenchurch, almost to the motorway, and then turn down towards Ibstone. At first the way is agreeable, wooded and unexceptional, but when the watershed is passed, the road dips gently into the soft green loveliness of the Hambledon valley. Here for once there is no need to hunt for associations. The present is with us and it is very good.

The direct valley route goes down Turville Hill, with tempting woods on the left, but it is worth taking a southward fork before the hill becomes steep in order to visit Turville. This is a village which may reasonably claim pre-eminence among Chiltern villages, not for any great distinction in its buildings but for their singular harmony with one another and with their setting. (A footpath south past some new houses provides a memorable view of the church tower and the cottage roofs set off by fine trees.) A little farther down the road, and on the northern side of the valley, comes Fingest, well known to all ecclesiologists for its Norman tower topped off with a later double saddleback. This is certainly handsome, but better still is the surrounding country whose wooded hills afford delightful glimpses of village and church. There is a tangle of highly rewarding footpaths.

The valley is narrow as far as Skirmett where there is an inn, then it opens a little for two miles and narrows again at the village of Hambledon. All the way the prospects are as fine as Chiltern country can offer. Hambledon itself has the advantage of being just off the through road and is a place of individual charm. Manor house and church are set in classic juxtaposition among the jumbled roofs of the village, and everything is beautifully to scale. The local family represented in the church monuments has the delightfully practical name of Sheepwash. Beyond Hambledon the woods move back and the valley comes to an unspectacular end beside the Thames. It has been only six miles or so from Turville, but in this brief distance the landscape has distilled the essence of the enclosed Chiltern scene. (The outward-looking Chilterns, to be seen later, are quite another matter.)

The Thames valley road to Marlow has too much traffic for comfort, but the miles pass quickly with no more than a single stop at Medmenham. Here a lane goes down past the church to the river bank not far from the site of Medmenham Abbey where Dashwood and his friend had fun—or was it more serious than this?—as the Monks of Medmenham. In our day we are unlikely to be shocked by stories of orgies here, and the strongest comment is that whatever went on was a waste of the talents of politicians, wits and poets. It is all the dimmest of memories now, and no aura remains.

Marlow has grown rapidly in recent years. It has still not lost all the style which once distinguished it among Thames-side towns. Here for once we can forget the politicians and pick up a memory of Shelley who came here in 1817. This was the period of *The Revolt of Islam*, and the unacknowledged legislator composed his poem on long walks beside the river. He would not do so well today, for the towpath, which is theoretically one of the longest footpaths in England, is now a constant scene of frustration because of the decay of bridges.

It is now a main road journey, and a mainly dull one, as far as Bourne End. On the Berkshire bank the river is splendid, but there is no hint of this on the northern bank. Beyond Cores End however, a secondary road follows the curve of the river before being deflected by the wooded heights of Cliveden. Here the Buckinghamshire Thames rises for once to heights of splendour, with woods piled terrace upon terrace up to the walls of Barry's bold and not-unlovely mansion. The house dates only from 1851, and succeeds two others which were each destroyed by fire. One may perhaps not be entirely regretful that memories of the disreputable George Villiers, second Duke of Buckingham, were purged in the flames, and at least his terrace has survived. The noble gardens date in part from a later revival of the house when it belonged to Frederick, Prince of Wales, that poor Fred who "was alive and is dead" and who might have made a better job of kingship than his son

George III. He was a patron of the arts and while at Cliveden he staged a masque to words by Thomson and music by Arne in which "Rule Britannia" first stirred the martial hearts of Britons. The great days of the house, and of the gardens, were when the Astors were here. William Waldorf Astor, American millionaire, was in the true line of landscape designers. The volatile Lady Astor helped to make the name of Cliveden synonymous with political influence, and for a time the house became, although more anachronistically than Bulstrode Park, one of the places where history was made over the dinner table.

Cliveden was given to the National Trust in 1942. Here was not a case for 'freezing' history by preserving the great house as it had been in the heyday of the Astor reign. It had to find a new function, and for preference one associated with the Astors' transatlantic interests. It was therefore let to the University of Stanford, California, and became the setting for courses which were themselves not without influence. This has not inhibited public access, and gardens and house are opened frequently. The gardens in particular call to be visited for their great charms and for the light they shed on three stages in the art of garden design.

The wooded park on the opposite side of the road past Cliveden belongs to Dropmore, another seat with a place in the history of politics and of landscape design. The estate was the creation of William Wyndham Grenville. There is room for two or more opinions of Grenville's abilities in government. He headed the disastrous Ministry of All the Talents in 1806, but the failure of that administration might be shared among its members. At least he was consistent in his unpopular support of Catholic emancipation, and he was a most vigorous and uncompromising opponent of the slave trade. His parliamentary activities came to an end in 1823 when illness forced him to retire to Dropmore. There he indulged a passion for trees and made a landscape as characteristic of the late Georgian age as West Wycombe was of the Georgian high noon.

The lanes around Dropmore are insulated from the industrial and residential tide of Slough by the wooded mass of Burnham Beeches. Between these and Dropmore, caught in a loop of narrow lanes, is yet another house, and this the last on this journey, which has a place in political history. In 1942 Lord Courtauld Thomson gave the modern house of Dorneywood to the National Trust to be used as a kind of Chequers by a Minister of State, that is as a quiet place away from the noise of London for thought and for uninterupted conferences. A tradition has grown up that this is the country house of the Foreign Secretary. For obvious reasons there is no general public access to house and grounds, although they can be visited, by appointment—and this might well be cancelled for urgent reasons of State—in the summer

months. In such a case as this access is indeed not important. What
matters here—even more than at Chequers, which is a building of high
architectural and historical value—is that a small piece of fine country
should be preserved from the pressures which in so much of the Home
Counties makes retreat impossible.

Travellers denied access to Dorneywood have ample compensation
in the green acres of Burnham Beeches which were, with Epping
Forest, the prototype of all country parks. The Corporation of the City
of London rescued the woods from destruction in 1880 and dedicated
a large part of them to public use. The Beeches have lost some of their
former popularity when they were the natural objective of Cockney
beanfeasters. Modern revellers and seekers after rustic delights alike are
prepared to travel farther for their pleasure. This is the Beeches' gain.
They are remarkably uncrowded and offer the opportunity for most
agreeable strolls among the ancient trees, now somewhat decayed but
still oddly attractive. The convoluted shapes are the result of centuries
of cropping by the local commoners. The old trees however form only
a small part of the forested area, and the newer plantations, linked by a
small stream and a chain of ponds, are equally pleasing.

The Chiltern round ends therefore, appropriately enough, among
beech trees in undulating country. A return to the starting-point might
be made past East Burnham Park, where the historian of Greece,
George Grote, lived; and the new housing estates of Burnham, in which
the church where Lord Grenville lies buried is almost lost; to the fragments of Burnham Abbey right under the motorway, or, perhaps
more pleasingly, across Farnham and Stoke Commons, skirting both
pinewoods and Pinewood Studios, and picking up, in the valley of the
River Colne one last literary memory. Here at Horton, within sight
and sound of Heathrow, is the site of Milton's youthful home. The jets
scream over the still-comely church where his mother lies. It is a nicely
incongruous thought that here he delighted in

> Meadows trim and daisies pied
> Shallow brooks and rivers wide.

10

The Way

IT is the most common of knowledge that our road
system was devised by the Romans. Until the
motorways changed our way of life in the last
fifteen years nearly every long journey in this country was made along
the lines laid down by military engineers in the first century.

These roads were surveyed according to scientific principles and
built, with methods approved by experiment as well as experience.
They were the product of an essentially sophisticated and complex
civilization.

In general the Romans started from scratch, taking their bearings
through forest and moorland in complete disregard of any existing
tracks. Only occasionally did their calculated route coincide with one
existing on the ground.

But when the forces of Claudius the God landed at Richborough
there was already in existence a network of ways used by traders and
war bands. The tribal system of prehistoric Britain may have produced
an essentially local form of administration, but there was regular communication between south-east and west, north-east and south-west,
along trackways which had been there time out of mind.

These were not roads in the modern or the Roman sense. They were
ways which came into being through use. No primitive genius had
organized a survey team and gone out with rudimentary theodolite

and markers—despite the ingenious and appealing theories of Hippisley Cox and Watkins. The trackways were produced by people travelling along them, finding out by trial and error what were the easiest and cleanest routes. So, unlike the Roman roads, the tracks are not definitive routes. A way which went well in the dry season might be impassable in winter; change in climatic conditions might make a popular route obsolete. Similarly the ways had none of the Roman road's straight lengths, charging ahead in disregard of natural obstacles. The early travellers found the easy ways which are rarely the straight ones. They followed contours, often adding miles to their journeys but avoiding laborious descents and climbs. The result of all this uncoordinated experiment was not one way but many. An aerial photograph of Britain in the first century BC would have shown country crossed with a seemingly haphazard hatching of ragged lines, rather like a modern photograph of Snowdon which reveals dozens of variants on the main Pig and Miners' Tracks where enterprising or foolish walkers have tried a new route and been followed sheeplike by others.

Because of the evolutionary nature of these ways and the absence of any artificial materials in their construction, it is impossible to prove their provenance or their history. Given time, resources and access, practically all the Roman roads could be established on the ground, because they followed fixed rules and used standard methods of construction. The only rules governing the trackways were those laid down by human nature, the only materials those lying immediately to hand, which a man might pick up to help him across a particularly boggy bit of ground. When the Roman roads superseded some of them, they tended to disappear. A natural way, unlike an artificial road, will quickly become overgrown when it is no longer walked and in a generation or two no trace will remain, even for the archaeologist. Then, in the Middle Ages, new trackways were developed, by methods similar to those of the prehistoric ways, and these can readily be confused with the originals. Even later still, when the turnpikes sent drovers and others off the roads to seek cheaper ways across country, while some took to the surviving ancient ways, others made new ways across the high and as yet unenclosed land.

The investigation of trackways is not therefore a fit exercise for those who like tidy answers to all questions and the scientific slotting into place of each proven piece of evidence. No one has ever written a triumphant Q.E.D. at the foot of a trackway problem. The ways appeal rather to those who hate the progressive smugness of life and who treasure its few remaining mysteries. For them it is more blessed to ask questions than to receive answers. To do this on the ground is singularly rewarding, for, whereas the Roman roads follow predictable routes, often through dull country and more often than not on

Ellesborough and Cymbeline's Mount

Ewelme school

Pitstone Mill and Ivinghoe Beacon

Dunstable Priory

routes now preferred by heavy traffic, the trackways rarely lend themselves to use by modern through traffic, they follow terraces with fine
views, and they pass many field antiquities.

These last are presumptive evidence in favour of the theory of prehistoric origin of the main trackways. It can scarcely be accidental that
the way links Iron Age hill-forts, Bronze Age barrows and Neolithic
great-stone tombs. It is notable too that, with some conspicuous exceptions, the ways do not go through centres of population. They may link
major ancient settlements, but between them they tend to pass through
empty country, or at least through country which has only become
populated—or repopulated—in recent times. In other words the Saxons
who established the pattern of English villages, and who were notori-
ously antipathetic towards the work of early man—or, as they would
say, of the Devil—took pains to avoid involvement with the ways. At
least they preferred not to have the way passing right through the
village; they probably took advantage of it in travelling.

In the south-eastern counties of England there are remains of two
major trackways and of many minor ones. Of the latter, the South
Downs are honeycombed with old tracks. Some of these, especially
those running counter to the main lie of the land, are probably medieval
or later. The track following the north-facing escarpment has all the
characteristics of a prehistoric way. It frequently splits into a mul-
tiplicity of alternative routes; it keeps wherever possible to a contour;
its passage is sown with prehistoric antiquities, including Stone Age
settlements and Bronze and Iron Age farmsteads; all the later villages
lie below the waterless chalk. This track has enjoyed a renewal of life
through designation as the South Downs Way.

The tracks all belong to the chalk, which was the favoured habitat of
prehistoric tribesmen. When the chalk country dried out, through
climatic changes, there was a gradual migration to the lower land, and
to this time, or later, belong the old tracks of the greensand country.
There seems to be the shadow of a way along the escarpment of the
greensand ridge through eastern Surrey and Kent, and westward in
Surrey there are the spectacular hollow ways which dig deep into the
soft stone of the hills. These may belong, like the greensand hill-forts,
to the iron-working communities of the Weald just before and after
the Roman occupation. There remain the two major southern trackways, the Pilgrims Way and Icknield Way. The Pilgrims Way owes its
title to a sentimental Victorian map-maker, and the concept of pilgrims
passing in a continuous flow between Winchester and Canterbury
throughout the Middle Ages seems to have been generated by this
whimsy. Of course pilgrims, together with other travellers, used the
way, and, as with any other medieval route, there is a string of chapels
on or near it. But the Pilgrims Way is clearly much older than the

15

pilgrimages. It has all the marks of a prehistoric trade route. What remains, and is clearly defined both on the map and on the ground, is the lower way. It runs at the foot of the steep escarpment of the North Downs, unlike the South Downs Way, sheltered from the harsh winds of the summit but free of the bog and dense woodland of the plain of Holmesdale. A parallel fine-weather route ran along the top of the down, and this still persists erratically. The Way passes through one of the most celebrated of all prehistoric sites, the great-stone monuments of the Medway gap, but otherwise, in its eastern route, it is not conspicuous for visible antiquities. The country it passes through was largely uninhabited from the Iron Age to late medieval times; few villages actually sit upon the Way although many are in sight of it. As for its destination, it led from the harbours of the narrow seas to the metropolitan centre of prehistoric Britain on Salisbury Plain and thence to the industrial area of the West. It therefore linked the South-east and the Continent with the cultural and religious heart of the country and with the source of vital raw materials. In very recent times the Pilgrims Way has been largely upgraded from bridleway to minor road, regrettably, I think, because it makes a poor motor road while the old track was a superb long-distance walking and riding route. The newly designated North Downs Way has been forced to abandon much of the old Way in favour of newly-defined tracks which sometimes follow the line of the lost fair-weather track on top of the downs.

Of all the ancient ways none has greater authority than the Icknield Way. Its name is no Victorian invention but an authentic—though as yet unexplained—original. It has an early documented history. It is mentioned, as one of the four main roads of England, in the apocryphal, but ancient, "Laws of Edward the Confessor", and it appears on a thirteenth-century map which, however oddly it portrays topography, is precise in showing the Way in East Anglia and at the crossing of Watling Street at Dunstable.

Here, among all the speculations, is an authentic ancient road. It still remains mysterious. We know what its course is today, and roughly where it went in the early Middle Ages; but why? Today it can be traced without difficulty and with only occasional controversy from Thetford on the southern borders of Norfolk to Wanborough in North Wiltshire. The way provides a useful cross-country route, but start and finish are inexplicable. Some clue must be missing. Thetford, it is true, is near Grimes Graves, the principal southern manufactory of stone tools and weapons, and Icknield Way provided a trade outlet for these essentials of Neolithic Britain. There must surely have been an extension northwards to the Wash. Similarly the Way, after crossing the Thames and traversing half the breadth of Britain, having witnessed the making of that monstrous and magnificent beast, the White Horse of Berkshire, comes tamely to an end at Wanborough near Swindon. The Vale of the White Horse is an area exceptionally rich in prehistoric monuments, but this is not enough in itself to bring the long Way to an end, especially when the cultural and religious centre of Avebury is so near. The explanation must lie in the close association between Icknield Way and the Great Ridgeway which pursues its course above the vale. The two must have amalgamated somewhere on the Berkshire–Wiltshire borders, and have continued their combined way to the West Country coast.

The relationship between Icknield Way and Ridgeway presents in an exaggerated form the traditional fine- and foul-weather routes of all the ancient trackways. In name at least the Ridgeway comes to an eastward end at the crossing of the Thames, but on its north-eastern course the Icknield Way still often shows a clearly defined division into upper and lower ways. The survival of the upper way is especially valuable because of what has happened to the lower. Everyone who travels about this country will know that there are very few effective through cross-routes. To get to any part of the compass from London is simple because the great trunk routes and motorways radiate from the capital. But to get from one of these radial roads to another is much less easy. Hence the popularity of such main roads as run counter to the general pattern—for example, the A25, which is a modern alternative to the Pilgrims Way, or the Lower Icknield Way. The old track below the chalk has become, not consecutively but frequently, a major traffic highway, and its intimate charms have consequently vanished. These are now to be found, if at all, in the upper way where this survives as a narrow lane or a deep track through the chalk uplands and the Chiltern beechwoods.

The Icknield Way represents the outermost limits of my territory. I may well be accused of stretching definitions beyond their reasonable limits by taking this into the Home Counties, but the Way provides so admirable and identifiable a link between interesting places and symbolizes so precisely the end of the chalk that I could not resist adopting it as the theme of a journey around the northern and western perimeter of the commuter country.

The problem is where to begin. The traditional advice to begin at the beginning begs too many questions, for a literal interpretation would take us into Dorset and Norfolk—both most desirable expeditions, but I fear that not even the most flexible of definitions would include these in the Home Counties. To stick rigidly to county boundaries, however, would not be helpful, for on the western edge Buckinghamshire merges imperceptibly with Oxfordshire in the soft folds of the Chilterns. I feel justified therefore—especially as the decision will make me free of much loved country—in starting this journey at the crossing of the Thames and ending it where the Way turns north decisively at Royston. One might, I suppose, argue for a logical extension of the journey to Newmarket, which, ever since Charles II gave up the real thrills and hazards of hunting in favour of the vicarious excitement of horse racing, has been a focus of the attention of the court and consequently of Londoners. But the Londoner went to Newmarket races for a day out. It never occurred to him that this was part of London's country, but rather a country which offered the additional attraction of unfamiliarity.

It is one thing to establish the principle of a journey, quite another to make an actual start. Everyone knows that the Icknield Way crosses the Thames from Streatley to Goring. But is everyone right? In order to make this crossing the Way turns south-east across the line of the Berkshire Downs, then turns north over the river in order to pick up the Chiltern escarpment. An alternative leaves the conventional Way just over Kingstanding Hill and goes past Moulsford to a crossing of the river at South Stoke. It is true that there is no bridge. There were no bridges at all when the Way was first extant. Yet another route leaves the Way at Upton and keeps below the hills, in the normal fashion, all the way to the Thames three miles or so south of Wallingford. It then rises to join the two alternatives at Ipsden. Each of the unofficial routes has a lane leading to the river, indicating the existence of a traditional crossing by ferry or ford.

Since there can be no conclusive decision as to the 'right' Way, and indeed, in the true style of these prehistoric wonderlands, all ways are right, we might skip the river, whose pleasure-boatmen and anglers somehow strike a more anachronistic note even than juggernaut lorries, and begin our journey at Ipsden. This is unquestionable on the Way.

(Authority has recently stepped in with its own definitive Way, for the Ridgeway has been designated as a long-distance footpath and walkers are able to follow a right of way from the Thames at least as far as Ivinghoe. This is fine, and one cannot but applaud the notable achievements in this area. It will not on the whole help us in our present dilemma because our journeys are necessarily tied to the car, and cars and walkers don't and should not mix.)

Ipsden is in open country alternating, in the typical West Chiltern way, with woodlands. The open land is mostly arable now and the most rewarding time for this journey is around harvest but not later, when the barbarous and doubtfully economic practice of stubble-burning turns the landscape into scorched earth and dying trees.

Having agreed a starting point, at Ipsden's little lonely church difficulties at once arise. The route of the Way is not in question, but here it is a trackway going roughly north across country, crossing in its course the mysterious boundary earthwork of Grim's Ditch, but cars must find a less direct route, either west towards Wallingford or past Well Place, where there are bird gardens, through the lovely beechwood of Ipsden Heath and then north past Nuffield to where the Oxford Road crosses Nuffield Common. Either way our objective is the same, the emergence of Icknield Way as a very minor road across Cow Common. At the top of the rise comes the first, and most essential diversion from the Way, for only a mile away lies Ewelme, the most priceless jewel of the Chiltern country.

Many villages are the result of one family's patronage, but Ewelme owes its unique loveliness to one generation. The manor belonged at the beginning of the fifteenth century to Thomas Chaucer, who was probably—the experts are divided on the question, but this need not concern us—the poet's son. Thomas had married well and had gained Ewelme as part of his wife's dowry. To this he later added the important manor of Woodstock. He was a notable figure, a man of great wealth and a warrior—he fought at Agincourt—and also Speaker of the House of Commons. When he died he left Ewelme to his only daughter Alice, who had already married, as her third husband, William de la Pole, Earl—and later Duke—of Suffolk. So Ewelme emerged from obscurity as the possession of one of the most prominent and controversial men of his age.

Suffolk's early career was military. He went to France with Henry V, but was wounded at Harfleur and therefore missed the battle of Agincourt. While he lay abed in England, his elder brother was killed in the battle, and so William inherited the title. In the next reign he had the distinction of being captured by Joan of Arc. His captain in these campaigns was the Earl of Salisbury, and he later married the earl's widow. He tired of the weary futilities of the French wars, and so became identified with the peace party in direct conflict with the king's uncle, Humphrey Duke of Gloucester. It was Suffolk's idea that the young king should marry the French princess Margaret. He negotiated the match personally and he and Countess Alice went to France to bring home the Queen, whom Suffolk had married as proxy for Henry VI. Suffolk won the struggle for power with Gloucester. Unfortunately he let himself be outmanœuvred by the French. The peace terms seemed like a defeat. Popular opinion turned violently against him. The king refused to have him condemned, but yielded to pressure enough to send him into exile. The ship carrying him to France was intercepted, and he was murdered.

The king's refusal to have Suffolk attainted meant that his estates were not confiscated. Ewelme remained intact, and his son had the title restored to him. (The Poles continued to be unlucky, however. Of William's grandsons one instigated the Lambert Simnel plot and was fortunate only in being killed at the Battle of Stoke and not on the block, another was beheaded, and the third spent his life intriguing against the Tudors and was killed on the French side at Pavia.) Alice, by now three times widowed, continued to live at Ewelme. She kept an interest in politics, was involved in Cade's rebellion and in the Yorkist struggle. (She was step-grandmother of Warwick the King-maker.) When she died at a great age in 1475 she was buried at Ewelme. Whatever the quality of Suffolk's public career, and it is by no means clear whether he was unlucky or culpable, his home life seems to have been singularly happy. His duchess was a person of character and an admirable manager of the estate.

The Suffolk's manor house has long disappeared, and the Duke and his wife would have equally gone into oblivion but for the energy and practical charity of—one suspects—the Duchess. During their days of prosperity and happiness they rebuilt the parish church of Ewelme and attached to it, as a twin foundation, a hospital and a grammar school. By an astonishing and joyful change this has survived, and three fifteenth-century buildings exist side by side, each still doing the work for which it was originally designed.

The ground is quite steep, and the three buildings are most effectively sited at different levels on the side of the hill. At the top is the church with its east end to the upper road and its western tower occupying the central position on the site. A little brick porch links church and bedehouse, and a flight of steps leads down to the cloister and the open court of the hospital. Around this are disposed the little apartments of the thirteen inmates. A domestic range on the northern side, providing shelter for a large walled garden, links the hospital with the grammar school—now the county primary school, a tall building in brick. Although the three elements in the plan make a highly satisfactory whole, each has an appropriate character. The church is a big building of sober magnificence in flint. The hospital is homely and intimate. The school has dignity and just a little swagger.

It is not clear how this foundation escaped the greedy hands of Henry VIII and his son, for it was doubtless a duty of the inmates to pray for the souls of Suffolk and his duchess, and this laid the place open to a charge of superstition. Then in the Civil War Ewelme had the incredible good fortune to come under the control of a parliamentary officer of rare sensibility, and he permitted no desecration. Even later restorers were kinder here than was their wont. The church has many points of interest, but its richest possession is the tomb of the foundress. Suffolk was buried at Wingfield on his Suffolk estates, but his duchess lies in a tomb of the utmost splendour. No other English woman, not even Queen Eleanor in Westminster Abbey, has so noble and perfect a monument. The Duchess, an austere figure in white alabaster, lies under a canopy with exquisitely carved angels at her head.

She was presumably herself responsible for the tomb of her father Thomas Chaucer, nearby, a more sober monument with brass effigies and heraldry. The latter include the arms of Roet, the Flemish family into which Geoffrey Chaucer married.

Apart from the monuments the most astonishing thing in the church is the towering fifteenth-century woodwork of the font-cover, a notably and highly sophisticated piece of work which suggests that the Suffolks employed craftsmen of more than local eminence for their foundation. Ewelme church indeed always seems to me to offer a yardstick by which all village churches can be measured. In its scale, its proportions, the excellence and the discretion of its fittings, the skill with which it is set into the landscape, it approaches perfection without —as the more majestic churches of East Anglia sometimes do— bludgeoning the visitor into admiration.

For the rest, Ewelme is a pleasant village with no buildings of out-standing quality. A little clear chalk stream, from which the place derives its name, comes out of the hills and widens out in the village to form watercress beds. There is a quiet distinction about the scene which even the proximity of Benson airfield cannot altogether destroy.

Few villages are harder to leave than Ewelme. However, the Icknield Way points steadily north-east and must be followed. For the motorist the obvious route is by the main road up Firebross Hill and so by Britwell—Britwell Salome, enchanting name!—to Watlington. I avoid obvious routes wherever possible, and the Way itself will take us over Cow Common on a narrow quiet lane heading in just the right direc-tion. On the downward side of the hill, however, the Way becomes a track and cars are forced eastwards around the flank of Swyncombe Down, a fine partly wooded spur of the Chilterns. There is a steady climb between the down and the handsome parkland of Swyncombe House, in which a very small Norman church nestles beside the bulk of the house. There was a small priory here, of French origin, but it was suppressed with the other alien houses by Henry V and nothing remains. Eventually the lane rises to the main road, literally a high road this with altitudes between 600 and 700 feet at Cookley Green.

For those with time to wander aimlessly this is rewarding country. Though not the highest, this is one of the finest parts of the Chilterns, their lovely curving lines enriched with typical beechwoods and with the parks of great estates, notably Turville and, best of all, Stonor. For the dedicated follower of ways the route must lie northwards along the main road around the flank of Watlington Park. The Way itself, still a trackway at this point, is crossed well down the hill and almost a mile out of Watlington town. At this point a glance half-backwards shows the steep face of Watlington Hill and down it the streak of the White Mark.

Chalk hill-figures, those characteristic expressions of the British genius for big, splendidly useless creations, always provoke lunatic speculation. They are so bold and elemental that they must surely be survivals from the dawn of man. The Watlington White Mark clearly offers evidence in support of such a theory; what is it but a phallic symbol? Look at it again, with more sophisticated eyes, and it suddenly looks quite different. In the eighteenth century there was a fashion among Georgian gentlemen for the erection on their estates of stone obelisks, often dedicated to the most improbable causes. At Watlington Edward Horne went one better. He cut an enormous obelisk (270 feet high) in the chalk and outdid all his neighbours.

The Way which we have seen intermittently in the last few miles is the Upper Icknield Way. The lower Way follows roughly the line of the main road out of Ewelme through Britwell. This road turns abruptly off the Way in order to go through Watlington, a rather dull little town enlivened only by the brick market-hall of 1664. It would be worth avoiding the congested town centre by going along the Oxford road for a few hundred yards and turning right past the parish church along a lane which leads to the pretty small village of Pyrton. There are Hampden associations here. John Hampden courted Elizabeth Symeon of Pyrton Manor and married her in the church. (She was

> The stay and comfort of her neighbours,
> The love and glory of a well-ordered family,
> The delight and happiness of tender parents,
> But a crown of blessings to a husband

on the authority of Hampden himself.) The church was practically rebuilt in the drastic Victorian manner.

The Lower Icknield Way follows roughly the line of a farm road skirting the back of Shirburn Castle and continuing as track or minor road behind Lewknor, crossing the main Oxford road and continuing, still as a bridle way, as far as Chinnor. Those enslaved to the tyranny of a car must be content with the road which runs almost equidistant between Upper and Lower Ways. This goes through Shirburn, past the boundary of the park containing the historic but unseen castle. Then road 'improvements', to use the cant term, take the traveller above Lewknor village, which is nice for the people of this charming village. Here in the combe between Bald Hill and Beacon Hill the Chilterns have acquired another 'white mark', made, in 1973, by the gash of the M40 motorway. There was a great row about this crucial section of the new road, and a battle which the conservationists lost. Obviously there will be bitter controversy whenever a new road passes through outstandingly fine country, and no route is going to please everyone—or anyone. However the damage has been done now, and one can find comfort only in the thought that the cars and lorries on the motorway cannot escape to congest these Chiltern lanes.

The old Oxford road is reached at the 'Lambert Arms'. Above is the big wooded bulge of Beacon Hill and the rich hanging woods of Aston Hill, safely—thank goodness—in the hands of the National Trust. That great and beneficent body holds all too little of this vulnerable Chiltern country. The Upper Way crosses half a mile up the hill and continues as a bridleway just below the steep rise of the escarpment. Our road passes through a string of little villages: Aston Rowant, Kingston Blount, Crowell and Oakley. None of these, except perhaps Aston, which has its church set away from the road in parkland, is of great interest or charm, but they make useful milestones on the road. The wooded line of hills looks well, and some fine roadside timber resists the efforts of road improvers and quick profit farmers to eliminate standard trees. At Oakley there is a sharp double bend, and then comes Chinnor, which has all the marks of a town except size. I remember when this was a place to delight in and a fine centre for the exploration of the western Chilterns. Now the charm has mostly gone, obliterated by overgrowth and traffic. A few good houses survive, and so does the big, rather grand church, which belongs largely to the end of the thirteenth century.

Here the road turns north for half a mile and then joins the line of the Lower Icknield Way on its north-eastern course. This line takes it away from the hills, while the upper way turns east across the wide dry valley which cuts deep into the Chilterns all the way to West Wycombe. Where the hills swing east, the last spur, heavily wooded, has in its face one small clearing in which the Bledlow Cross gleams white. It occupies a position roughly corresponding to that on the other side of the valley where the bigger and altogether more interesting Whiteleaf Cross stands. It will be better to consider these enigmatic chalk monuments when we come to Whiteleaf. Bledlow Cross is easily missed. It can be seen best about a mile out of Chinnor, and even then it may be mistaken for a small chalk quarry.

The road nearly touches the fringe of Bledlow village, but a diversion south is essential, for this is one of the most attractive of Chiltern villages. It is quite small, just one street with the inn at one end, the church and manor house in the middle, and all harmonizing most rarely. We are now in Buckinghamshire, but only just, and the scenery and buildings show no subtle changes. This country is neither Ox nor Bucks but Chiltern. Bledlow church is not one of the biggest but certainly one of the loveliest on this journey, a perfect village church because it has no aspirations above its station. The detail is as pleasing as the general design, and there is a good Tudor brass.

As Bledlow marks a turning-point in the journey, and the next mile
or two are markedly duller, this might be the place to leave a car in
favour of a little walk. A triangular stroll of barely three miles, including
a climb almost to the 600 feet contour, starts just beside the inn and
takes in the fringe of the woods on Wain Hill where the skirting
track is the upper way. The dense woods doubtless hide the site of the
burial mound of a Saxon warrior Bledda from whom the village
derives its name. The views across the plain towards Thame and Oxford
are exceedingly fine.

At Bledlow upper and lower ways move apart. The lower way
goes very straight from Chinnor to Little Kimble. The ultimate authority
in this field, Mr I. D. Margary, has identified this as a Roman road to
which the name of Icknield Way has become traditionally attached.
Might it not be both? For once the Romans found that an ancient
trackway served their needs, and they updated it and got rid of its
occasional waywardness. As far as Little Kimble this lower road is
rather dull. The upper way, which turns east around the spur of Wain
Hill and goes across the neck of the valley without much loss of height,
has more scenic interest. It is reached from Bledlow church by a
southward turn on a lane which eventually climbs to the top of the
hills, leaving it by the second eastward (left) turn. The modern lane
reaches the main Wendover–Wycombe road in two or three miles.
What happens to the Way is less certain. The Ordnance Survey shows
it passing around the new developments of Princes Risborough on a
steadily ascending line; this is doubtless correct but we can only follow
it on foot. Except by becoming entangled in the steep Chiltern lanes
to the east, the motorist is forced to enter Princes Risborough.

This is the first sizeable town on this journey, and it should prove
useful for supplies and refreshment. Like other towns which enjoyed a
revival in the eighteenth century it is generously provided with inns.
In general I find Princes Risborough slightly disappointing. Recent
growth has been considerable but reasonably well contained. New and
old do not cohere very well, and neither is of high quality. The
'Prince' is popularly identified as the Black Prince, but is more likely
to have been Richard of Cornwall, Henry III's brother, who held the
manor late in the thirteenth century. For visitors the most attractive
part of the town is around the sharp double bend in the middle. In a
back street past the church there are some pretty timbered cottages,
and immediately adjoining the churchyard is a very handsome town
house from late in the seventeenth century with a characteristically
civilized façade; this now belongs to the National Trust. The church
itself does not quite rise to the demands of its effective central position;
it is an adequate building of the early thirteenth century but lacks the
distinction one might look for in a royal manor. For the rest the curious

modern process which reduces all towns to a common level, architectural and social, seems to be at work here.

If Princes Risborough is not royal enough, Monks Risborough benefited from its monastic connections. It belonged to Christ Church Priory, Canterbury, and has an admirable church. Risborough was a grange of Christ Church and had no resident religious community in the ordinary sense. Probably there was a brother who looked after the affairs of the estate, or the manor might have been left in the care of lay officials. The farm beside the church probably stands on the site of the grange. The immediate area has stood up well to the pressures of development and is still remarkably attractive.

Looking east from Monks Risborough the scene is dominated by the high wooded sweep of the Chilterns, which just beyond rise above eight hundred feet. The centrepiece of the view is a very big chalk cross, quite different in character from either Bledlow Cross, which we have recently seen, and the modern memorial crosses of the North Downs. It rises from a very large pyramid-shaped white wedge cut, or eroded, from the turf. At present the Whiteleaf Cross is about 250 feet high and the base is all of 400 feet wide. A giant among hill figures indeed and most impressive in its gaunt simplicity. Modern measurements, of course, are no guide to the intentions of the original designers. Rain and ice play havoc with the work, and restorers, without whom the figure would disappear under grass and weeds in a few generations, involuntarily enlarge the outlines as they scour the chalk.

Controversy has been busy for more than two centuries over the origin and purpose of the Whiteleaf Cross. All that is known for certain is that it existed, much smaller, in 1742 when it was drawn and measured. The topographers of Tudor times, often good witnesses and especially interested in ancient and mysterious objects, have nothing to say about it, but that is merely negative evidence. Like all the ancient hill-figures the cross is sited near prehistoric burial mounds; its situation in relation to Monks Risborough is precisely similar to that of Wilmington Long Man in Sussex with its neighbouring monastic grange. Like the prehistoric White Horse of Berkshire it keeps close company with an ancient trackway. Some of these parallels are shared by the Bledlow Cross, but there is no hard evidence for the existence of the latter before the nineteenth century.

In an area where speculation must take the place of proof, I am prepared to come out with the confident guess that the Bledlow Cross is a product of the great age of follies in the late eighteenth century, when many of the White Horses were cut by enthusiastic romantics. About the Whiteleaf Cross I must be more cautious, for evidence, probabilities and theories are at variance. It might be a prehistoric marker on the Way, a white mark later Christianized by the addition of arms. It could be medieval, a Christian symbol made by monks of Risborough grange in an excess of devotional zeal. It might be yet another folly; if so it must have anticipated the fashion by an improbable number of decades, for it was obviously old when the Reverend Francis Wise described it in 1742 and identified it, in pursuance of his obsession, as the work of Saxons. Morris Marples—in *White Horses and Other Hill Figures* (1949)—is inclined to give the cross a mid-seventeenth-century date. But the puritans would not have tolerated such an idolatrous symbol, and after the Restoration who would have bothered?

The Whiteleaf Cross must remain a mystery, but a stimulating and strangely moving one. Scenically it is enhanced by the setting, for the cross is cut in a very steep face of the downs, and it is framed in fine beechwoods. I have always had a special feeling for the Whiteleaf Cross, for it belongs to almost the earliest of my memories. I sat in its arm at the age of about four, with the Oxford plain a limitless expanse of green and blue, a vision of infinity which I have never lost.

This view is not to be missed. By driving around the base of the cross it is possible to gain height and then walk along the ridge, through beechwoods which are at their finest in autumn and winter, to emerge just above the gleaming head of the cross. The prospect takes in the low country of the Thames valley. It is closed in the distance by the dim wall of the Cotswolds, and in the haze twenty-five miles away lies Oxford, which, by confused and obscure traditions, is associated with Whiteleaf Cross and its ritual scouring.

Back to the main road, and in a mile we are at Great Kimble, where a stately church stands by the road. This was the scene of Hampden's formal challenge to the legality of ship money, for here he answered the summons to pay his assessment—it related to property which he owned in Stoke Mandeville, a village down in the Aylesbury plain—a trivial event with large consequences. Just beyond the church the road divides, the major road continuing north to Aylesbury, the lesser—the upper way—turning right at Little Kimble church. This is a pretty, unassuming building from the early fourteenth century in an effective setting. Beyond lie the wide green police-protected acres of Chequers.

The next village on the upper Way is Ellesborough, which has as fine a situation as any. The Way has risen considerably at this point and views are opening up over the plain. The church stands on a little hill with no neighbouring building sufficiently large to detract from its dramatic position. Across the road the Chilterns surge upward in an unusually exciting fashion to the bald crown of Cymbeline's Mount. Although this is barely 250 feet above the village it seems twice that height, so distinctive is its shape and so marked its isolation, for the spur thrusts well out from the line of the hills. Across the re-entrant rises Combe Hill, higher by a hundred feet and mostly wooded. On the top of Cymbeline's Mount are the traces of a hill-fort with a single rampart. The view is very extensive towards the north-west, and especially attractive south-west along the richly wooded line of the Chiltern face. Ellesborough is the parish for Chequers and the church has monuments of Tudor and Stuart Hawtreys who lived in the great house. The charm of this very pleasant place is at present marred by controversy over the security of the Prime Minister's home, jeopardized by the existence of a beautiful footpath over which many citizens are inconsiderate enough to exercise their right of way. Hampden might have had a word for it.

The upper Way continues to Wendover, still at a high altitude and following the edge of some of the finest of Chiltern country. Coombe Hill (National Trust) and Bacombe Hill clamour for attention, and if time allows nothing could be more enjoyable than a walk over their wooded flanks. Coombe Hill was the scene in 1973 of the formal inauguration of the Ridgeway, an event of major importance in the history of man's struggle for the right to enjoy the land in which he lives.

The road drops quite sharply to Wendover, a little town which straddles the neck of a gap in the chalk. A main road runs through the gap and down into the Misbourne valley. Wendover itself stands up quite well to its modern pressures. It is at about the limit of normal commuter range, and there is consequently a considerable amount of modern building which has not yet gone to the point of suffocating the old community. Some pretty cottages survive, especially at the southern end where the church tower marks the heart of the original settlement. The building is of much interest, but it is not for buildings that one visits Wendover but for the exceptional charm of the setting. High wooded hills rise on either side, each offering walks of a characteristic Chiltern greenness.

From Wendover the obvious route is by the main road towards Tring, which the Ordnance Survey designates as the Upper Icknield Way. This is very pretty as main roads go, but too busy for enjoyable motoring. The lower Way crosses the Aylesbury road at World's End and then goes astray. The Ordnance Survey shows it as a secondary road at Weston Turville and again near Wilstone, but this seems improbable. For once the modern road system has abandoned the old Way, and the Way has been swallowed up by a leat feeding the Grand Union Canal. This straight waterway passes beside the church at Halton and very close to the isolated church of Drayton Beauchamp, a building which briefly entertained, if not angels, at least a saint unawares, for here Richard Hooker, apologist extraordinary of the Church of England, was rector for a year before being carried off to more influential office in the Temple Church. Walton in his brief 'life' painted a charming picture of the great man interpreting his pastoral duties very literally. This route is not very satisfactory as a through-way for cars, and it would be better to follow the Ordnance Survey's advice and turn right by the Marquis of Granby at World's End, then coming right through Weston Turville. This is now largely suburban in character, acting as an overflow for Aylesbury. It is mostly modern and socially superior. The old village is on the southern edge of the developed area, and the church is the last building in the village, with only the brick manor house for company. Most attractive in its setting, the church also has interest in its very mixed architectural styles and in its fittings.

At the main London road (A41) there is no real alternative to a mile of trunk road eastward through Aston Clinton, a once-attractive village which has had the spirit hammered out of it by traffic, and then the road to Ivinghoe turns off north-west. We are here not far from a summit of the Grand Union Canal, and in the background of our view is the green swell of Ashridge, on which stands the monument to the only begetter of that great industrial enterprise, the Duke of Bridge-water. The reservoirs beside the road were cut to maintain the level of the canal which between Aylesbury and Tring has twenty-two locks. We cross the canal at Startop's End. The scene is now dominated by big cement works. These are visually very fine of their kind. I wish that the additions to Pitstone and Marsworth villages, built to house workers in the factory, were half as good of *their* kind. Our century has found its outlet for architectural expression in great industrial buildings, but it seems quite unable to design a tolerable housing estate. At least these mean houses are not built to last. The rows of domestic built-in obsolescence bring us to Ivinghoe, and at once we are surrounded by demonstrations of the art of building for people.

We have it on the authority of the 'King of the Chiltern Hills' himself, Sir Bernard Miles, that Ivinghoe is "what they call inter-denominational" and that the noble parish church contains "the finest bit of sharpening stone in all Hertfordshire"—but we are still in Bucks! It is certainly an exceptionally attractive place, grown up around complex crossroads. All the essentials are here, inn, town house—now a youth hostel—admirable cottages, and a big cruciform church, almost a mini-cathedral in the way it dominates its community and the surrounding flat land. Since we left Ewelme the churches we have passed have been charming, individual but not architecturally exciting. Here is one in the manner—if not to the standard—of the great churches of East Anglia, even to the angel roof. The grandeur, so much more than the modest size of the modern village—one-time market town—warrants is explained by the Bishops of Winchester's lordship of the manor. The church was built perhaps to the greater glory of God, certainly to that of My Lord Bishop.

Ivinghoe has a very small place in literary history, because the name, imperfectly remembered, gave Scott the title of his famous historical romance. He presumably never came here, or he would have got the name right; he remembered it from an old jingle—itself historically inaccurate—about a medieval Hampden who surrendered the manor to the Black Prince in compensation for an offence; he was supposed to have hit him during a tennis match!

Upper and lower Ways converge here, at least on the map. (The modern Ridgeway is probably more correct in keeping along the top of the downs.) A small layby at their junction provides parking for a visit to Pitstone Mill, standing alone in a field to the west. This little post mill now belongs to the National Trust, who claim—but this might be disputed by other ancient mills in the Home Counties—that it is the oldest in the country. It is certainly a fine example of the most primitive form of windmill, in which the whole structure turns into the wind on a great central pole.

The road to Dunstable is not in itself interesting, but it skirts one of the most spectacular areas of the Chilterns. The great beech woods have been left behind and the chalk downs are bare and boldly profiled. They drop abruptly into the plain from Ivinghoe Beacon, which looks much more than its 700 feet and gives the most uninterrupted view of the whole range. Behind are the commons, Ivinghoe, Pitstone, Aldbury, Berkhamsted with their rolling views and fine walks. Ivinghoe Beacon makes an appropriately dramatic conclusion to the Ridgeway.

From the beacon the view is mostly across flat country, the wide seemingly endless Midland plain. Immediately in the foreground there is one interruption of the general horizontal lines. A hillock, rather like a diminutive parody of the beacon itself, rises conspicuously, the more so because it is capped with a very large church. Not even the church at Ellesborough, which is comparable to Edlesborough in some ways, is more effectively sited. If you make a worthwhile diversion to visit it, you will see that the mound on which it is built is obviously artificial. Here surely is one of those very early foundations, a place in which Christian missionaries chose a mysterious pagan 'work' on which to plant symbolically the victorious cross. The church, less magnificent in scale than Ivinghoe's, is, despite some villainous restorations, exceptionally rich containing, as it does, rood screen and carved stalls and one of the most lavish and early of pulpits in the county, with a pinnacled sounding-board imitating in wood the liern vaulting which was just then going out of fashion. This is work of the utmost sophistication and remarkably successful. Whoever put it in this out-of-the-way place? Those who have so far resisted the charms of English village churches might use Edlesborough as a test case; if it does not appeal, then they may as well give up.

Edlesborough Church, once picturesquely isolated, now keeps company with modern houses which spill across the county border into Bedfordshire. In spite of them it is probably more acceptable to keep this side of the Icknield Way in order to avoid the worst of the traffic around Dunstable. This alternative route goes through the fringe of Eaton Bray and Totternhoe—where a famous limestone was quarried in the Middle Ages. These were on the northern edge of the village, near the great castle mound, and the area is of exceptional antiquarian interest. Totternhoe Castle looks across to Maiden Bower, the biggest and most impressive Iron Age camp in the Chilterns. South of Totternhoe there are views to the main wall of the hills at Dunstable Downs, where gliders circle and the Whipsnade Lion ambles tamely across the chalk.

Dunstable is the first real town—in the modern sense—which we have encountered on the Icknield Way and it is historically the most important in the whole length of the Way. It was a place, or at least a neighbourhood, of some importance from the earliest times. Maiden Bower is almost inside the modern town, and where Dunstable Downs sweep down to the built-up area they terminate in Five Knolls, a group of Bronze Age round barrows. Just to the south-east, at Caddington, there was an important Neolithic stone-implement factory. When the Roman military engineers made Watling Street Dunstable was an obvious site for a staging post. It was at the right distance from Verulamium, at a point where the hills sloped down towards the plain, and to clinch the matter here was an east–west trackway creating with Watling Street a model crossroads settlement. This was known as Durocobrivae. The Roman town was destroyed comprehensively by Saxon raiders. No doubt something grew up in its place, for the site was too valuable to lie neglected for long. Its full revival dates from the beginning of the twelfth century when King Henry I built a palace in the manor and endowed a house of Augustinian Canons on land close to the ancient crossroads. This enjoyed royal favour for several centuries, and several kings stayed here, including the mourning Edward I on his melancholy journey to Westminster with the body of Queen Eleanor. The Queen lay in state in the priory church on the night of 12th December 1290, and an exquisite cross was put up at the crossroads. It stood there until the pious barbarians of the Parliamentary forces blew it up during the Civil War. The last great event in the life of the priory took place in 1533, when proceedings for the divorce of Henry VIII and Catherine of Aragon were held in the priory. At the Dissolution the King was probably more eager than usual to get rid of this evidence of past unhappiness, and the priory buildings, except

Icknield Way below Telegraph Hill

Ashwell

for the nave of the church, were effectively destroyed. The nave was spared and sold to the town for a parish church.

What is left is still profoundly impressive. The nave is late Norman work, with as yet no hint of the transition to Early English, dignified, restrained, avoiding extravagance—and remarkably well cared for. It is in marked contrast to the west front, which shows an incomplete reconstruction of the original. The flanking towers fell early in Henry III's reign, making drastic rebuilding necessary. The restorers completed the northern side and then presumably funds ran out leaving the front a most magnificent hotch-potch. To the south is a huge Norman arch of five orders, on the north a most elegant and rich doorway from the high noon of Early English architecture above which are inserted three slender arcades. It looks curious, certainly, but memorable. Part of the site of the conventual buildings has been turned into an attractive small garden, a refuge in the heart of what is admittedly a noisy town.

After the decline caused by the loss of the priory Dunstable revived in the seventeenth century when straw-plaiting and hat-making promoted an industrial boom. The town also prospered as a result of the increased mobility of the eighteenth century when traffic on Watling Street produced business for a number of inns. Some of these survive to grace the main road with their dignified façades. Later ages have added little which enhances the appearance of the town. It has never quite recovered from the excessive congestion which preceded the opening of the M1 motorway, and the central area, which might have been as handsome as, say, Stony Stratford and Towcester, bears a battered, shabby aspect.

So much—or so little—for central Dunstable. As for the outer areas, words, or at least polite words, do not come easily. It is sad, and a defeat for the principles of good planning, that no green belt has been preserved between Dunstable and Luton. The four miles between Dunstable Cross and the M1 are my idea of Hell, not a fearful place but one utterly devoid of individuality, from which all spirit has been drained. I awake at night in a sweat after dreaming that I have been condemned to drive these miles in perpetuity. And this is the Icknield Way!

Perhaps we might cheat for once, and make a big loop around Luton, avoiding most of this big urban and industrial mass. Not that Luton itself lacks interest. It is a fascinating example of a small ancient town coming to terms with the demands of the twentieth century and accepting the necessity of growth. It is an interesting—even an exciting —town, but it is not a Home Counties town. Luton turns its back on London and looks inward to itself.

To avoid the town, we follow Watling Street for a mile northwards, and then turn off to Houghton Regis. The one-time village has grown

16

considerably and lost its charm, but a minor road near the church escapes into the country in another mile or two, following the watershed between the Lea and the Ouzel which flows west to the Great Ouse. There is a slightly confusing junction beside the M1 and then we are out in true country among different hills from those we have been in throughout this journey. Instead of the bald chalk downs and the beechwoods, the hills are more rolling and imperfectly defined. Sundon, which stands at about 450 feet, is the first real village we have seen for a long time, although it is barely a mile from the northern outpost of Luton. It is a quiet unassuming place grouped around church and manor house, remarkably peaceful except when, as at my last visit, it is suffering from an incursion of 'wind on the heath'. The road rises to the larger and less attractive village of Streatley. Having come so far in what is admittedly the wrong direction, we may as well go a little farther north to see the edge of the Chilterns at Sharpenhoe. Here a wooded spur, safely in the care of the National Trust, gives long views across the Bedfordshire clay towards the greensand hills of Woburn.

This, however, is an essentially Midland scene, and we must return to our brief, not even to be diverted by the continuation of the Chiltern range to Barton Hills, where another Iron Age camp lies buried in the woods. So we return to Streatley and follow a high straight lane almost due east with the central ridge of the chalk full in view. Where this lane meets another we are within a few yards of the Icknield Way at one of its finest and least spoilt stretches. Having survived the passage of Luton the Way rises steeply over Galley Hill and for the next ten miles or so becomes, with few interruptions, a trackway which resembles, if not its primeval original or the Saxon herepath, at least the drove-road which it became in the eighteenth century.

This calls for exploration on foot, and happily there is room to park beside the road. I hope you will not, as some selfish visitors do, drive along the green way, destroying its peace and integrity in order to avoid a little exertion. The Way rises steadily to the top of Telegraph Hill—from which the news of Trafalgar and Waterloo was flashed into the Midlands—and it then becomes the boundary between Bedfordshire and Hertfordshire. As it drops towards Ickleford it loses the views to the north behind the shoulder of Deacon Hill, and then joins for a mile the secondary road between Hitchin and Barton. It then becomes a rough trackway again following the valley of the Oughton into Ickleford. Here the modern village intervenes for less than a mile, and the Way continues, this time as a bridleway right to the edge of Letchworth.

This very direct route is for walkers only. The car-bound must adopt a more wayward course, unless, which would not be my choice, they simply take the main road into the centre of Hitchin. A beautifully roundabout route heads into the border country below the Chiltern ridge, by way of Apsley End—with another almost irresistible excursion into Bedfordshire, lured by the tremendous bulk of Shillington Church—and Pirton, which is a nicely compact village with some excellent houses, notably the really charming Rectory Farm. Then the road goes well to the north to Holwell, a plain village with a rebuilt church on a sharp bend. This is worth a quick visit because it contains, on a brass, the representation of two green men, or woodwoses, those mysterious savage creatures of the Middle Ages about whom controversy will always rage. But surely they must have been drop-outs from medieval society who took to the woods and became a half-dreadful, half-fascinating legend.

The main road from Bedford goes south to cross the line of the Icknield Way at Ickleford. Here is another village which must once, and not so long ago, have been very charming. It has become a little overgrown and suburban, being now almost overtaken by the northern spill of Hitchin. Here the River Oughton joins the improbably named Hiz, flowing north to the Bedfordshire Ivel and eventually joining the Great Ouse. Coming east out of this valley we may enjoy the last of the open country before entering the well-mannered and slightly demodé rows of Letchworth Garden City.

It is one of those pleasant ironies in which the Home Counties are rich that the central highway—although it goes nowhere in particular—of the garden city, the characteristic first fruits of the social thought of the twentieth century, should be the prehistoric Icknield Way. For part of its course it is flanked by Norton Common, a piece of open woodland preserved as a small lung for the new 'city'. The turn of the last century was a time of earnest and idealistic theorizing. Where Ebenezer Howard's theories on urban environment differed from others is that they were acted upon. Within five years of the publication of Howard's *Living in Cities*, the first bricks were being laid on a virgin site at Letchworth. It was a good idea, and one from which latterday planners have benefited much. They have profited too from Letchworth's mistakes, for, at least in architectural terms and perhaps in others, the garden city did not really come off in practice. The civic buildings are rather mean, the domestic mostly dull and to modern eyes old-fashioned. The designers planned for a new age, but they could not anticipate the impact of the motor car. The trouble with Letchworth is that its theories have been taken over, and its performance bettered, in a hundred modern developments in other places; and the pioneer is left looking just a bit shabby and elderly.

If one must live in cities, this nevertheless would be no bad place. It stands consciously apart from the older towns of Baldock and Hitchin, carefully avoiding any traditions not of its own making. In its original plan it had no main road. It was a town of the railway age, and its centrepiece is not the town hall or the church but the railway station.

It is typical of Letchworth that the only direct link with Baldock, barely a mile away, is that provided by the Icknield Way, and this is here only a bridlepath. The motorist has to go south to pick up the main road from Hitchin, or northwards, more agreeably, leaving the garden city abruptly in Norton, which suddenly ceases to be a housing estate and becomes a pretty rural village with a church standing high among cottages.

Baldock used to be familiar to all travellers on the Great North Road. It was a celebrated bottleneck, and there was ample time to study the fine eighteenth-century architecture of the high street while waiting for some movement in the traffic. Now the improved A1 bypasses the town, and it is beginning to recover itself. I like Baldock very much, but it always seems to me a Midland town, having none of the characteristics of the Home Counties. Visually it is made by the wide high street, almost a square rather than a street, which narrows effectively to central crossroads. Behind this the parish church pokes up a perky spike of a spire, a nice homely touch. In fact the church, when seen whole, is impressive, very much the church of a prosperous town and having that air of being just a little indifferent to everything—including God. The style is strong and solid, admirable if not endearing. In interest and general appeal it is outclassed in Baldock by the domestic architecture in which are alternated, most democratically, big dignified mansions and casual, almost cheeky, little houses.

The last miles of the Icknield Way in Hertfordshire lead uncompromisingly from Baldock to Royston. Surely there can be no question about the direction of this last stage of our journey. However, the Way is here also the A505, one of the busiest cross-routes north of London, and only those who relish the thought of sharing the road with juggernauts will choose to drive this way. The road is visually very good indeed, for the chalk down rises steeply from the south side of the highway and there is evidence along the Way of the populous character of this country in prehistoric times in many barrows, could one spare attention for them. I prefer to follow the Way at a distance.

This journey proper began with a village of character, Ewelme, one with a long history and buildings to prove it. Before the journey ends I should like to visit another such, a place utterly unlike Ewelme in setting and architecture, but almost its equal in interest. In order to reach Ashwell one must leave Baldock on its northern edge, as if intending to join the A1, then turn sharp right along a minor road across the low undulations north-west of the Icknield Way. At two miles Bygrave provides a small incident in a most uneventful ride; then the road rises steadily to Claybush Hill and below in the dip soars the slim spire which is Ashwell's centrepiece and pride.

The 'well' of Ashwell is the Cam, the western of two streams of this name which join to flow through Cambridge. This Cam rises in the heart of the village and goes north through the quietly beautiful Cambridgeshire countryside, making for a time the county boundary. Ashwell is rather freakishly in Hertfordshire, for it has little of the character of that county, being essentially a town of East Anglian type. I say 'town' deliberately, because, although it is a village administratively and in size, it has the complexity of a town in miniature. Historically, too, it had urban status, but it has stood still, very sensibly, while neighbours like Baldock and Biggleswade have grown and, in growing, lost some of their quality. Ashwell has an air, immediately recognized, of belonging to itself, of having a concern with objectives and values quite other than those pursued by most modern communities. Civic pride, which has produced a good small museum and an impressive list of local activities, is part of the story but not all. It would be good to feel a part of this community, but honorary citizenship, one feels, is not to be had for the asking. One has to deserve Ashwell and its standards are very high.

It is manifestly absurd to claim this place for the Home Counties. It is untouched by the pressures which bear upon places only a few miles to the south. There is nothing to justify its inclusion in this book, except that having come so near I cannot pass Ashwell by.

And yet, what is there here for the casual visitor? Not much in conventional terms, apart from a church which is of national importance. The hurried tourist will put his head in at the church door and be away, having missed the essence of the place. It must be savoured at leisure, by wandering the neatly paralleled streets—an example of unconscious medieval planning, or was it deliberately replanted after the disasters of the Black Death?—and idling in the pubs. None of the houses within immediate view is of the first interest, but none is poor or unworthy of its setting. New developments have been kept out of the central area. There at the hub of the community stands the church, Ashwell's pride and the most thrilling sight in Hertfordshire (I am not forgetting the cathedral).

St Mary's Ashwell is more of a piece that one usually finds in this country. It was entirely rebuilt around the middle of the fourteenth century, at a time of social crisis and architectural transition. The flowing lines of Decorated tracery were just about to turn into the soaring formality of Perpendicular, and there are examples of both. It is a very big church; the tower is all of 176 feet in height, and out of it grows a a tall slim spire, a feature which in this low country is astonishingly effective. There are other big, spacious churches around, and a few with towers almost as tall and fine. What makes Ashwell unique is that the fabric bears contemporary evidence of the conditions under which it was built. Someone, perhaps the presiding mason, scribbled on the wall of the tower his wages' bill. Another, or the same hand, poured out his anguish when the plague raged in the little town, halving the population and leaving only 'the dregs', and then gale swept through the desolation. One would be dull indeed not to feel the poignancy of this cry across six centuries. The lettering is exquisitely carved, for all its informality, and it must surely have been cut by a professional hand. Perhaps the same man was responsible for a brilliant sketch, surprisingly 'modern' in technique, of a cathedral tower and spire which must have been cut by someone who had seen St Paul's. Pestilence and storm slowed but did not halt the building, which was completed after twenty years, years of economic crisis, national humiliation in the French Wars, religious and social unrest. With all this in mind, look at the soaring, confident lines of this noble building, and marvel at man's unconquerable spirit.

One should complete the circuit of Ashwell by driving around the Bury, the big park at Ashwellbury. This is a comely house belonging to the first half of the nineteenth century, past the golden age of English domestic yet clearly unconscious of any decadence. It looks most pleasing in this lush woodland setting.

We are almost at the end of the road now. A lane comes across to the Way at Odsey and for those who have had enough it is a straight run into Royston. If anyone still wishes to explore, a lane south climbs the open chalk hill to Therfield, where there are very fine views into the Cambridgeshire plain, and then another road crosses Therfield Heath, a nature reserve among the golfers and an area rich in barrows recalling the Bronze Age users of our ancient Way. Royston, a brisk busy modern town yet not unmindful of its antiquity, brings to an end this journey, but not the Icknield Way itself which veers north-east to its destination among the wastes of the Wash.

11

Native Fields of Hertfordshire

WHO is the patron saint of Hertfordshire? Not St Alban, proto-martyr, but St Charles of Widford.

Charles Lamb was born in London and died in Edmonton. The farthest he lived into the country was Enfield where he yearned for 'the fresher air of the metropolis'. Lamb was a townsman by birth and inclination, yet Reginald Hine found material for a long and eloquent book—*Charles Lamb and his Hertfordshire*—out of his country connections. It is a paradox in which Elia himself would have delighted.

There was a small conflict between townsman and countryman in Lamb, just as there was a conflict between Lamb and Elia. It would be easy to exaggerate both, but they were indeed aspects of a personality by turns sentimental and shrewd, wayward and sincere, and always appealing. At least I suppose this last is so. In recent years, the members of the Charles Lamb Society excepted, there seems to have been a sharp decline in interest in Lamb. Few people read Elia nowadays. He has nothing of interest to say about burning questions of our day. On labour disputes he was a Tory of Tories. The only black people he wrote about were chimney sweeps. He wrote off conventional sex early in life and thereafter showed no interest in deviations. What a man to speak to the late twentieth century!

Not only was Lamb a townsman, he was a man of artificial light.

For him happiness was a tall folio and a brace of candles (brought by Betty, of course), or an evening at the theatre with Munden or Fanny Kelly on the bill, or the company of friends and much good talk. Yet this was the man who yearned for "the green plains of pleasant Hertfordshire", to whom childhood memories of the countryside were infinitely dear.

This is not quite the paradox it seems. Lamb's feelings for the countryside were largely retrospective. He had been happy in childhood—or thought that he had—in visiting his grandmother and other relations in Hertfordshire. These memories fed his imagination and produced some passages of inimitable prose as well as a great deal of more informal writing. But when he "left the d—d India House for Ever", with a very respectable pension of £450 a year, he did not use this freedom and affluence to buy himself a place in the country. Indeed, thirteen years earlier he had inherited a country cottage, had put a tenant in, and three years later had sold it. No Hertfordshire Arcadia for Lamb. The "wholesome Temple air" suited him better, and when this failed he "rusticated" in Dalston or by the New River in rural Islington.

Apart from Hertfordshire, Lamb rarely ventured afield. He and Mary went on a sight-seeing trip in 1816, visiting Bath and Bristol from Calne in a "vertigo of locomotion". This adventure was mild compared with the visit to Keswick during the summer of 1802. Then the Lambs climbed Skiddaw, Mary being excessively tired until refreshed by an icy spring, and they enjoyed Coleridge's cottage in its "net of mountains: great floundering bears and monsters they seemed, all couchant and asleep". It was a traumatic experience for Lamb, who could bring himself down to earth only by thinking of the ham and beef shop he patronized in London. Not a Pantheist, in fact. Haydon reports him, in his cups, abusing Wordsworth as "You old lake poet, you rascally poet". This was in 1817 when the stimulus of the mountains had worn off.

It was not the high hills which haunted Lamb's memory but the softer hills of eastern Hertfordshire. His rivers were not Derwent or Duddon but Lea and Ash, and if he returned to them more often in thought than in person they were not, perhaps, less dear to him for that. It suited him well to live at Colebrook Cottage, in the most productive years of his life, beside the New River. This derives its waters from the springs of Amwell just across the watershed from his own favourite village of Widford, which held the dust of the Grandame, the ruins of Blakesmoor, and the ghost of the mother of his dream children.

The direct evidence of his concern with Hertfordshire is slight: three essays, his tale of *Rosamund Grey*, a couple of poems, and a few hints in letters. Then there is *Mrs Leicester's School* in which most of the stories, and all those about Hertfordshire, are Mary's. In all the writings except the letters he is looking back to boyhood. This is markedly different to his London writings, in which as often as not he records the everyday events—if George Dyer falling into the New River may be called everyday—of the town.

This does not mean that he did not visit the country. We have his own evidence, and that of his contemporaries, that he was a formidable walker. Mary did her share, too, even if, as Tom Hood showed in a jolly sketch, she had some difficulty with stiles:

> But having climb'd unto the top,
> She could no further go.

Writing to Cowden Clarke in 1828, in the first flush of enthusiasm for Enfield, Charles described a walk on the Hertfordshire borders. Although he was handicapped at the time by a strained tendon "got by skipping a skipping-rope at 53", his performance would shame most modern ramblers. We shall not follow his route, even by car, for time and the overspill of London have dealt severely with much of his Enfield countryside. Only here and there a little survives precariously of his 'paradise', and we cannot altogether echo his verdict—"a sweeter spot is not in ten counties round"—on Northaw Church. (But it is still good by the standards of this hard-hit country.)

There is a real dilemma about where to start this journey. Not that direction is important. We have here the authority of Lamb himself who revisited Mackery End, near Wheathampstead, from London by way of St Albans and Luton Hoo—"somewhat a circuitous route"! The problem is how to make all the journey, including the devastated bits, enjoyable. One interesting way, for those with ample time and an instinct for exploring suburban deserts, would be to follow Lamb's New River from its outflow near Sadlers Wells, past Lamb's old house off Islington Green—where the statue of the deviser of this pioneer waterway, Sir Hugh Myddleton, gazes aghast at what has happened to his merry village—through the northern suburbs past Lamb's "prettiest compactest" house at Chase Side.

For much of this course the river, if one can come up to it, makes its own tiny green belt, and beyond Bulls Cross there is a hint of real country. Here it passes through Theobalds Park, where there is no hint of the splendours of James I's palace and only a sad glimpse of Wren's Temple Bar crumbling into melancholy ruin. This is within diversion distance of Waltham Cross, where Lamb, on a stroll from Enfield, was moved to write an unwontedly sharp poem about two queens, Eleanor and the ill-used Caroline who in her life-time had her "share of crosses". The New River passes the nursery country of

Cheshunt, Turnford and Wormley, crosses the main road at Brox-
bourne and skirts the churchyard of the fine church. Here New River,
River Lea and Lea Navigation are very close and they keep company
all the way to Amwell. The New River just avoids housing estates at
Rye Park, within sight of Rye House, and then by way of St Margaret's
it reaches its head-waters at Great Amwell, whose "perpetual stream"
is celebrated in elegant verse in an exceedingly charming landscape
design just below the church. This scene was new in Lamb's day, and
perhaps he did not care for its calculated artifice. Age—it is not far
short of 175 years old—has mellowed the stone ornaments and the
trees have matured to produce a most refreshing haven.

In fact Great Amwell is likely to rank high in any list of the most
delectable places on London's doorstep. The original planners followed
tradition in choosing a high point for the church whose plain chancel
arch and apse hint at an early Norman origin. They did not foresee
how much more dramatic this setting would become when the New
River was cut out at its base. Myddleton's contribution to the scene
was a piece of strictly utilitarian engineering, and he too did not
anticipate the enthusiasm and, it must be confessed, the self-satisfaction
of his successor Robert Mylne, who tricked out the river with twin
islands and their ornaments and whose mausoleum adds a suitable
neo-classical note to the churchyard above.

Mylne, although doubtless a very sound engineer, does not inspire
much affection. Another Amwell man spans the centuries effectively
and seems as dear to us as he was to Dr Johnson and his other contemporaries. This was John Scott, 'Scott of Amwell' as he will always
be known although he was born and died elsewhere. The little Quaker
poet came to live here in 1770 and wrote his celebratory poem *Amwell*
six years later. The verse is unmemorable, but no one could question
the sincerity of his tribute to an adopted home. Lamb, who was born
too late to know him, made fun of his verse and commended instead
his energetic campaign for improvements in the Hertfordshire turnpike
system.

Just beyond is Ware, which we might take as our true starting point,
for it was a town very familiar to Lamb. Ware has changed much since
John Gilpin arrived here involuntarily. It still preserves something of
the atmosphere of a market town, and the Hertfordshire spike on the
church tower competes on the skyline with the vents of innumerable
maltings. A brisk and busy town, owing at least as much to the countryside as to London. For me Ware always has a might-have-been sadness.
Had my parents postponed for a few years their decision to move from
here to London I could have claimed a share of Hertfordshire instead of
being a Cockney, a citizen of no mean city—but I would rather have
been country-born.

There is something especially precious about country on the edge of great cities; one cherishes it as one does a child under sentence of a perhaps-fatal illness. Can it survive? At least we must make the most of it while it is still there. So, instead of getting on with our Lamb pilgrimage, we will taste the country between Lea and Stort, towards which the tentacles of London grope ever closer, while only the river stands between us and Harlow New Town. Marvellously it survives. So, out of Ware by the Hadham road, over the Lea, and then a minor road turns back beside the river—not the navigation. Just beyond the town the road crosses Lamb's River Ash a quarter mile above its confluence with the Lea, and then we are quickly in Stanstead Abbots. Here is a fascinating mixture of big and little, humble and flamboyant, fine rambling inn and domineering Victorian factory. My personal favourite here, one remembered from earliest childhood, is the little clock house which has a cosy absurdity which creeps deeper into the affections than more admirable qualities.

The road climbs steeply out of the village to the hilltop on which stand, in companionable isolation, the big house and the church, the latter a characteristic Hertfordshire product—though barely a mile from the border—with its slim spire, timber porch and general air of quiet confidence in its own merits. Just before the church the main road swings left and runs high with pleasant views right across the Stort into Essex. The distant sight of Harlow's towers and factories gives added spice to the rural delights of the road. Then, in two miles, a lane goes due north to Hunsdon. In true Hertfordshire fashion house and church come first, and then there is a long gap before the village proper is reached. At first the road is enclosed and leafy, then suddenly the green turns to red in a riot of Tudor brick. Hunsdon began its brief season of more than local importance in Henry VIII's reign when William Carey rebuilt the house and extended the church. He came into the inner circle of the court when he married Mary Boleyn, Anne's sister. The Careys survived the disasters which followed the fall of Anne Boleyn. William's son Henry was created Baron Hunsdon. As first cousin to the queen he enjoyed royal favour, and his sound and unspectacular talents took him to a variety of public offices. Then, in 1580, Queen Elizabeth came visiting during one of her royal progresses —a grievous honour for any householder to sustain—and a fine new chapel was added south of the chancel of the parish church. So house and church grew with the fortunes of the family. Structurally the church underwent no major revolution after the death of the great queen, although it was greatly enriched with fittings and monuments in the following century. The house however was extended, then drastically reduced, and its character changed early in the nineteenth century. For the passer-by the place, apart from its memories, is chiefly appealing because of its setting and of the close association of the two buildings. One might fear that the village would suffer by comparison, but one finds, on reaching it at last, that it sits most effectively around the crossroads. No single building is of really outstanding interest, but the whole has a harmony—of a kind we shall find elsewhere on this journey —which is rare in commuterland.

The main road continues the direction of the church lane northwards and goes uneventfully to Widford where it encounters the more important highway from Ware to Bishops Stortford. The situation of the village is almost identical with that of Hunsdon, but it is a little less attractive both in outline and in detail. However we have come here, not to look at minor domestic architecture, but to visit a major shrine of St Charles. A long half mile west along the main road brings us to Widford Church and across the fields to the north are the swelling acres of 'Blakesmoor in Hertfordshire'.

Blakesware was a house of the Plumer family, who bought the estate and the mansion—dating from the time of the Civil War but a rather old-fashioned building of its time with a rambling front and an addiction to Dutch gables—in James II's reign. The Plumers lived there until William Plumer died in 1767, when the heir, another William, transferred his allegiance to New Place at Gilston, five miles away towards the Stort. (He later dignified his house, and gave it a fashionable neo-Gothic facelift, as Gilston Park.) William Plumer was Lamb's 'Fine old Whig', who sat in the House for nearly sixty years, venerated Pitt, despised Portland, and—like a true Whig—hated the common mass of people. When he abandoned Blakesware, which held too many memories of a domineering father for his liking, his mother stayed on in the old home in the care of a housekeeper, Mrs Mary Field. Old Mrs Plumer died after eleven years of widowhood, and the housekeeper was left alone, apart from the servants, for another fourteen years. Mrs Field was Charles Lamb's grandmother.

Lamb was only three when Mrs Field was left in undisputed control of the rambling old house. He and Mary often came to stay with her, and for both its echoing emptiness was a formative experience. "Nothing fills a child's mind like a large old Mansion," he wrote to Barton towards the end of his life, and certainly these childish impressions went deep and stayed with him always. Mary too, although she was older when she first went to Blakesware, recalled the house when, in the Lamb's jointly composed children's book *Mrs Leicester's School*, she drew herself as Margaret Green wandering in loneliness around the marble hall and memorizing the names of its twelve marble Caesars, while she enjoyed "as perfect a solitude as Robinson Crusoe".

Old Mrs Field died in 1792 and was buried in Widford churchyard, and the house was left to moulder away. In 1822, when William

Plumer's long life ended, his widow pulled the old mansion down, so giving Lamb's receptive mind an additional nostalgia to feed upon. He continued to visit the place on and off. Writing to Southey in 1799, when he was only twenty-four, he hints at a recent visit and the emotions it had aroused. "Of this nature are old family faces, and scenes of infancy." His affectionate melancholy found full expression in 1824 when, walking in Hertfordshire, he diverted from his road to take another look at Blakesware and found that "the demolition of a few weeks had reduced it to—an antiquity". The result was one of the finest of the reminiscent Essays of Elia, the first in his last sequence in the *London Magazine*. Had the demolishers spared 'Blakesmoor' Lamb's eloquence might have been fettered by the realities before him; the house down, his fancy roamed in glorious freedom through the vanished halls and galleries. "The solitude of childhood is not so much the mother of thought, as it is the feeder of love, and silence, and admiration," he says in one of his most penetrating dicta; and that love, stored up for half a lifetime, spilled over into the enraptured memories of "Blakesmoor in H—shire".

Lamb's Blakesware of dust and rubbish has long vanished. A later owner rebuilt the house in Tudor style on a more congenial site up the hill. The new house was built in the Wilderness, a neglected pleasance in Lamb's day and one recalled in his imperfect romance of *Rosamund Grey*. Even Gilston Park, Plumer's preferred house, was demolished, and another mock-Tudor mansion put in its place. This was long after Lamb's time, and his spirit doubtless relished this further evidence of the activities of Time's scythe. "I feel like a grasshopper that chirping about the grounds escaped his scythe only by my littleness. Ev'n now he is whetting one of his smallest razors to clean wipe me out."

As the senior servant of the great house, Mary Field must have enjoyed considerable status in the village, but she was of Widford, not merely in it, and Lamb got to know the neighbourhood and its worthies. He recalled some of them not long before Time used his "smallest razor", in a poem called "Epicedium". By this time the poignancy had gone out of his childhood memories, and he is content to rhyme frivolously and affectionately about Widford folk "Going and Gone". Here are servants of the household, farmers, knaves, fools, great ladies and paupers, all "intomb'd by fair Widford".

Lamb is one of those writers who are more interesting than their works. He was not much of a poet, yet his poems are important because they help to fill in some essential lines in his portrait. Of these is "The Grandame", written at twenty-one when he was still under the spell of Mary Field's memory. A fragment and undistinguished as verse, it captures the mood of Widford, and the affection of a child for a wise and tolerant mentor.

What is for some readers the finest of Elia also comes out of Widford. This is "Dream Children", in which Lamb recalls, tenderly but with an emotion far removed from its source, his boyish love for Ann Simmons of Widford. He renounced marriage when he was only twenty-one, after the disaster of Mary's madness and his mother's death, and by 1822 when "Dream Children" appeared in the *London*, any bitterness had long since been dissipated. His vision of John and Alice, who are not the children of Alice but are "nothing; less than nothing, and dreams" is exquisite, sentimental without mawkishness. His feelings were fresher and sharper when he wrote, in 1798, in his most familiar poem: "I loved a love once, fairest among women; Closed are her doors to me". Of Ann, who lived at Blenheims, a cottage in Helham Green on the edge of the Blakesware estate, only the shadow of a memory remains. Like Willy Lott and the Dark Lady she enjoys the faintest breath of immortality because her path once crossed that of genius.

All these reminiscences came crowding in on me as I stood not long ago in summer sunshine in Widford churchyard, within sight of the Grandame's grave and with, surely, Lamb's wayward ghost not far away—for he would not willingly let himself be confined in Edmonton, a place of few memories and those sad. Widford still makes a pretty scene but not a readily evocative one. Much of Lamb's Widford must be seen with the eye of imagination. Blakesware has been renewed, and the park is closed to visitors. The church has suffered restoration since his day. It is much tidier than the building he knew, lacking the typical dilapidation of early nineteenth-century churches as well as the festoons of ivy which the age regarded as an essential accompaniment of antiquity. Even the "slender-tapering length of spire" has been renewed. He would recognize as a familiar and friendly sight the red-brick wall of the churchyard, borrowed from a vanished Tudor house called Widfordbury which still retains its stylish doorway leading into nothing. Nearest of all to Lamb's Widford is the view behind the church, which looks across his "pretty brawling brook" to the wooded slopes of Blakesware, a view which by some miracle includes at present no obvious evidence of the twentieth century.

There is a strong temptation to explore from Widford the valley of the Ash, an inconsiderable stream which drains some of the loveliest and least spoiled country of the Hertfordshire border with Essex. A twelve-mile diversion would take in the Hadhams and the Pelhams, with the little village of Albury set delectably between them, a country of village streets, modest 'great' houses, and many fine farms combining Tudor brick and New Elizabethan wheat. The soft hills top four hundred feet only around Stocking Pelham, but no one would call this flat country. It undulates in the most seductive folds with a satisfying rise and fall. There are commuters, certainly, but in sufficiently small numbers to enable them to integrate and not to form their own exclusive societies. Here if anywhere in Hertfordshire is genuine 'country' instead of the bastard town-country of the normal commuter belt.

However, this may have to be a journey saved for another day, and at best travellers may spare time for a short stroll behind Widford Church along the footpath which follows the Ash up to Hadham Mill. There is plenty here to surprise those who still think of Hertfordshire as all New Towns and motorways.

From Widford Church our Lamb journey continues along the Ware road for the best part of two miles to Wareside, passing the entrance drive to Blakesware just beyond the railway bridge. At Wareside a lane turns north and this, successfully followed—and there are generous opportunities for error—will keep the traveller away from main roads all the way to Puckeridge. The first sharp rise lifts the road out of the Ash valley up to the watershed and then there is a steady fall to the River Rib. After heavy rain the first acquaintance with this little stream may be dramatic, for there is a watersplash at Great Barwick Farm, and then lane and stream are closely associated all the way to Standon. Nothing of outstanding interest is passed by the way, but the country is exceedingly relaxing with its utterly unobtrusive charms.

Puckeridge is on the Roman Ermine Street, a crossroads hamlet which grew up suddenly under the stimulus of the coaching age and which is now on the way to recovery from the effects of heavy main-road traffic after the completion of a bypass. Just on the northern edge of the built-up area, a lane turns west towards the inappropriately named Nasty. Here another lane, narrow and winding, leads northwards through open and attractive country to the hamlet of Cherry Green. The road turns east at this point, but a still smaller lane may be followed west for a few hundred yards to another shrine of St Charles.

Lamb's godfather, Francis Fields, died in 1809 and left all his property to his wife. She three years later conveyed part of the estate, a little cottage near Puckeridge, to Charles Lamb. So Charles gained "the only landed property which I could ever call my own". Elia describes how he took possession and trod his three-quarters of an acre with a land-owner's pride. This pride did not however prevent him from letting the house and after only three years as a landlord selling it to a Thomas Greg for £50.

The bequest came too soon. Lamb was chained to his desk in the East India House and was condemned to stay there for another thirteen years. Had he been free, would he, I wonder, have chosen to live at Cherry Green? It is doubtful. The cottage was in the heart of his favourite country. The isolation would mean little to a man of Lamb's formidable walking powers. Removed from the scene of her tragedy and in tranquil surroundings Mary might have enjoyed at least partial immunity from the attacks of her demon. Here was the answer to many problems. But Lamb, for all his nostalgia for his "native fields", belonged to London, the theatre and the company of friends.

The cottage is still there. Button Snap—most perfectly Elian of names—was acquired and restored by the Charles Lamb Society, and is in admirable condition. With its low walls, its huge enveloping cap of thatch, and its pretty garden, it seems the cottage of every city-bound Cockney's dreams. It huddles into the ground as if indifferent even to the life of the cornfields which stretch northwards into infinity and certainly oblivious of the ubiquitous pylons. A lovely house. Perhaps Lamb's errant ghost, regretful of that opportunity squandered for fifty pieces of gold—a pitiful sum, for Lamb, though by no means wealthy, was never badly off—walks contentedly among these quiet lanes and fields.

The return journey—if one can bring oneself to leave so perfect a place—is made to the Rib valley at either Westmill, an example of unconscious planning achieved through five centuries of evolution, or Ashenden, which in a very different way is equally attractive. Then the streets and the traffic of Buntingford close in.

Although it is so small, Buntingford is a town and a very typical Hertfordshire highway town. It is essentially contained in a quarter mile of Ermine Street, and within this area are some very pleasing houses mostly presenting seventeenth- and eighteenth-century front-ages—there may be older work behind. A native of Buntingford who remembered his home town was Seth Ward, who became Bishop of Salisbury in Charles II's reign. Ward was a typical man of his day, a scientist and a friend of the leading intellectuals. His contribution to Buntingford's welfare was, for so forward-looking a man, slightly archaic, an almshouse whose effective and unassuming buildings stand just behind the church in the most effective position in the town. (He seems to have been an almshouse man for he also founded the exquisite College of Matrons in Salisbury Close).

Just past Ward's Hospital a major road goes west, and we with it, towards Baldock. This, which was once a peaceful winding lane, has now been taken over by heavy lorries, and we shall not wish to stay long with it. However, in four miles there is a turning, the first through road available, left in the village of Cottered. Most of this village is contained within a triangle, at one apex of which stands the large and stately church. Someone got to work on this in the fifteenth century and opened it up with very big Perpendicular windows. The effect was startling, making the building so light that it seems even bigger and finer than it is. Happily one wall was spared, and with it an enormous

Therfield Heath

Farmhouse at Pirton

New River Head, Amwell

painting of St Christopher—symbolically placed so that it was the first thing the traveller sees on entering—in which the giant, himself somewhat decayed, is set in a recognizable local landscape. The practice of thus bringing home the contemporary relevance of the saints is a medieval commonplace, but it always brings with it a sense of pleasurable shock. Altogether a very delightful building, for its spaciousness, the interest of its bygones—hatchments and Royal Arms of Queen Anne, and its tall spire—by no means a 'spike' this.

Our road continues south-west for a mile and then turns abruptly to follow briefly the line of a Roman road. At this point there is a very lovely red-brick Tudor house set back with attendant dovecot—complete with doves. Before the effect of this has passed the road turns again, and there stands a remarkably perfect post mill gleaming white above the way. We pay for these pleasures with the comparative dullness of Cromer, where the road picks up and follows the valley of the River Beane. Like most streams of this gentle country the Beane is a sensitive barometer; in fine weather it is mostly dry. Nevertheless it is the principal maker of this landscape.

Walkern, the next village, no doubt owes its existence to a watermill on the river; and to the same cause we owe one of the most charming of all Hertfordshire villages. It is just a single street with a detached church-end, and it has the artlessness of a community which 'just growed', and who could wish otherwise? Walkern is beyond the achievement of planners, who would scarcely approve its reckless mixture of styles and periods. Only one or two houses call for individual comment—the manor form has an elegant façade and a garden to match, and alongside stands a big brick dovecot beside the pond—and this is not important compared with the rewarding harmony of the whole. One could not easily find a more satisfying place in which to live and find a niche in rural society. To the east lies a tangle of lanes and tracks mostly going nowhere in particular, following forgotten boundaries and forgotten objectives; a real bit of country this, insensitive to the appeal of London. To the west, by one of those paradoxes which help to make the good things of the Home Counties even more precious, four miles of open land separate Walkern from Stevenage New Town.

On the edge of Walkern the main road turns west to Stevenage, but we continue south in the Beane valley, lush with ripe corn. It might be tempting to take the diversion left to Benington, another enchanting place with a ruined castle and Gothic accompaniments. If so we would continue across country all the way to Watton, which the valley road reaches more soberly.

Watton itself—full title Watton-at-Stone (was the stone a 'foreign' sarsen stone like the one beside the churchyard wall at Cottered—no doubt a boundary stone anyway marking a very ancient administrative division?)—sits uncomfortably on the Hertford-Stevenage highway. A pity, this, because it is not far short of attractive. A fine flinty church stands well above the road, and there are agreeable houses on both sides. We turn west in the middle of the village, passing at the corner Watton's most precious possession, a gorgeous iron pump. The next three miles are quiet and uneventful, and the next village, Datchworth, is also unexciting. The old village and church lie off to the north among new buildings. Beside the green I saw the skeleton of a great timber barn placarded "To be sold for redevelopment"; it was the most distinguished building in sight. There is a big green here, lined with quite good houses, but nothing of irresistible quality. Here a narrow lane turns south across Gover's Green and Bull's Green, deceptively attractive country, open and leafy; only slowly does one realize that the commons and woods are littered with 'developments'. The commuters have crept up and taken us unawares. However, it has all been carried out very well, with the minimum of visual damage.

An even narrower lane forks right in the woods and comes out opposite Queen Hoo Hall. From time to time this ancient house has been shown to the public, but it is currently inaccessible. The bridle track to Tewin which passes beside the house gives a good view of its pretty gabled garden-front. Houses of this style and period—early Tudor—are not uncommon in this country, but Queen Hoo is unusually perfect. It has a very small place in literary history, and serves to recall an attractive personality of the Georgian Age.

If you follow the bridle track past the hall through the cornfields and copses, gaining on the way views which are incredibly flawless in the heart of this crowded county, you come at length to a farm road serving Bacon's Farm, in the parish of Bramfield. This became the home, late in the eighteenth century, of James Strutt, the son of the miller of Springfield Mill at Chelmsford. Strutt became a professional engraver, and enjoyed a considerable reputation as an illustrator of books. He was a man in tune with the antiquarian fashions of his day. He preferred to illustrate books which called for a detailed knowledge of the dress and manners of the past, and he had real claims to medieval scholarship. Queen Hoo Hall appealed strongly to his imagination, which peopled the house—not altogether correctly—with men of the later Middle Ages. He was stimulated to write a romance of which the Hall was the leading character, filling it with all he knew and imagined about the past. The novel got out of hand and he died leaving it incomplete. The manuscript might have been lost for ever, but somehow it drifted into the publisher Murray's hands, and he showed it to Walter Scott. Scott was so greatly taken with the story that he completed it— admittedly in a scrappy fashion—and the novel, called *Queen Hoo Hall*, was published in 1808. It made no deep impression and is now utterly forgotten. It has however a small place in history, for it was the fore-runner of the socio-historical novel of the Victorian Age, and Scott himself confessed that Strutt's work set him on the road which led to the Waverley Novels.

It is now a short run downhill to the commuter village of Tewin, built not ungracefully around the core of the old settlement. The church stands away from new and old houses, on a small eminence above the Mimram valley. As the arm of London stretches so near this point it is good to find that this is still a village church and a pretty one. The original Norman building has evolved over five centuries without losing touch with its proper scale. Not important in architectural terms, certainly, but very pleasing in its modesty and aptness. Footpaths go downhill from the churchyard to the river.

River? This is the Mimram, which is never big enough to merit any more ambitious description than 'stream', but it is perhaps the prettiest of all Hertfordshire's streams and an important element in the land-scape. The lushly wooded banks keep company with the Welwyn road, making this as rewarding a main road as can be found hereabouts. Then the Mimram enters Panshanger Park and achieves a moment of glory as it becomes the key to Repton's wonderful landscape design.

However we are going upstream, not down, to the fringes of Welwyn Garden City. Here the Mimram, at its most insignificant, fathers a colossal engineering work. The Great Northern Railway line crosses the miniature valley on a magnificent brick viaduct, whose soaring arches express all the self-confidence of the Victorian high summer—it was built just before the Great Exhibition.

The Garden City planners have made a little public garden under the shadow of the viaduct, from which its splendours can be well seen. I admire their enterprise, but I cannot but be glad that this journey does not include a close examination of this great social experiment of the 1920s and its post-war expansion.

In fact the Digswell valley road barely escapes the tentacles of the expanded Garden City. However, the Great North road, now of motorway standard and character, acts as a fairly effective barrier against westward sprawl and once across it one comes quickly and with a pleasant shock of surprise into Welwyn town. This shows all the characteristic signs of a settlement on a great highway. The houses, even if none is of the very highest individual excellence, are stylish, the inns prosperous; everything has the civilized appearance of the eighteenth century, an age which knew how to make money and spend it well. In this age Welwyn had a vicar who effectively countered the popular image of the Georgian sporting parson; this was Edward Young, whose natural and cultivated melancholy found expression in his *Night Thoughts*, poems sententious, reflective, occasionally satirical, whose stupefying dullness is lit by rare flashes of eloquence as well as gnomic utterances—such as "procrastination is the thief of time"— which have achieved an independent existence. Young was a successful poet of his time. Despite popular acclaim and a judicious marriage, however, he missed preferment and spent thirty-five years as the parson of this minor parish. He is buried in the church, which strikes the one positive note in the urban scene.

Just past the church a very narrow lane turns off left across the Mimram and follows the river upstream for a mile or two. It would in fact be most enjoyable to trace it farther through the mild and fertile Whitwell to its springs in the high land of the Waldens. Richly satisfying territory this, hinting at an awareness of London only in the cottages, whose standard of fabric and repair is that of the wealthy townsman turned countryman, not that of the farm worker for whom these modest buildings were first raised.

Our objectives, however, are farther south, and so we follow a narrow and winding lane westwards out of the Mimram valley to the most celebrated and perhaps the most perfect of Hertfordshire villages. A combination of circumstances have made Ayot St Lawrence a tourist attraction. When I first came here fifty years ago it had not lost its innocence. Nearly all the residents belonged to the village, if not by heredity, at least by economic involvement in the land. Now it is a show village and also, if the two things are not irreconcilable, a place to live in by choice. The twin attractions are Shaw and silkworms, to which may be added—a long way behind—ecclesiastical architecture and harmony. The last is a most miraculous survival, for the relaxed and peaceful atmosphere of Ayot is proof against waves of visitors in cars and coaches.

The transformation of a typical medieval village began in the eighteenth century when a Tudor manor house was superseded by a stately mansion in brick. This was the seat of the Lyte family. Sir Lionel Lyte wished to beautify his estate and to improve the outlook from his house. What was needed to close the view effectively was some neo-classical building. An ornamental 'temple' would have done, or a triumphal archway leading nowhere, but Sir Lionel had bigger ambitions. In the village street stood the old parish church, shockingly out of date and fashion in its thirteenth-century Gothic. Surely it would be both wise and beneficial to get rid of this anachronism and replace it with a more suitable church, one moreover in the right setting. So Sir Lionel, with Georgian self-assurance, put in hand the building of a new church and the demolition of the old. In the latter course he was not wholly successful. The building was unroofed and dilapidated and then left to make a highly satisfactory ruin, much more to the melancholy tastes of the age than a complete and operational building. Meanwhile the new church arose at the far side of the park, facing the great house. The architect was Nicholas Revett, a pioneer of the revival of Greek art, and if Revett had not really grasped the principles of Greek building, this worried neither him nor his patron. What Lyte got was what he wanted, a fine and fashionable eye-catcher, a central portico, tall and pillared, flanked by smaller open-sided wings—rather like gazebos—which were destined to hold the ashes of the patron and his lady. The effect was most solemn in grey-gold stone. (The body of the church, which could not be seen from the house, was of red brick!)

For once a highly artificial exercise in a natural setting came off triumphantly. The old church in its arrested decay makes a most lovely and affecting feature of the village scene. The new looks splendid against its backcloth of trees and is even lovelier inside, with its subtly balanced proportions and the calculated simplicity of its decor.

Sir Lionel's house has now become the home of the silk farm which had its beginnings at Lullingstone Castle in Kent, and this deservedly has its endless flow of visitors. These invaders also go to the other end of the village for an encounter with the sardonic spirit of George Bernard Shaw.

Shaw came to live in the house called Shaw's Corner in 1906, and it was his country house thereafter. His ashes were scattered in the garden. House and garden are alike in possessing only moderate attractions in themselves, but both are so rich in memories of the old man that a visit should not be missed. (The house was presented to the National Trust by Shaw in 1944 and was opened to the public after his death in 1950.) In the course of a journey devoted primarily to Lamb, an hour or so in the company of Shaw is a useful corrective. The two men could scarcely be less alike, having in common only a love of the theatre, and even here their tastes were diametrically opposite. I have always felt a highly personal and deep affection for Lamb, for Shaw a wry and reluctant admiration. His astringent humour is a necessity of life, and there is evidence of it all around Shaw's Corner. No ghosts, however. Unlike Lamb Shaw was insensitive to the genius of place; his possessions are in Ayot but not his personality.

Renewed by this interlude, we may now go on joyfully for a last encounter with Charles Lamb. Between Ayot St Lawrence and Mackery End lies a tangle of back lanes, always agreeable but without memorable incidents. Mackery End itself is half-way down the sloping side of the Lea valley. Below, on the other bank of the river, Harpenden sprawls along the sides of the A6, but of this there is no hint at all, for Mackery End has miraculously survived intact. The roads are better made, the houses in better repair, the husbandry more efficient, but in essentials the hamlet is as it was when Charles and Mary made their sentimental pilgrimage, some time after the year of Waterloo.

This was a return to childhood. Lamb had stayed here when he was very small. Mary Field, the Grandame of Blakesware, had been a Miss Bruton, whose sister married a farmer of Mackery End called Gladman. Although this never became as Blakesware had been, a second home to the Lambs, they both came here and retained tender memories of the house and its family. Mary probably drew on her store of Mackery End experiences when, in *Mrs Leicester's School*, she told her story of "The Farmhouse".

Lamb's friend Thomas Manning lived four miles away at Redbourn on Watling Street and knew the Brutons and Gladmans as neighbours. Writing to him, probably soon after his return visit, Lamb recalls how he had once projected a great poem but got no further than "Hail, Mackery End!" Knowing Lamb's verse and his tendency to go on, one may feel that this was just the right length. But when he came to write in the *London* in 1821 about the return to this childhood scene his touch was at its surest, his sentiment most delicately balanced. He captured that paradox, that a house, although quite forgotten, can seem familiar, with which every maker of a sentimental journey is acquainted. "We had been talking about Mackery End all our lives, till memory ... became a phantom of itself." Lamb himself was too shy to go in, but Mary was of tougher material; she knocked up "the image of Welcome", a handsome Gladman who took them straight into her house and her heart. So Lamb renewed his compact with "hearty, homely, loving Hertfordshire".

The Mackery End of the Gladmans and the Brutons was a farmhouse, and the slaughtered fatted calf and the wine alike were home produced. This is the house, nicely backed by a great barn, which stands a little back from the road junction in the middle of the hamlet. Although a very fine house it was, and I suppose is, subordinate to Mackery End proper. This latter house lies off the lane which drops downhill to the Lea and to Harpenden. Among all the delightful houses of the Home Counties here is one to awake the sin of covetousness. It is not a great house, but plenty big enough; a house to live in, not just one which establishes the right status symbol. It is, as all the best houses are in this stoneless county, of red brick, an Elizabethan manor house which was given a new look, including curved Flemish gables, in Charles II's reign. A garden which happily keeps the balance between formality and naturalism closes it in. (This is open to the public on some days.) Following the immemorial tradition of such hamlets, the women of the farm helped in the big house, and Mary Field's sister was housekeeper here just as Mary herself was at Blakesware.

Lamb's cousin insisted on taking her rediscovered kinsfolk to Wheat-

hampstead to introduce them "as some new-found rarity" to the rest
of the Gladman clan. There we may follow them, for this, although
much overgrown, is still a small town of character, disposed pleasingly
around the bridge over the youthful Lea. In the large church, which is
essentially town-like in scale, you will see a Lamb prominent among
past rectors, but no relation, and monuments to Garrards who owned
Mackery End for two centuries. Wheathampstead, which has no pretensions among Hertfordshire towns today, could claim pre-eminence
in the remote past, for this, if tradition is as true as seems likely, was the
site of the capital city of Cassivelaunus. In the years immediately pre-
ceding the Roman invasion the Catuvellauni of Hertfordshire were the
dominant force among the Belgic settlers of south-eastern Britain, and
Cassivelaunus was reluctantly accepted as the paramount chief of this
loose confederation when the tribes were driven to unite under the
threat of Caesar's invasion. Had the union remained intact Caesar
might well have been held at the line of the Thames, but one by one
the chief surrendered until Cassivelaunus was left alone. His last stand
may have been made at Wheathampstead, or possibly at Beech Bottom
nearer St Albans.

The Belgic *oppidum* stood above the Lea just to the east of modern
Wheathampstead, and one impressive relic is easily accessible. Coming
out of the town on the Hatfield road, which follows the Lea valley,
open country is reached in about a half-mile. Here a lane goes right
with houses on one side and woodland on the other. In a hundred
yards or so there is a gate into the woods with a panel proclaiming
that this is the Devil's Dyke. Our Dark Age and medieval ancestors
alike attributed anything ancient and contrary to nature to the Devil,
and here obviously is some of his work, a deeply-cut ditch with high
banks, now heavily overgrown. This was the western defence of the
fortress and there are less conspicuous remains of the eastern wall across
the fields.

In following the footsteps of Charles Lamb through the "green
plains of pleasant Hertfordshire" I have claimed the authority of the
master for adopting a "somewhat circuitous route". I propose to end this
journey at St Albans, which Charles and Mary visited *en route* for
Mackery End, but before coming to this noble, historic and sadly
overbuilt city there should be time for one more brief taste of the
rural county and two memories of the great.

The road eastwards out of Wheathampstead rises to a breezy height,
and then drops away gently. Half-way down the slope a lane crosses
diagonally. Not even continuous use over eighteen hundred years has
altered the straight line which proclaims its Roman origin. This was a
road leaving Verulamium for Ermine Street at Braughing. Along the
lane towards the Ayots there is a crossing of the Lea and above the ford

a brick farmhouse of quite spectacular loveliness. It has that slightly
swaggering style which characterizes some of the building, even in so
remote a place and on so small a scale, of James I's reign. Water End
belonged to the Jennings family, and here lived Sarah Jennings who
married the greatest English commander of his time—possibly of all
time—John Churchill, Duke of Marlborough, and who as Mrs Freeman
to Queen Anne's Mrs Morley helped to rule England over the teacups.
Did she, I wonder, ever tire of Hampton Court and Blenheim and long
for the simplicities of Water End? Probably not. She was the last
person to indulge in personal sentiment if it conflicted with personal
power.

The Lea flows past Water End, with an accompanying footpath,
into Brocket Park where it is artificially widened into a long serpentine
lake in front of the house. The severity of the big red-brick house is
softened a little by its setting which is in the best eighteenth-century
landscape manner.

This part of Hertfordshire is a statesman's corner. Politicians found
the county, like parts of Essex and Buckinghamshire, conveniently
removed from the capital and yet easily accessible. Cecil at Hatfield
and Bacon at Gorhambury set the fashion, and it was followed much
later at Brocket by another politician, one who was a great deal more
amiable than his illustrious and ruthless predecessors. Brocket belonged
early in the eighteenth century to Sir Thomas Winnington, who
gained it through marriage. Winnington, who is now scarcely even a
name in the history books, had been a man of exceptional promise,
and Walpole marked him out as a potential Prime Minister. This
promise was not redeemed. In 1746 Sir Thomas sold his Hertfordshire
estate to Sir Matthew Lamb, and William Lamb was born here in 1779.
He spent his childhood in the house, under the conflicting influences of
a jolly spendthrift father and a devoted, intelligent and cultivated
mother. He seems to have learnt the right lessons from both. His
education was conventional in form—Eton and Oxford—and unusual
in academic brilliance. Possibly there, and certainly at home in Brocket,
he laid the foundations of cultural and intellectual interests which
supported him through the disappointments and frustrations of
political life, and even through the anguish of a disastrous marriage.
Whatever did Lady Caroline make of the relaxed and mild air of
Brocket Park? William at last found his true metier when, as Lord
Melbourne, he acted as tutor in statecraft to the young Victoria.
Opinions will continue to vary as to the quality of his performance in
government and opposition; no one is likely to deny his personal
appeal or the interest of his many paradoxes, as sympathetic cynic,
hard-swearing connoisseur of the good life, ruthless in-fighter and
kindly friend of monarchy. Brocket must have seen the best of him, for,

although no recluse, he was most completely himself away from the brittle artifice of society and the greed of Parliament, living the life of the eighteenth-century gentleman which essentially he always was.

Brocket Park is bounded on the eastern side by the A1. It is in the parish of Lemsford, which consists of a few houses towards the river and a Victorian Gothic church—quite effectively done—on the corner. Almost opposite this, a lane wanders erratically towards Sandridge. As this is the last we shall see of unspoilt rural Hertfordshire we must make the most of these four miles which alternate cornfields and broad-leafed woodland. Then comes Sandridge which offers no great interest except the church, and even this at first looks dull. Inside it is quite another story. The core of the building is early Norman and there is a ponderous chancel arch in Roman brick, on to which was imposed a later rood screen of stone. To complete the list of incongruities the Victorian restorers topped the screen and arch with open timber tracery. The result may not be beautiful but it is certainly unique.

It is now a quick and uneventful journey down the main road to St Albans, a dull approach except for its culmination in the tree-lined breadth of St Peter's Street. Given time I should prefer to work around and approach the city from below the hill, where the dramatic situation of the abbey can be best appreciated.

St Albans was the dream city of my childhood. Its position, its small size, the long unbroken line of its history, the great church and the ancient streets, all combined to feed a hungry imagination. The city provoked, I remember, at the age of nine or so my first piece of topographical writing. I still find it difficult to think of St Albans except in the terms of the 1920s.

Today's reality is very different. St Albans is no longer small. It has spilt down the hill southwards and has sent tentacles out towards Hatfield, Harpenden and Hemel Hempstead. Only on the north side has its growth been contained. The old streets have been largely rebuilt or transformed. What I remember as the wide green emptiness of Verulamium is now a public open space, noisy with happy, rowdy, relaxing citizens. All the secret places are exploded wide open. As for the cathedral, it is certainly no smaller than I have remembered it but it is far more of a hotchpotch. Can this medley of styles, some of them not represented at their best, be the abbey in which I first learnt to read a building's story in its fabric?

There remains the history, which time and change can only enhance. Of all the ancient settlements seen on these journeys only Canterbury and Colchester can match St Albans for continuity of history.

After Julius Caesar destroyed Wheathampstead, if not before, there was a Belgic settlement below the steep hill here. The site commended itself to the Romans and they made it a key settlement for their network of roads, the first important stage northwards out of London on their most important route, Watling Street. Verulamium may even have enjoyed unique status among Romano-British cities as a *municipium*.

It lay across Boadicea's track on her fiery way to London, and she wiped it out. The rebuilt city was larger and more impressive, and at its height it must have been almost the most Roman of British cities. Walls, gates, forum, theatre, all aped the manner of the eternal city. To gain only a slight idea of its scale, consider how many Roman bricks were taken from the ruins to build the abbey tower. This was after the Roman city had lain in ruin, subject to weather and robbery, for six centuries.

In Roman Verulamium history and legend became confused. During the persecution of Christians in the reign of the Emperor Diocletian (284–305) a Roman soldier of Verulamium was arrested, tried and executed. The bald facts later became decorated with much colourful speculation. The soldier was Alban. He had discovered a Christian priest named Amphibalus on the run, had hidden him, and been arrested in his place by mistake. So Alban had died not just for his faith but as a sacrifice for a friend. Roman custom decreed that executions should take place outside the city walls and a high place was preferred for symbolic and propaganda reasons. Alban died therefore on top of the hill overlooking the city. When imperial policy was reversed, and Christianity was first tolerated and then approved, a church was built at the place of execution in memory of the first Christian martyr of the province. At the height of his power the great Mercian king Offa replaced this humble building with an abbey dedicated to St Alban. Around this a town grew up while the Roman city decayed, useful only as a quarry for building materials.

With the Normans legend becomes firm history. St Albans did not form a part of the Conquerer's strategy and he built his castles at Hertford and Berkhamsted. As an important religious and pilgrim centre St Albans called for development. Through the influence of Lanfranc a fellow monk of Caen was appointed abbot, the monastery was reorganized, and a great new church replaced the Saxon building. Paul of Caen built his church in conscious rivalry with Lanfranc's at Canterbury, and he certainly made it bigger. It was in the massive, spectacular, dull style in vogue in Normandy, very long, heavy and dark. There was a great square tower beyond the nave and an eastern nest of apsidal chapels.

In the difficult days of Richard I and John another abbot, John of Cella, began additions to the church. His reasons are obscure. St Albans already had an abnormally long nave. The nave played the least important part in the Benedictine ritual. Yet John added to the length of the nave, pushing it westward and planning a grand west front. This was not the soundest period, in terms of economic stability, for such work, and it was never completed. Then part of the Norman nave fell down and had to be rebuilt, while the short Norman chancel was replaced on a larger scale to create a more spacious setting for the saint's shrine.

Every English cathedral is a mixture of styles, illustrating a process of growth spread often over many centuries. In some, as at Canterbury, the good sense or the luck of successive builders has produced a strange harmony out of these incongruous elements. Sense and luck were largely lacking at St Albans. Individual details are lovely, but they do not often coalesce. The beautiful Early English arcades at the west end of the nave draw attention to the gracelessness of the Norman nave and crossing. Having acquired a uselessly long nave the monks cut the eastern section off with a stone screen, so producing a division which, whatever its functional validity, makes aesthetic nonsense.

Last of all in this chronicle of architectural ineptitude comes Lord Grimsthorpe. The abbey had fallen into a terrible state by the nineteenth century. At the Dissolution the church had been sold to the town for a parish church, all 521 feet of it. It was quite impossible for any town to maintain so vast a white elephant, and it became delapidated almost to the point of ruin. The pundits argued long about what should be done, but there was no real basis for agreement. At this point Sir Beckett Denison took a hand. He was living at Batchwood in St Albans and was widely known as a troublesome, aggressive and interfering millionaire. He had been a lawyer, and had made a fortune at the Bar, more by persistence and fighting spirit than through excellence in the law. He then retired to devote his enormous energies to the indulgence of his personal interests. These included clock-making, for which he had a real genius—he made Big Ben; ecclesiastical controversy, and the frustration of successful architects who disagreed with his own dogmas. Denison threw himself with great gusto into the arguments about the future of the abbey. Money was very short, and he launched a restoration fund, contributing generously himself and bullying others into benefactions to the total of £130,000. Then in 1880, by which time Sir George Gilbert Scott, the principal architect in charge of restoration, was dead, he persuaded the cathedral authorities to grant him a faculty to carry out further work to his own design and at his own expense. The extraordinary west front is his, and so are many other peculiar and sometimes effective features of the building. At least when he died in 1905, the abbey—by now a cathedral—was out of debt and danger, at a price.

If the design of St Albans is more often strange than beautiful, much of its detail is of enormous interest.

The martyr's shrine is oddly moving, despite its battered and fragmentary state—at the Dissolution it was broken up and the bits used as rubble to fill up the arches between the saint's chapel and the ambulatory. The wooden watching chamber above it is as lovely as it is rare. On the opposite side of the saint's chapel is a monument of the greatest historical interest, the tomb of Good Duke Humphrey of Gloucester—good to the scholars and artists whom he befriended, but the wicked uncle of the young king Henry VI. The two chantry chapels which flank the high altar are more beautiful, with the lace-like tracery of the last age of Gothic. On the south is Abbot John of Wheathampstead's chantry, restrained and chaste; inside a place has been found for the magnificent memorial brass of Abbot de la Mare who predeceased Wheathampstead by half a century. On the north is the early Tudor Abbot Ramryge, whose chantry is most elegant and delicate in its fine details, including a vaulted roof. We may also admire unreservedly the great stone reredos behind the high altar—while realizing that in terms of liturgical drama the building was probably more effective when the saint's shrine, all gilt and gems, towered above the altar.

As for the city this is probably at its best in the byways. The centre has been mangled in the name of progress and commerce. Away from the main crossing many smaller roads wander away quietly and without through traffic, often lined with brick and plaster houses which survive from the city's mellow years of the eighteenth century. Here the illusive urban style, which has been so signally lost in other parts, endures and flourishes.

One such street is George Street, which becomes successively Romeland Hill and Fishpool Street, ambling gently down from the highest point of the city, crowned with its curfew tower, past the great gate of the abbey, and coming at length to the village of St Michael's. The museum, the Roman theatre, the zoo and the playing fields have brought hordes of visitors here, and yet by some strange inner integrity St Michael's remains itself, not a suburb of the city. Here is the little church which was standing when Abbot Paul raised the tower of the abbey, a church in which Francis Bacon, Lord Verulam, still sits at ease, indifferent to the changed world outside and to the controversies still surrounding his name. Beyond the church lie Gorhambury Park, which the great chancellor's father built, and more of the "native fields of Hertfordshire" which miraculously resist the commuter pressures on this toughly resilient county.

12

The Forest of Essex

I N William the Conqueror's reign the whole of
Essex was under forest law.
This does not mean that the county was covered
by unbroken tracts of woodland. The word 'forest', which came into
England with the Conquest, meant a waste, and referred to an area
which consisted of wide acres of rough open ground alternating with
wooded thickets. The latter provided shelter and food for the beasts of
the chase, the former unobstructed country over which to hunt.
Today the term is most correctly applied to the great forests of Dart-
moor and Exmoor, which still exhibit these characteristics, while the
Forestry Commission is historically incorrect in applying the term to
its often dreary plantations of conifers.

The original Forest of Essex was a very mixed area of woodland,
heathland and pasture, sewn liberally with settlements. There were as
many villages and townships as in other parts of the country, but all
were subject to the restrictive operation of the forest laws.

That at least was the theory. It is difficult to believe that it was ever
completely the practice. The forest laws promulgated by William
had their origins in the remote past. In the beginning—could one ever
isolate and identify a society so primeval—"the Earth was the Lord's
and the fullness thereof", as the Royal Exchange ironically proclaims,
and it was for the enjoyment of all. Very soon some men became more

equal than others and established proprietary rights over certain products of the soil. By the time of the late Saxon kings the hunting of the bigger and more worthy quarry had become restricted to the king and such nobles as he chose to honour with the privilege. It was this situation which William recognized, formalized and intensified in his forest laws. They were, however, more wide-reaching, more strictly applied, and reinforced by more severe penalties. Those who lived in Essex under the forest laws lived hungry in a world of plenty, surrounded by food which they might not eat—and which might indeed destroy their livelihood, for they were forbidden to drive the royal deer out of their crops. Breach of the law meant for the freeman fines or loss of liberty; the serf who took the king's deer lost—literally—his skin.

Laws as narrow and punitive as these bred resistance, not only from the poor who suffered most but from the nobles who used the forest laws as a lever against the Crown. Successive Norman and Angevin kings tried to extend the operation of the laws. Successively the barons resisted and forced restrictions upon the king. The climax came in Magna Carta. This was followed by a forest charter of 1217 which appointed a commission of knights to perambulate the country and establish what was actually and not merely nominally forest. The commissioners did their work faithfully, quartering the area on the ground and looking into traditions and precedents. In 1225, after seven years of very hard work, they ruled that in Essex three-quarters of the county lay outside forest law because the formal processes of afforestation had taken place after the accession of Henry II. At this early date the Forest of Essex ceased to exist, and its place was taken by the Forest of Waltham. Henry III, who had been forced in infancy to accept these restrictions, tried to set them aside after his maturity, but Edward I, a great statesman or perhaps a king who was always too busy for hunting, appointed a new perambulation in 1301. This confirmed the findings of the earlier commission with the addition of royal demesnes around Colchester, Writtle, Hatfield and Felsted. By the sixteenth century the proportion of forest land was down to one fifth. James I characteristically tried to set the clock back by blocking the process of disafforestation and banning sheep farming, and his son tried first to extend the forest land and, when this failed, to sell it. By this time the pattern of conflict over the forests was established: the Crown clung to hunting rights, the lords of the manors maintained rights of ownership over land, and the commons held tight to their rights of grazing and lopping. This struggle went on in a modified form right into the Victorian age, and had a spectacular climax which we shall look at when we get to Epping in this journey.

By the reign of Charles I the forest land of Essex was for all practical purposes the area bounded by the River Lea, the Roding and the Rom. The Long Parliament, acting to frustrate the King's plans for the forest, passed an Act to establish these boundaries and to fix the forest at 60,000 acres.

So, while the unfortunate peasants of Essex suffered grievously from the operation of the forest laws under the Norman kings, the position changed dramatically in the next two centuries, although the king continued to chase the royal beasts in those parts of the county where the law ran. The old authorities classified the quarry into beasts of venery—hart, wolf, boar and hare; beasts of chase—fallow and roe deer, fox and marten; and beasts of sport—badger, cat and otter. These distinctions probably meant little except to the theorist, and the king confined himself to deer and boar. The wolf had disappeared from Essex by the Conquest and the fox was considered vermin and so beneath the attention of royalty. The noble and ancient hare, which has always occupied a very special place in rustic lore, had a somewhat anomalous position in the hierarchy of hunting. It was not preserved by law, at least in the Essex forest, and belonged not to the forest but to the warren, an area outside the forest, the hunting rights over which were granted to certain foundations or persons.

The fascinating story of hunting in the royal forests attracted the attentions of numerous writers of the nineteenth century and a library of books grew up, culminating in a valuable and still readable summary by Dr Charles Cox, the celebrated antiquarian of Edwardian times— *The Royal Forests of England* (1905). Incidentally Cox dealt briefly with Essex in this volume because the subject had been studied exhaustively in the fullest and most scholarly of all these forest books— W. R. Fisher's *The Forest of Essex* (1887), now excessively rare. The subject has not been over-written in recent years, and there is room for a full modern study.

The disafforesting of much of Essex was completed by the beginning of the seventeenth century. The contrary process, by which much of the wilder parts of this country has been transformed, not always for the better, through the operation of the Forestry Commission, has had relatively little effect in this county. When Mr H. L. Edlin made a survey in 1958 he found only 3·2 per cent of Essex under timber, a figure much below the national average. The area has increased since that date but not enormously. The reason is clear. Forestry is an economic use of poor land, even if the conflicting claims of ecology and economy have not been satisfactorily reconciled. In Essex most of the available land is much too precious to be wasted on conifers. It grows good wheat—and good houses. Where the Norman kings rode now lie the golden acres of North Essex and the commuter estates of the south.

It may be that the tradition of the Forest of Essex held back the development—to use the curious cant term for over-building—of the county. When, in the years before the war, the banks of London burst and flooded Middlesex, Surrey and West Kent with houses, the flood waters were held back by the not very formidable barrier of Epping Forest. Perhaps the developers were intimidated by stories of wolf and bear, woodwose and troll. The completion of the District Line to Epping and Ongar marked the beginning of the end of this period of respite, and now the housing estates have leapfrogged the forest easily. Yet still rural Essex beyond the main trunk roads is far more rural than the most remote parts of other Home Counties. The tradition of the waste lands still retains some of its ancient potency.

Apart from the Waltham area Essex escaped the tyranny of the forest at a comparatively early date. Place-names are often a sound guide to early history. The village names of north-west Essex do not suggest a country which was exceptionally wooded or wild or rich in beasts. They reflect the conditions which the original Saxon settlers found. These retired warriors made their homes in the valleys of the low hills; the winding valley of Wenden Lofts and Wendens Ambo, the valley of Walden where, long centuries afterwards, saffron was cultivated, the deep valley of Debden. Water was vital to these farmers. They made a home beside the sandy ford through the Pant at Great Sampford, and gathered thatch for roofing in the reedy valley of the Chelmer at Thaxted. They cleared the waste and made a field out of the heath at Hatfield and Finchingfield—this was settled by descendants of a tribal leader named Finc. They pastured their sheep—their *tegs*— on the lea at Takeley, and found a badger's holt at Broxted. All these names are commonplaces of Saxon England. They paint no picture of a land more than usually given over to the wild. The forest, in fact, was largely an arbitrary creation of the sporting kings, and when the land was released from forest law it quickly reverted to normal.

In this journey through western Essex, therefore, the forest will after all feature only occasionally. There will nevertheless be plenty of fine trees to see and much evidence of the virtuosity of our ancestors in remedying the lack of building stone by a wide and brilliantly skilled use of wood. These clay soils produced oak; they still do— Forest Commission plantations apart, more than half the timber of modern Essex is oak, providing immensely durable roof-trees and the frames of innumerable black-and-white houses. There is a notable example of the latter, lying off our present route but worth a separate visit, in the charming main-road township of Newport. The general impression which the traveller gains is of eighteenth-century brick, for Newport reacted to the stimulus of the coaching age and many

Widford churchyard

(*above left*) Gate to the old churchyard, Ayot St Lawrence (*above right*)
Gate of Widfordbury

Farmhouse at Walkerne

of its houses acquired face-lifts in the fashionable material and in formal symmetrical styles. Among these, however, stands a house which clearly does not belong here—although it would look quite at home in the Weald of Kent or Sussex. It is a characteristic hall-house with overhangs, one of which is decorated in a crudely vigorous manner with a Virgin and angels. Newport is not far from Hatfield Forest, but other spectacular timber-work is found all over Essex from Moynes Park and Steeple Bumpstead in the north to the noble timber refectory roof of Prittlewell Priory in the south. There will not be time to look at more than a few examples on this journey, but enough remains for a lifetime of travel.

Our journey into the Forest of Essex begins on Icknield Way at Royston in the farthest north-east corner of Hertfordshire. A road runs south-east out of the town, keeping close to and occasionally crossing the boundary with Cambridgeshire. This is chalk country, the last we shall see of this most characteristic of all south-eastern landscape features except for the outcrop on Thameside. Here the chalk produces not the beechwood curves of the Chilterns or the steep escarpments of North and South Downs, but long undulating slopes and shallow valleys. Compared with the "dim blue goodness of the Weald" seen from the Downs the views are never extensive. They are however singularly satisfying in the harmony of all their elements. These prospects of field and copse are free of irrelevance, unless one counts the ubiquitous overhead wires. It is prosperous country, growing excellent wheat and barley. Unlike some intensively cultivated country, however, it is not inhospitable to the visitor who wishes to see it from the standpoint of his two feet. In addition to some delectable and not overbusy lanes there is a reasonable sufficiency of footpaths passing ancient moated halls and leading to hamlets—nearly always called 'greens'—and picturesque villages. As usual in chalk country, too, there is surviving evidence of the remote past, in barrows, field systems and a Roman road leading from Ermine Street at Braughing to the military station of Great Chesterford.

There is a last outpost of Hertfordshire at Barley—not named after the prevailing crop but recalled a lost *leah*, a grove in the woodland—which is made memorable by its inn sign, on which fox and hounds span the street. Long may they remain to the confusion of giant lorries! Then the road climbs to the 300-foot contour where a white-painted post mill dominates the scene most handsomely. Still rising, the road—now in Cambridgeshire—traverses the pretty village of Great Chishill and then achieves an incredible 478 feet. All height is relative and we are really in the highlands here. The chalk is here overlaid with gravel as the village name—compare Chislehurst and the Chesil Bank—proclaims. After this the road declines somewhat as it

passes through a wood and enters Essex. We are in one of the most
densely populated counties in England, and one of the emptiest. There
is not a house in sight and no village actually straddling the road for
seven or eight miles. If you crave human society you must diverge
from the route to find charming and remote settlements a mile or
more away—at Chrishall, for example, neatly disposed around
crossroads and with the big stately church away on a wooded hill; or
Elmdon, which is larger but less distinctive. A single diversion will take
in these two villages and also Wenden Lofts, where there is no village
at all, only a church in the park of Lofts Hall. Even better things lie off
to the south or our road, enchanting country, around the extremely
pretty village of Arkesden, and Clavering which is as comely as it is
historical. Here is a memorable row of houses leading up to the great
church with its splendid wooden roof, and an open site nearby which
displays earthworks thrown up by Edward the Confessor's Norman
friends and abandoned when Earl Godwin chased them back home.
This has, however, tempted us far to the south, and other delectable
sights may lure us even farther afield. So back to our little B1039 as it
drops steadily towards the valley of the Cam, and at last reaches human
habitations at Wendens Ambo. Essex is rich in place-names which are
charming and slightly grotesque, and here is one of the best. There
were two parishes originally, Great and Little, which became amalgamated. So Great and Little Wenden become Both Wendens in fine
lawyers' Latin.

Wendens Ambo is in commuter country and right next to Audley
End Station—itself a classic example of Victorian railway architecture.
Astonishingly it has survived the test and remains an outstandingly
unspoilt Essex village. The tiny side street framing church and great
barn is as pleasing as one may hope to find anywhere. The barn is a
grand piece of traditional construction in timber. The church is almost
excessively picturesque, and remarkably interesting too. It has retained
its old benches, despite a late Victorian clean-up. These are mainly of
homely rural carpentry, but one illustrates, in a very crude way, the
medieval beast fable of the tiger who is caught by the hunters with a
mirror. Spellbound before her reflection she is easily snared. There was
never such a tiger as this!

Less than a mile separates this quiet rural village from the main
Cambridge Road, noisy with heavy traffic. To the south lie Newport
and other good things, but our way must take in the most celebrated,
perhaps the most beautiful and certainly the most accessible of Essex
great houses, Audley End.

The park of Audley End straddles the main road a mile or two to the
north, taking in as an integral part of the design a rounded and wooded
hill capped by the rampart of a hill-fort. Ring Hill was always an eye-

catcher, and Robert Adam accentuated the effect when he set a classical round temple on it in celebration of the Seven Years War. I mention this before coming to the house partly because it is reached first, partly because it helps to emphasize that Audley End is not just a very big and handsome house but a great and successful exercise in landscape design. This came much later than the house, which originally had the geometrically formal gardens which the Jacobeans admired. The new layout was devised by Capability Brown—one of the comparatively few works not only traditionally but actually carried out by this master—during the second half of the eighteenth century, and it is imaginative, resourceful and discreet as any. Water was an essential element in Brown's designs, and here he had a small, very clear stream, the infant Cam. This was widened to form an ornamental sheet of water in front of the house. It was crossed by a stately ceremonial bridge on the main approach, and later by a most enchanting classical fantasy, complete with summer house, which provided a scenic accent to the circuit of the estate. Another temple stands at the rear of the house, and elegant works of art and artifice capture, or surprise, the eye around the park.

All this is so satisfying that on most visits I should be content to pass the house by. This however would be to miss a major example of English domestic architecture and a house of character.

The first impression of Audley End is of a Jacobean palace and this is, broadly speaking, accurate. Most great houses proceed by a natural process of growth, each age adding its own characteristic wing or court. Thomas Howard, who built Audley End around the time of James I's accession, worked on so huge a scale that his successors were left with little to do but repair, modernize and demolish. Roughly half of the original has gone, but what remains is still one of the biggest houses in the country. James I said, with that sour irony which was in him a substitute for humour, "too much for a King, but it might do well for a Lord Treasurer", and for once one sees things his way.

There was a Benedictine priory (later abbey) at Walden, founded by that fascinating and sinister figure who dominated Essex during the anarchy of Stephen's reign, Geoffrey de Mandeville. This, according to custom, was built out of sight of the little town in the river valley. After the Dissolution the property was granted to the Lord Chancellor Sir Thomas Audley, who made a house out of the domestic buildings of the abbey. Audley's daughter married the Duke of Norfolk and it was their son, Thomas Howard, who cleared the site and built himself a new house appropriate to his dignity as Earl of Suffolk and Lord Treasurer. The house stayed with the Suffolks, on and off, for a century and a half, when it was sold to the Countess of Portsmouth, who carried out a scheme of modernization and reduction and laid out the grounds. This work was completed by Lord Braybrooke towards the end of the century. It is now in the care of the Department of the Environment and both house and park are opened regularly.

There is neither space nor need for a detailed description of the house here. (The handbook on sale at Audley End is a model of its kind.) Sufficient to say that it displays that happy genius of the Jacobean builder in giving a traditional tone to an entirely modern style, "twixt antique and modern" as Evelyn said. The great hall is in the grand manner of its day and yet it is clearly akin to the medieval hall—like that of Penshurst—which was by then long outdated. Here is a rich array of wood, panelled walls, carved timbers framing and supporting the plaster ceiling, and a quite extraordinary screen which all but occupies the end of the hall. (It is challenged at the opposite end by a stone screen of altogether different character.) If the detailed motifs of this are baroque the concept is medieval, and here the centuries war agreeably with one another.

The rest of the house is grand, or homely, but nothing eclipses the memory of this. It is in a way a comfort to escape into the garden to establish contact with a less exciting but more relaxed age.

Before going on to Saffron Walden it is worth making the short journey along Audley End street to the charming brick buildings of the College, almshouses dating from Tudor times and perhaps a surviving offshoot of the abbey.

Saffron Walden is a brisk, busy and attractive small town, a place which I always visit with enjoyment without once feeling in the least at home. Walden had the dangerous privilege of association with Geoffrey de Mandeville, who built a castle on a high point above the town. A few fragments, too faint to be interpreted by any but experts, stand near the admirable museum. The town acquired its distinctive first name some time during the late Middle Ages when it became a centre for the production of saffron, a plant used extensively in medicine, cookery and dyeing. With this and more conventional industries the place became wealthy enough to replace the old church with one built at the very height of English Gothic. This was begun early in Henry VI's reign and finished in that of Henry VIII. The soaring spire is an addition from the nineteenth century. This church, with its stone arcades and great windows, has the lightness and dignified spaciousness which we associate more with East Anglia. (We shall soon see an even finer example at Thaxted.) The detailed carving calls for examination. In the south aisle lies the Lord Chancellor Audley who founded Audley End, a grand piece of Tudor monumental extravagance.

The town is a jolly mixture of good and bad buildings, with a share of indifferent. There is one famous example of Essex pargetting, but the most effective buildings in the town are timber-framed, notably in

Bridge Street and High Street. The narrow back streets and alleys repay the explorer.

To the east of Saffron Walden a subtle change comes over the landscape. So far in this journey we might have been in almost any part of the chalk belt of East Anglia. Now, although the contours continue their slow sweeping lines and the wheat is almost as golden there is a faint smell of the city in the air. This is unmistakably a Home County, and London reaches out to touch the most remote farmhouse. Yet only the most leisured executive commutes from these parts and there is no unsightly semi-urban sprawl around the villages. The scene is still very beautiful, but that marvellous feeling of emptiness which marked the miles from Royston has gone and will not be recovered before this journey ends.

The main road to Thaxted is high, direct and rather dull. A much longer alternative to the north has a rather messy start and then takes in some attractive and interesting villages in the valley of the young River Pant. Perhaps the best route is by way of a byway through Debden. This is the slowest way, for the road is narrow and as direct as only Chesterton's drunkard could make it. It stays mostly on or above the 300-foot contour—high for Essex—with agreeable views. Then, at about the highest point, it enters the very pretty village of Debden. Here, although there is nothing of particular distinction, the general impression is most pleasing. The old woodlands have been felled to some purpose to produce some good half-timbered cottages, and there are others which look more as if they belong to the West Country with their whitewash and thatch. One thing seems lacking, a church. This is a long way off, on the edge of Debden Park in a pleasing setting of wooded parkland, in which the little Debden Brook, a tributary of the Cam, has been widened into an ornamental water for the benefit of a mansion which is no longer there. The church is largely late Georgian in a kind of Gothic style, built under the inspiration of a local gentleman who rests herein from his labours. It was an absurd and extravagant exercise, but we are sufficiently remote now from the event and may enjoy a badness which almost acquires merit.

This country is so agreeable as to claim the better acquaintance of a walk. Something of the essence of the landscape might be got from a round trip by way of Rook End to Mole Hall—where the park of a handsome house provides the setting for the friendliest and most informal of wild-life reserves—returning by a track behind the church at Widdington and across Debden Park.

From Debden the road keeps high and undulating past Debden Green where it reaches the highest point, and then most pleasantly and uneventfully heads for Thaxted. Past Cutlers Green—recalling the craftsmen of the town's staple industry, there is a memorable view

across the lower gathering grounds of the River Chelmer of Thaxted
spire, and the last half mile goes uphill past the windmill to the crossroads of the most perfect small town in Essex.

Thaxted is a town of superlatives. (It lost its charter under James II
but still has the characteristic complexity of a town; only the most
imperceptive would confuse it with a village.) It is high in my list of
favourite places, for it has contained its growth—every town changes,
and not for the better, when it grows beyond 20,000 population—and
kept its sense of purpose. Some of the loveliest of small towns—I am
perhaps thinking of Lavenham—are marred by a slight air of precious-
ness; like a professional beauty they are too consciously lovely. Thaxted
is under no delusion about its loveliness, but it makes no fuss about it.
This is a town for living in as well as looking at. Certainly I should
dearly like to live there—especially now that the threat of a major
airport nearby has gone, surely for ever—and there is scarcely a town
which gives me greater delight in an idle and purposeless perambulation
of its streets.

Not that there are many streets. Thaxted is principally a main-road
town, its ancient buildings disposed around the central guildhall and
reaching uphill to a little beyond the church. It can all be contained in a
single short stroll—and understood after a lifetime of contemplation.

Although the forests were scarcely a memory when Thaxted had its
heyday in the fifteenth century, there were still plentiful supplies of
building timber, and the town is still, despite its many eighteenth-
century brick frontages—as usual they often mask older buildings—
essentially one of black and white. The keynote is struck at the very
heart of the town by the Guildhall of the Cutlers, a square block rising
upwards and outwards with two storeys overhanging the open market
hall on its oak stilts, and with a hipped roof over all. A remarkable
building this and impressive, but just a little comical too. It inspires deep
affection. At its side one of the few byroads runs narrowly up towards
the church with more timber-framed overhanging houses, and there
are more of the same just below the guildhall in the High Street.

Part of the secret of Thaxted's appeal lies in the differences of level.
The church and its immediate neighbours are on a higher plane than the
commercial centre of the guildhall, giving the arrangement both
symbolic and visual significance. On the way up the hill there stands on
the right, as a contrast to all the half-timbering, a very distinguished
brick house of the early eighteenth century, Clarence House. The name
is a reminder that, in addition to the support of the woolmen and the
other craft guilds, Thaxted Church benefited from royal and noble
patronage. One of the early benefactors was Lionel, Duke of Clarence,
second son of King Edward III whose daughter married Edmund
Mortimer, Earl of March. Their grandson, another Edmund, built the

north aisle and the great stone spire. The March earldom died with him, but his grand-nephew, Edward IV, continued the association with Thaxted and with his encouragement the chancel was completed. The resultant building is appropriately regal and noble. Its spire, the oldest in Essex, greets the traveller on whichever road he approaches the town. The exterior of the church is a treasury of medieval art and allegory, for every corbel, label-stop and gargoyle is carved richly and with fine humour and fantasy. The interior can stand comparison with any non-collegiate parish church in England. The soaring lines are clean and unfussy. There is an abundance of ornament when one looks for it, but it does not obtrude; the general impression is one of economy which stops short of austerity. It is very light. There is plenty of plain glass, and light floods in above from a Tudor clerestorey. No heavy Victorian pews obstruct the nave. Here is a building stripped for action; as functional as a power-house and, one feels, as effective. Over all, and the only dark note in the building, is the magnificent wide-span flat roof, of fifteenth-century timber.

Even those visitors who are normally resistant to the charms of ecclesiastical architecture—and only recently has it occurred to topographical writers that such exist—should enter here, for this is a building which represents one of the lofty achievements of its two centuries and one which, under a succession of inspired rectors, remains highly relevant to our time.

For those with time to spare, Thaxted may be made the base for a visit to the upper valley of the Pant, a district which is for many connoisseurs the best of Essex. This includes Finchingfield, just beyond the Pant but linked with it by a tiny stream. Finchingfield is one of the show villages of England, with all the charms and all the drawbacks attached to this status. It is certainly exceptionally pretty, with the graces which come from a combination of rising ground, a foreground of green and pond, the happily careless grouping of cottages—mostly timber-framed but with the timbers hidden behind plaster—which make up in harmony for their lack of individual quality, and a very fine church half hidden behind the long range of the guildhall. No one could deny these charms. I like equally, or even more, Great Bardfield, which has a rather more sophisticated air with its elegant town houses in brick and wrought iron. The Sampfords are most attractive too. Better still is the surrounding country, so relaxed for all its productivity, and dotted with choice farmhouses and halls. Among these is one of the most celebrated, Spains, which lies just to the north of Finchingfield, a very handsome mansion in Tudor brick standing in a fine park; and also one of the most intimately charming, Tewes, near Little Sampford, which opens its doors most generously to the visitor. The catalogue of delights might be extended indefinitely.

The main route goes south from Thaxted, diverging quickly south-west to cross the infant Chelmer at Dairy Green. A narrow lane follows the stream downwards past the fragments of Tilty Abbey, but our road climbs briskly to the vantage-point of Broxted. Here, open for viewing on certain days, is one of the finest medium-sized gardens in Essex—or in England. There is not much else in the village but the breezy atmosphere. Across the fields, and most pleasantly reached by footpath, is the little Saxon church of Chickney.

At Broxted the main road may be followed to Elsenham, famous for the aristocrat among English jams, and Stansted. This way however gets entangled with the Cambridge Road traffic, and although it is arguably the more interesting route, I prefer to come south off the road in Broxted village. There is no village all the way to Takeley, but Molehill Green, a straggle of mostly undistinguished cottages, is as big as most villages in this part of Essex. Just below the green the River Roding has its source.

As the lane drops towards its crossing with the Roman Stane Street a green lane right leads to the lonely church of Takeley, which had been dedicated as one of the sacrifices on the altar of the third London Airport. Was it worth saving? Of course. There are dozens of buildings as good or better in this county, but none which summarizes and testi-fies to the history of this village alone. A village church is more than a more-or-less comely arrangement of bricks and rubble and Roman tiles and flint, as those charged with the disposal of 'redundant' churches might remember. The showpiece of Takeley, and the only thing which gives the building national significance, is the tall, extrav-agantly decorated, timber font-cover. Had the worst happened, this would no doubt have found a home in the Victoria and Albert Museum where it would have received loving care. But it belongs to, and in, Takeley.

Of Takeley on the Street little need be said. Main roads have a habit of knocking the character out of any village through which they pass. But it is along this road that we must go for a long mile until at Takeley Street a turning south offers escape. We are now at last within reach of a surviving fragment of the Forest of Essex, a most delightful and quite untypical tract of woodland preserved miraculously and now safely in the care of the National Trust.

Hatfield Forest is a good corrective to those who still imagine that a forest must be full of trees. There are plenty of trees, it is true, though few of any age, but the scenic effects of Hatfield are made by the open spaces, the wide green rides and the central lake. Much of its charm belongs to the eighteenth-century love of contrived landscape, com-paratively little to the medieval king's love of hunting.

The forest is nevertheless in essence a genuine descendant of the royal forest. If one takes into account not only the thousand acres of the National Trust land but also the woods and open land of Hallingbury Park which essentially belongs to it this is a goodly expanse of green country. From Anvil Cross to Takeley Street the crow will fly a good four miles, and on foot or by car the way is much longer. All this area is specifically included in Henry III's Perambulation, when the forester was Richard de Montfichet—whose family gave their name to Stansted Mountfitchet. By Elizabeth's reign the royal forest was largely fragmented, and a sizeable chunk came to the Barringtons of Hatfield Broad Oak and more to the Morleys of Hallingbury. In 1729 Hatfield Forest was bought by trustees of the distinguished Houblon family, and it was they who set about the deliberate beautifying of the estate according to the current principles of landscape design. This work included the formation of a big ornamental lake, while a lady of the family indulged in a typical conceit of the time by decorating the lakeside cottage with designs in seashells.

The forest remained with the Houblon family until 1923 when Major Houblon sold it for its timber. Mr E. N. Buxton, one of the most stalwart advocates of Epping Forest and an informed lover of the forest country, stepped in and bought back the freehold of Hatfield Forest. Most of the timber was felled, but a few of the finer old trees were preserved. Mr Buxton presented the forest to the National Trust, and subsequent gifts by Major Houblon and members of the Buxton family extended the estate to its present size.

What the Trust acquired, therefore, was not woodland but an estate with trees. Most of the latter were ancient oaks with a few hornbeams, both typical trees of the Forest of Essex and perhaps direct descendants of trees in the royal forest. Most of the existing trees however are in coppices of oak and birch and other fairly young trees. There are also some trees not of forest character, and these belong to the landscape developments of the eighteenth century.

This, then, is the forest which we visit today. At first impression it seems disappointing. There are no 'forest giants', no hint of a forest primeval. But the appeal of Hatfield Forest grows with fuller acquaintance. I wish the Trust had not decided to admit motor traffic, for cars and forests do not go well together. It is a grand place to walk in, away from the motor tracks, hunting in the many boggy areas for wild flowers, and rewarded too by glimpses of birds and butterflies. The lake, where refreshments may be had, is nearly always crowded—though beautiful—while wide acres to the west are almost empty and so are the detached woodlands reached from Woodside Green.

The very wet forest land drains south-west into the River Stort. Just to the east there is a narrow watershed, and then the drainage is south-east to the Roding.

The early history of Hatfield Forest is much concerned with the de
Veres, Earls of Essex, who dominated the county's affairs for several
centuries. They were the founders of the fortunes of Hatfield Broad
Oak, a village right on the watershed to the south-east of the forest.
Here Aubrey de Vere founded a priory of Benedictine monks around
the year 1135. The village grew up at the gate of the monastery. It was
never a house of great importance or wealth, and was dissolved as a
'lesser' monastery in 1536. The conventual buildings were destroyed
and also about two-thirds of the church, leaving only the nave to serve
the parish. Very little of the present church dates from the foundation
of the priory, belonging rather to improvements carried out in the
fourteenth and fifteenth centuries. It makes a very handsome parish
church, a little reminiscent of that at another centre of de Vere activities
farther north, Earls Colne. The west towers are markedly similar. As
befits a forest church the woodwork is exceptionally good, but it is all
much later than the wild forest. The splendid roof is early Victorian,
the chancel lining and stalls Georgian. The representations of the four
Evangelists: angel, lion, bull and eagle, are strong and dignified,
worthy of a collegiate setting. There are good eighteenth- and nineteenth-century monuments, but the dominant feature of the church is
the battered knight in the middle of the chancel. He is alleged to be
Robert de Vere, the third earl, who died in 1221.

There is plenty of exposed timber in the little village, which for all
its small size manages to convey a feeling of importance. There are no
big houses in sight but no poor ones either. The great house is Barring-
ton Hall, a later house of the woodwards of Hatfield Forest, and their
big park comes right up to the churchyard wall, taking in the site of
the priory buildings. The whole scene is self-contained and remarkably
unspoilt.

Between Hatfield Forest and Epping Forest lies a sizeable tract of
country which has not been afforested for many centuries and which
has developed its own characteristic way of life. It consists in fact of
two quite distinct areas. To the east the Roding, here a stream of very
modest proportions, gives unity to the string of tiny villages known
collectively as the Rodings. To the west, in country sloping very gently
to the Stort, is a group of '-ing' villages and then come the Lavers, all
places of great charm and so far successfully resisting the pressures of
Harlow New Town. It would not be difficult to surrender to the
temptation of lingering long in so leisured and agreeable an area.

The Rodings, which provide material for a book to themselves,
must be encompassed in a paragraph or two. The Roding, whose
beginnings we saw at Moleshill Green, is still only a trickle when it
crosses Stane Street within sight of Little Canfield church. It then goes
past the more impressive village of Great Canfield, where it flows

around half the circuit of a large and overgrown motte dating from
the Conquest and very close to the charming church. If you venture
inside, disregard some of the aggressive modern fittings and concentrate on the exquisite Norman chancel, built not very long after the
castle. Here is the treasure of Canfield, and one of the loveliest things
in the county, a wall painting of Virgin and Child, set here behind the
altar when the building was in its second century. We owe its survival
to the insensitivity of a later age which put a wall monument over it
and so preserved it from both decay and vandalism. We are still not
at the Rodings proper, but in two miles the stream passes not far from
the remote church of High Roding, while the road goes right through
this high-road village with its half-timbering. Next comes Aythorpe
Roding, marked by a very fine post mill just off the road and a pretty
church on a hillock above the river. Here too is one of the moated
sites which abound in this part of Essex, and another is in sight, with its
great barn, just to the north of the side road. This same road, if followed
round a right-angle bend, leads past a beautiful timbered farmhouse
and then comes to Leaden Roding. (The church roof was of lead when
the normal covering was thatch.) To the west, and well out of sight of
the river, is White Roding—the church was whitewashed—and to the
south from this Abbess Roding—belonging to Barking Abbey—
where there is an exceptionally charming church with a spire. From
here it is a short journey to the main road through the valley and to
Beauchamp Roding, where there is scarcely anything except a church
with a tall slim tower standing all alone in a field. To complete the
tally, Berners Roding, with a church even plainer than High Roding's
beside a brick manor house, lies away on the east side of the valley, and
Margaret Roding is on the busy Chelmsford road. The church of
St Margaret has no particular charm as seen from the road, but a closer
look reveals several good things: a richly carved doorway which is a
textbook example of Norman work, a curious and not fully explained
arcade in the north wall with elegant detail, and an enormous oak
chest. Necessarily, in dealing in this summary fashion with the Rodings,
one mentions only the old buildings, but the real appeal of this country
lies in the quiet, intimate landscape in which billowing clouds and
ancient willows and alders are reflected in the lazy waters of the little
river. Its beauties cannot be assimilated in a hurry.

Across the westward ridge, which at best falls short of three hundred
feet, the scene is subtly different. The villages are a little larger and
rather more sophisticated. In addition to the characteristic moated
halls there are substantial mansions standing in their small parks, like
Durrington Hall at Sheering, whose Georgian confidence and self-
consciousness make it a perfect foil to the Jacobean timber of Aylmers
which stands just across the road. Sheering, while we are there, also

has a fascinating church with grotesque carving—so crisp in its detail that it must surely have been renewed. The next village is Matching— all these village names hint at very early settlement by Saxons carrying on their colonizing mission up the Lea and Stort and at last beating their seaxes into hoes in these peaceful clearings in the forest—which has no direct communication with Sheering by road, although a farm road cuts across to the wooded corner in which church and hall stand in traditional companionship. There is a third and rarer building in this group, the pretty Marriage Feast House which stands behind the church, a nice piece of timberwork and an unusual survival. Most of Matching village is at Matching Green, where there are some good houses and some bad, but the best is at Matching Tye where one exquisite small house displays lively and tasteful ornament.

South of these 'ings' come the Lavers, with villages at Little Laver, Magdalen Laver and High Laver. These are all worth a visit, but the best in scenery and buildings is at High Laver, which still recalls its connection with John Locke. The great philosopher who anticipated the age of enlightenment came to live here towards the end of his life, and he was duly buried in the churchyard in 1704 with an austere monument to mark the place.

Some of the attraction of these places derives from the savouring of the miracle of their survival. We are now well within commuter range of the City, with High Laver roughly equidistant between the two railway lines, and yet, with one or two lapses, this is the genuine rural Essex. It needs to be savoured while it lasts. Harlow New Town has now jumped the A11 and grows into Potter Street and Harlow Common, and a finger points tentatively towards Foster Street. To the south Ongar has spread across the A122 and driven a wedge into the valley of the Cripsey Brook. Anything may happen—planners permitting— in the next few years.

There is some evidence here in support of the New Town principle. Those who remember the little villages of Great Parndon and Nettes-well, which in their day were as individual as High Laver and Match-ing, may mourn their passing. Nevertheless Harlow has developed not as a great amorphous sprawl but as a group of related communities each of which preserves whatever village quality it brought to the New Town. Harlow is not yet in the true sense a town, but it is a cluster of villages which may, without loss of integrity, one day cohere to make a town. And imagination sees only too clearly what might have happened to Essex if this development, instead of being concen-trated, had been distributed haphazard over the country between Epping and Bishops Stortford. Harlow is arguably the best of the New Towns, in its plan, its architecture and its solution to social problems. Enjoying, perhaps selfishly, the quiet lanes which wind just out of sight of its tower blocks, I am thankful for the existence of the New Town. But I should not care to live there!

Coming south out of the Laver country we encounter the A122, busy with heavy lorries making a big loop around North London, and then the small urban eruption around the airfield of North Weald. There are stories to tell about this station in the early days of aviation and in the Battle of Britain, but not here. The houses cease and in half a mile genuine forest country, the detached Lower Forest of Epping, appears beside the road.

This humble patch of woodland is an outpost of the only true survivor of the great Forest of Essex. As we have seen, the forest, which after the Conquest nominally covered the whole county, had by the reign of James I become limited to the 60,000 acres of the Forest of Waltham. In the next two centuries this area was whittled away by the unplanned but persistent enclosures of the landowners, a process resisted only by commoners who wished to preserve their common rights. The Crown was no help, as it had been in the great days of royal hunting. Charles II was the last king to hunt the forest deer, and after his time the forest law, although theoretically operative, had no real force. In the past it had been the king who stopped the lords of the manor from fencing their land, because this would have hindered hunting. Now there was a straight fight between lords of the manor and commoners, with all the odds on the former.

The largest concentration of enclosures took place between the Napoleonic Wars and the middle of the nineteenth century, an age which gave unsentimental favour to the landowner who wished to increase profitability and had no stake in traditional rights, especially those unsupported by written evidence. In this climate the Forest of Waltham, already shrunken to the Forest of Epping, disappeared gradually into private estates until little remained but the central strip, at most two miles wide, which enclosed the high road to Epping, and a smaller detached fragment at Hainault, well to the east and close to the old royal manor of Havering.

The climax to this process of enclosure came in 1851 when by Act of Parliament Hainault Forest was disafforested and parcelled out among its seven manors. The Crown's share was 2,842 acres, and this was all promptly grubbed. This was the ignominious end of an historic forest. Much fine timber disappeared, although the most famous tree in the Forest of Essex had gone, all but a few fragments, some time before. This was the Fairlop Oak, a real giant according to reliable accounts; the trunk had a girth of 36 feet and the boughs covered an area 300 feet in circumference. Legends and traditions clung to it, and it provided the focus for popular junketings. The oak caught fire in 1805 and was badly damaged, and a gale fifteen years later put an end to its eventful life. One small patch of Hainault, of about 300 acres, was granted to Lambourne parish by the Inclosure Commissioners, in 1862, and this remains. It serves as a precious 'lung' for the residents in the vast housing estates of Chigwell and Havering.

With the destruction of Hainault Forest the commoners lost a battle. In their next test it seemed that they were likely to lose the war. The lord of the manor of Loughton, one of the largest villages within Epping Forest, was the Reverend Mr Maitland, the local parson. He owned some 1,300 acres of forest land and this he enclosed with a fence. He acted with scrupulous regard for law, if not for custom, buying out his tenants. This left unaccounted for the lopping rights of the commoners. From the most ancient times the commoners of Loughton had been privileged to cut firewood in the forest. Branches were cut and stacked, and then drawn from the forest by sledge. To this practical arrangement a number of traditional details became appended. Cutting had to begin at midnight on St Martin's Eve. The commoners met for a celebration, accompanied with drinking, and on the stroke of midnight they began cutting. The first load had to be dragged out by a team of white horses. These picturesque trivialities were important to the commoners, although the lords whose timber was being mangled did not always appreciate the celebrations.

Festivities and lopping alike seemed to be at an end in Loughton after Parson Maitland put up his fences. One man of Loughton did not agree. A Mr Willingale—a grand Essex name—took his two sons into the forest on St Martin's Eve and carried out the traditional lopping. Maitland prosecuted them, and they were sent to gaol. The incident might have attracted little attention, but one of the sons died in prison and the Willingales were on the way to becoming martyrs. The Commons Society became interested in the case, and with their support Willingale started legal proceedings to restrain Maitland and to confirm the rights of the people of Loughton to lop winter firewood.

The case dragged on. Willingale died, and it seemed as if there might be indefinite stalemate. At this point there was an improbable intervention. The City of London took a hand. The corporation owned land in the forest and consequently had a theoretical interest in forest rights, and they decided to support the cause of the commoners. This not only brought the big battalions on to the commoners' side against the lords of the manors; it gave their case valuable publicity and attracted the attention of Parliament. The government set up a commission, linear descendant of those perambulations which had studied the forest in the reigns of John and Henry III, and this body looked into all the evidence of rights and privileges in the forest. The corporation's law case and the commissioners' report both came to similar conclusions: all further enclosures were forbidden, and this judgement was backdated by twenty years. It was a striking victory for the Willingales of the forest—or so it seemed.

However, all was not quite as it seemed. An Act of Parliament placed Epping Forest in the care of the Corporation of London, and ensured that it should remain open freely to everyone for all time. The freedom did not extend to lopping. The lords might have lost the war, but so had the commoners.

This decision provoked yet another row, this time between the Commons Society and the corporation. In the end a compromise was reached by which the corporation paid the parish of Loughton compensation for loss of lopping rights, and this money was spent on a new village hall, called Lopping Hall. At this point the saga of Loughton, which had embraced high drama and tragedy, concluded on a note of pure comedy. The parish invited the Lord Mayor of London, the very head and symbol of their oppression, to open their hall, and Rector Maitland dedicated it with unctuous prayer. It was a situation to which only Trollope could have done justice.

Whatever the rights of the men of Loughton, we are all beneficiaries of the Epping Forest Act, which in 1878 formed a landmark in the history of man's struggle to enjoy his environment. It antedated by a year the Corporation of London's acquisition of Burnham Beeches and by seventeen the foundation of the National Trust. Almost for the first time, and certainly for the first time on this scale, it was recognized publicly that the desire to walk in the country was a basic human need which had to be guaranteed. With comparatively minor—but very disturbing—changes, the area dedicated to public enjoyment in 1878 is that which exists today. The future is less clear. Pressures on the forest grow daily as roads threaten to eat up more open land and the housing developers cast eager—that is to say greedy—eyes on the green belt. The time may not be far distant when another Willingale will be called upon to sacrifice himself for the cause, but he will face a more formidable adversary than Maitland.

At present the forest consists of about 6,000 acres, one-tenth of the Forest of Waltham which existed three centuries ago. The wooded area is about six miles long from Chingford to Epping and at most two miles wide. To this should be added the numerous 'flats' which penetrate deep into the built-up acres of East London. These are mostly open spaces sown with a few battered trees and with a pond or so, unlovely perhaps but very important to the inhabitants of the crowded inner suburbs. One of these, Wanstead Flats, merges with Wanstead Park which is an example of landscape design on the grand scale, disposed about the site of the prototype of English Palladian architecture. Colen Campbell's masterpiece vanished long ago, but there are reminders in the park—the grotto, a charming temple, and the glorious church added half a century later—of one of the most splendid estates on the fringe of Georgian London.

Wanstead, however deserving of a visit, is a long way, spiritually and geographically, from the quiet heart of Epping Forest. It is still quiet, however noisy the gear-changing on the A11 as the monster lorries grind up the hill from Wake Valley to Mount Pleasant. Most of the motor traffic is confined to four roads, and even the motorist, if he goes cannily and chooses his time and season, may see much to enjoy. But obviously the forest will yield its secrets fully only to those who get out and walk. For them Epping Forest is full and open and inexhaustible, despite its small scale. They alone are likely to see the fallow deer, introduced in the nineteenth century to replace the noble beasts who were the quarry of kings, the rarer birds, and the exquisite play of light on leaves in full summer, the pattern of frost and snow in winter.

It is hardly necessary to advise the walker in the forest. It is sufficiently small for everyone to follow his fancy without risk of getting lost or even excessively muddy—although good boots are more than desirable. After a few visits each explorer will establish his own favourite rides and thickets, his special route to the ramparts of Loughton Camp, the unexpected outward glimpses of Lea and Roding valleys. On hot days there will be a call to cool dappled glades in Monk Wood, or for hardier souls and skins the sun-soaked expanse of Honey Lane Plain. Everywhere there will be reminders of the activities of Tom Willingale and his friends in ancient hornbeams and other trees, their trunks contorted into shapes at once ugly and highly intriguing as a result of lopping. And if one wants an eloquent and informed guide there are admirable books by James Brimble (supremely well illustrated by this master photographer) and William Addison.

In the course of these walks the wanderer will certainly encounter some of those officers whose business is the care of the forest. He will probably not meet the Ranger, who represents the Crown and so is a direct descendant of the Lord Warden who watched over the king's interests in the Middle Ages. The office of Forest Ranger was established by the Act of 1878 and the first holder was the Duke of Connaught. (The big pond on Chingford Plain, the largest expanse of water in the forest, is called Connaught Water.) Nor are you likely to see a verderer, although this is not impossible. There are four of these officers, who represent the forest parishes on the committee of the corporation which administers the forest. They are forest residents and so have a real stake in its proper maintenance. The practical work of keeping the forest in good heart is in the hands of a superintendent and his team of keepers and woodmen. It is these who patrol the rides, with a keen eye for overgrowing, vandalism and other natural and man-made hazards to the forest's health. It is through them that these acres, which absorb

Digswell Viaduct

The 'Greek' church at Ayot St Lawrence

Mackery End, Hertfordshire

probably more visitors than any comparable area in the country, remain fertile, beautiful and incredibly free of litter.

There will be visitors who have not the time, or the strength, or the inclination to get to know the forest at close range, but for whom a road itinerary will at least give some hint of the delights of this unique London playground. Coming in from the lower forest they will pass along the wide high street of Epping Town, now considerably developed and terribly busy with traffic, but still a place of real character. This is a new town, as English towns go. The old settlement was two or three miles away to the north-west at Epping Upland, where the parish church, mangled in a nineteenth-century restoration, still rears its brick tower above the rolling country. New Epping grew up with the coach and has some nice brick houses to show for it. There is not a great deal of timber despite the nearness of the forest, but some weatherboarding crops up on the edge of the built-up town. The most memorable thing in Epping belongs to a later age and is in a sense quite out of place in this setting. The new church of Epping Town is a spectacular exercise in neo-Gothic, largely from the inspiration of Bodley. Not one of his greatest works, certainly, but grand, consciously splendid and consistent. The tower dominates the street as it should and one readily forgets its incongruity in this Georgian scene.

South along the A11 there is a turning opposite the 'Bell' which may tempt you if the traffic is tiresome, and it will take you most pleasantly to Theydon Bois. However, if one can endure the exhaust fumes for a little longer, it will be worth while to persevere for another mile until, just before a turning goes off right, there is a chance to park and visit the second Iron Age camp of Epping Forest, Ambersbury Banks. This is close to the road and, before the leaves are out at least, the rampart can be seen from this range. The bank and ditch are much eroded, but enough remains to give some impression of an enclosure which must have been formidable when there was a twenty-foot slope from the floor of the ditch to the top of the bank. There are picturesque stories about Boadicea's involvement in this work. She may indeed have come this way in her retreat from London, but the camp was a century or two old in her day.

In another mile the road comes to the main crossing in the forest at Wake Arms. Here a turning should be taken sharp left towards Theydon Bois. (You will see the *bois* all the way, but the pronunciation has long been anglicized to Boys.) The road runs out of the forest in little more than a mile at Theydon Plain, but in this space you will see some fine timber, in autumn some dazzlingly beautiful tints, and catch a passing glimpse of the Green Ride which is one of the loveliest forest paths. Theydon Bois itself is commuter country with a station on the District Line, and it need not attract us now. Before the main village is reached there is a turning right which quickly leads to another going right to Debden Green. There is another patch of woodland by the way, but this is mainly interesting as showing how even near the railway a country lane can still persist, however precariously.

Debden Green is not very green nowadays while southwards to the Roding stretches a wide residential and industrial belt, some of it by no means uncomely. A turning right climbs up to a high point on the Wake Arms road above Loughton. A sharp turn right and another left provide an escape off the main road to Baldwins Hill with views especially to the west across the main body of the forest. Here we may regret the cessation of lopping because the trees have grown unrestrictedly and limit the prospect. Beyond this point the lane briefly becomes a suburban road and then joins the road from Loughton to the 'Robin Hood'. Turning right on this will bring us back into the forest quite quickly and up to the A11 again. On the right lies some of the best of the forest, its delights restricted to walkers and riders. This is the principal catchment area and many little streams join below Loughton Camp before ambling off to join the Roding.

At the 'Robin Hood' one ought to turn left and then second right after two unmemorable miles to visit the present headquarters of Epping Forest on Chingford Plain. Next to the Royal Forest Hotel, in bold black-and-white 'Tudor' from between the wars, and utterly eclipsed by it, stands Queen Elizabeth's Hunting Lodge. The great queen's name is so often quoted in vain that one accepts almost with reluctance that this is a *bona fide* Tudor building and that Her Majesty came here, not this time to sleep but to watch the hunt from the top of this admirable belvedere. The Lodge is very tall for its ground plan and is obviously entirely functional. It was built as a grandstand, and so the upper floors, now enclosed, stood open to give an uninterrupted view. It is a neat, practical and by no means unattractive building. It now houses a permanent exhibition of the history and natural history of the forest.

Having come quickly down the Ranger's Road we may now return at leisure, stopping to look at the big expanse of Connaught Water, which nowadays looks rather too much like an East London park lake to be entirely pleasing in this natural setting. If you are here early in the day or in winter it will recapture its past charms. Back on the A11 there is a fork left into Fairmead Lane which crosses the open green of Fairmead Bottom. When I first knew Epping here stood the battered tree called Fairmead Oak, which was probably the oldest in the forest and certainly the one about which clung most legends. It, too, had marked the start of the famous, or notorious, Epping Hunt out of which Tom Hood and others had much fun. It was an Easter meet, originally honoured by the Lord Mayor and other London dignitaries.

Later it became a more plebeian affair in which high spirits replaced ceremony, and the carted stag provided less in the way of sport than the fights among the huntsmen. It had died out before the passing of the Epping Forest Act. The Fairmead Oak lingered on for the best part of another century.

Beyond the Bottom trees crowd in again, and it is a shady wooded lane which comes up to High Beech Church, which seems to be in the heart and which now stands almost on the edge of the forest. It is a pretty enough piece of Gothic Revival, given a distinction which the architecture scarcely merits by the enchanting setting. A little farther on the trees cease and the land falls away in front of Dick Turpin's Cave— the Essex-born rogue lived near here—to give long views across the Lea valley ashimmer with reservoirs and cloudy with industrial towers and chimneys. The scene, purged of the grossness introduced by dozens of parked cars, is enshrined in *In Memoriam*, on which Tennyson was working when he stayed in a house just beyond the church.

The "single tower below the hill" of which he wrote is visible from this point, and it is for that ancient church that we shall now head, cutting across the front of the Kings Oak and across Rushy Plain. The lane, followed left at the fork, drops slowly and then more steeply through very fine woodland, and suddenly emerges into the green expanse of Honey Lane Plain. On this route this is the last of the forest, and it makes a fitting climax. At the foot of the hill there is an endearingly comical well-cover, gabled and thatched. At this junction we pick up a busy main road coming down from Wake Arms to Waltham.

When the generic term Forest of Essex first became limited to the south-western corner of the old Forest Law area, it became known as the Forest of Waltham, named after the most important township on its fringe.

Waltham—the homestead in the weald or forest—was a place of some importance from early times, standing as it did where a forest track came down to a crossing of the River Lea. In the reign of Canute the manor belonged to a warrior called Tovi—reputedly the king's standard bearer. Tovi also had an estate at Montacute in Somerset, and there a marvellous rood was dug up. Tovi had it loaded upon a cart and attempted to take it to the nearest great shrine at Glastonbury, but the oxen would not budge. After a number of fruitless attempts he thought of Waltham, and the team at once started pulling. This much has the doubtful authority of a chronicle of the twelfth century. What is certain is that a famous rood existed at Waltham, and the town acquired in consequence the title of Waltham Holy Cross. The church of Waltham came to Harold Godwinson in the reign of Edward the Confessor, and Harold, who had a manor nearby at Nazing, rebuilt the church and founded a college of canons to serve it. This building was dedicated, the King being present, in 1060. There is an appealing story, which deserves to be true, that Harold came here to pray before setting out on the forced march through the Weald to a wooded hill north of Hastings.

Legend and history are inextricably mingled in the story of the Conquest. It is reasonable to suppose that Harold wished to be buried at Waltham, and probable that William, his battle anger over, would not have denied this privilege to a brave enemy and a former companion. In Henry II's reign Harold's college was dissolved and replaced by an Augustinian priory, later an abbey. The church was enlarged and big conventual buildings added. The abbey was long in building and was not consecrated until 1242. It was a rich and influential abbey, and the abbot exercised important rights in the forest. It was still prosperous when Henry VIII's Commissioners came this way. After the Dissolution the nave was sold to the town for a parish church, the choir demolished by gunpowder—so destroying among many beautiful things the tomb of King Harold the founder.

Although it is only a pitiful fragment, Waltham Abbey is one of the most interesting and impressive churches in the Home Counties. The nave, very short in proportion to its height and to the grandeur of its conception, is majestic Norman work which reminds one of nothing so much as Durham Cathedral. The great drum pillars with their deep ornamental grooves are unforgettable. One would like to think of this part as Harold's work, and he could easily have called upon Norman craftsmen in 1060, but, unless all our ideas on the dating of Norman decorative masonry are wrong, it must be later, but not much after the Conquest—say the reign of Henry I. It is maddening to think what splendours were destroyed by Cromwell's gunpowder. Only a pretty south-eastern chapel survives from a later extension to the abbey. The central tower, included in the deal with the parish, soon fell down, its stability upset by the general destruction around, and a low, very white stone tower was added at the west end.

Many details—carving, fittings, glass and paintings—are worth study. I particularly like the modern statue of the founder, outside on the south-west corner, which was executed by Elizabeth Muntz. She is the sister of Hope Muntz, whose novel *The Golden Warrior* is incomparably the best of many fictional chronicles of the Conquest and whose portrait therein of Harold is here given three-dimensional form.

Although the destruction of the abbey buildings was unusually thorough, there is still a little to be seen: a vaulted passage and the fine double-arched gatehouse. In the water-meadows to the north, now disfigured by a ring road, is a fragment of a medieval bridge called, with no historical validity whatsoever, Harold's Bridge. The new road, however destructive of the rural surroundings which had survived so long the industrial growth of the Lea Valley, has at least taken traffic out of the old town, which, with its pretty houses and its busy market, has the quality which belongs to an ancient place which has carried its old traditions intact into the twentieth century. How sad that Henry VIII did not keep his original promise—when did he ever?—and make the abbey into the cathedral church of Essex. The town might have made almost as convincing a small city as Wells.

One of the memorable dates in the history of Waltham Holy Cross was 1290, when the funeral cortège of the great Queen Eleanor stopped here and the queen's body lay beneath the holy rood. As in other places King Edward had a memorial cross erected not outside the church but on the highway which was the main route of his melancholy journey. A mile and a half away, across the Lea into Hertfordshire, the Eleanor Cross survives in the modern township of Waltham Cross, its battered and much restored loveliness in strange contrast to the dreariness around.

Here at Waltham our forest journey seems at an end. One visit has so far been omitted, and this belongs so firmly to the story of the Forest of Essex that we ought to backtrack in order to conclude this chapter more fittingly. So back up the hill to Wake Arms—or more agreeably by way of Upshire and Copthall Green—to the main forest road, north towards Epping, then a turn right opposite the 'Bell' on Epping Common, and a twisting journey by byways through Colliers Hatch— where the charcoal burners operated—and Toot Hill to Greensted.

In 870 King Edmund of East Anglia fell in battle against the Danes. He was buried in London but in 1013 his body was translated to a new shrine in the minster of Bury St Edmunds. The procession went through the forest and stopped for a night near Ongar, and the royal saint lay in a wooden chapel deep in the forest. The chapel was not new then. It was probably similar to hundreds of other humble buildings in Saxon England, most of which were swept away to make room for the proud stone churches of the Norman conquerors. It may have been Greensted's remoteness, or the special sanctity acquired by association with St Edmund—who until the crusaders brought back St George from the Holy Land was the patron saint of England—which led to its preservation. At any rate, at Greensted, a parish without a village, is the unique phenomenon of a Saxon church of wood. A church of logs, in fact, oak trunks split down the middle and set with the rounded side outwards. Originally they were probably about ten foot high and laid straight into the ground. The base rotted and had to be cut away, so that they now sit upon a brick cill. A new chancel replaced the original one in early Tudor times, and the weatherboard tower is medieval.

The building has an obvious claim to attention for its immense antiquity and its unusual construction. What is less obvious is its emotional appeal. This is a church which breathes out the atmosphere of the remote past, and in that atmosphere the building, which is quaint rather than impressive, takes on a strange and deeply moving beauty.

13

Essex Brick

THE chalk which has been the common element in all these journeys forms a wide band across the top of Essex and then spreads northwards through the middle of East Anglia. The greater part of the county consists of tertiary beds overlaid by clay, sand and gravel which produce the great wheatlands of central Essex. A fertile and, for those attuned to its subtle qualities, a beautiful land, but not a land of building stone. Apart from flint in the chalk belt, there is indeed nothing except septaria, a curious material formed by chemical action in clay. This crops up in many ancient buildings mainly in the north-western part of the county, but it is neither versatile nor attractive. In the south ragstone was ferried across from Kent for the more important buildings. But mostly, and almost invariably in domestic building, wood was the rule. The forests promised an apparently inexhaustible supply, and traditional methods could produce houses inexpensively and quickly.

Yet the Essex clays and sands offered vast resources for the manufacture of the most versatile of all building materials. That they lay undisturbed for so many centuries is one of the mysteries of history, for brick is the oldest artificial building material in the world. Its use was a commonplace of biblical times, and in Essex, as in all other places where the Romans had been, there was abundant evidence of the effectiveness and the durability of the wide flat brick tiles which the

Roman builders favoured. These were regularly pillaged by medieval builders and re-used in such buildings as St Botolph's Priory in Colchester. No attempt however was made to revive the craft of brickmaking, although travellers must have seen the new brick churches which were rising in Europe.

There is, as we shall see, one freakishly early example of native English brickwork extant in Essex, but this was so isolated as to have only curiosity value. It was not until well into the fifteenth century, when brick was in use in many other parts of England, that the material became adopted in Essex. After that, however, Essex builders took the new medium to their hearts, and during the next three centuries it became the most characteristic element in Essex architecture. Even if the county cannot claim outright supremacy, it can offer as wide a range of styles and as rich a range of textures and colours as any.

A journey through the heart of this neglected and most attractive county will give an opportunity to see, often in most charming settings, all the stages in the history of brick-building, from its abortive beginnings late in the twelfth century, through the exuberance of the Tudors to the grave formality of the classical age, past the restrictions of the brick taxes and the shamefaced early nineteenth century, which gave brick a modest clothing of stucco, to the introduction of mechanized brick-making and the end of individuality. There may even be some examples of modern success in exploring the aesthetic possibilities of machine-made brick. As always I shall not scruple to depart from this general theme in order to visit some attractive scene, or to recapture a memory, which may be irrelevant to the quest of brick.

A good starting point is the county boundary at Dedham Bridge where the very best of Essex landscape meets the best of Suffolk in the heart of the country which made Constable a painter. Dedham, I must admit, is not my idea of an Essex town. It belongs in spirit to the opposite bank of the Stour, and so does the church which is a cousin of the great 'wool' churches of Stoke and Lavenham. Brick is here used, in conjunction with freestone and rubble, with great exuberance and freedom from inhibition. The general impression is one of lightness and whiteness, and the tall slim tower, of which Constable never showed any signs of tiring, sets the tone of the fine high street. Elsewhere the keynote is brick. Part of the charm of Dedham lies in its informality; houses big and small stand cheek by jowl in casual neighbourliness. Many of the most pleasing are quite unpretentious. By contrast, just opposite the church stands Shermans, which is a solid prosperous town house, stiff, conscientiously stylish, the homeliness of its gabled roof concealed behind a high parapet which displays a sundial. The brick is varied, window surrounds and pilasters in deep red in contrast with the lighter walls, and a splendid white doorcase strikes a classical note.

This northern sector of Essex, in which I must confess that I could wander contentedly for a couple of lifetimes, is profoundly unlike the popular concept of this county. It is, the trunk roads apart, easily the quietest part of the Home Counties. A great deal goes on. The farming is highly efficient and successful; the society of small town and village goes its busy way; yet the stresses which are so essential a feature of other places are here absent. One has the unfamiliar feeling that there is time to live. The landscape has that happy and characteristically English partnership of use and appearance. Many modestly prosperous landlords of the eighteenth century laid down the ground plan with their landscaped estates, each provided with good specimen timber and a little ornamental water, each provided with its well-proportioned, not too large brick hall. Most of these remain, and even when the parkland has shrunk under the demands of farming the pattern remains. Stately two-hundred-year-old oaks planted as elements in a landscape picture may rise above a field of barley, but they still make their contribution to a memorable scene. The lanes are as apparently lacking in motivation as any in England. They make their wayward course between villages, delighting in sharp bends and often turning right back upon themselves, not out of perversity but because they follow long-forgotten boundary lines or the paths of lost settlements.

The Constable country apart—and this is popularly taken to mean only Flatford and Dedham—this is not for the tourist. The few people who find this country keep the discovery to themselves. Indeed there is no great need for secrecy because the landscape is in a low key, and villages, houses and churches eschew both the dramatic and the picturesque. Nothing could be farther from the normal tourists' objective. This means that those who live here are not called upon to meet outside and alien demands. They live to themselves in a way which is rarely possible in this country, not for any selfish ends but because circumstances have placed them in communities which are largely blessed with immunity from interference. Coming to these parts only as a visitor I have always been met with great courtesy but I have never been left with the illusion that I, or any other stranger, really matters. This, which might distress some people, suits me very well and leaves me free to come and take delight in the countryside without obligation.

It is essentially by-road country. Necessity will take us occasionally to small towns like Kelvedon which straddle the old highways—and these are very fine—but they are not the true Essex. To find this we cross the main roads and lose ourselves in a tangle of lanes, bridle ways and streams—for this county which has no major river except the

Thames is a land of innumerable waterways, all of them adding individual and discreet touches to the scene.

So, although Colchester is not ten miles away and this is well up among the ten most interesting towns in the Home Counties, we will postpone a visit to a later occasion and take a perilous course westwards into the unknown. Constable's great tower is lost behind a low hill and the land drops gently towards the Stour. The first village in this direction is Langham. Village, did I say? Hardly that; just a trail of cottages beside a road junction with hall and church in the classic North Essex position away towards the river. The church has Constable associations; the hall has a fine park and gardens—sometimes open to the public—looking into Suffolk across the water-meadows.

The route continues to keep to the outside edge of the county with nothing on the right but farm tracks and the river. At one point it is possible to make a mistake and cross into Suffolk at Thorington, but a course through the scattered village of Boxted and a lane almost into Nayland will eventually lead, by anything but a direct way, to Little Horkesley. I like to come this way, partly for the quiet, partly because here is one of the most satisfying of all modern buildings in a rural setting. When the village church was destroyed in the war the response was unequivocal. There were two alternatives, one to write the whole thing off and send the half-dozen worshippers along the road to Great Horkesley, the other to be bold and contemporary and to put up a new building as a spiritual expression of the mid-twentieth century. Little Horkesley, to its eternal credit, did neither. The new parish church is new, certainly, but, taking full advantage of modern techniques and materials, it is unashamedly traditional. In its modest, unfussy English Gothic it is reminiscent of a good college chapel. Above all it shows the kind of clean efficient craftsmanship for which the county is distinguished. Very good wood and metal work, appropriate and quietly elegant fittings and furniture, every detail is in scale and is in the right mood. One realizes at once that here was no striving after a false archaism, but a building following styles which were native to the country and its craftsmen. It graces the quiet churchyard and has the hall as a good neighbour.

Not everything was lost in the destruction at Little Horkesley. Out of the ruins was salvaged one of the finest of the wooden monumental sculptures for which Essex is renowned. The lady and her two husbands, life-size, in thirteenth-century costume were unharmed. The figures are rendered with unusual realism and with great grandeur. Remounted on a brick plinth, they help to recreate the sense of continuity which every country church must possess.

After Little Horkesley all my inclinations are to go west and north into the country between Stour and Colne, the land of the Beauchamps,

the Hennys, the Maplesteads and the Hedinghams. This is country of
low hills and long views, good cornland, solid, dignified halls and fine
churches. There are far more spectacular areas of the Home Counties,
and many which in the general view are more beautiful. Nowhere
else is one aware of the irrelevance of London. Distance and poor
communications have kept this out of the commuter belt. Rural communications are focused not on distant cities but on little market
towns. For once the country is not an extension of suburbia but the
genuine thing.

For this very reason, I must exclude the area from my itinerary,
which is necessarily devoted to exploration of London's country. Until
some fool puts a motorway through the middle and opens it up to
'development', may it continue to enjoy its quiet, sane, useful isolation.

So, turning our backs on Eden, let us head southwards towards the
Colne, passing through only one village—Fordham—before reaching
the river at Ford Street. Due south is more interesting country, rather
too far off our route, including Marks Tey, long famous for traffic
jams and having, within sight of the main road but for most travellers
no more accessible than the moon, a charming little church with a
wooden font, which may seem odd but is surely most appropriate in
this forest country. Beyond the main road are other good things:
Copford with the best preserved Norman church in Essex, and then,
standing in isolation above the levels, the brick and terracotta fantasy
of Layer Marney Tower.

Leaving these attractions for another day, our journey goes by way
of Aldham across to the country of the Teys. Great Tey has grown a
little, not altogether attractively, but the village is still dominated, as
it has been these eight hundred years, by the huge central tower of the
church. (I call it central, because that is obviously its function, but
restorers early in the nineteenth century made nonsense of the design
by destroying the nave.) In its bulk, and in its free use of Roman brick,
it is rather like a rustic St Albans. The lane beyond Great Tey crosses the
watershed between Colne and Blackwater and descends to Coggershall.

This is one of the most satisfactory of small towns. The Roman road
to Colchester goes right through the heart of the town without
damaging its unity, and there is none of the straggle into the country
which disfigures most towns in the South. There are some good brick
houses, but Coggershall is essentially a black-and-white town. The
pervading forests were harvested profitably in the sixteenth century to
make the timber frames and the heavy roof beams of Paycockes and
the Woolpack and a dozen notable others. Paycockes, the house of a
prosperous merchant of Henry VII's reign, is one of the finest of the
National Trust's smaller properties. Corporate ownership has destroyed none of its intimacy, and a loving tenant keeps house and garden

in immaculate but homely order. The architectural unity of so much of Coggershall comes from the town's involvement in the cloth trade, which brought rapid prosperity and resulted in massive projects of building and rebuilding. The fine half-timbered inn near the church recalls the trade, and curly-horned rams form appropriate decorations on corbels of the church. This building was badly damaged in the war, and with rebuilding came much enrichment of the interior. There is some superb modern craft-work.

Any town is the richer for possession of a river, and the Blackwater, flowing discreetly behind the high street, makes an effective appearance at the town bridge. It then turns abruptly south and passes through the site of Coggershall Abbey.

The Cistercians, who occupied the site in 1147, always looked for lonely river-valleys in which to build their houses. They chose a position reasonably remote from whatever settlement then occupied a crossing of the Roman Stane Street, and town and abbey grew together. Here, as elsewhere, the Cistercians were defeated in their search for holy poverty by their own industry. They farmed efficiently and were caught up with the town in trading in wool. They managed to retain their isolation, however, and there is still a break between Coggershall, on the north bank of the Blackwater, and Little Coggershall on the south. The abbey lies down a narrow farm road opposite Grange Farm —the 'grange' was the abbey farm. The complex group of abbey buildings, church, cloisters, frater and the rest, have gone without trace, except from the air. There remains an attractive cluster of farm buildings built from materials of the abbey or adapted from its structure, all close to the mill-stream which flows parallel with the river. There is also, nearer to the road, a neat small church which was the chapel-at-the-gate of the abbey. (Cistercians, to preserve their traditional insulation from the world, habitually provided a chapel outside the walls of the abbey for the benefit of the laity and so were able to use their own church without interruption.)

The remarkable feature of both the chapel and the abbey buildings by the river is that they are built partly of brick. Although this is Roman-occupied territory, these are not Roman bricks re-used, but native-made brick from about the year 1200 and the earliest known in this country. Were Essex builders of King John's reign encouraged by the sight of Roman bricks lying about to try their hand at making them? If so, they did not attempt a direct copy. The Coggershall bricks are much thicker, crude and irregular, and a particularly deep red. The revival of brick-making, which was in time to transform the appearance of the whole country, began here and here abruptly died. No more bricks were fired for more than a century.

The road from Coggershall keeps pace with the winding Blackwater all the way to Kelvedon, where the great central artery of Essex—the A12—now happily bypasses the old coaching town. As usual with such places—the same phenomenon can be seen down the road at Witham—the original settlement lies north of the road, and the town grew with the development of road travel in the seventeenth and eighteenth centuries. This produced some fine town houses in brick as well as coaching inns which line the main street most impressively.

Kelvedon almost merges with Feering to the west, but again the old village stands off to the north. This is a place which I like to visit for the sake of its church, as well as for some very charming old cottages. The church, tenderly cared for, is of many periods, styles and materials. The building was extended early in the Tudor period by the addition of a splendid south aisle in brick, entered by a brick porch which shows how exuberantly these pioneer craftsmen handled an apparently intractable material. They seemed determined to prove that whatever a mason might do in freestone they could do in brick, tracery, pinnacles, vaulting.

While we are here we should see the Constable altar-piece—an uncharacteristic rarity—and also a movingly beautiful relic of monastic Essex. When Henry VIII's Commissioners moved upon Earls Colne Priory, one of the brethren took the precaution of hiding a statue of the Virgin and Child, and there it lay for four hundred years. Then it was discovered, broken and headless, and brought to Feering. Here, with newly carved heads for both figures, it stands in the angle of the Lady Chapel, as lovely a piece as even this rich country can show.

South of Feering the Maldon road, on its way to the newly developing industrial area of Tiptree, passes an inconsiderable village at Inworth. Here one may observe almost the end of the long story of Essex brick. In the late 1850s, when the abolition of the brick tax had given a boost to building, the additional demand was met by the supply of machine-made bricks. The price fell sharply, and so inevitably did the quality. Until then brick-making had been essentially a local industry. In Essex, where there was an abundance of clay and gravel, materials nearly always came from close to hand. The bricks varied greatly, not in size—for a uniform standard based on what would fit snugly into the bricklayer's hand had been established long ago—but in colour and texture. Freakish variations in the chemical constituents of the clay might produce unexpected blues and yellows; so might the fuel used in firing or the duration of the firing process. Sometimes these variations were designed; more often than not they were accidental. They ensured that each locality, and almost every building, had a marked individuality. The great brick factories of the East Midlands, on the other hand, turned out millions of bricks almost completely uniform and utterly lacking in individual quality. Thereafter every newly developed town or housing estate would look just like every other, regardless of geology or topography.

How quickly this revolution reached remote parts of the country is in doubt. Inworth church was restored and extended in 1873 and a new tower and porch were provided in red brick. The workmanship is good, the colour not unworthy of its setting. Was it the last flourish of local craftsmen in face of the coming revolution, or did the builders get delivery of a supply from the factory which by chance matched the old Essex style? Whatever the answer, here at Inworth is almost the last of the traditional Essex towers, and very well it looks. It is contrasted in the fabric with Roman brick salvaged just after—or possibly just before—the Norman Conquest from one of the numerous Roman ruins which lay around the legionary *colonia* of Colchester.

Just beyond the church a lane goes south through quiet country to Great Braxted. Here is one of the finest parks in central Essex, designed as the setting for a large brick mansion. The parish church, with much Roman brick, is in a corner of the park and the churchyard affords delightful glimpses of the wooded estate with a great ornamental water in the foreground. From here another lane, even narrower and more winding, leads to Little Braxted, a tiny village in a setting of almost excessive picturesqueness at a crossing of the Blackwater. Here is the hall, the church, the mill, a cottage or two and very little else— the elements of a medieval community. A Victorian rector of Little Braxted was deeply involved in the church-restoration business, and here he really let himself go. He took the little Norman building and accentuated its gloom by a scheme of sombre decoration which is really rather good in itself but not in scale with so humble a building. The hall and the mill are less ambitious and look much better in their quiet country surroundings.

Witham, a mile away on the A12, is, like Kelvedon, a town which grew under the stimulus of the coaching trade. There is plenty of good brick in the long high street setting off neat and elegant doorcases. Witham, which was made by traffic in the eighteenth century, was in danger of destruction from the same cause in the twentieth, but a by-pass has rescued and restored its soul. Industry has come to its economic aid without spoiling the civilized small-town atmosphere.

As at Kelvedon the older settlement is not here but away on higher ground to the north. Here the Georgian Age gives way to the Middle Ages, where pretty black-and-white cottages frame the old, and very interesting, church. This was largely rebuilt in the fourteenth century when the Roman brick used in the old structure was salvaged for re-use with flint—a curious mixture but not unattractive.

The road past old Witham rises gently above the valley of the little River Brain and on the right, well seen from the road, is the tall battlemented tower of Faulkbourne Hall. Here building in brick, which had enjoyed a brief and abortive revival at Coggershall Abbey, began again in the reign of Henry VI, when the owner of an earlier house was given licence to fortify it and carried out the work in deep-red brick. At Faulkbourne therefore begins the consecutive story of Essex brick, and several chapters of the story are told in this single building, which was extended over the next century and greatly remodelled and altered in the nineteenth century. The work, as may be seen even at this range, is remarkably ornate, the tapering pinnacles competing with the characteristically elongated Tudor chimneys. It is ironical that this house, set in so sophisticated and civilized a manner in its park, should have had a defensive origin.

Northwards the road passes through the Notleys, two agreeable villages separated by the great bulk of the hospital. There have been few human associations so far on this journey, so one might pick up briefly at Black Notley a memory of John Ray. Essex is a county of scientists, and in this little village lies one of the greatest, the first English field naturalist, a man of enormous physical energy and close observation. He shared the spirit of enquiry which characterized England after the Restoration. He was a prodigious walker; the record of his journeys in search of wild flowers, in a country lacking tolerable roads or conveyances, is enough to humble the toughest of Pennine Way enthusiasts. From these travels he returned to his native village, not surprisingly in ill health, to write the conclusions of his research and eventually to be buried in the churchyard.

The southward creep of Braintree has almost reached Notley. The town occupies a neck of high ground between the Blackwater and the Brain—here renamed the Pod. Braintree is a comparative newcomer, grown in the Middle Ages from an original settlement to the north at Bocking. It flourished in the cloth boom of the seventeenth century and again in the coaching age, but recent developments have taken away much of its individual quality. Travellers may avoid the town by a slightly tortuous route west out of Black Notley and then by way of the A131 and a byroad across to Rayne, a village on Stane Street. Here there is a fine brick group just set back from the main road. Church and hall stand in classic relationship behind a pretty green. The hall is largely timber and half concealed behind a fine but crumbling brick wall. In front is the church, rebuilt except for a fantastic brick tower. Here is remarkable Tudor work of about 1510, demonstrating the adventurous spirit of these early craftsmen who played with patterns of blue and red, with textures and improbable elevations. The effect is strangely alien. Did the Fleming weavers who emigrated to the valley of the Pant see in it a symbol of their lost homeland?

At Rayne we are again under the strongest temptation to turn off our proper route and go north into the country of the Salings, where there is an abundance of old green roads and the latest and the most enigmatic of the Essex round-towered churches; and to Stebbing where there is a stone screen which blends, in typical medieval fashion, lyricism and earthy vulgarity. However, these are attractions which must be resisted, for the way lies south and for the moment west through country in which for once the hamlets tend to straggle and trail between one 'green' and the next. The largest of these is Bannister Green and then comes Felsted, village by size but town in character and a place of outstanding charm and personality.

The general impression here is of timber and plaster, not brick. Apart from a big mill too far removed to affect the town scene, the most notable brick is to be found in the charming Victorian almshouses, the most conspicuous the buildings of the public school in which charm plays no part at all.

The hero of Felsted is most people's idea of a villain, the astonishing Richard Rich, who in the heyday of opportunism around the Reformation was conspicuous for ruthless pursuit of ambition and scrupulous avoidance of commitment. One by one the heads of the wise, the statesmanlike and the self-seekers fell, and over their corpses Rich clambered stage by stage to the Chancellorship. He trimmed his sails brilliantly to the changing winds of Edward and Mary and found haven among the tempests of the early Elizabeth. Rich assisted at the Dissolution and made his home—which we shall pass shortly—in the ruins of the Augustinian Priory at Little Leighs. From this vantage point he dominated local politics for many years. He was on the whole a benevolent tyrant in Felsted, where he endowed a grammar school and almshouses. The school flourished and gained—and retains—a national reputation. The almshouses survived and were rebuilt in 1878. The old school house, which has all the visual attractions which the later buildings so conspicuously lack, forms the centrepiece of the town. It overhangs the main street, lying across the line of the church and having the church tower rising, apparently, from its roof. The church, large, of varied styles and periods, and with an elegant porch in Tudor brick, is dominated, in death as in life, by Rich himself. He was buried here in 1568, but his son restrained his filial piety and omitted to build him a monument. It was not until James I's reign that the third Lord Rich provided his father and grandfather with—in words quoted in Katharine Esdaile's masterly book—"a comlye and decente tombe". This appears to be the work of the Jacobean master Epiphanius Evesham—which suggests that it is a good idea to wait for one's monument until a worthy sculptor comes along—and is one of the major works of its kind. The complex design is dominated by the reclining figure of Rich, in robes as Lord Chancellor, on one elbow and

Abbey gatehouse, St Albans

Central tower, St Albans

Priory church, Hatfield Broad Oak

gazing with disconcerting intensity straight at the observer. The sculptor could never have seen his subject in the flesh; by what insight therefore did he capture the haunted eyes, reviewing a life of betrayals and false testimonies, of blocks and stakes? It is a disturbing work.

Rich's house, Leez Priory, lies south-east. The canons established their house in a typical setting beside a little stream—the Ter, a minor tribuary of the Blackwater—which provided them with water and drainage. The foundation enjoyed a modest prosperity and was still in fair order when it was dissolved in 1536. Rich acquired the site and buildings and built himself a new house, using the spoil from the church and the conventual buildings for some of his materials. This house has largely disappeared, but what remains are two gatehouses in the grand Tudor manner, less extravagant than Layer Marney but in the same mood. The buildings are privately owned but may be reasonably well seen from the road.

Just beyond the priory the land rises to a low watershed and then descends, at Howe Street, to the Chelmer Valley. Hereabouts are some very attractive houses in timber-frame—a notable one at Hillhouse Farm on our route—and in plaster with examples of the characteristic and still current Essex craft of pargetting, in which the smooth plaster is ornamented with incised or relief designs. The engraved decorations are usually geometrical, made by combing; the reliefs may be formal ornaments, swags, cornucopias and the like, or human and animal forms. When well done—and the most pleasing examples may well have been executed during the last decade or two—the effect can be enchanting, especially when it is done on quite a small scale and selectively.

The parks which were a feature of the early stages of this journey disappeared many miles back and the country has been mostly pasture, arable and orchard. At Howe Street the scene changes to the unmistakable informal patterns of the landscaped park, in which stands a great brick mansion. Langleys—which may be seen at close range on the rare occasions when the gardens are shown—is a singularly rich house originating in the last days of Elizabeth's reign and later encased and enlarged early in the eighteenth century so that its general appearance is that of the golden age of English domestic. It combines great dignity with a warm homeliness, both qualities accentuated by the very delightful gardens. Where the main drive begins just beyond the village centre there is an exceptionally stylish lodge-house in brick with just the same elegance and restrained good taste as the mansion.

There is also good brick to be seen in Great Waltham village, including Roman brick in the fabric of the predominantly Norman church. Quite the most delightful thing in the village, however, is the so-called guildhall which stands with its back to the churchyard. This is a compact Tudor box in timber built around a brick chimney stack which rises exuberantly high—a heart-lifting sight.

Whilst in this attractive and remarkably peaceful country it would be reasonable, if not strictly relevant to our theme, to visit the celebrated village of Pleshey which lies off to the west. This, it should be stated, is a place which reserves itself for the antiquarian, or at least for those whose sense of history is sensitively developed, for there is comparatively little to see on the ground. Of the great Norman castle literally no masonry survives; the only structure is a brick bridge spanning the moat, and this dates from the last stage of the castle's history. What does remain, and this gives the village its distinction, is the ground plan of a major castle. The huge motte lies just off the village street. Around it is flung not only the conventional bailey but also a great earth rampart in which literally the whole village is embraced. Only the church, a sad and largely rebuilt remnant of a great collegiate foundation, stands outside the embankment.

The whole complex may well antedate the Norman castle by several centuries. The castle itself belonged to the sinister genius of Essex, Geoffrey de Mandeville, who played a dangerous power game during the reign of Stephen, changing his allegiance whenever self-interest required it. He set a standard of treachery which was maintained and extended later by Richard II, who at Pleshey played out the penultimate act of the tragedy which culminated in the murder of his uncle Thomas, Duke of Gloucester. With the destruction of the Duke Pleshey's history came to an end, and the castle, deserted, gradually crumbled. Its masonry was robbed for building in the area until nothing remained but the bare earthworks. There ought to be ghosts here, if anywhere, but the mounds and banks seem obstinately untenanted.

Around Pleshey, as in the Saling area, there are many green roads. Travellers bound to the metalled road have a long round before they reach the Chignalls, a route enlivened by the sight of several characteristic Essex farmsteads. Most of the houses are of timber and plaster and nearly all stand within the moats which are recurrent symbols of this country. Eventually the way turns north with the red tower of Chignall Smealy Church in sight. Here surely is the very last word in brick, for the whole building is of bright early Tudor brick, including the piers of the nave arcade and even the font. It is good work, too, less ornate than some Tudor brick but used resourcefully and with plenty of variety, both in colour and in treatment of detail. A most appealing building and beautifully situated in the neat small village.

To the south lies the spreading mass of the county town. There are good things in Chelmsford, including Georgian brick in the heart of the town around the cathedral and in the cathedral itself, which is the old parish church made large, interestingly but not always harmoni-

ously, by the additions necessary to the administration of a large diocese. It is sad that Essex did not rate a see earlier in its history, or that
there was no existing great building, as for example at St Albans or
Bury St Edmunds, awaiting elevation to cathedral status. Chelmsford
has sufficient admirers to be in no need of my advocacy. I find the
town too big, too congested, lacking in that indefinable but unmistakable atmosphere which identifies the county town. Lewes has it, and
Hertford, but not Maidstone or Chelmsford. I must emphasize here
my personal limitation and acknowledge that in not relishing the
quality of Chelmsford I am undoubtedly the loser. That sensitive and
shrewd observer, Mr Lynton Lamb, has celebrated his adopted home
in word, in line, in an enchanting book *County Town*.* I deeply regret
my inability to share his vision. I must therefore take the bypass and
head briefly in the wrong direction northwards along the A12 to gain
a glimpse of another brick house and this perhaps the most splendid of
them all. New Hall stands well off the road to the north, along a road
which goes only little beyond it. The house has been a convent for
nearly two centuries. It is only a fragment of the original, but enough
remains as witness to splendours lost.

New Hall was built originally for the Earl of Ormonde, and came,
as attractive houses had a way of doing, to Henry VIII, who extended
and enriched it. He renamed the house Beaulieu, but the name barely
survived him. It remained a royal palace and was a principal residence
of the Princess Mary in her unhappy days—but when was she ever
happy? Elizabeth granted it to Thomas Radcliffe, Earl of Sussex, who
carried out further changes. It did not long remain the seat of the Earls
of Sussex but passed to George Villiers, Duke of Buckingham, in the
next reign. It returned to the Buckinghams after the Restoration and
was much altered and reduced a century later. Despite all these vicissitudes the remaining building is a noble fragment. The basic brickwork
is much disguised with stone, and the general impression is one of remarkable restraint with little of the usual flamboyance of the Tudor
builders.

The Earl of Sussex is buried in the parish church at Boreham, a little
farther along the main road, and so are his father and grandfather, who
were originally buried in London. They have handsome memorials all
erected at the same time in the bold monumental style of the Elizabethan period.

After Boreham the land to the south drops to the Chelmer—here
the Chelmer and Blackwater Navigation, a place of fishermen, birds
and wild flowers—and then follows the Essex highlands, rising dizzily
to beyond 350 feet. The tangle of commons and woods, variously
named, are usually referred to as Danbury Common after the village

* Eyre & Spottiswoode, 1950.

which occupies the central and nearly the highest position. Much of the land is National Trust, and here for the first time since Dedham we encounter genuine wastes, a rare sight indeed in this intensively cultivated country. Here too for the first time, except for Chelmsford, we find *urbs in rure*; a sinister trickle of houses and bungalows percolates the green places as evidence that here the commuter has come to rest. There are good things as compensation: Little Baddow, where the emphasis is on wood, with a fine timber-framed hall opposite the church, and inside the latter two wooden effigies even better than those at Little Horkesley; Woodham Walter, where there is a church all in brick, with stepped gables, and also an exceedingly picturesque inn; Danbury, a little bare and exposed but with some handsome brick mansions grouped around the common.

Much the best brick in these parts is at Sandon, below the hill to the west, where there is a most pleasing tower. In Kent, where the design would seem quite at home, it would be built of ragstone. Here it is in patterned brick, in which battlements and corner turret are rendered with splendid virtuosity; but it is no showpiece, just a good, sound and workmanlike job. Very satisfactory too. At Great Baddow, nearby, the brick is much more showy. Little pinnacles rise somewhat frivolously above the nave clerestory as if they were making mock of the very tall spire. There are notable brick houses all around, making the most of what remains of the village atmosphere before Chelmsford once more closes in.

There is however an escape route for us immediately opposite the church. This goes through suburban country to Galleywood and then, shrugging off the town very successfully, descends to the valley of the little River Wid. All the streams in this county are so small, until they become great tidal estuaries, that bridges are crossed in a flash. It is always worth stopping to look underneath; as often as not in the byways the bridge will be neatly arched in brick and will be well into its second century. Over one such our road rises to meet the trunk road at Margaretting Street.

Traffic has knocked most of the charm out of main-road Margaretting. Just south of the road, however, beyond the railway there is a miniature haven where the church stands away among orchards. This building has one of the most complex of the Essex timber-framed towers, although in this setting the effect is more endearing than impressive. It was presumably a tower-nave and a very big one too, exceeding the width of the later stone nave. The building is well kept with some very good modern craftsmanship to match the old. Charming as the church is, it gains additional appeal from its position. It stands so solidly for durability and goodness against the rush of Progress just up the lane. Those who love this spot—and for some it may repre-

sent one characteristic and highly valued aspect of the Essex scene—
may feel inclined to hug themselves in a glow of melancholy satisfaction that it endures when so much decays.

There are few enough sensations of this kind all the way along the
A12, which can scarcely be anyone's favourite trunk road. The road
improves steadily, which means that year by year more of the towns
and villages are bypassed, too late to save them from the destruction
or ruin of much of their charm. As always it is the villages just off the
old road which fare best. Fryerning, for example, has grown but not
with the feverish haste of the main-road villages. On a high point
stands the church, revealing Roman bricks re-used by the Norman
builders and having a really splendid tower of early Tudor brick. This
shows what can be done in the medium, not by pushing it beyond its
natural limits but by pressing it into the service of good proportions
and good taste. The only exotic note—and this much restrained—is
struck by the patterning in blue brick.

I am disposed to prefer Fryerning's tower to the more celebrated one
at Ingatestone. In this I may well be influenced by the surroundings,
for Fryerning, although commuterized, is still a village at heart while
Ingatestone has abandoned its village character without gaining the
essential qualities of a town. The great tower, as fine in its way as the
famous stone towers of the West Country, is hemmed in somewhat
and cannot be as well seen as one would wish. This being said, let us
admit that here is one of the wonders of Essex. The contrasting brick
here is in black, not blue, a distinctive note and an effective one. As
at Fryerning, the tower impresses not by extravagance of ornament
but by fine proportions, although here the composition is a trifle
elongated.

Ingatestone and its church are dominated by the memory of the
Petre family who have been here since the reign of Henry VIII. The
manor was a grange of Barking Abbey, which was one of the largest
and wealthiest nunneries in England and much the most important
religious house in Essex. One of the King's servants in the Dissolution
was a William Petre and he received as his reward the manor of Ingatestone. From the researches of the former county archivist of Essex,
Mr F. G. Emmison, we know as much about Petre as about any of his
more celebrated contemporaries. He had in abundance one of the most
valuable qualities of his age, the ability to survive. He grew up in pre-
Reformation England, took part in the Dissolution of the Monasteries,
played an important part in the politics of Edward VI's reign, survived
Mary, and died peacefully and with honour under Elizabeth. He was
roughly contemporary with Richard Rich of Felsted and his political
career was not dissimilar—although he never aspired to the highest
office. No two men could be less alike. In public as in private Sir

William Petre walked modestly, worked hard and precisely and avoided calumny. He was indeed not in the strict sense a politician at all but a civil servant, one who eased the transitions of those tormented decades by his quiet, unobtrusively efficient management of affairs. He made his principal home at Ingatestone, a rural retreat but one well placed for quick access to Whitehall or Greenwich, and here in due time he lay under a handsome but characteristically unextravagant monument. Here again there is a strong contrast with Rich at Felsted. Sir William, his work done and put aside in order, lies beside his wife, relaxed and with just the hint of a smile at the corners of his mouth. The alabaster sculpture seems certainly to have been a close likeness.

Sir William lies beside the altar. The Petre chapel was built in brick on the north side, and here lie others of the family, including Sir William's son John, the first Lord Petre, represented by the more extravagant fashion of James I's reign. The family seat was at Ingatestone Hall, which stands over towards the river in very attractive country. Sir William built in style, providing himself with a large brick mansion on the open courtyard principle with which he was familiar at Hampton Court and elsewhere. When the house lost favour with his descendants in the eighteenth century much of this was pulled down, and what remains, still the residence of the Lord Petre, is only a handsome fragment, its scale understated and its splendour deliberately diminished by such homely touches as the picturesque stepped gables.

Even in its truncated state Ingatestone Hall is still a large house, bigger than most owners need or want in the twentieth century. Such a situation may breed difficulties; there must always be the temptation to demolish or abandon. A most happy solution has been found at Ingatestone. Essex was one of the first counties to set up a county record office run on modern archive principles and it still has one of the best. The county is custodian of a great wealth of historic documents, many of them absorbingly interesting and beautiful. It is usually the fate of such archives to lie in store, awaiting the call of an occasional researcher. The Essex Record Office have collaborated with Lord Petre in setting up in a wing of Ingatestone Hall a permanent showroom in which documents are displayed in a setting which would hardly—bearing in mind the profession of the founder of the Petre fortunes—be more fitting. It is indeed especially good to see this lovely and friendly house so suitably set to work.

At this point it is necessary to think what to do about Brentwood, which fills the map to the south. There are far worse towns than this. On the other hand it has no special attraction to offer, either of irresistible general interest or in our quest of Essex brick, and it may therefore seem best to work out how to avoid the urban barrier. This will have the advantage of postponing for a few miles the inevitable clash with the urban mass of Thameside.

We therefore refrain from a return to the A12 and instead continue along the lane from Ingatestone. This continues with scarcely a hint of the commuter's presence until it comes up to Mountnessing Church, which stands, not as it might in more conventional counties in the middle of Mountnessing, but all on its own except for the sober eighteenth-century brick hall beside a roadside pond. There are prettier scenes in Essex but not many. Mountnessing itself lies off along the trunk road with nothing memorable about it except the fine post mill. Church End might be in another world. Here is another of the famous Essex timber towers, supported by a complicated structure which stands open within the building, not, as at Margaretting and other places, enclosed as a separate tower or tower-nave. There is plenty of brick in the fabric too, from some fragments of Roman brick in the medieval core to the Victorian aisle. The chancel, of Georgian brick, is sober and unenterprising; the west front is much more distinguished and is dated 1653, a surprising time to find an addition to so remote a building. The whole church makes an agreeable hotchpotch, set off by fine trees.

By following the lane past the church and continuing to the outskirts of Billericay, it is possible to avoid the town centre—but it is really quite attractive with elegant frontages in brick and timber to offset the inevitable supermarkets—by a sharp southward turn through the urban fringe and then through open country almost to the centre of Little Burstead. This is New Town territory but still remarkably rural with fine open views across to the factories of Basildon. To avoid these, there is a lane westwards which emerges on the Tilbury–Brentwood road at Herongate. Here a tiny village green lies incongruously beside the busy road, and beyond this a very curious brick structure takes the eye. The first guess is that this is one of those water towers which our Victorian ancestors loved to disguise as castles. A closer look dissolves the illusion. Ingrave Church is that rarity, a genuine piece of English baroque, such as might have arisen without comment in post-Wren London but which looks at once impressive and odd here. This is a style which does not easily acclimatize, and Ingrave Church has never quite settled down in this semi-rural setting. Although undeniably distinguished it is not quite right. The church replaced a medieval building in 1735 and it was built under the patronage of Lord Petre, whose seat, replacing Ingatestone Hall as the favourite family home, was just opposite. Thorndon Hall was one of the very biggest Georgian mansions of Essex, a place of great dignity but, in its rather grim white brick, not much charm. This element was supplied by the setting which was a successful essay in landscape naturalism. Much of the park remains, fairly successfully adapted to the needs of a golf club. The house, however, was ruined by fire in Victorian days and never fully restored. Its façade, even more gaunt now, shows up well from the road, and helps to make architectural sense of a scene which is confused by the intrusion of much modern housing.

The timely fire at Thorndon sent the Petres back to Ingatestone and so ensured the survival of the older and—to modern tastes—more pleasing seat.

Ingrave has another claim to a place in history. It was here, in 1903, that young Vaughan Williams heard Charles Pottipher sing "Bushes and Briars", and as a result of the experience dedicated himself to the pursuit and the transformation of English folk songs.

There are attractions around Ingrave. The country beyond Thorndon Park, accessible by footpath from Herongate and by byroad from the outskirts of Brentwood, is agreeably wooded and astonishingly remote —considering that Greater London is now very near indeed. To the south the Southend Road makes a barrier which at times seems utterly impenetrable, and just beyond the road Little Warley Hall and church have been divorced from their community by the tarmac boundary. They make a charming group. The church has Tudor brick in the choir, Georgian in the neat little tower. The hall is almost unadulterated Tudor, brick at its reddest and warmest and altogether delightful.

Just along the Southend Road, or reached direct from Ingrave, is East Horndon, whose church stands all alone on a little rise just above the traffic. The surroundings have become a small country park in the care of the local authority, one of those modest enterprises, so unimportant and relatively inexpensive and so immensely welcome, in which this county excels. Here is one of the most complete of all brick churches and one of the prettiest. It is mostly of quite early date for brick, and the enterprising design is doubtless due to the patronage of the famous Tyrell family who lived at Herongate—but their house has vanished all but the moat. The church included a Tyrell chapel which housed monuments salvaged from an earlier building. I wish one could believe the romantic legend that Anne Boleyn's head was buried here, having been rescued from the Tower by a Lady Tyrell. Altogether this is a church of character. One wonders how long it can survive in a harsh society which lacks a sense of history; there is no parish to speak of.

To the south lies the unaccountable district of Thurrock, which includes Thameside industry, the docks of Tilbury, solidly-packed housing estates, little compact villages, and wide-ranging fields. Thurrock has everything, except unity. It is all very puzzling. However, in order to complete this journey, we must continue to traverse Thurrock. At first there is no alternative to the Tilbury road, which indeed here offers pleasant enough prospects on either side; but after about three miles there is a more interesting option on the right to the village of Bulphan. Not that there is much to see here apart from a church with a good timber bell-tower, but I find these small communities which resist the urban threat to their individuality most appealing. Beside the church a lane goes south through the village and quickly finds open country again. This goes through some contortions before straightening out to make for Orsett village.

In a way Orsett is a more remarkable survival than Bulphan. The town crowds up close here, and there is a big and aggressive hospital with large associated buildings. Still Orsett remains a real village, tightly knit and self-sufficient. One might not give it more than a couple of glances in the Stour or Colne valleys, but here almost within sight of the towers of Thameside it is phenomenal, an occasion for rejoicing.

Orsett was a manor of the Bishop of London, which may account for the big and elaborate church and certainly accounts for the earthworks just to the north which are the foundations of Bishop Bonner's palace. Orsett Hall, the principal house, stands apart in a large and finely wooded park and forms no part of the village scene. The central domestic feature of the village is Orsett House, whose grave, almost severe Georgian brick frontage looks to the road. Here the Augustan Age presents its most sincere, least fussy face. There are no tricks, only restrained good taste and a delicate feeling for proportion. I like it greatly. It is the only notable brick building in sight, for the church is of flint and much of the old village is homely in its traditional timber-framing. There is a little green complete with lock-up and pound.

If one closes one's eyes to what is happening around, Orsett can still be seen as a genuine Essex village, untouched by London. It is the last of its kind. For the rest of the journey, even if by careful navigation one avoids the densest traffic and the most dreary of housing estates, the end cannot be in doubt.

The way lies just to the north of the main road, through Stifford, which must once have been a village of the Orsett kind but which has lost its battle. Beyond, where a road turns north through the Ockendons, there is a very handsome house, rather earlier than those we have seen recently. Ford Place belongs to the Restoration and wears its symmetry with an engaging air of unfamiliarity. It stands in a miniature park on the banks of the Mar Dyke. Make the most of its charms, for the next mile or two are rather grim. The new houses of Aveley are not lovely. Just to the north there is a green haven where a fragment of the great park of Belhus survives precariously among the estates and the new roads. Most of the big house has gone. Aveley itself shows how doggedly village tradition persists under the enormous pressures of the town. The church is a beauty.

Even this is not the end. Just beyond the old Southend road, with traffic building up towards the Thames Tunnel, there is the ghost of another village at Wennington. From a distance, where the church tower dominates all, it looks a village unscathed. At close range the illusion is shattered—it is still possible to see in imagination the wide flats of the Thames marshes through whose creeks Kentish rag was ferried for the plain sturdy tower, but present-day realities are assertive. The road past the Norman church and the drab mid-twentieth-century houses has one more brief illusion of countryside and then settles for the urban gloom of Rainham.

Rainham, which has the undeniable atmosphere of a town, is still a town apart and not just a semi-detached bit of London. It turns in upon its centre where the church stands beside a road junction. Essex has reserved its last two surprises for us here. First there is the church, which is all of one piece from the reign of Henry II. It must have been finished just about the time when the quarrel between King and Archbishop moved to its climax. Very dark, heavy and severe, the building offers no hint, except possibly in the enriched priest's door, that architecture was about to take one of its decisive steps forward. This rich, sombre and impressive work is hemmed in on two sides by grim buildings. On the third side is our second surprise, Rainham Hall. In this grubby setting stands the last of the brick halls of Essex and one of the best. It is a town house rather than a hall in the true Essex sense, quite modest in size and exceptionally harmonious in proportions. The red brick is enlivened with stone, especially in the noble central doorway protected by a most elaborate and yet restrained porch. In typical town-house style this building stands back from the road behind railings with elegant wrought-iron gates. This most admirable house, which we have not seen bettered on this long journey, belongs to the early Georgian Age. It came to the National Trust in 1949, having been acquired by the Treasury in lieu of death duties. A house on this scale, however, is essentially a home and not a showplace. While it can be seen by appointment it is not opened regularly to the public, and so it is able to preserve intact its intimate quality.

Beyond stretch the square miles of Dagenham, Barking and the Hams—not to be despised, for there too are surprises and unsuspected charms, but these are altogether overwhelmed and swallowed up in the brick and concrete jungle of Greater London. We will venture no farther, but rest content with Rainham Hall as the fitting crown of this quest of Essex brick.

14

Viking Coast

THE profile of Essex, more almost than that of any other English coast, seems designed by nature for the invader. The deeply indented coastline, the low shore which at no point offers even the pretence of a cliff, the wide deep-water estuaries, all invite penetration.

Yet Essex does not seem to have had more than its due share of attention from the Northmen. In all the long years of the Danish wars only two major battles are on record in this county, and of these one alone was of decisive importance; the other is remembered because by chance a poet of genius was on hand to record the events in unforgettable verse. These however were wars of movement, not of set pieces. The Northmen preferred the swift raid and the quick withdrawal to the formality of battle, although when pressed they fought with ferocity and surprising discipline. Through all the centuries of terror from the North the Saxon villagers of Essex were familiar with the bellow of the war horn and the flame in the thatch.

It was a war between cousins—but softened by no family feelings. The Saxons had themselves sailed up these estuaries and creeks, burning the villas of Romanized Britons and winning for themselves a patch of land and a well. Then they had settled down, becoming efficient farmers and evolving a society based on the community of the village and the rule of law. In time they abandoned their grim, humorous and human northern gods in favour of Christ—and, although the change was delayed by almost a century in Essex, it was inevitable. Thor and Wodin and the promise of Valhalla are relevant to a race dedicated to warfare; when the warrior becomes a farmer he needs a different kind of heaven as well as earth. So the ruthless, brutal East Saxons became industrious rural citizens, their natural melancholy fed with a philosophy dominated by the acceptance of fate.

They were no immediate match for their volatile cousins from Denmark and Norway. The sea robbers who came storming up the Blackwater were not, as the Saxons had been, moved by the land hunger and the westward racial urges which had motivated Celts and beaker folk and all the previous waves of invaders. They sought an outlet for energy as much as loot. The same lust for adventure which drove them to Essex sent them south to the Mediterranean, east to Russia and south-east to Byzantium. They fought for the sheer joy of battle, and for plunder, on their own account or as mercenaries—but always preserving their individual freedom. Race meant nothing to them. They would fight their neighbour as readily as the Saxon or the Frank, and they gave loyalty only to the head of their clan, and to him only so far as he earned it. This independent spirit allowed them to change sides at will and to break sacred oaths quickly and cheerfully. They followed, after all, the example set by their own gods, and if the followers of the White Christ were distressed by such double dealing this bothered them not at all.

In warfare, as in other aspects of life, they were strongly conservative. They had no wish to experiment with strategy. In their coastal raids they brought their longships as far upriver as they would float, beached them, commandeered horses from the nearest farmsteads, and then rode inland burning and slaughtering. Any disadvantage these tactics suffered from being entirely predictable was offset by their extreme mobility; the raiders would strike and be away before a defensive force could be mobilized.

The true Viking wanted no other kind of life. He might, like Harold Hardrada, be successively Captain of the Imperial Guard at Byzantium and King of Norway, but the idea of a settled life was utterly repugnant. But not all the Northmen were Vikings. After the raiders came the settlers. The Danes brought into England qualities of energy and shrewdness which most usefully complemented the Saxon industry. The Danes were essentially town dwellers and traders, the Saxons countrymen and agriculturists; both were, in markedly different ways, fine craftsmen. When at last the wars ended there was good hope that the two races, working together and intermarrying, might settle down to an age of prosperity. These hopes were destroyed when Duke William and his Norman host, themselves descended from

Vikings of an earlier generation, tilted history in a contrary direction.

The spirit of the Vikings is best captured in the sagas, those cheerful, gay and brutal accounts of family feud and revenge pursued from generation to generation and of voyages to Orkney, Ireland, Iceland and Vinland the Good. The sagas however are Norse. They have nothing to tell of the southern and eastern raids or of the invasions of East Anglia and Essex. For these we are dependent upon the necessarily partial accounts of the Anglo-Saxon Chronicle. The monkish chroniclers, being both English and Christian, could not be expected to view the pagan aliens with critical detachment. There are no jokes, even black ones, in the Chronicle as there are in the sagas. Yet the Chronicle does manage to convey something of the miracle of integration which succeeded the wars, as it does the desperation of Alfred's resistance to the earlier pressures. The Chronicle helps to prove too how necessary the earlier conflict was to the resolution of the later. Alfred won for the English a breathing space, as perhaps Arthur had done four centuries before. Life under Guthrum would have been intolerable; England under Canute was a better place than it had been under Ethelred. It was Alfred who won the century in which the Danes could achieve moral and political maturity.

There was no political wisdom among the raiders who first sailed up the Blackwater and the Crouch, only a joyous lust for plunder or, at worst, the determination to avoid the ultimate disgrace of death in bed. Although their activities were of the greatest moment to the East Saxons for a century and a half—probably longer, for, although the Norman Conquest put a stop to the Anglo-Danish experiment, it did not end the Viking raids—there will be few certain reminders in this journey around the Essex coast and estuaries. The pattern of Essex life was established long before the Danes, and most of the villages which we shall see are of Saxon foundation. The great rivers are dedicated now almost exclusively to pleasure sailing. Only on the low, muddy, inaccessible coast can one capture, of a misty morning or as twilight fades, a little of the terror which struck without warning.

In a sense this is an impossible journey. It would be wrong to take no account of the coast of Essex, one of the most fascinating and for the most part undervalued phenomena of the Home Counties, but the motor car on which these itineraries are necessarily based is irrelevant to this country. Only the wild-fowler and the small-boat sailor can come fully to terms with some of these coastal stretches; even the walker is at a disadvantage although, theoretically at least, there is a coastal path for much of the way. We shall see much that is very beautiful—as well as much that is not—and pick up memories of the remote and recent past, but more than anywhere else in these journeys we shall have to evoke imagination in support of visual observation.

There are four major waterways into the Essex interior. In the north, and forming the boundary with Suffolk, is the Stour, navigable to Manningtree—and indeed to a degree as far as Sudbury. Then comes the double estuary of the Colne and the Blackwater. To the south lie the Crouch and the Roach. The southern county boundary is the Thames. Of these rivers only the Stour—and this only at the mouth—and the Thames have commercial significance. One of the curiosities of Essex is that these great salt-water estuaries are associated for the most part with insignificant rivers. The Stour is sizeable up to Dedham, but Colne, Blackwater and Chelmer are little streams for most of their length; as for the Crouch, which offers a deep-water channel for almost twenty miles, above Battlesbridge one is hard put to it to identify the trickle which drains the rather nondescript country north of Basildon New Town. (This is not to say that these upper waters lack interest. Scenically striking or not, the rivers determine the character of the country and their exploration—as we have in part discovered—is always rewarding.)

We shall therefore start this journey at Manningtree and follow, as best we can, coast and estuary southwards until the coastal narrative of Essex ends prematurely in the enormous question mark of Maplin.

The estuary of the Stour, more than a mile wide in places, has only a narrow passage beyond Wrabness and is quite outclassed by the Suffolk Orwell. So Manningtree has remained a modest market town while Ipswich increases in size and prosperity. Only at its mouth does the Essex river acquire national importance in the port of Harwich. Manningtree itself is a town of some character but of no special appeal to the visitor. There is more to see in the suburb of Mistley. This was an ancient village on the road to Bradfield which was deliberately abandoned in favour of a Georgian new-town project. The original church of St Mary fell down and was demolished, all but the porch which survives. The appeal of ruins is inexplicable if undeniable. St Mary's was probably a building of no great distinction; had it survived intact it would have attracted no more comment than any one of the hundred medieval buildings. In its quiet decay the remaining fragment is evocative, its decorative flintwork holding a promise of architectural distinction which the reality would scarcely have sustained. Old St Mary's was supplanted by New, a plain Georgian building which was later transformed beyond recognition by Robert Adam. The dream of an imaginary Classical past which resulted itself lasted for barely a hundred years, and was replaced by another church at the height of the Gothic revival. Adam's strange masterpiece was largely demolished, leaving the two classical towers in splendid isolation beside the river. The subsequent development of Mistley, which linked it with Manningtree, has been less interesting. Only among the industrial buildings beside the river does one catch a little of the spirit which enlivened the place during the Georgian Age.

The villages of the Stour estuary stand well back from the water, reflecting perhaps the caution of Saxon settlers who knew the wisdom of not disclosing their position to an enemy from the sea. All the church towers are post-Norman or later, and in the tenth century a raider would have glimpsed from the water level no hint of a settlement. Essex is famous for its curious place-names, grotesque, humorous and beautiful, and the villages hereabouts have names whose harshness seems to hint at an alien, perhaps a Scandinavian, origin. But no. Wix and Wrabness are sturdy Anglo-Saxon. Wix is *wics*—dairies—and Wrabness is the cape of a homespun Saxon named or nicknamed Wrabba. At Wix there was a small nunnery which fell victim to Wolsey's collegiate ambitions, thereby anticipating its inevitable dissolution by fifteen years or so. Not a stone of the buildings shows above ground, and a Tudor brick farmhouse occupies the site next to a homely church. There is even less of an antiquarian kind to seek at Wrabness, but here there is road access to the shore of the estuary, with views across to the low wooded slopes of Suffolk. If there is activity to be seen here, and it is mostly a restful, sleepy scene, the energy is being expended on pleasure. Scarcely a hint of commerce. In a few miles beyond Ramsey, however, where the Tudor brick tower stands high above the estuary, the old village of Dovercourt—now a suburb of Harwich—gives access to Parkstone Quay and the neighbouring promontory is occupied by the ancient borough and port of Harwich.

Harwich has been the principal port of North Essex at least from medieval times when Edward II recognized its significance by the award of a charter. It has had its vicissitudes since then. The port received a shot in the arm from the railway in the 1880s when Parkstone was developed, and it now enjoys a reasonable degree of prosperity, from the Holland ferry as well as from the sandy beaches of Dovercourt.

Harwich is not to my mind a particularly attractive town. Apart from the normal excitements of the sea traffic there is little to see beyond what the average small town provides. The original Edwardian town—later protected by walls—was laid out very typically on a grid system and this remains, much changed through later and especially recent developments. The buildings old and new call for little comment, and atmosphere, which in most ancient towns is so distinctive, is lacking.

(This is of course an outsider's view. Harwich no doubt seems very different to those who know it from within and who can identify and interpret each change of level and style. Certainly the place is rich in memories, of the Elizabethan voyagers and of Nelson.)

At Harwich estuary becomes sea, and our route turns southwards along the coast. At least it ought to do so, but there are no means of following it. After Dovercourt's beaches and holiday camps the coastal strip becomes marshy and is soon deeply indented by the erosion of Hamford Water. This strange area, more sea than land, is an estuary without a river, for the few streams which drain Tendring Hundred do not merit the name. A tangle of creeks, saltings and marshy islands penetrate inland for upward of five miles, and make a bird-haunted—and small-boat-haunted—wilderness which contrasts sharply with the watering-place urbanity of Walton and Frinton.

The main road out of Harwich is forced well inland by Hamford Water, and it proceeds by a series of fits and starts, contortions and changes of mind, all the way to Clacton. Not an engineered main road at all, in fact, but the upgrading of a series of lanes linking old settlements and, as such roads tend to be, a lesson in local history. Each abrupt turn has a story to tell to those disposed to listen. By the way lanes, tracks and lost roads lead down to deserted wharves, hinting at a time when Hamford Water enjoyed a busier life than it does today. By way of the Oakleys Little and Great the road comes to Beaumont, in full Beaumont-cum-Moze. Moze has gone, more or less, apart from its two halls off towards the marsh, and there is not much of Beaumont except a straggle along two lanes and a restored church under the wing of the fine Tudor-brick hall. Then comes the road down to Beaumont Quay, and shortly afterwards a chance occurs to escape the main road and to regain the coast at Walton. We are now within the ancient liberty of the Sokens. The capital of the liberty, Thorpe, is away to the west, but we pass through Kirby-le-Soken, where the church tower dominates the low country.

Walton-on-the-Naze—although it has an honoured place, as indeed the whole of this stretch of coast enjoys, in the study of archaeology—is a product of the early nineteenth-century craze for sea-bathing. Weymouth and Margate were well established when the developers reached Walton in the 1820s and built the first hotels and terraces on the coast below the Naze. Growth continued at a modest pace through the century until in the last decade it reached south to Frinton. We have here, therefore, however changed by the years, a miniature history of the English watering-place in its heyday, and more recent developments help to illustrate the decline of the vogue.

Geology and history have continued to prevent the joining-up of Frinton and Clacton, and a belt of creek-drained fields and golf courses provides welcome relief before seaside-urban takes control again at Holland-on-Sea. (This used to be Little Holland, and we pass Great Holland on the way.) Clacton was a creation of mid-Victorian times, of which some fragments remain among later developments. It is not, I must confess, my favourite kind of place, but few resorts can match Clacton's miles of beach, with sand, and the climate blends the typical

(*above left*) Queen Elizabeth's Hunting Lodge (*above right*) Pollarded
hornbeam in Epping Forest (*below left*) The founder's statue, Waltham
Abbey (*below right*) Essex brick, Great Bardfield

Lees Priory

east coast freshness with a softness derived from the southward curve
of the coast.

Martello towers, of which there was a specimen at Walton, are
prominent along the coast here. They were built during the Napoleonic
invasion scare at vulnerable points along the east and south coasts. Not
even the passage of one hundred and fifty years has invested them with
romance or charm, but they remain, like the blockhouses of a later war,
as permanent—because it is too much trouble to destroy them—reminders of the perils which through all the centuries threatened these
low shores.

Only the most conscientious of coast-followers will pursue the
route right through Clacton and Jaywick and the new developments
beyond. A brief taste of Clacton would do for me and I would then
escape north through the parent settlement of Great Clacton. This is
now merged with the new town, but there is a real village feeling
around the fine Norman church, where old red brick and black-and-
white bring relief to eyes sated with stucco and concrete. After that the
route is plain and largely undistinguished all the way to St Osyth.

We are now, although we have not yet seen it, under the influence
of the River Colne. A creek of the Colne estuary reaches almost to the
village street, and this played a vital part in the history of the community. St Osyth was originally called Chich, a Saxon settlement on a
site which represented almost the ideal sought by warriors weary of
strife. It was on water, fertile, and having access to the sea.

The transformation of Chich into St Osyth is clouded in mystery.
Osyth seems to have been an Anglian princess who married Sighere,
King of the East Saxons. He was the son of the first Christian king
Sigebert. Whether, as a tradition claims, she left him on their wedding
day and took a vow of chastity or, as was more common, she took the
veil after performing her royal duties for a reasonable period, the King
gave her the manor of Chich for a nunnery and Osyth became the
first prioress. This was late in the seventh century. Here the story becomes more confused. Dear old Dr Cox, who wrote the 'Little Guide'
to Essex, follows earlier hagiologists in saying that Osyth was martyred
by Danes in 870. This would give her an unusually ripe old age! It was
of course the fashion to blame the Danes for everything. Perhaps it was
a crew of pirates who came raiding up Chich Creek and burnt the
nunnery. They took Osyth off with them, attempted her virtue without success, and then cut off her head. Whereupon the Queen picked it
up and walked back to Chich with it, presumably under her arm. Her
canonization duly followed.

It is not clear whether the original priory survived the Danish raids
of the ninth and tenth centuries. At any rate the house was reformed,
as a priory of Augustinian canons, in the reign of Henry I, the founder

21

being Richard, Bishop of London. It was soon upgraded to the status
of an abbey. St Osyth—strictly the abbey of SS Peter and Paul and St
Osyth at Chich—enjoyed a high reputation from the start. One of the
original canons, William of Corbeuil, became Archbishop of Canterbury in 1123, and the abbot was usually a man of some standing in the
world. Almost the last of these dignitaries was John Vyntoner, who in
the early years of Henry VIII's reign—and as if, sensing the doom of
his house, he wished to make one final demonstrative splash—rebuilt
with a splendid disregard of economy and signed his work with his
rebus—V and a bunch of grapes. Then came the King's Commissioners and after them the Vicar-General himself, Thomas Cromwell,
who acquired the property for himself. Cromwell fell; the abbey
buildings reverted to the Crown, and were sold, early in Elizabeth's
reign to Lord Darcy. By this time the great church had gone, and
Darcy built himself a house—or rather a lavish, randomly designed
palace—on the site and partly from the materials.

Of all these and later developments the remains are extensive and
generously shown to the public. They are highly confusing. Continual
use—for the building has remained a residence—has blurred the outlines of the abbey, and it is now to be admired as a nobleman's estate
and house, illustrating stages in the story of man's cultivation of his
environment and only thinly that of his involvement with God.

The first sight of the abbey—which popular usage, reversing the
normal process, persists in downgrading to priory—is the most memorable and exciting. At the back of a small green beyond the centre of
the village stands a gatehouse. Essex is full of architecturally good
things, but for me this is visually the most magnificent. An abbot late
in the fifteenth century, perhaps with renewed confidence after the
end of the civil wars, replaced an older entrance with a building which
proclaimed to the world outside the monastery, if not the glory of God,
at least the message of the Church Militant and the belief of Essex men
in the versatility of flint and stone. Dazzling white stone is matched
with the glossy blue of split flints in the most elaborate flushwork
which this county affords. Such unrestrained exuberance might become
vulgar were it not for the feeling for proportion which informs the
whole work. The concept is grand enough to contain the lavish detail.
I like particularly the soaring canopied niches, one to each of the three
entrance arches, which cry out for effigies of a corresponding beauty.
The elegant central arch has a square-headed surround, in the spandrels
of which the Archangel Michael, winged and armed, confronts Satan
in the form of a dragon in endless conflict.

Within, if there is nothing to equal this, much of interest and beauty
remains, not least the very charmingly landscaped garden which
comes perhaps from a Georgian or Victorian scheme of improvements.

Against these formal walks and clipped yews the tall flint buildings look very well indeed. A few elegant fragments of the medieval buildings are incorporated in later work, but much the most spectacular feature is the tall chequered tower which Lord Darcy contributed. Darcy was living in a world fully exposed to the intellectual and artistic revolution of the Renaissance, but one would never know this from his work, which is entirely medieval in style and spirit. There are other good things to be seen during a stroll around the site, including the great oriel window which is the most remarkable of Vyntoner's surviving additions to his abbey, and one which is purely secular in mood.

Behind the abbey the eighteenth-century landscape park stretches almost to the creek. The village has not much to offer apart from the church. The canons of St Osyth, unlike their brethren in some other places, did not encourage the laity to share their church, and the parish church stands just across the road from the abbey gatehouse. This building represents the continual development of a Norman original, perhaps dating from the foundation of the abbey, which culminated in a remodelling, so lavish as almost to amount to rebuilding, around the time of Abbot Vyntoner. Brick was used for this, as it was for Vyntoner's abbot's lodging, and the material gives the tall nave a pleasingly austere appearance. Here, for once, a Gothic building depends on scale and proportion rather than on detail.

This is a peaceful place because, thanks to the waywardness of Essex waterways, the road past the abbey has no outlet. The creek which protects St Osyth from road traffic presumably carried the raiders who brought the saint her martyrdom. The settlement is a standing invitation to the invader, whether Saxon or Viking. But there is no record, other than the sweetly absurd legend, of those Dark Age commonplaces of murder, fire and rape in this delectable spot.

The creeks dictate the next stage of this journey. Colne mouth is barely five miles away, but for the motorist it might as well be a thousand. The shortest way forward is by way of Thorrington, from which the objective is Brightlingsea, near the mouth of the river and in a classic position for the development of a medieval port. As we saw in Chapter 4 Brightlingsea is associated with its neighbours of Wivenhoe and Rowhedge, not only as a port but as a member of the Confederation of Cinque Ports, the only ones outside Kent and Sussex. Whether the association was of material benefit to Brightlingsea is not on record, although there were no doubt advantages to the parent port of Sandwich to have a far-flung member and especially one well on the way to the North Sea fishing grounds and the herring fair at Great Yarmouth. Anyone expecting to find Cinque Port picturesqueness and a generous accumulation of antiquities will be disappointed. If you do not sail there is not much to interest you in the town which has grown, not ill, but without distinction. Even the river makes little impact. The only substantial link with the past is the church, and this is two miles away on a little hill overlooking not the Colne but Alresford Creek. Here is the big church of a prosperous late medieval community, developed out of a Norman building and added to right into the Tudor period. The building is dramatic. Inside there are monuments to generations of Brightlingsea merchants, culminating in the memorial to a German businessman of the Georgian Age, whose wealth and enterprise are remembered, indeed unforgettably, by an extravagant display of monumental cliches. This is, once one has got over the shock, rather impressive. It does not help to an understanding of Herr Magens, for whom the cherubs weep unconvincing tears, but we do learn something about the age in which he lived and died. By 1764, when he found his rest in this splendid building, Brightlingsea had outlived its importance as a port, but it was still notable enough to attract men of substance to settle there.

The road is forced inland now—it is indeed the road by which we approached Brightlingsea. A mile or so beyond Tenpenny Heath, there is a turning left to Alresford where there is another isolated church on the way down to the creek, and beyond comes a turning to the shores of the Colne at Wivenhoe.

Wivenhoe is best seen from the river or, failing this, from the opposite shore, approached by way of Fingringhoe. At close range it is more difficult to assess the quality of the little town, which is essentially one grown up to serve the river and not the road. From the river its profile is exceptionally pleasing, and distance helps to diminish, or at least to put into scale, the messiness inevitable in a place dedicated to maritime pursuits. The various layers of the town slip naturally into perspective, and one is unaware of the narrowness and congestion of its little streets. At close range some of the enchantment disappears, and one is forced to see not just general outlines but details which are mostly undistinguished. One house displays an exceptionally extravagant example of Essex parge-work. The dullish church has a pair of enormous monumental brasses, of late date for such elegant work, to a Lord Beaumont and his widow. The group is completed by the brass of the lady's chaplain. There is material here for a study as much human as aesthetic.

Again the road forces the traveller away from the river, skirting Wivenhoe Park—where are the massive and not altogether unsightly buildings of the University of Essex—and encountering the Colne again at The Hythe, the port of Colchester and the beginning of the principal town—but not the administrative centre—of Essex, perhaps the oldest and certainly one of the most historically interesting towns in England.

Colchester stands well inland, and the Colne is today an insignificant feature of its scene. It would be inappropriate to devote a large
amount of space to the town in a tour of the Essex coast, but having
come so near it would be intolerable to continue the journey without
a brief stroll through its busy and—one must admit—not invariably
attractive streets.

The trouble with Colchester today is that it is between periods. It
has the makings of a major tourist centre. It is an important shopping
town. It has been a garrison town. It stands at major crossroads. It has
some industrial importance. All these elements are at present imperfectly reconciled, so that to the stranger—and I cannot speak for the
resident—it gives the impression of a place struggling to find itself.

The visitor comes to Colchester to find, among other things, evidence
of the past. This was a tribal capital before the Roman Conquest and
the site of the first Roman *colonia*, created for time-expired imperial
soldiers. It was the objective of Queen Boadicea's devastating raid. It
was chosen by the Conqueror as the site of a major strategic castle.
Here, if anywhere, is history on the ground. Can it be seen? The
answer must be yes, for those willing to eke out their sight with imagination. There are great historical monuments, but they need to be
interpreted. And, as in all towns where occupation has been uninterrupted over nearly two thousand years, the centuries jostle one
another. One has to be prepared for Roman and Norman to be inter-
mingled, Georgian to sit beside post-war. This is no place for harmony
or for a clinical segregation of elements, but a glorious, stimulating
jumble.

This having been said, it must be added that an astonishing amount
remains to be seen. One may curse Fairfax, who did a terrible amount
of damage during the siege which formed the penultimate operation
of the Civil War; or the contractor who, with less excuse, took the top
off the castle; or modern developers who, with no excuse at all, for
these are enlightened times, have knocked down some fine buildings
and substituted some—but not all—which are vastly inferior. It is still
possible to pick up many threads of the past.

First come the enigmatic earthworks which occur, often in incongruous settings, all around the town. These, whatever their origin, were
closely connected with the story of Colchester, immediately before the
Roman invasion when Cunobelin—old King Cole himself—ruled
here. They can be followed fairly well on the western edge of the town
where a footpath behind the hospital follows Gryme's Dyke—Gryme is
the Devil of course—for a mile or two southwards. It extended, but
not now visibly, to the Roman river which seems to have constituted
the boundary of the tribal capital. Some magnificent objects found
during excavations around the dykes are shown in the museum, and

they form convincing evidence of the extravagant prosperity and the artistic virility of first-century Colchester.

Some visitors may not be responsive to the appeal of earthworks. The town walls are quite another matter. Few towns in England have retained so completely the original defences, and these are often still of most dramatic height. The walls are substantially those of the Roman city, although the bastions were added in the Middle Ages. The most impressive survival from Roman Colchester is the main entrance, named the Balkerne Gate, which still retains its entrance arches and flanking towers. All this massive work is of the chunky limestone called Septaria which occurs in the Essex clay. It is cemented with Roman mortar and reinforced with courses of thin brick. If there was a short list of wonders of Roman Britain, the walls of Colchester would rank not much below Richborough and Hadrian's Wall and they would have few other rivals.

The great sight of Roman Colchester was the temple of Claudius the God. This was the centrepiece of the newly-founded *colonia* and a symbol of the might of Rome. Very naturally Boadicea destroyed it after slaughtering the colonists. When William the Conqueror—or more probably his engineer—surveyed the town for a site for his royal castle he chose the site of the temple, largely because it was centrally placed and level, perhaps because debris from the Roman days was still on hand for building materials, an important point in such a stoneless county. Whatever the reason he built the castle over the foundations of the Claudian temple, so protecting them for the next nine hundred years.

Next to the Roman walls, much the most impressive and interesting thing in Colchester is the castle, which has the largest keep in existence. Its proportions are lost through partial demolition, and the roof is an incongruous addition from the eighteenth century, but it is still, if not beautiful, a staggering demonstration of Norman arrogance. (It now houses one of the finest local museums in Britain.) Apart from the castle, the Normans are best represented by St Botolph's Priory, a house of Augustinian canons on the eastern edge of the old town. The noble church, built before the end of the eleventh century almost entirely of Roman brick, survived intact until the Civil War. Then it got in the way of Fairfax's artillery and was ruined. Much of the church, roofless and melancholy, remains, displaying the severe, almost grim lines of very early Norman work.

Of Saxon Colchester there is nothing to be seen now but the tower of Holy Trinity Church, tall, slim and elegant in Roman brick, attached to a medieval building which, when I saw it last, was in a pitiable state of disrepair.

Colchester flourished during the Middle Ages, carrying on a substantial trade in the celebrated oysters of the Colne beds, and later taking a share in the national boom in cloth. There are many relics of these days. St John's Abbey was one of the greatest, perhaps the greatest, of religious houses in Essex. From its foundation in 1096 to the Dissolution it was prosperous and influential. Henry VIII took the resistance of the last abbot badly and awarded him the full severity of the penalty for treason. Then he took the abbey into his personal possession, and it disappeared, all but the great flint gatehouse, second only to St Osyth, which now stands somewhat sadly by the roadside. Eight of the medieval parish churches survive in part, some still doing parochial work, others finding new functions. The pretty church of All Saints opposite the castle is now a natural-history museum and a good one. None of the churches is, in historical or architectural terms, of the first importance, but together they contribute substantially to the atmosphere of the town. So do the many old houses, some medieval, more of seventeenth- and eighteenth-century date, which make a stroll through the back streets so rewarding an experience. The best individual house is probably 'Hollytrees', near the castle, a distinguished Georgian town house with elegant doorway and porch. It has that relaxed urbanity which came so easily to that age and which seems to elude our own architects. 'Hollytrees' is now a museum, and provides as appropriate a setting for its domestic contents as the castle does for the archaeological discoveries. To these buildings must be added the Victorian contribution, notably a rather fine town hall which justifiably takes itself seriously and 'Jumbo', the absurdly elephantine and strangely appealing water tower which dominates the Colchester scene today. This the Victorian designers placed, with that bland consciousness of rectitude which endears our ancestors to their detractors, right behind the Roman Balkerne Gate.

A minor road southwards runs through suburbs no lovelier than those of most large towns. A short diversion will take in one delightful survival, Bourne Mill, which belongs to the National Trust. The approach road is discouraging, but the pretty building set behind and reflected in a mill pond is exceptionally charming. The original building may have belonged to St John's Abbey, but as we see it now it is Elizabethan, its gables following the popular Flemish fashion of that day. After use as a fishing lodge it was adapted, after two centuries or so, as a mill without losing any of its picturesqueness.

The southward road at last shakes off the town and comes to Rowhedge, which, with Wivenhoe, had a share in the Cinque Port activities of Brightlingsea, and which still is aligned to the riverside. Then comes Fingringhoe, where a narrow lane leads down to the Colne, giving the celebrated view of Wivenhoe across the water. Fingringhoe consists of pub, church and little else. The church is neat and heavily restored, and has over the porch a Michael and dragon which is closely related to the group at St Osyth and almost as effective.

This, however improbable it may seem, is earthquake country. On 23rd April 1884 the most severe shock of recent history occurred. It was felt extensively across the northern half of Essex, but the effect was most devastating in the peninsula between Colne and Blackwater. About twenty parishes were affected, notably Wivenhoe, Fingringhoe, Langenhoe, Peldon and Great and Little Wigborough. All the ancient churches were severely damaged, and the lonely church of Langenhoe, almost a mile outside the village, was an almost total loss.

The church at Langenhoe, now rebuilt, with its attendant hall, is almost the last building east of the main road. Beyond are roadless marshes and saltings, producing the kind of desert which one finds nowhere else in the Home Counties except along this wonderfully unexploited coast. The road skirts the deserted area, passing an isolated and celebrated inn, and then becomes a causeway joining, except at high tides, the mainland and Mersea.

Mersea—the second element in 'Mersea Island', which is in common usage, is tautologous—is a place with a very long history. Wealthy Romans and Romanized Britons found the climate pleasing and the oysters edible and they settled both island and adjacent mainland. Coming on to the island one sees a conspicuous mound on Barrow Hill. This covered one of the most sophisticated Roman burials discovered in the country, and there have been other notable finds hereabouts. Mersea itself is a mixture: lightly populated arable land in the north, a semi-urban seaside resort at West Mersea, caravans and chalets farther east. A persistent walker can still find some pleasingly lonely spots. As usual the small-boat sailor gets the best of it. The original village of West Mersea still persists, encased like a fly in amber by modern housing. Church and hall and a few nice houses may seem even better than they intrinsically are by contrast. I prefer East Mersea, a very small and largely unspoilt village on the central low ridge of the whaleback island. The fine fifteenth-century tower of the church stands tall above the fields which drop away to the coast. This is a church dedicated to Edmund King and Martyr, and there is a good modern sculpture inside showing the saintly king with his attendant wolf. (Legends cling to this king, who was much loved in southern England, in life and for centuries afterwards; according to one of these the King's severed head was guarded by a wolf until it could be reunited with the tortured body.) The dedication is appropriate, for Mersea saw much action during the Danish wars. The island, slung between two deep estuaries, was ready made to be a Viking base, and here the Danish chief Hasten set up headquarters during the later campaigns of King Alfred. Hasten was a great maker of earthworks; at least two survive in Kent, at Appledore and Milton Regis, and it is just possible that traces of artificial works near the church may be his. Certainly the church seems to occupy the best strategic site on the island. From this the Danish host went by sea and river up the Lea, where Alfred trapped their fleet in one of his most brilliant manœuvres.

There is now no alternative to back-tracking across the Strood and taking the first westward turn to Peldon. The dominant feature of this landscape is man-made, a great reservoir at Abberton. This wide expanse attracts sea birds in very large numbers. On the northern shore are the Layers, and near the head of the lake the great red tower of Layer Marney dwarfs the nearby church. To the south the villages are smaller and the countryside emptier. The settlements have one Essex characteristic in common. Almost invariably the church stands not in the heart of its community but apart, partnered only by the hall. This is true of Peldon, and conspicuously true of Langenhoe and Great and Little Wigborough. The churches, drastically repaired after earth-quake damage, are not particularly interesting, but the settings make them all worth the visit. I find these little groups of mellow brick and timber most appealing, not least for the isolation and the wide empti-ness of the surrounding fields.

These places mostly have their backs to the sea. Only Little Wig-borough has its creek running down to the saltings. Salcott and Virley, however, are clearly committed to the sea. The two tiny villages share a creek. Salcott's church was damaged in the earthquake of 1884, but Virley's must have fallen down before then. It lies in picturesque ruin. Beyond is nothing but a tangle of waterways and marshes.

Next comes the country of one Tella, a forgotten Saxon warrior who gives his name to a group of parishes: Tollesbury, Tolleshunt D'Arcy, Tolleshunt Knights, and Tolleshunt Major. Here we are on the fringe of the Essex jam country and the birthplace of scientific farming. Tiptree and jam are synonymous—and to jam is now added minor industry but before jam and seed-production became staples, a London businessman, in the spirit of Victorian self-help, which was soon to achieve its most spectacular demonstration in the Great Exhibi-tion, moved in to Tiptree Hall and applied to its unproductive soil the scientific discoveries of his day. The arrival of this specialist unfettered by tradition heralded the most profound change in the appearance of the countryside since the decline of the feudal system.

Tiptree is however beyond the range of this present journey; and, indeed, notwithstanding the enormous importance of Mechi's ex-periments, the area has comparatively little to appeal to the modern traveller. Our way lies south to Tollesbury, a large village traditionally involved in fishing and for a time standing on the light-industrial railway which was built between Kelvedon and the estuary. This enterprise is now dead. There is access to a typical Blackwater creek and on foot as far as the decaying pier of the lost railway. The village— almost a town in plan though not in size—has a little individuality, especially in the pretty group of buildings around the church, which here for once stands in the heart of the community. The church, which is picturesque rather than impressive, is celebrated for the unique inscription on the font, proclaiming for all time the repentance of a Georgian drunkard who interrupted divine service with his cursing and was condemned to pay for a new font. It is an unusual way of achieving immortality.

Of the Tolleshunts, Tolleshunt D'Arcy which comes first is the largest and the most interesting. It is notable for a Tudor manor house, moated, close beside the church, and is enlivened by some neat cottages around a complex system of crossroads. Cutting out Tolleshunt Knights, which is scarcely worth the diversion, the way lies west along a minor road to Tolleshunt Major. Before the main village is reached, a narrow land turns south to the parish church, again neighboured by a Tudor hall. Much good brickwork is to be seen in both buildings. Then, by a tangle of lanes, the route passes by Little Tetham hall and church—another pretty group with some Norman detail in the latter —until it reaches Heybridge, crosses the Chelmer and Blackwater Navigation among big brick Victorian warehouses, and enters the ancient borough and port of Maldon.

Historically Maldon is second only to Colchester among the towns of coastal Essex. Today its interest is a little obscured, so far as the casual visitor is concerned, by extreme traffic congestion. It is not a town which yields its secrets readily, and one needs time, patience and a sound historical imagination to get to know it. I must confess that I have never really managed this, although I continue to hope for ultimate enlightenment.

There are essentially two Maldons. The original town, founded by Saxons as a strong-point to resist Danish attacks, was built beside the Chelmer about a half mile above its confluence with the Blackwater. The medieval town grew up just to the east of the Saxon earthworks and had its hub where the fish market joined the corn market. There was a church on the corner, preceded according to the practice of the early Christian Saxons by a wayside cross at the highest point—the *mael-dun*, the cross on the hill—which gave the town its descriptive name. Farther east, and detached from this settlement, was the hythe, the port of Maldon with a church of its own. All these elements remain, so overlaid with later buildings and with the outlines fuzzed by modern development that their story is not easily read upon the ground.

The Saxon *burgh* may originally have formed part of King Alfred's strategy during the first Danish wars. It suffered its greatest pressure during the later wars of Edward the Elder's reign. The King was there in 913, according to the Chronicle, using the town as his base for defensive works in central Essex, and again seven years later when he repaired the Maldon fortifications. These stood test in the following year. The Saxon *fyrd* had scored a success at Colchester when they took the town from the Danes. The latter retaliated by attacking Maldon. The siege was raised when a Saxon force arrived, but the men of Maldon streamed out after the retreating enemy and routed them. This was Saxon Maldon's most successful hour. Its finest came nearly seventy years later. The Danish invasions which followed the peaceful years of King Edgar and the accession of the egregious Ethelred were at their height. The Danish host had sacked Ipswich and now came south against Maldon. On the marshy southern shore of the Blackwater below the port an English army was drawn up under the command of Alderman Brithnoth. It was a long and desperate battle, and at its end Brithnoth was dead and the English army shattered. A disaster? Militarily, the battle was not of the greatest significance. It merited one line in the Chronicle. But a poet was present at the battle. His identity is unknown, but the poem he wrote has the obvious authenticity of an eye-witness account. The battle speeches of the war leaders, although true in spirit to the age, were no doubt heightened by the poet's licence, but the brief phrases of defiance which the defenders, faced with defeat, grunt out in time with their strokes have the genuine ring.

The battle of 991 was the last appearance of Maldon in the Chronicle. Whether Dane or Saxon was in control the town prospered until at the Norman Conquest it was one of the largest and richest in Essex. Through the centuries town and port grew until they merged, probably in the sixteenth century. The borough was incorporated in Henry II's reign, making it one of the oldest in the country.

Fair evidence of all this history remains in the town, for those who stop to look. The medieval town had three parish churches. All Saints is the key building and a strange one too. It was put up on such a restricted site that there was no room for a conventional tower; the walls were fitted as best they would go, producing not a square but a triangle. This necessity gave Maldon its unique architectural possession. The effect is not unpleasing. The church has suffered, as town churches do, from restoration and reduction, but its south aisle is a masterpiece of mid-fourteenth-century Gothic, with exceptionally lavish detail. Lower down the town, on the main road from the bridge, stood St Peter's. This was abandoned in the seventeenth century and became ruinous. A distinguished clerical benefactor of his native town, Dr Plume, cleared away the debris, leaving only the tower. In its place he built a neat brick box which he presented to the town together with his collection of books. By a most happy arrangement, which neatly balances tradition and modern needs, the eighteenth-century library has been preserved on the first floor, while the ground floor has been given over to the public library. St Mary's was the parish church of the hythe. Its massive tower, topped by a spiky spire, is the most familiar sight in Maldon. It stands right down at the water's edge among the masts of numberless pleasure craft and, on occasion, the sturdier masts of sailing barges. The church is Norman and earlier and the oldest surviving building in the borough.

According to the usual practice, Maldon's abbey was established outside the town's bounds. Praemonstratensian canons at Great Parndon—now swallowed up in Harlow New Town—decided in 1180 to move to a new site, and found one fulfilling their need for solitude and a good water supply on the Chelmer a mile west of Maldon. The house, subsequently known as Beeleigh, survived until the Dissolution. The abbey church was then destroyed, and the conventual buildings were incorporated in a mansion built on the site. The present house, which the owner opens with generous frequency, is a very charming building in stone and half-timbering of which the most impressive feature is the vaulted chapter house. Medieval Maldon also possesed a hospital dedicated to St Giles and founded at about the time that the white canons were moving to Beeleigh. Later the abbey took over responsibility for the hospital administration. Ruins of the hospital chapel stand in a little garden near the modern hospital.

D'Arcy's Tower, the moot hall which is the focus of municipal activity, rises in the centre of Maldon. The original Tudor brick has been much altered to match the growing civic pride of the community. Around it are some of the best domestic buildings in the town, although it is not exceptionally rich in good town houses. Perhaps one captures the essential spirit of Maldon not among these staid Georgian façades but among the fishy smells and the organized muddle of the hythe.

The road past the hythe soon turns back and joins the southward road which crosses the neck of the peninsula between Blackwater and Crouch. This soon passes a farm road leading towards Northey Island, straddled across the channel at the bold last bend of the river before Maldon. On the low marshes here, according to tradition, the Battle of Maldon was fought. The road soon loses contact with the water, and the long and fascinating shore of the Blackwater estuary must be abandoned to its birds and to those hardy walkers who are prepared for the long and twisting trek along the sea wall. Turnings to the left lead only to farms and to the lonely and unspoilt parish church of Mundon—but where is the village? At Latchingdon the road turns abruptly east and then a minor road maintains this direction while the major road makes another right angle. This leads by way of Steeple and St Lawrence for Bradwell. There are no highlights on this part of the journey, unless two Victorian Gothic churches appeal, but the way is open, breezy and by no means unattractive. A road and track go off near Steeple to the estuary at Stansgate where a few fragments of a Cluniac priory are built into the farm. After St Lawrence the towers of the nuclear power station at Bradwell dominate the horizon, and we leave the main road before it reaches Waterside to go into the little townlike village of Bradwell-juxta-Mare.

Bradwell seems to promise well from the start. The neat streets have style. There are some unassumingly pleasing cottages, a brick lock-up and a fine church. Just behind stands the old parsonage, now Bradwell Lodge, an elegant late-eighteenth-century mansion designed by the most celebrated of Essex architects, John Johnson, and rich in the culti-vated atmosphere of the pre-revolutionary intelligentsia. This is opened from time to time.

It is not these things, delectable as they are, which make Bradwell one of the major objectives of pilgrims through Essex. Near the church a minor road goes east for two miles, ending in a car park opposite Eastlands. This little road for most of its length is most uncharacteristi-cally straight. Thus Essex lanes do not behave. Beyond the car park a farm track continues the direct progress to the sea. You have guessed it. This is a Roman road, heading straight for the almost vanished walls of a Saxon Shore fort. In the centre of our view stands a small barn-like structure. This was the springboard of the Christian mission to the pagan East Saxons, and one of the places where the smell of the past still hangs in the air.

Othona was one of the third-century coastal forts referred to in Chapter 4. The choice of this site may seem strange today, but Othona effectively covered the mouth of the Blackwater and, if the garrison had ships under their command, also the Colne. When the fort was four hundred years old and presumably disused and in ruin Othona had another invasion, whose results were more lasting than any earlier ones.

When St Augustine had established his base at Canterbury he sent his lieutenants out to take the gospel to the other Saxon kingdoms. His original intention was to make London the capital of Christian England and he therefore chose his best man for this mission. Mellitus accord-ingly set out along Watling Street to win the East Saxons for Christ. The East Saxon kingdom included Middlesex and part of Hertford-shire and the capital city was London. Mellitus had some initial success, but when the old king died his sons reverted to paganism and chased the bishop back into Kent, where he accepted the softer option of becoming archbishop. The plan to base the Primacy on London was abandoned and never seriously revived. For the next half century the East Saxons enjoyed their freedom from Christianity. Then Sigebert became King of the East Saxons. He was a friend of Oswy, King of Northumbria, and a frequent debater with the northern king of the relative merits of Thor and Christ. At length, during a visit to Northumbria, Sigebert accepted baptism, and invited Oswy to send him a missionary. The choice fell on Cedd, one of four celebrated brothers who had worked under Aidan at Lindisfarne. Cedd and his brother Chad were at the time in Mercia where the old pagan king Penda was at last softening in his bitter antagonism to Christianity. Cedd chose as his base in Essex the old disused fort on the Blackwater and here in the year 653 he built his 'minster'. There was precedent for this. Augustine had built a church within the walls of Richborough and there was also an early minster at Reculver. One of the advantages of such a site was symbolic; the fort was older than the Saxon invasions and was invested with the mystery and the potential sanctity of a pre-pagan building. Cedd saw an additional and practical advantage. He built his church across the wall of the fort, giving its foundations the strength of Roman masonry and mortar. No wonder it lasted while later buildings crumbled to dust.

Cedd was duly consecrated as Bishop of the East Saxons. Although he is sometimes described as the second Bishop of London, it is probable that he never entered the city. At that time the control of London was a matter of dispute between East Saxons and Mercians. The Mercians were in the ascendant, and in this moment of decision there was no place for a controversial religious figure. Cedd probably was content to have his cathedral at Bradwell—Ythancester to the Saxons—with a secondary base at Tilbury. Like Wilfrid, the apostle to the South Saxons, Cedd clearly looked upon his task in Essex as a job, not a life's work. When the church was reasonably firmly established, he returned to the North and ended his days, dying young, as Abbot of Lastingham. The tradition of Lindisfarne, in which he had been raised, favoured discipline and a tough line rather than gentle persuasion, and Cedd organized his church and controlled his diocese rigidly. The East Saxons' respect for him was based on fear, not affection. When his strong hand was removed they lapsed into paganism, but not for long. The spirit of the age was against them.

This was the origin of St Peter-ad-Murum, St Peter's literally 'on the wall', which still defies the sea winds of this stormy coast. St Peter's is arguably unique among English churches. St Martin's in Canterbury is older, because it was there when Augustine landed, but the ancient walls of St Martin's are almost obliterated by later additions. St Peter's has lost its original apse and porches, but virtually nothing has been added. There could be no plainer building, yet it has a strange beauty

which comes not from lush detail but from proportion and pure line.
It has the Saxon characteristic of extreme height in relation to width. It
has also that indefinable quality which comes from great age, an
atmosphere which grows with silence. More than any other building
known to me it illustrates the psalmist's "Be still and know that I am
God".

There is so little to see here that tourists may be inclined to make
this a brief visit. This would be a mistake. The spirit of St Peter's is
not to be taken by storm. There must be time to sit between church
and sea, watching the changing patterns of the sky and the ceaseless
wheeling of birds while the tide creeps over the pale grey mud, time
too to potter among the grassy hummocks which hide the foundations
of the Roman walls of Othona, noting how the soil had slipped back in
places to reveal cement-bonded flints. And to bring home the continuity of history and to provide an appropriate time scale, across the
flats from Roman Othona and Saxon Ythancaster looms the huge
bulk of Bradwell's power station.

The low, but by no means dead flat, land to the south is the hundred
of Dengie, which in its own way is as typically Essex as Epping Forest
or the Pant valley. It has not conventional attractions to lure the visitor
and, I suspect, no wish to possess them. A beautifully self-contained
and self-absorbed area, crossed by one main road and a few lanes, most
of which seem to go nowhere in particular; in fact they go where local
needs require them to go, sometimes ending in the middle of the
marsh. For most people not bred in these parts Dengie hundred would
have no charms; it needs a very special kind of stranger to recognize the
quality of a landscape in which everything is in a low key and the most
important factor is the sky. There is no drama, and the contrasts are so
delicate as to be almost imperceptible.

Most travellers on this long journey may therefore be inclined to
hurry through the miles to Burnham, saving themselves for more
exciting experiences. The minority will not need much guidance from
me, for this is country in which the best discoveries are self-made.
Some may find satisfaction in the empty marshes—empty, that is, of
humans but rich in wild birds and flowers and in the sleek black-and-
white Friesian herds; others will look at the over-restored churches:
Tillingham with its soaring tower, Asheldham compact and historically
all of one piece, Dengie humble and self-effacing but with a gorgeous
Victoria sun-lion on its little belfry. Others may prefer the relaxed
life of the villages and the easy talk of the public bar where Essex
speech may still be heard. I will not prescribe.

By whatever means, we all come at length to Southminster which
is the largest inland village of the peninsula and not the most attractive.
The name and the big church may offer hopes of grand monastic

architecture, but Southminster was a minster in the Saxon, not the medieval sense. Apart from a fine porch, almost the best in this county, there is little to encourage delay. The road southwards loses by degrees its Dengie-hundred quality as it descends to the estuary of the Crouch. A big handsome church stands at a road junction, the parish church of Burnham, and then the town closes in as we come towards the high street and the quays of the classic sailing community of Essex.

Burnham must look different from the river. It is so obviously dedicated to and orientated to the water that the mere landsman feels acutely out of place. Its pre-eminence comes from a commanding position on an estuary which, by Essex standards, is straight, wide and free of mud. Medieval Burnham, as we realized as we passed the church, turned its back on the river. The town is Georgian, Victorian and modern, in for the most part descending order of attractiveness. There are pleasures to be had, even for landsmen, among the bustle and the small visual attractions of the quay, but when the rise and fall of tides and the manœuvres of small and medium craft pall it is time to go back by the way we came.

The main road back to Maldon turns west a little before Burnham church and we stay with this as far as Althorne. The road then turns abruptly north, and we continue west on a minor road. Minor road it may be, but for me this is one of the major pleasures of this country. The road occupies a small ridge, at most little more than 150 feet high but enough to give views across the river. The quality of the scene lies in its trees. This may seem strange, for few parts of Essex are less wooded. The very sparsity of the trees gives them importance, and the lines of tall trees marching down hill, marking the boundaries of fields or offering shelter from the east winds, have a rare beauty.

The miles from Althorne to Woodham Ferrers are uneventful. There is an interesting church at Althorne and a tiny one—adapted to other uses—at Latchingdon, but otherwise only the scattered farm-houses punctuate the journey. One lane goes down to the water's edge at North Fambridge passing on the way a Georgian brick church characteristically withdrawn from its community and partnered only by the hall. The Crouch is a good half mile wide here, and plenty of river traffic is to be seen, while the marshes to the west offer delights to the naturalist.

At Woodham Ferrers these rural delights seem lost for ever. There is more than a hint here of the metropolitan Essex which lies to the west, and although the road runs out of the built-up area quite quickly there is a subtle change in the air. The river lies well to the south and when we see it again at Battlesbridge it has shrunk to a stream. Over the bridge and sharp left past the mill, we turn back downstream. At first the scene is undistinguished and, at Hullbridge, downright unlovely,

Essex pargetting

(*below left*) Chimneys at Great Waltham (*below right*) Lord Rich in
Felsted Church

Margaretting Church tower

Orsett House

Corinthian porch, Rainham Hall

Chequered flintwork, St Osyth

(*above left and right*) St Michael and
the Dragon, Gatehouse, St Osyth
(*below left*) Mourning cherub,
Magens monument, Brightlingsea

The shore, Mersea

Essex mud, Wallasea Island

but then the country opens out with something of the quiet beauty of the northern road.

This is Viking country again and the scene of the most decisive battle on Essex soil. The next village is Ashingdon, which is on the whole visually unexciting or even unattractive, except for a pretty little church on a knoll overlooking the flats. Here, in a struggle distinguished by heroism and treachery, the Danish wars came virtually to an end.

The year was 1016. The miserable reign of Ethelred had come to its appropriate close, and the Witan turned to Edmund Ironside and elected him king. Edmund had already shown his quality when he was the atheling, exhibiting the characteristics of decision and courage which his father so conspicuously lacked. Now he took the offensive in Wessex and won an encounter at Brentford. The Danes next turned up in the Medway, and Edmund followed them and contained them on Sheppey.

At this point treachery took a hand in the campaign, in the person of Edric. Here is an enigmatic figure. One regrets more deeply than ever the fragmentary evidence of the chroniclers, for it would be interesting to know all the facts and to speculate on the basis of knowledge about the motivation of this most evil of the Anglo-Saxon lords. Edric was Alderman of Mercia, and he turns up at intervals in the chronicles, always in an equivocal role. Early in 1016 he had been campaigning on the Danes' behalf. Now he turned up in Kent and advised the King against pressing his advantage against the enemy. King Edmund agreed, which is strange because he had ample evidence of Edric's unreliability, not to say treachery, and he should have known better than to trust him. At any rate the Danes were allowed to pull out of Sheppey and they promptly went raiding in Essex.

Edmund mobilized his army again, and crossed over into Essex. The two forces met "on the down called Assandun". It was the biggest conflict of the war, with both sides committed to the limit. At first the English had the advantage, but at the crisis of the battle Edric ordered his Mercian force to flight and "so betrayed his natural lord and all the people of England". One story says that he caused a panic by shouting that the King was dead. The defection of the Mercians tilted the balance, and the English attack collapsed. "And all the nobility of the English nation was there undone," the Chronicle declared in a rare outburst of personal feeling. It was the final battle. Edmund and Canute patched up a truce, and the English king was murdered soon afterwards. Tradition blames this on Edric too; and probably tradition was right. Canute very sensibly had him killed in the next year; this was too poisonous a snake to leave loose in the kingdom.

The next few years saw the settlement of England under Canute's rule and the transformation of this Viking warrior into a Christian

22

ruler of exceptional wisdom and integrity. In 1020 the king came back to Essex and visited the scene of his greatest victory. In the presence of the leading earls and bishops he dedicated a site above the battlefield and founded a minster "of stone and lime" for the ease of the souls of those men, English and Danish, who had died there. He appointed his own chaplain to be the priest of Ashingdon, a man called Stigand who was destined to achieve fame and some notoriety as Archbishop of Canterbury, the last in that office before the Norman Conquest.

There can be no reasonable doubt that the little church on the hill at Ashingdon stands on the site of Canute's minster. Whether any of the original structure "of stone and lime" remains is more doubtful. There is no visible architectural detail of Saxon character, and the story of the building is greatly obscured by additions and restorations right up to the nineteenth century. Some of the fabric could well be pre-Conquest. Perhaps the memory of the great king's foundation lingered and protected the little building from the fate of most Saxon churches under the rule of their conquerors. The story of the battle and its sequel is unusually detailed, and it is worth remembering in this otherwise undistinguished place. In one respect at least it must be unique. It is the only Saxon parish church whose foundation is attested to by contemporary record.

The country between Ashington and Canewdon is more evocative. Here the beauty of the Crouch valley, temporarily lost, is recovered and increased. The country is unusually hilly and the gentle rise and fall of the land is most appealing. Soon the scene acquires an architectural accent as the tower of Canewdon church comes into view on its little hilltop. This, the most distinguished building of the peninsula between Crouch and Roach appropriately occupies the highest point, and if this amounts to only 128 feet such heights are significant in country like this. The hill was possibly the command post of Canute's army in 1016.

Canewdon tower is associated, if only by tradition, with another battle. It belongs to the first half of the fifteenth century, and it displays the royal arms of England and France. Tradition claims that it was built in celebration of the victory of Agincourt. How good it would be to believe this! Certainly it is a fine tower, so much more elaborate and costly than any of its neighbours that it must have been undertaken for some special purpose. The ragstone was brought by water, at considerable expense, from Kent, and the design has more sophistication than would come easily to a local rustic designer.

Canewdon is the central village of the peninsula and the most interesting. There are some good houses around the church, as well as the village lock-up and stocks, and all the signs of a self-contained community. The road beyond quickly loses height and at length crosses a muddy creek and comes to an end in the big, marshy and almost roadless island of Wallasea.

Our necessarily road-bound journey must go south and east to allow a visit to the most remote of the peninsular villages and one of the most charming. A twisting narrow lane comes at length to an end at Paglesham and finds very little there, just a church, an inn and a row of cottages. Not much to make a fuss about or justify a special visit, except that the buildings are singularly perfect of their kinds and the setting one of great harmony. Here we seek not important architecture but something equally precious, the blending of disparate elements which produces the English villages, and the search is not in vain.

To complete the exploration one might follow the southern arm of the Paglesham road till it fades out a half mile from the muddy shore of the Roach. The return route is past Ballards Gore, and then south through Great Stanbridge to its isolated Norman church, and so to Rochford, the town of the River Roach which preserves somewhat precariously its cardinal-point ground-plan. Here there is a grand church tower and nearby the much-altered brick towers of Rochford Hall with its memories of the Boleyns. Rochford is not the town it was, but it will make a not unsatisfactory conclusion to a journey through the often lonely and delightful land between Crouch and Roach.

I wrote these words on the day that the proposals for Maplin and its new town were published. These make any commendation of this countryside not so much an elegy as an exercise in bitter irony. The whole of the peninsula is thrown into the new town. It is true that parts are designated, in the vile jargon of the planners, "open areas of sub-regional significance". The concept, like most concepts of rural amenities, is one which could only occur to the townsman, who sees the country not as an entity in itself but as a cow to be milked for the benefit of the town. Such a mentality classifies rural areas as 'country parks' or 'beauty spots', and preserves them, as one preserves a body, by the removal of the vital organs. Paglesham is not a 'beauty spot'. It is a community, a complex organism of people, buildings and land, developed by an evolutionary process over many centuries. Its elements are interdependent. It is not a raree-show for Cockneys to gawk at.

This journey along the Viking coast, started in beautiful and as yet unthreatened country, ends sadly and bitterly, in a part of Essex faced with hazards as great as those posed by the Danish hordes, dangers which cannot be set aside either by battle courage or the payment of Danegeld.

South across the Roach lies Southend, the south end of the parish of Prittlewell which has so monstrously outgrown and swallowed its parent. Much might be written about Southend, its sociology, its architecture—which reflects, not always at their highest, the changing fashions of the past century—the psychology of its residents and its rulers. This is not the place for any of these. In the context of this book Southend is interesting in that it illustrates in an advanced form what can happen to the commuter town of a metropolitan county when growth outstrips planning. To the east, where the solid ranks of houses at last ease their grip on the landscape, the way is barred. Where Hasten the Dane had his military headquarters, the army now holds the flats, sharing the muddy foreshore with a multitude of sea birds in the forbidden emptiness of Foulness. Mud or concrete? The question symbolizes a basic dilemma of all the Home Counties.

Bibliography

Addison, W. *Epping Forest* (Dent, 1945)
Barr, H. A. *In Saxon Sussex* (Arundel Press, 1953)
Betjeman, J. *Buckinghamshire: architectural guide* (Murray, 1948)
Branch-Johnson, I. *Hertfordshire* (Batsford, 1970)
Brentnall, M. *The Cinque Ports and Romney Marsh* (Gifford, 1972)
Brimble, J. A. *Londoner's Epping Forest* (Country Life, 1950)
Brown, A. F. J. *Essex people 1750–1900* (Essex County Council, 1972)
Bulfield, A. *The Icknield Way* (Dalton, 1972)
Camp, J. *Portrait of Buckinghamshire* (Hale, 1972)
Church, R. *Kent* (Hale, 1972)
Cracknell, B. E. *Portrait of Surrey* (Hale, 1970)
Crosher, G. *Along the Chiltern ways* (Cassell, 1973)
Crouch, M. *Essex* (Batsford, 1969)
Crouch, M. *Kent* (Batsford, 1967)
Dickson, A. *Portrait of the Chilterns* (Hale, 1957)
Edlin, H. C. *England's Forests* (Faber, 1958)
Fitzgerald, K. *The Chilterns* (Batsford, 1972)
Hine, R. L. *Charles Lamb and his Hertfordshire* (Dent, 1949)
Jennett S. *The Pilgrims' Way from Winchester to Canterbury* (Cassell, 1971)
Lamb, L. *County town* (Eyre and Spottiswoode, 1950)
Massingham, H. J. *Chiltern Country* (Batsford, 1949)

Meynell, E. *Sussex* (Hale, 1947)

Millward, R. and Robinson, A. *South-East England: The Channel Coastlands* (Macmillan, 1973)

—— *South-East England: Thameside and Weald* (Macmillan, 1971)

Murray, K. M. E. *The Constitutional History of the Cinque Ports.* (Manchester U.P., 1935)

Nairn, I. *Surrey* (Buildings of England) (Penguin Books, 1971);

Nairn, I. *Sussex* (Buildings of England) (Penguin Books, 1965)

Newman, J. *North East and East Kent* (Buildings of England) (Penguin Books, 1969)

Newman, J. *West Kent and the Weald* (Buildings of England) (Penguin Books, 1969)

Pevsner, N. *Buckinghamshire* (Buildings of England) (Penguin Books, 1972)

Pevsner, N. *Essex* (Buildings of England) (Penguin Books, 1959)

Pevsner, N. *Hertfordshire* (Buildings of England) (Penguin Books, 1953)

Spence, K. *The Companion Guide to Kent and Sussex* (Collins, 1973)

Straker, E. *Wealden Iron* (Bell, 1931; David & Charles, 1969)

Surrey County Council *List of Antiquities in . . . Surrey* (Surrey C.C. 1965)

Vine, P. H. L. *London's Lost Route to the Sea* (David & Charles, 1973)

White, A. *Tideways and Byways in Essex and Suffolk* (Arnold, 1948)

Willard, B. *Sussex* (Batsford, 1965)

Williams, G. *The Heraldry of the Cinque Ports* (David & Charles, 1971)

Woodford, C. *Portrait of Sussex* (Hale, 1972)

Wright, C. J. *A Guide to the Pilgrims' Way and North Downs Way* (Constable, 1971)

Index